KOREAN STUDIES OF THE HENRY M. JACKSON
SCHOOL OF INTERNATIONAL STUDIES

MARGINALITY AND SUBVERSION IN KOREA

The Hong Kyŏngnae Rebellion of 1812

SUN JOO KIM

UNIVERSITY OF WASHINGTON PRESS

Seattle and London

This publication was supported in part by the Korea Studies Program of the University of Washington in cooperation with the Henry M. Jackson School of International Studies.

University of Washington Press
PO Box 50096, Seattle, WA 98145
www.washington.edu/uwpress

Library of Congress Cataloging-in-Publication Data
Kim, Sun Joo, 1962–
Marginality and subversion in Korea: the Hong Kyongnae rebellion of 1812/Sun Joo Kim.—1st ed.
p. cm. — (Korean studies of the Henry M. Jackson School of International Studies)
Includes bibliographical references and index.
ISBN-13: 978-0-295-98684-5 (hardback : alk. paper)
ISBN-10: 0-295-98684-0 (hardback : alk. paper)
1. Hong Kyŏngnae Incident, 1811–1812.
2. Korea—History—1637–1864.   I. Title.
DS913.25.K58 2006   951.9'02—dc22   2006034636

IN MEMORY OF JAMES B. PALAIS

Contents

Acknowledgments

It is often remarked that writing a book is a joint intellectual venture, and nothing could be truer of the present volume. I owe a great deal to many wonderful people who encouraged me, guided me, and assisted me in various ways.

My advisor and mentor, James B. Palais, professor emeritus of the University of Washington, read at least three different drafts of the manuscript over the years. Each time, he wrote dozens of pages of comments. How then could I possibly claim that this book is the result solely of my own intellect and sweat?

I am equally indebted to John B. Duncan of UCLA and Martina Deuchler, professor emeritus of the University of London, who reviewed earlier versions of the manuscript and made invaluable comments that enabled me to sharpen my presentation and avoid apparent errors. Elizabeth Perry also kindly read the whole manuscript and made helpful suggestions. Clark Sorensen, who assumed editorship of the publication series following James B Palais's retirement, also provided helpful suggestions for tightening my arguments from a social-science perspective.

I have been immensely blessed with the good will of my colleagues in the field of Korean studies all over the world. Oh Soo-chang of Hallym University and Anders Karlsson of the University of London happened to engage in research on the same topic, the Hong Kyŏngnae Rebellion of 1812, around the same time I did. Although we arrived at different conclusions as to our understanding of the rebellion, their insights and comments inspired me in many ways and helped sharpen my focus. Yi T'aejin of Seoul National University and Yi Hŏnch'ang of Korea University took precious time to read an earlier draft of the manuscript and send a list of suggestions to me.

Although the field of Korean history is relatively small, the intellectual vigor and generosity of those who are committed to it are unrivaled. And I have certainly been the beneficiary of such an intellectual environment. It is impossible to list all the people who have shown great interest in the progress of my work and given me unbounded encouragement. I would, however, like to recognize the following colleagues: Kyung Moon Hwang, Gari Ledyard, Eugene Park, Ken Robinson, Andre Schmid, Vipan Chandra, JaHyun Kim Haboush, Mark Peterson, Donald Baker, Ross King, Gi-wook Shin, and Hyaeweol Choi.

I am grateful that my colleagues at Harvard University have provided a productive and dynamic environment over the last few years. Carter Eckert and David R. McCann have been the source of intellectual stimulation as well as comfort. Peter Bol in particular has been a wonderful supporter of my work and of Korean studies as a whole. Mikael Adolphson, Adam Kern, Wai-Yee Li, Philip Kuhn, Michael Puett, Hue-Tam Ho Tai, Wei-Ming Tu, and others have graciously shared their expertise, advice, and experiences, thus making my life much more meaningful and manageable. Members of the Korea Institute, Susan Lee Laurence, Myong-suk Chandra, Edward Baker, and Mrs. Namhi Kim Wagner, in particular, deserve my special thanks. I am also thankful for my graduate student assistants, Jungwon Kim, Aeri Shin, Joohang Cha, Joe Wicentowski, and Junghwan Lee, for their meticulous research work.

A number of researchers and librarians in the United States and Korea helped me obtain copies of rare books and of the images that appear in the book. Yoon-whan Choe, former librarian at the University of Washington, not only helped me locate books and articles but also showered me with warm thoughts and support. Choongnam Yoon, former librarian at the Harvard-Yenching Library, has also been a strong supporter of mine. Seunghi Paek and Hyang Lee at the Harvard-Yenching Library did not hesitate a moment in fulfilling whatever requests I made. Jaeyong Chang, a librarian at the University of California at Berkeley, alerted me about and provided a copy of a rare manuscript that no one had yet used for the study of the 1812 rebellion. A number of researchers at the National Institute of Korean History (Kuksa p'yŏnch'an wiwŏnhoe) guided me to acquire copies of rare books preserved at the institute and of the images inserted in this book. I would also like to acknowledge the National Library of Korea (Kungnip chungang tosŏgwan) and the Kyujanggak at Seoul National University for letting me use their collections.

Fellowships and grants were indispensable to me in carrying out research and completing the manuscript. I would like to thank the following institutions for their generous support: Korea Foundation Advanced Research Grant; AAS Northeast Asia Council Small Grants for Korean Studies; Asia Center Faculty Grants; Clark/Cooke Funds; and small grants from the Korea Institute and the Department of East Asian Languages and Civilizations, Harvard University. Institutions that have provided venues to present earlier versions of this research and to interact with their scholars include the Harvard University Korea Institute, the Harvard-Yenching Institute, the Asia/Pacific Research Center at Stanford University, the Center for Korean Studies at UC-Berkeley, the Korea Forum International in New York, Kyungpook National University, UCLA, and the University of Utah.

I should note that my copyeditors, Victoria Scott and Julie Van Pelt, have made this book much more readable than it was. Michael Duckworth and Mary C. Ribesky at the University of Washington Press managed the whole publishing process efficiently and seamlessly. I would like to thank them all.

The completion of this book would have been impossible without the everlasting friendship and emotional support from the following warmhearted friends: Soon-mi Yoo, Hwasook B. Nam, Nancy Abelmann, Mark Caprio, Seunghee Jeon, Og Lim, Yoon Taek-lim, Pak Yangsin, and Kim Sunja. Finally, I would like to thank my family for their unstinting love and understanding.

Writing acknowledgements is a very personal journey. It is even more so because I would like to dedicate this book to my mentor, James B. Palais, who sadly passed away in 2006. If I have made or will make any contribution to Korean studies through this book and any other academic work, it will be largely due to his enduring guidance, inspiration, and enthusiasm, and the example that he has set for me. I would like to share with the reader one most memorable lesson, among many others, that he imparted to me: "Don't be afraid of criticism." Thus I hope this book is not the end but another beginning of useful conversations with my critical readers, colleagues, friends, and family.

Author's Note

The Korean terms and names in the text are rendered in McCune-Reischauer romanization, the Chinese terms and names in pinyin, and the Japanese in the Hepburn system. Korean names in the text are given in Korean order (surname first, without comma). Korean and Japanese names in the bibliography are also listed in that order, except for those authors who have published in English. The references to Chosŏn rulers use their posthumous titles, which are listed in appendix D along with their reigning years. In the text, dates have been converted to the Western calendar from the original lunar calendar unless noted otherwise. Lunar calendar dates appear as year. month.day (1813.1.1), and Roman calendar dates appear as month/day/year (2/15/2006).

Weights and Measures

1 *chu-ch'ŏk*=20.795 cm*

1 *po*=6 *chu-ch'ŏk*=1.25 m

1 *chang*=10 *chu-ch'ŏk*=2.08 m

1 *ri*=360 *po*=2,160 *chu-ch'ŏk*=449.17 m

1 *sŏm*=15 or 20 *mal*=one picul of grain
   by volume=89.464 or 119.285 l (liters)

1 *mal*=10 *toe*=5.96 l

1 *toe*=10 *hop*=0.596 l

*Pak Hŭngsu, "Toryanghyŏng chedo"; and "Toryanghyŏng," Online EncyKorea, http://www.encykorea.com.

MARGINALITY AND SUBVERSION IN KOREA

CHINA
Tuman (Tumen) R.
Amnok (Yalu) R.
Kanggye
HAMGYŎNG
P'YŎNGAN
Ch'ŏngch'ŏn R.
Ŭiju
Chŏngju
Taedong R.
Anju
Yŏnghŭng
Tonghae
(Eastern Sea)
P'yŏngyang
Wŏnsan
Anbyŏn
Yonggang
Koksan
HWANGHAE
Han R.
Kaesŏng
KANGWŎN
Kanghwa Island
Seoul
KYŎNGGI
CH'UNGCH'ŎNG
Hwanghae
(Yellow Sea)
Andong
KYŎNGSANG
Naktong R.
Kyŏngju
CHŎLLA
Tongnae
N
W   E
S
Tsushima Island
0   100 miles
JAPAN
Cheju Island

MAP 1. Chosŏn

Introduction

In the Confucian tradition, a rebellion could be a sign of misrule and of a lapsed Mandate of Heaven. The right to rule was given by Heaven; therefore, when a king ruled unwisely, Heaven would be displeased and would transfer the mandate to someone else. Heaven's will would be expressed in various extraordinary natural phenomena and popular protests. Mencius (Chinese Confucian philosopher, ca. 371–288 B.C.E.) even maintained that the people could revolt if the ruler failed to bring peace and order. This political ideology often conferred legitimacy to Chinese and Korean rebels in their challenge to existing rule and efforts to bring about a dynastic change.[1] Over the long life of the Chosŏn dynasty (1392–1910) there were relatively few such challenges, and even fewer that erupted into an armed struggle, for most uprisings were aborted and none was successful. The main focus of this book, the Hong Kyŏngnae Rebellion of 1812, is one of the rare events that terrified the Chosŏn court. It required deployment of the central army and took the combined efforts of the central army, provincial forces, and local militias four months to suppress.

It all began as a small armed attack on the magistrate's office at Kasan[2] by a group of people led by Hong Kyŏngnae, U Kunch'ik, Yi Hŭijŏ, and Hong Ch'onggak in the late evening of January 31, 1812. The rebels killed the magistrate, Chŏng Si, and his father, and swiftly took control of the town. The same evening, another group, led by Kim Sayong, rescued rebel collaborators from Kwaksan who had been arrested and were being taken to Sŏnch'ŏn, and the group succeeded in capturing Kwaksan the next day.

These acts marked the beginning of the famous Hong Kyŏngnae Rebellion, which had probably been conceived in the minds of its top leaders for a number of years. The rebel enterprise, ultimately aimed at destroying the existing dynastic rule, was initially successful. The rebels took over the seven district seats of Kasan, Pakch'ŏn, Chŏngju, Kwaksan, Sŏnch'ŏn, Ch'ŏlsan, and T'aech'ŏn, as well as a much larger rural area north of the Ch'ŏngch'ŏn River—the Ch'ŏngbuk region[3]—within the first ten days of the rebellion without meeting any substantial resistance, primarily because they had secured support from the local elite in charge of district governance before taking action. However, the rebels' defeat at Pine Grove (Songnim), 10 *ri* (approximately 4.5 km) north of Anju, on February 11, 1812, and at Four Pine Field (Sasongya) ten days later, put a stop to their advances toward more strategically important towns. These included Anju to the south, where one of the military headquarters of P'yŏngan Province was located, and Ŭiju to the north, which was an important border town just south of the Amnok (Ch.: Yalu) River. Even after losing key leaders (such as the top strategist Kim Ch'angsi and the valiant commander Yi Chech'o) and being forced into a defensive posture inside the administrative walled town of Chŏngju—known for its security because of its location and sturdy perimeter walls—the rebels managed to survive for about four months. But government troops dug a tunnel beneath the wall, planted a charge of gunpowder, and blew up part of the fortifications, enabling more than eight thousand government troops to enter Chŏngju and round up almost all rebels inside on May 29, 1812.

This antidynastic movement in Korea, popularly known as the Hong Kyŏngnae Rebellion, has fascinated historians, poets, and writers, nationalists, rebels, and revolutionaries, and ordinary citizens of Korea for the last two hundred years.[4] The relative wealth of documentation on the event partly explains the sustained interest expressed by both academics and nonacademics. In addition, this kind of popular movement in the premodern era provides a valuable window through which historians can look at the social and economic conditions of ordinary people, because the bulk of the source material consists of records of trial proceedings and testimonies of people involved in such uprisings. This firsthand information on the lives of rural residents differs from that found in other official records, which are preoccupied with the concerns of the ruling elite about the institutional structure and internal dynamics of the high court. Finally, in looking at events like those in 1812, historians can picture the dynamics of social change because the process of popular rebellion exposes the strengths and

MAP 2. P'yŏngan Province

weaknesses of the existing social and political structure and sheds some light on the direction of future change.

In the English-speaking world, a more general interest in popular rebellions has developed since World War II as scholars have generally found that peasants played an important role in bringing about social change. In fact, the major revolutions in world history occurred in agrarian societies, as seen in the French, Russian, Chinese, and Vietnamese revolutions. In particular, the communist revolutions in Russia, China, and Vietnam emerged and succeeded in backward, agrarian societies with major support from peasants—whom many scholars of historical sociology, including Karl Marx, had thought to be politically impotent. This theoretical anomaly has further stimulated scholarly investigation of the political behavior of peasants, the nature of the peasant economy, and the causes of peasant rebellions in traditional society. Thus the idea that popular revolt often triggers a change in regime—indeed, that the transition to modern society has been heralded by popular rebellions in many regions of the world—has made the study of popular movements indispensable for those who want to understand the nature of epochal social changes in any early modern society.[5]

It is not surprising, then, that the popular rebellions in nineteenth-century Korea have been a fashionable subject of study in Korea. The nineteenth century in Korean history is often called an age of popular rebellions, principally due to the frequent outbreak of larger-scale popular movements.[6] Besides the major rebellions—such as the Hong Kyŏngnae Rebellion in 1812, the rebellions in 1862, and the Tonghak Rebellions in 1894–95—there were numerous and various forms of popular protest movements throughout the nineteenth century.[7] The Confucian ruling elite of the time were quite alarmed by the recurrent outbreak of popular uprisings, which were regarded as a sign of dynastic decay or as withdrawal of the Mandate of Heaven, as mentioned above. In a similar vein, one of the main approaches in the study of nineteenth-century popular rebellions sees them as the stage in the dynastic cycle (the prime mover of traditional history in East Asia), in which an erstwhile vigorous government begins to degenerate, to be eventually replaced by a new, stronger one. This colonial perspective characterizes Korean society as fundamentally rural, stagnant, faction-ridden and unable to make spontaneous development. More detailed studies based on various primary sources have appeared in both North and South Korea as well as in Japan, but their interpretations have often been clouded by the postcolonial discourses on Korea that have recently dominated academic environments. For example, contemporary scholars of popular uprisings have almost all been interested in identifying progressive social and economic developments during the late Chosŏn dynasty, the resultant emergence of class conflicts, and the formation of vanguard revolutionary social forces in order to "prove" the progressive direction of nineteenth-century Korean history that was "distorted" by Japanese aggression.[8]

The present work proposes a more comprehensive and integrated view of the causes and developments of the 1812 Hong Kyŏngnae Rebellion, not only by examining the rebellion itself but also by exploring the social, political, economic, and cultural conditions that led to the rebellion. Special attention is given to the nature of the rebellion's leadership, because its composition defined the nature and the course of the rebellion itself. A number of previous studies have acknowledged that the main body of leadership was composed of the local elite, but these studies' subscription to certain perspectives, such as the theory of class struggle, has diverted their attention to people at the bottom, who rarely surface as spontaneous participants, not to mention as leaders, in the written records available to us. This rebellion, however, does not simply fit the previously popular interpretation that it was a peasant rebellion, despite many peasants having participated in it. This becomes apparent when one traces why the local elite of the Ch'ŏngbuk region revolted. To complicate matters, the local elite not only became leaders of the rebellion but also stood at the front lines of the government's counterrebel campaign. Explanations for this can be found by closely investigating local culture and politics, which were, in turn, intertwined with local finance and its relation with the center.

To understand popular rebellions in the late Chosŏn period, it is critical to analyze power relations at both the national and local levels and the social status of different types of residents in the areas of rebellion. This is because social status stratification, rather than class differentiation in the strict sense, most powerfully underlies the social dynamics of collective action in these rebellions. In particular, we need to pay close attention to the formation of the "marginalized elite" during the latter part of the dynasty. During the Chosŏn period it is commonly understood that society was dominated by the *yangban* status group—a status stratum marked by inherited ascriptive privileges and a group of bureaucrats defined by their access to power through monopoly of learning and examinations.[9] What is less commonly recognized is that many yangban families were alienated from central political power and were under constant threat of losing their privileges and prestige in the local system because of intra-elite competition for the control of local resources. In the broadest definition, most yangban literati living in the countryside (except the capital-based aristocracy, called the *pŏryŏl* or *kyŏnghwa sajok*) could be categorized as marginalized elite: they were largely excluded from central politics, were distanced from real power at the center, and stood on the margin in the sharing of privileges and prestige.[10] Within each locality, moreover, this large pool of marginalized yangban was further divided into several different status groups according to their family background, their involvement in local politics and culture, and, to a lesser extent, their financial situation.[11] They thus were ripe for fragmentation based on political and economic interests.

Jack Goldstone's approach, a demographic/structural model of state breakdown, is helpful in understanding the political propensities of the marginalized elite in the late Chosŏn period. Emphasizing demographic changes as an independent force in early modern history—and relating demographic changes to prices, conditions of state finance, elite recruitment, and popular living conditions—Goldstone argues that population increases have a particularly nonlinear effect on marginal groups who face some sort of boundary conditions, such as peasants who are seeking to gain new lands or younger sons of elite families who are in search of new elite positions. He points out that "increases in total population generally produce a much, much larger increase in marginal population—that is, in those groups competing for some relatively scarce resource—than in the population as a whole. The increase in competition is therefore much greater than the increase in overall population, by itself, would suggest."[12] He further proposes that the relative inflexibility of early modern state institutions with traditional systems of taxation, of elite recruitment, and of economic organization in responding to accumulating pressures leads to state breakdown at a variety of levels.

Unreliability of demographic data and the near absence of a price index in traditional Korea make it difficult to apply this well-formulated framework, designed to explain "waves" of state breakdowns in early modern world history, to the history of the Chosŏn dynasty or, more specifically, to explaining the causes of the 1812 rebellion itself. Yet Goldstone's essential point—namely, that overall population increase would have a much greater impact on marginal elites than on other groups, by heightening division and competition among them—does help us understand the structural and institutional problems that the northern elite faced in the late Chosŏn period. Notwithstanding erratic demographic statistics during the Chosŏn period, it is generally accepted that population grew steadily, especially until the late eighteenth century.[13] The combination of such prolonged population growth in the late Chosŏn period with the elite recruitment system—in which only a fixed number of official positions were available while those passing the higher civil service examination (*munkwa*), and thus official candidates, almost tripled by the late eighteenth century—generated an unprecedentedly large pool of marginal elite who were unable to penetrate the central political arena.[14] This, in turn, resulted in heightened division and competition among various groups of elite at the center as well as in the local areas.

The competition among elites in P'yŏngan Province—which produced dramatically more *munkwa* passers in the late Chosŏn period, thereby creating a much larger elite group—must have been intense. On top of the fact that the number of aspirants to official positions increased, P'yŏngan residents were routinely discriminated against in their promotion to higher-ranking prestigious positions at the court. Central yangban had invented prejudice against the northern region, maintaining that northerners lacked scholarship (though they respected militarism) and that there were no yangban at all in the region.[15] The elite in the northwestern region, whose successful performance at the *munkwa* outnumbered that of their southern counterparts in the late Chosŏn period, shared social and political concerns deriving from this regional discrimination by the center, which provided a focal point for collective discontent.[16] Political discrimination alone may not fully elucidate the making of the rebellion, for by the early nineteenth century almost all the provinces outside the capital region had become subject to political discrimination, since political power and authority were dominated by the central yangban elite. The reasons that the P'yŏngan elite became more resentful of exclusionary central politics than other regions deserve attention. One possible explanation may be that their much improved capabilities, as displayed in the *munkwa*, were not just unrecognized but even fell prey to contempt.

The creation of a larger pool of aspirants to official posts from P'yŏngan Province also contributed to divisive local politics because these educated elites had to compete for local power and limited resources more vigorously. Exploration of local power relations, the local elite's cultural practices and expectations, and their source of discontent stemming from local society as well as from their interactions with the center thus shed important light on the surprisingly divergent ways the local elite responded to the 1812 rebellion. One group enthusiastically supported it while the other participated in its repression.

The ideological dimension of the 1812 rebellion also proves to be important. Although subversive ideology does not fully account for the causes of the rebellion, the influence of both (1) the Confucian idea of challenging the Mandate of Heaven and (2) prophetic beliefs in the inevitability of dynastic change in unifying leaders of and participants in the rebellion is affirmed repeatedly in the written records. Previous research has tended to overlook this because any emphasis on the impact of folk beliefs, which were presumed to be backward and irrational, might undermine the progressive nature of rebellion that scholars of modernization theory have tried to champion. The present work recognizes that no matter how archaic and superstitious popular beliefs may have been, they could be transformed into a very subversive ideology.[17] When folk beliefs could find sources of legitimation in the dominant Confucian ideology, they could appeal to the marginalized elite and commoners alike. Such beliefs could then become an effective tool to bind believers together for collective action and to provide legitimacy for their protest.

The data as I see them, then, lead me to a multifaceted analysis of this historic event rather than interpreting this rebellion as a manifestation of evolving class conflict. The comprehensive examination of social and political structures and institutions at the central as well as local level; the careful reconstruction of the local social structure and its changes in the late Chosŏn period, especially in its relation to the central government; the complex implications that the economic changes, especially the expansion of commerce and trade in P'yŏngan Province, had caused in the late Chosŏn period; cultural norms and popular beliefs in prophetic teachings; and the close readings of attitudes of various strata involved in the incident—all these, combined, can truly illuminate the proper historical space of this popular movement.

Among all these causes, however, I believe particular emphasis must be placed on the traditional resentment of the northern population toward the central government because of its discriminatory treatment of people from the region. In investigating various regional reactions to that discrimination (including an armed revolt like the 1812 rebellion), I think taking a regional perspective is important precisely because it gives the region itself a voice.[18] For a number of political and historical reasons, including colonization and the division of Korea into two political regimes in the twentieth century, historical studies have been dominated by nation-centered approaches that have rationalized the writing of Korean history as a single narrative while effectively muting diversity and variant explanations.[19] Some local-based studies that focus on the southern provinces have appeared in recent years, mainly because scholars in South Korea had access to primary sources kept by private collectors in the south. As a result, the history of the southern provinces has tended to stand in for the history of the entire peninsula. Although the size of the Chosŏn kingdom was relatively small, especially when compared to the land area controlled by neighboring Chinese states, the geopolitical conditions and particular experiences of each region within even this small kingdom shaped distinct regional cultures, customs, and histories. It is thus desirable to consider regional subjectivities, particularly concerning the experiences of the northern provinces and a major popular uprising such as the one under investigation in this book, to begin to appreciate the vital importance of subnational subjectivity in Korean history.[20]

The unusually rich sources primarily concerned with the 1812 rebellion make it possible to retell the event in great detail.[21] Taking advantage of this material, this study therefore highlights human actions, voices, and motivations in addition to analyzing structural and institutional backgrounds. Because the examination of the physical and historical environment in which the rebellion took place and the human actors lived will provide proper context for our understanding of this event, this book begins with an investigation of place. The regional history and its social structure, the political spectrum in the national as well as local arena, the economic and financial challenges that this region faced, and, finally, the ideological aspects embedded in the popular culture are laid out in part 1 before turning to the event itself in part 2.

PART I

State, Region, Regional Elite, and Culture

1 Historical Development of the Ch'ŏngbuk Region and the Regional Elite

In many ways, the Hong Kyŏngnae Rebellion of 1812 was caused by regional particularities. Social and political discrimination against the official advancement of residents of P'yŏngan Province resulted in growing discontent among expectant officials as well as among ordinary people.[1] The rebels fiercely resented discrimination against people from P'yŏngan Province, as clearly expressed in their rebel manifesto:

> The central government abandoned P'yŏngan Province as one abandons rotten earth. Even when the slaves of powerful families saw men from P'yŏngan Province, they always called them "the common rabble from P'yŏngan" (p'yŏnghan). How unfair and what a source of resentment this is for the people of P'yŏngan Province! Whenever the government faces a dangerous situation, it always depends on the military power of P'yŏngan, and it also borrows the talents of literati from P'yŏngan Province at the time of the civil service examinations. In the last four hundred years of the Chosŏn dynasty, have the P'yŏngan people ever turned their backs on the government?[2]

It is quite difficult both to pinpoint when this regional discrimination emerged and to locate the sources of it. The discrimination itself is closely related to the particular regional history of P'yŏngan Province, which was, of course, also conditioned by the larger structural changes in Chosŏn society. What is important is that the discrimination alone did not necessarily create favorable conditions for a rebellion. We know this because all marginalized elite living in peripheral regions in the late Chosŏn period were subjected to political discrimination, because power and prestige were dominated by the relatively few nationally renowned elite residing in the capital or its vicinity. In the case of P'yŏngan Province, the regional elite, who seem to have been relatively undistinguished in the central political arena in the early Chosŏn period, came to invest their resources in learning and in the examination system, joining the central court in increasing numbers in the late Chosŏn period. Yet despite their phenomenal growth in numbers and their aspiration to acquire high prestige and privileges at the center, their careers ended early, and with less than expected honor, because of the political as well as social discrimination against the people of P'yŏngan Province, which was firmly entrenched by then. After experiencing this contradiction between the Confucian ideal of meritocracy and the exclusionary political practices of the central elite, these self-empowered regional elite became extremely frustrated and acutely resentful of the central government, providing a well-grounded pretext for a rebellion. At the same time, regional politics had been creating schism and conflict among members of the local elite, resulting in divided allegiances concerning the rebellion. To understand this complicated landscape of national and regional politics and social conditions, I trace the regional history of P'yŏngan Province, the formation and growth of the northern elite, the emergence and nature of the prejudice and resultant discrimination against people from this region, the dynamic construction of regional identity, and the regional elite's negotiations with various conflicting identities.

EARLY HISTORY OF THE NORTHERN REGION

P'yŏngan Province is often remembered as the founding place of the Korean people and states, although it underwent a long history of territorial conflict among various political entities before it finally became a part of Koryŏ (918–1392).[3] Old Chosŏn, whose territory may have included the northwestern part of the Korean peninsula, appears in Chinese sources as early as the fourth century B.C.E., but the location of this early state has not been confirmed.[4] Historical records reveal a more detailed and clearer picture of the history of the northwest region after Wiman (Ch.: Wei Man), a refugee from the Chinese state of Yan (?–222 B.C.E.), usurped the throne from King Chun of the Old Chosŏn kingdom sometime between 194 and 180 B.C.E. Wiman Chosŏn fell in 108 B.C.E. to the Chinese Han dynasty (194 B.C.E.– 220 C.E.), which subsequently set up commanderies, including Lelang commandery (Kor.: Nangnang, 108 B.C.E.–313 C.E.) in the former Chosŏn territory.[5] Lelang occupied the plains of northwest Korea, directly controlling lowland areas, but on the periphery it simply recognized indigenous rulers by giving them titles. Lelang survived the disintegration of the Han in China. The Koguryŏ state (?–668), which from early on controlled highland areas on northern Korea and Manchuria, began advancing onto the plains of northwest Korea in the third and fourth centuries A.D. and successfully took over Lelang in 313. Koguryŏ ruled the region until it failed to defend itself from the joint attack of Tang China (617–907) and the Silla kingdom (?–935) in 668. After the demise of Koguryŏ, this area was occupied by various tribal groups, including the Mohe, Khitan, and Jurchen, as well as the remnants of Koguryŏ's people. The Parhae state (Ch.: Bohai, 698–926), whose ethnic composition and rulership are quite controversial, controlled a part of northern Korea at some point.[6]

As soon as Wang Kŏn established Koryŏ dynasty in 918, he pursued a northern expansion policy, pushed the borders north to the Ch'ŏngch'ŏn River, and rebuilt P'yŏngyang, the former Koguryŏ capital, which had been abandoned since the fall of Koguryŏ. With the reconstruction of P'yŏngyang as a secondary capital and with the northward expansion policy, the tradition that Koryŏ was the successor of the Korean-Manchurian state of Koguryŏ was established during the early years of the Koryŏ dynasty.[7] Koryŏ's northern expansion effort brought constant conflict with northern tribes, which often built a strong military and posed a threat to Koryŏ. After going through three major invasions by the Khitan, which formed the Liao dynasty in 947 and successively occupied northern China and Manchuria, Koryŏ gained a foothold on the lower reach of the Amnok River. Koryŏ built a long wall stretching from the mouth of the Amnok a thousand *ri* eastward to the modern city of Yŏnghŭng on the Eastern Sea over a twelve-year period, from 1033 to 1044.[8] In addition, the government built forts and walls around the towns and moved people from other regions to this newly acquired area to secure the border region.[9]

The Jurchen tribal people, who inhabited Manchuria and the northern part of the Korean peninsula—including modern-day Hamgyŏng Province and P'yŏngan Province north of the Taedong River—posed another military challenge to Koryŏ soon after the Koryŏ court made peace with the Liao. The Koryŏ dynasty tried to secure its northeastern territory by establishing military garrisons in the region in 1107, but its efforts were blocked by the Jurchen people, who were consolidating tribal groups into a state. The Jurchen at last founded the Jin dynasty in 1115 and defeated the Liao dynasty ten years later. In 1127, the Jin successfully drove the Chinese Song dynasty south of the Yangzi River and occupied north China proper. Meanwhile, Koryŏ, which had severed its formal relations with the Song when it had concluded a peace with the Khitan Liao in 1022, acknowledged its tributary status to the Jin by 1116.[10]

Not only external forces but also internal rebellions threatened the security of this northern region throughout the Koryŏ period. Most prominently, Myoch'ŏng's conflict with the Kaesŏng-based aristocracy led him and his followers to revolt in 1135. Couching his strategy in geomantic terms, Myoch'ŏng maintained that the court should move its capital to P'yŏngyang because Kaesŏng, the capital of Koryŏ, had lost its geomantic virtue, when in fact he wished to remove the king and the center of power out of reach of the existing capital aristocracy. He also believed that the Koryŏ king should declare himself emperor and adopt his own reign name, thus asserting Koryŏ's equality with the Chinese Song and Jurchen Jin dynasties. Furthermore, Myoch'ŏng proposed launching an attack against the Jin. Although the rebellion was pacified after a year-long campaign and the region was again put under the control of the court, P'yŏngyang lost its previous luster.[11]

Political and social tensions that had built up in the Koryŏ court exploded in the form of the military revolt of 1170, after which a handful of military men usurped power and authority from civil aristocrats for almost a century.[12] In 1174, Cho Wich'ong, secretary of military affairs and concurrent commandant of the western capital (Sŏgyŏng, present-day P'yŏngyang), and his followers from the northern border region (Pukkye)[13] rebelled against Chŏng Chungbu and Yi Ŭibang, de facto rulers of the dynasty ever since the military coup of 1170. All the local government officials in the area north of Chŏllyŏng Pass except one, Yŏnju, joined Cho Wich'ong's force when Cho sent a message asserting that the military rulers in Kaegsŏng had already sent out an expeditionary force to repress the northern border area, which had become too strong militarily. The message urged the local elite in the northern region to immediately gather a force to defend themselves, rather than being wiped out by the military rulers. It took twenty-two months to quell the revolt, and even then, the remnants of Cho's forces entrenched themselves on Mount Myohyang and continued to cause disturbances for many years.[14]

Upon the rise of the Mongols, a nomadic herding people in the steppe region of north central Asia, the northern border area of Koryŏ became a place of constant turmoil. In the early thirteenth century, the Khitan entered the area, driven by the pressure of the Mongols, and made a defensive stand at Kangdong Fortress, east of P'yŏngyang. Even after the Khitan surrendered to the combined Mongol-Koryŏ forces in 1219, the region suffered a series of attacks by the Mongols. In 1269, Ch'oe T'an and Han Sin, low-level officials at the military commander's office in the northwestern border region, revolted against Im Yŏn. Im Yŏn was a military commander who had seized power by eliminating his predecessor, Kim Chun, and who had even deposed King Wŏnjong, who had put the pro-Mongol policy into effect. The rebels, who controlled the western capital and other walled towns in the border regions, surrendered to the Mongols, who subsequently set up the Tongnyŏng Administration in P'yŏngyang in 1270 and appointed Ch'oe T'an to rule the area north of Chabiryŏng Pass. Upon a request from the Koryŏ court, the Mongols returned the territory to Koryŏ in 1290 and moved the Tongnyŏng Administration to Liaodong in southwestern Manchuria. The Mongols also established the Ssangsŏng commandery in Hamgyŏng Province, north of Chŏllyŏng Pass, which was only recovered by force of arms in 1356.[15]

The trouble, however, continued with the invasions of the Red Turbans, a large Chinese rebel army from northern China. On two occasions, in 1359 and 1361, they swept across Manchuria and devastated the northwest region of Korea temporarily. They sacked and burned the capital, forcing the Koryŏ court to flee to Kanghwa Island while the invading forces pillaged the countryside. Although Kaesŏng was retaken in 1362 and the rebels were pushed back across the Amnok River, small bands of rebel soldiers continued to disturb Koryŏ territory from time to time.

Koryŏ had incorporated the area up to the lower Amnok in 993, as a result of a treaty with the Khitan, but it had never been able to place the area under secure government control because of constant incursions launched by tribal groups and because of internal disturbances as well. After the founding of the Chosŏn dynasty in 1392, one of the new court's most critical concerns was securing the border area to the north, which was widely inhabited by various Jurchen tribes. The Chosŏn court adopted a two-pronged policy of appeasement and military subjugation, depending on the situation. The court's conciliatory measures operated within the "ritual space" of Chosŏn diplomatic order, which placed the Ming at the top, Chosŏn in the middle, and the Jurchen at the bottom. Within this hierarchical order, Jurchen leaders enjoyed the privileges of conducting tribute trade; receiving ranks, titles, and even stipends; and participating in tribute rites by "moving up to" the capital and the king. In return for providing economic and political security to the

Jurchen, the Chosŏn court was able to alleviate their predatory behavior, thereby introducing stability to the area. This policy, however, did not silence the Jurchen completely. When Jurchen, especially those living north of the Amnok and Tuman (Ch.: Tumen) rivers, posed a heightened security concern, the court sent out expeditionary forces to put them down. At the same time, four districts in the upper reaches of the Amnok River and six garrisons in the lower reach of the Tuman River, along with numerous military stations, were established in the fifteenth century for administrative and defense purposes.[16]

Together with strengthened defense measures along the two rivers, organized transfers of people to the northern border region took place in the fifteenth and sixteenth centuries. People living in the southern part of Hamgyŏng and P'yŏngan provinces were moved to the northern part of those provinces first, and migrants from the southern three provinces were then placed in three northern provinces. Although yangban, public and private slaves, and those who provided special services to the government were exempted from forced migration by certain stipulations, the government found commoner households who were wealthy and who had more than three able-bodied men more suitable for relocation because their economic resources and manpower could be utilized for a successful settlement. Many of those who were selected to move apparently resisted the relocation policy, realizing that the northern terrain was barren, that customs there were different, and that the inhabitants of northern provinces were taxed more heavily, both to accommodate frequent foreign missions to and from China and for defense purposes. Emotionally, people also hated leaving their homesteads where they had built their lives and where their ancestors' tombs were located. Consequently, the government tried to provide all possible incentives to encourage relocation. It provided transportation and other moving expenses. The settlers were given land to reclaim and various tax breaks so as to stabilize their settlement. Those who volunteered to move to northern locations were also offered opportunities to earn local ranks and titles (*t'ogwanjik*), which in principle opened up an avenue to entering the central bureaucracy.[17]

In addition, some criminals and their households were forced to move to the north as a punishment and as a way of populating the region at the same time. Criminals who were sentenced to "the punishment of relocating their whole household to the border region" (*chŏn'ga sabyŏn yul*) were frequently sent to the area, especially in the sixteenth century. The crimes to which mandatory relocation was applied ranged from simple theft and robbery to concealment of public and private slaves from the government, forcible conversion of commoners into slaves, arbitrary occupation of land, evasion of taxes and of payment of debts, forgery of documents, the wrongful impeachment of district magistrates, and violation of Confucian social norms such as filial piety.

Those corrupt clerks (*wŏnak hyangni*) who committed crimes at the time of land, household, and military registrations were also moved to the northern provinces.[18] This particular policy was intended to root out indigenous power holders (*t'oho*), such as local strongmen (*hyangni*) in the southern provinces, who were hindering the central government's efforts to integrate the whole country under its control by reorganizing local administrations and by registering land under cultivation and enlisting adult males in the military roster in the early Chosŏn.[19] The *hyangni*, who played a dominant role in the Koryŏ period by hereditary succession, control of land, and domination of local politics, had been reduced to inferior status as unsalaried clerks in the district magistrate's administration office through various measures taken in the late fourteenth and early fifteenth centuries, such as prohibiting them from taking the civil service examinations and prescribing distinguishable dress codes. Although such legal measures certainly contributed to downgrading the social and political standing of *hyangni* in the countryside, the process of differentiation between *hyangni* (as merely local administrative clerks) and *sajok* (hereditary yangban who were primarily central office-holders and scholars) and their respective descendants evolved throughout the early Chosŏn period. The physical detachment of *hyangni* from their places of origin, by forcibly relocating them to border regions and post stations, thus had the dual effect of removing indigenous power holders from their power base and of supplying administrative experts to these newly acquired areas, which did not have indigenous *hyangni*.[20]

THE NORTHERN ELITE IN THE EARLY CHOSŎN PERIOD

What was the social condition of the northern region when these migrants of various status backgrounds tried to settle there? First, the northern region—except for Sangwŏn, Chunghwa, Anbyŏn, and Yŏnghŭng—did not have any indigenous surname groups (*t'osŏng*) that represented the powerful families of the area, both because the ancestral seat system (*sŏnggwan chedo*), which identified descent groups by geographic place of origin, originated from late Silla and very early Koryŏ times and because the region north of the Taedong River and Wŏnsan in Hamgyŏng Province was not yet Korean territory at the time.[21] Subsequently, individuals from prominent descent groups in other areas relocated there and established separate lines of descent groups (*ipchinsŏng, ipsŏng, naesŏng*) from their places of origin, which came to compose the ruling stratum in this region during the Koryŏ and early Chosŏn periods.[22] Although the fortunes of these families fluctuated greatly, due to the frequent military engagements and major rebellions in this region, some descent groups produced prominent officials and scholars active in the central court during the late Koryŏ, for they played an important role as power brokers between the Yuan (1234–1368) and Koryŏ and also as military commanders.[23] Nonetheless, the area's relative paucity of indigenous hereditary elite families and its instability as a frontier border region resulted in the underrepresentation of this region in terms of producing prominent personalities (*inmul*) throughout the Koryŏ (see table 1). For example, the Chosŏn compilers of the *Sinjŭng tongguk yŏji sŭngnam* (Augmented Survey of the Geography of Korea), probably the first dynastywide geographical survey of Chosŏn, found only 24 (3.87 percent) out of 619 prominent personalities under the Koryŏ court to be from the area subsequently designated P'yŏngan Province by the Chosŏn dynasty. This trend of underrepresentation continued in the early Chosŏn, for only 16 (3.18 percent) out of 503 prominent personalities in the new dynasty came from the same province.[24]

Although the northern region produced relatively few prominent personalities in the Koryŏ and early Chosŏn, this does not mean that there was no hereditary ruling stratum in the area. The ruling elite in the area were incorporated into the specially designed institution of the indigenous office and rank system (*t'ogwan chedo*), which had originated in the late Koryŏ, when special offices to be filled by native residents (*t'ogwan*) were created in three areas restored from Mongol occupation—Cheju, P'yŏngyang, and Yŏnghŭng. The system had been adopted in ten more districts along the northern border area by the end of King Sejong's reign (r. 1418–50), to strengthen the security of the area. Like the central bureaucratic structure, *t'ogwan* were divided into civil and military branches; the officials who filled them were appointed from among local residents by the provincial governor and military commander, respectively. They could earn as high as the fifth rank, received a salary, and were given the privilege of potential entrance into the central bureaucracy, in which case their central rank was reduced to one lower than their *t'ogwan* rank.[25]

In addition to the *t'ogwan* system, the northern elite could enter the central bureaucracy through various lower-level military positions, which they obtained via simple selection processes. In particular, a number of positions

TABLE 1. Prominent Personalities (*inmul*) of the Koryŏ and the Chosŏn Dynasties

Province	Koryŏ	Chosŏn	Total inmul (Koryŏ + Chosŏn)	Population
Kyŏnggi	104 (0.206) ((16.8))	78 (0.154) [15.5]	182 (0.361) {16.22}	50,352
Ch'ungch'ŏng	76 (0.075) ((12.27))	51 (0.05) [10.13]	127 (0.126) {11.31}	100,790
Kyŏngsang	189 (0.108) ((30.53))	212 (0.122) [42.14]	401 (0.23) {35.73}	173,759
Chŏlla	122 (0.129) ((19.7))	72 (0.076) [14.31]	194 (0.205) {17.29}	94,248
Hwanghae	51 (0.07) ((8.23))	48 (0.066) [9.54]	99 (0.137) {8.82}	71,897
Kangwŏn	50 (0.172) ((8.07))	22 (0.075) [4.37]	72 (0.248) {6.41}	29,009
Hamgyŏng	3 (0.004) ((0.48))	4 (0.005) [0.79]	7 (0.01) {0.62}	66,978
P'yŏngan	24 (0.022) ((3.87))	16 (0.015) [3.18]	40 (0.037) {3.56}	105,444
Total	619	503	1,122	

SOURCE: *Sinjŭng tongguk yŏji sŭngnam.*
( ) = percentage of total area population
(( )) = percentage of total Koryŏ *inmul*
[ ] = percentage of total Chosŏn *inmul*
{ } = percentage of grand total *inmul*

in the royal guard units, such as Kyŏmsabok and Ch'in'gunwi, were set aside for northerners.[26] All these measures were devised to integrate and appease power holders of the border region, including Jurchen leaders, since the constant military attention and cooperation of the natives were needed there. As these military needs diminished, the prestige that accrued to indigenous offices seemed to dwindle. Indeed, it was rare for *t'ogwan* to advance into the central bureaucracy, and even when this happened they only obtained low-rank military positions. Nevertheless, this institution must have provided these local elite with a strong foothold for maintaining their privileged status and with some leverage for establishing an elite tradition in the northern provinces.

Early Chosŏn migrants from the south supplied fresh blood for the ruling stratum in the northern provinces, as Paek Kyŏnghae (1765–1842), a late Chosŏn literatus from Chŏngju, remembered in 1802. He wrote, "From 1484, during the reign of King Sŏngjong, [the court] selected wealthy and powerful families [from the south] and relocated them there [to Kwansŏ] to populate the area. Now, if examining great families of Kwansŏ, eight or nine of the ten began to reside there from that time."[27] The phenomenon of elite families of southern origin relocating to the northern region was not unlike the exodus of the same elite families to southern provinces other than their place of origin in approximately the same time period. That is, relocation of residence took place frequently in the early Chosŏn period for various reasons, such as uxorilocal marriage, banishment, reclamation of land, and scenic attraction.[28] It was rare for members of the southern elite to move into the northern area via marriage relations because the Chosŏn elite generally practiced regional endogamy. Thus the most likely reasons for them to establish residence in the north were the voluntary and forcible relocation policies in the early Chosŏn.

Some general remarks in the middle of court discussions on the relocation policies shed some light on *sajok* migration to the north. In 1442, the state councilors remarked that many migrants were family members of the powerful local elite and previous officials (*hyanggok uho yup'um chaje*) from the south.[29] And discussions during the reign of King Chŏngjong (1398–1400) about waiving the punishment of forcible relocation to the northern region for *sajok* criminals show that until then the *sajok* were indeed sent to the north when they were sentenced to the punishment of "relocation of the whole household to the border region." According to the advice rendered by the Ministry of Punishments (Hyŏngjo) in 1525, those who concealed more than three public or private slaves from the government roster had received this punishment even when they were incumbent officials, descendants of merit subjects, or lower examination passers, pursuant to the 1485 regulation.[30] The policies had not been strictly instituted all the time, but the southern elite's fear of the punishment of relocation was very real when the government tried to tighten its grip on human resources; even an incumbent scholar-official, Yi Hwang (1501–70), showed great concern in 1554 that those who evaded military duty would be relocated to the border region once discovered.[31]

Although the extreme paucity of primary sources renders it difficult to reconstruct exactly which status groups of people migrated to the northern region when and for what reasons, it is possible to document a few specific cases.[32] Based on his field survey conducted in the early 1930s, the Japanese scholar Zenshō Eisuke (1885–?) found that a number of same surname villages (J.: *dōzoku buraku*, Kor.: *tongjok purak*) in northern P'yŏngan Province had been established by those banished to the area in the early Chosŏn period. For example, Kim Segyun of Kyŏngju Kim committed a certain crime in the early Chosŏn period and was banished to Yŏngbyŏn. Even after he had served his full sentence, he decided to stay in the area because he saw economic opportunity there. Kim Ŭijin of Kyŏngju Kim, one of the literati purged by Yŏnsan'gun (1494–1506), was exiled to Yŏngbyŏn and founded his residence there with his wife, Madame Kil. And Kim Chusŏ of Andong Kim, a proctor of the Hall of Worthies (Chiphyŏnjŏn Haksa), was banished in the early Chosŏn to Yongch'ŏn, which was subsequently the home of his descendants.[33]

Three genealogies compiled by prominent yangban descent groups resident in Chŏngju and Ch'ŏlsan also disclose the origins of the northern elite. The case of the Yŏnan Kim was the result of the state's relocation policy, whereas those of the Haeju No and the Ch'ŏlsan Hadong Chŏng were driven by banishment.[34] The Yŏnan Kim, one of the moved-in surname groups (*ipchinsŏng*) recorded in the *Sejong sillok chiriji* (The Veritable Records of King Sejong, Geographic Survey) and the *Sinjŭng tongguk yŏji sŭngnam* (Augmented Survey of the Geography of Korea),[35] claim that their ancestor Kim Anju, chief magistrate of Kaesŏng, migrated to the north in observance of the state's relocation policy, which mandated that a household with numerous sons must move. Kim's four sons settled in different locations in the Ch'ŏngbuk region, though the descendants of the first son, who established his residence in Chŏngju, flourished the most. The case of the Haeju No descent group is a clear example of an early Chosŏn official who set up a permanent residence in the northern region after he was exiled there.[36] No

Segŏl (?–1529), who held the junior sixth position of ritual preceptor (Inŭi) at the Office of Ceremonies (T'ongnyewŏn), was accused in 1521 of participating in the conspiracy allegedly led by An Tang (1461–1521) and his son An Ch'ŏgyŏm (1486–1521) to oust high ministers from the court. King Chungjong listened to the accusation, leveled by Song Saryŏn, and purged a large number of officials close to the An family.[37] No Segŏl was first banished to Haeju, Hwanghae Province, then removed to Chŏngju.[38] He was posthumously pardoned in 1533.[39] Another example of the relocation of criminals to the north is the case of the Ch'ŏlsan Hadong Chŏng descent group, which had established its residence in Ch'ŏlsan in the early Chosŏn period. Chŏng Lim, the founder of a Ch'ŏlsan branch of the descent group, held the position of historian (Hallim) when he was banished to the area after offering his views against the king's will.[40] All his family members probably moved to Ch'ŏlsan and began to form a separate line from its southern counterpart, which was one of the top yangban descent groups that produced famous officials and scholars throughout the Chosŏn period.[41]

THE LOCAL ELITE: CONSOLIDATION, DIVISION, AND COMPETITION

How the local order had been shaped in P'yŏngan Province in the early Chosŏn period is not very clear. Gazetteers sporadically mention that distinguished scholars and officials in the early Chosŏn introduced Confucian learning and rites to the region. For example, in Chŏngju, Cho Hŏn (1544–92), who held the position of preceptor (Kyosu), was remembered as the person who had laid the foundation of Confucian learning in the area;[42] Kim Sangyong (1561–1637), who had once served as the magistrate of that district, was known to have greatly promoted Confucianism; and two other magistrates, Maeng Sehyŏng (1588–1656) and Maeng Chusŏ (1622–?), were also renowned for spreading Confucian teachings to young scholars in the area.[43] According to the gazetteer of Yŏngbyŏn, Kim Kyehwi (1526–82), the distinguished Neo-Confucian scholar Kim Changsaeng's father, and Yi Wŏnik (1547–1634) established two provincial learning centers in P'yŏngyang and Chŏngju to propagate Neo-Confucian teachings there. In addition, the gazetteer states that the Confucian tradition was fortified by a publication drive initiated by Special Commissioner Min Yujung (1630–87), who supported publication of *The Elementary Learning* (*Sohak*, Ch.: *Xiaoxue*) and essential ritual manuals.[44] Gazetteers also noted that the local elite participated in various Confucian cultural practices, such as wine-drinking and arrow-shooting ceremonies, and organized themselves into local yangban associations in the sixteenth century.

A more concrete picture of local society can be reconstructed for the period after the major invasions by the Japanese (1592–98) and Manchus (1627, 1636). As was the case for local yangban elite in the south, these wars gave the northern elite optimal opportunities to consolidate power and prestige in their own communities. During the war years, most local yangban were successful in organizing militia units (*ŭibyŏng*) and defending the immediate areas in which their interests lay. The Chosŏn state, unable to defend the country against its invaders and on the verge of demise, had to endorse the yangban's military activities—and, indeed, viewed these activities as a manifestation of loyalty toward the court, which subsequently rewarded militia leaders with honorary ranks and offices. Hence local yangban not only confirmed their status as a ruling class in their local societies by establishing their military merit and earning honorary ranks and offices, but also reestablished local order and their own power and prestige by reconstructing various Confucian institutions.[45]

Members of the Ch'ŏlsan Hadong Chŏng descent group for example established a record of distinguished merit during the Japanese and Manchu invasions. Two major figures, the brothers Chŏng Pongsu and Chŏng Kisu, played a critical role in defending strategic areas in northern P'yŏngan Province. As a reward for their military services, Chŏng Pongsu was given the honorary title "Duke of Cultivating the Military" (Yangmu-gong) and went through various offices as high as a senior third rank position in the Military Training Command (Hullyŏn tojŏng), while Chŏng Kisu was appointed to a junior sixth rank magistrate post (Hyŏn'gam) and a junior fifth rank military office (P'anggwan).[46] The wars gave members of this descent group the opportunity to enhance and perpetuate their position as a prestigious family in the area, as they were in the southern provinces. Their descendants thereafter established a powerful yangban family in the Ch'ŏlsan area by producing twenty *munkwa* passers and numerous military examination passers.[47]

Chŏngju—which turned out to be the rebel stronghold during the 1812 rebellion—provides an excellent window through which to learn how reconstruction of the Confucian order took place in the late Chosŏn period. Surviving records testify to the fact that three men from three descent groups—Kim Samjun (1608–76) of Yŏnan Kim, Im Taejik (1599–1681) of Anŭi Im, and No Chinjong (1611–90) of Haeju No—displayed splendid leadership in reestablishing social order after the major invasions by the Japanese and

Manchus. The three men were actually relatives by marriage, for their ancestors had married one another at least from the sixteenth century on.[48] They established themselves as leaders during the Manchu invasions by either organizing militia or supporting government forces to defend the area from the Manchu invaders. For example, No Chinjong of Haeju No, a sixth-generation descendant of No Segŏl, led a militia against Manchu invaders. After the wars, No Chinjong accrued wealth by reclaiming wasteland and building irrigation infrastructure. He did not spare his own wealth in rebuilding the local Confucian order and even assisted fellow members of the local elite who were in financial trouble.[49] Im Taejik, together with Kim Samjun, established a shrine in 1666 to commemorate the aforementioned Kim Sangyong and his younger brother Kim Sanghŏn (1570–1652), who had played such a significant role in propagating Confucian mores in the area. The shrine received a royal charter of Pongmyŏng private academy (*sŏwŏn*) in 1671. Im and Kim also promulgated rules for the local school and for Confucian wine-drinking rites.[50] Most importantly, the three men put genuine effort into revitalizing the local yangban association in the mid-seventeenth century.[51]

The institution of the local yangban association deserves special examination because it sheds important light both on the consolidation and preservation of the elite group in local northern society and on the competition and conflict within that elite community. The conflict—and resultant division—among local elite was heavily reflected in the memberships of the rebels as well as counterrebels in 1812, as discussed later in this book. Compilation of the local yangban roster and participation in its members' association (*hyangan*)[52] were two of the most outstanding cultural practices of the elite in the late Chosŏn period. The *hyangan*, which represented major local descent groups, was self-regulating and self-disciplined institutions whose basic purpose was the preservation of local elite descent groups and their interests. The members of the association were supposed to promote a sociopolitical order based on ritual and ethical Confucian thought and action in the local community. The institution also undertook the maintenance of local security and welfare through supervision of personnel in the public administration bureau (Chakch'ŏng) and the military administration bureau (Much'ŏng). Through the local yangban bureau (Hyangch'ŏng)[53]—whose officers, such as director (Chwasu), assistant director (Pyŏlgam), and granary supervisor (Ch'anggam), were elected by the local yangban association—the local yangban association was deeply involved in local administrative affairs, especially taxation and military service.[54]

The local yangban association was an exclusive organization; only local yangban with the proper family background were admitted to it after earning unanimous support from the original members. Thus degree-holders of civil and military service examinations and even prominent scholars did not automatically qualify for membership, and yangban who had relocated from other districts were often excluded from the organization.[55] As a corollary, the association became an increasingly attractive institution for an ever-growing number of rural yangban who sought to preserve their status in the local community. Membership not only enhanced members' social standing but also provided material benefits, such as exemption from labor and military service. Moreover, since local taxation and other local affairs were under the command of the association, membership conferred some ability to control local resources.

Due to such attractiveness and the exclusivity of the *hyangan*, the repeated compilation, revision, and rescinding of membership over the years became a source of local struggle. By the eighteenth or nineteenth century, depending on the internal social and political conditions of each district, the nature and function of the *hyangan* had gone through changes. The yangban population grew during the late Chosŏn dynasty, both because of natural population growth and because the perceived definition of yangban—by which all the descendants of a prominent ancestor were qualified to claim yangban status—inevitably resulted in more and more yangban. Social and political changes during the late Chosŏn further complicated the membership composition of the associations. For example, nothoi (*sŏŏl*) began to demand to be included in the yangban category after the legal abolition, in 1695, of the earlier prohibition against their taking the civil service examination and holding office in the regular bureaucracy.[56] And after the military tax reform of 1751, local yangban previously excluded from an association wanted their names listed in the roster to verify their yangban status and to receive exemption from military service.[57]

The responses to such unforeseen changes were manifold. In some districts, the number of new members admitted to the *hyangan* increased dramatically beginning in the early eighteenth century. In others, the updating of membership ceased and the roster itself was sealed off in storage to prevent unqualified members, such as nothoi, from penetrating the institution. When non-yangban members began to encroach upon this exclusive organization, the established yangban in local society tended to form similar but separate institutions and rosters to clarify the distinction between the established, original yangban members (*kuhyang*) and the new members (*sinoyang*).[58]

In extreme cases, the exclusivity of the institution and the ever-increasing number of aspirants in the late Chosŏn combined to create local strife (*hyangjŏn*)—namely, a power struggle among various groups of yangban, and even non-yangban, in the local society.[59] Although the stratification of local yangban in the late Chosŏn period was indeed too diverse to generalize about, it is very clear that the effort of the established yangban to maintain their grip on power and prestige met with various challenges and generated considerable friction in local society.

Such discord is evident in the case of the Chŏngju yangban association. The original rules and functions of this yangban association were very similar to those found in the south. The Chŏngju yangban roster was restored by the initiative of the Kim Samjun, Im Taejik, and No Chinjong in 1646, based on the earlier rosters lost during the Japanese and Manchu wars. This roster included sixty-six members representing twenty-eight major descent groups in Chŏngju, and these original members were later designated "established yangban" (*kuhyang*). In principle, membership was given to the brothers and sons of the original members. The only exceptions were granted to those who excelled in scholarship and who then received unanimous approval from existing members. The roster was subsequently revised to update its membership several times, but all rosters, including the 1646 one, were destroyed in 1766 because of unknown conflict, probably between members and nonmembers over qualifications for membership. Right after the incident, the roster was restored again, but the compilers of the 1766 roster decided to record only those 158 original members from four previous rosters (1646, 1672, 1691, and 1706) who represented forty-one prominent descent groups and their branches in Chŏngju, for local people knew the descendants of those original members even though their names were not recorded in the roster.[60] After 1766, a copy of the roster was kept in each member's house, in order to deny physical access to the roster to new aspirants and thus maintain the roster's authenticity. Interestingly, Kim Poman, who wrote the prologue of the 1766 edition, pointedly commented that the yangban association was a matter of local yangban, not something to be determined by the state authority, suggesting that the state had played a role in destroying the original rosters.[61]

As hinted in the 1766 incident, the elite society of Chŏngju must have already been experiencing division and conflict. One later source reports that the Chŏngju elite were divided into the established group of yangban (*kuhyang*), the new group of yangban (*sinhyang*), and those who had not yet been able to participate in the yangban association (*hyangoein*).[62] A close investigation of four extant rosters and genealogies reveals that only those members of the 1646 roster and their descendants were called *kuhyang*, while those from three later rosters and their descendants were called *sinhyang*. And the division between *kuhyang* and *sinhyang* is observed even within a single descent group, in which one branch belonged to the *kuhyang* while the other belonged to the *sinhyang*. Interestingly, the *kuhyang* group was most successful in producing *munkwa* passers and was also most active in local politics.[63]

To further complicate matters, the Chŏngju yangban association granted membership in return for monetary contributions (*yejŏn*) from the early eighteenth century on.[64] The funds raised in this way were used for various public matters, including repairing public buildings and relief of the hungry, orphans, and widows. Although the central court prohibited this method of fundraising, the local government was actively involved in such enterprise for this was a handy way of raising funds and an opportunity for self-aggrandizement as well. The original members of the yangban association (*wŏnhyang*) assisted the district government in selecting new members (*sinhyang*) and collecting contributions. Yet the sale of membership did not really bring immediate changes in local power relations because the original yangban members set up a separate roster for new members on such occasions as the sale of membership (*maehyang*), which enabled them to preserve the authenticity and authority of their exclusive elite membership.

A brief examination of an incident in 1789 involving the sale of membership reveals dynamic aspects of local politics and social conditions. The incident caught the court's attention when the widespread misappropriation of collected funds by the district magistrate, O Taeik, was discovered. In 1789, O Taeik allowed 384 new members to register for the Chŏngju roster (*ŭban*), and 364 new members for the provincial yangban roster (*yŏngan*), in return for monetary contributions of 500 to 600 *yang*[65] from each new member, for a total of more than 45,000 *yang*. A portion of the funds raised was used for district finances, but more than half was taken by O Taeik and officers at the local yangban bureau who were in charge of selecting new members. Coercive fundraising and large-scale misappropriations of the funds by local administrators invited a thorough investigation by the central government and punishment of magistrates and other officials.

First of all, the original association members who worked closely with the local yangban bureau officials and the magistrate were the most prominent people of the district, who had passed the *munkwa* exam and who held central government positions, representing the most powerful and successful descent groups in Chŏngju.[66] New members were selected according to five categories: (1) local military and civil title holders; (2) nothoi of the original members; (3) (yangban) migrants from other districts; (4) descendants of the original members; and (5) anyone with official permission from the local yangban bureau. This set of principles in the selection of members of course defied the original purpose and nature of the association and must have offended most of the original yangban. Apparently, a number of non-yangban, such as commoners obliged to military service (*p'yŏnojiryu*) and people of low status (*ch'ŏllyu*), earned membership, and those yangban who felt gravely ashamed of their names being listed side by side with these undesirable elements submitted appeals to the provincial governor's office and even wanted to leave the district. Today it is impossible to investigate the social status of new members because the 1789 roster is unavailable. However, it stands to reason that the representatives of the most renowned descent groups of Chŏngju and the highly esteemed local leaders in charge of issuing new membership would not have admitted someone of lower status into the original association, because this would have downgraded their own reputations in the local society. What really happened was that the original members kept their own original roster (*wŏn'an*), which was beyond the reach of these new members. Consequently, the new members acquired membership with their wealth but were never able to infiltrate the secure community of authentic yangban or exercise social and political power and authority in Chŏngju.[67]

Indeed, Paek Siwŏn (1776–1839) of the Suwŏn Paek of Chŏngju, who passed his *munkwa* in 1814, informs us of the highly restrictive and exalted nature of the original yangban association in the district of Chŏngju. Writing in 1813 to support the award of membership in the original roster to Han Houn (1761–1812), a *munkwa* degree-holder since 1800 who had been killed by the 1812 rebels because he preached to them on the Confucian value of loyalty, Paek Siwŏn stated that the stipulations of the yangban association were different in each district. According to him, membership in the Chŏngju yangban association had been awarded to members of established descent groups (*hwabŏl*), to those recognized as filial sons, and to prominent scholars. He regretted that no one who had earned fame with loyal behavior had yet been named a member. As for Han Houn, he had obtained a membership at some point for being a filial son but was still labeled a *sinhyang*. Thus Paek Siwŏn proposed that Han be promoted and recorded as a *wŏnhyang* to reward and pay tribute to the loyalty he had demonstrated during the rebellion.[68]

Another example, in contrast to the case of Han Houn, illustrates the insecurity of a purchased membership. Yi Hŭijŏ from Kasan, one of the original conspirators in the Hong Kyŏngnae Rebellion, had been a post-station slave but somehow passed the military examination and made his way in life by listing his name on the Kasan yangban roster. However, his membership was rescinded by the magistrate of Kasan, and he may have sought vengeance against both the magistrate and the social system at large.[69] This, in part, explains why Yi and some local wealthy residents stood by the rebels. They felt that the restrictive and closed nature of the social status system and the barriers against upward status mobility were unfair, and this may have induced them to join the upper social stratum of the new dynasty established by the rebels.

Despite government prohibition and punishment, the sale of yangban association membership was ongoing in P'yŏngan Province.[70] In Kwaksan in 1811, eight people were allowed to list their names in the roster by contributing 100 to 500 *yang* each, in order to raise a relief fund. According to the testimony of Pak Sŏnggan, a close relative of Pak Sŏngsin, one of the yangban rebel leaders, he himself had been selected as one of contributors and asked to pay 500 *yang* for the membership, though he had had great difficulty raising the money because of the shortage of copper cash (*chŏnhwang*). Pak Sŏnggan was obviously agonized by the pressure to make swift payment. He supported the rebels by contributing grain, even though he was not an active participant in the rebellion.[71] Another close relative of Pak Sŏngsin, Pak Sŏngni, was also allowed to obtain membership in the yangban association, but he asked Pak Sŏngsin, who happened to be in charge of raising the relief fund by offering memberships in the yangban association, to help him by loaning him the money, whereupon Pak Sŏngsin told him not to worry since there would be an armed rebellion soon.[72] At the time of the rebellion, Pak Sŏngni also gave 2 *sŏm* of grain in support of the rebels.[73] In the same year, twenty-eight wealthy people were selected to buy membership in the Chŏngju yangban association. One of those selected, Pak Humun, testified that each candidate was supposed to contribute 1,000 *yang*, and some even had to sell their land to do so.[74] Pak Humun himself was a close friend of rebel leader Kim Idae, the director of the yangban bureau and was suspected of supporting the rebels by contributing money and grain.[75] A portion of the contributions made by new members before the rebellion was taken over by the rebels for their expenditures.[76]

After all is said and done, does competition between old and new elites account for the makeup of rebels and loyalists in the Hong Kyŏngnae Rebellion? There is insufficient evidence to suggest that the rebellion was caused by a "newly emergent elite." Local society at the time of the rebellion was certainly very complex, multilayered, and crisscrossed with diverse networks based on kinship, village, social status, and interest group. The elite community in particular had been experiencing acute competition and conflict among themselves in terms of holding local power. It is unclear how the stratification and division of this elite group played out at the time of the rebellion, because surviving documents do not provide enough information to verify each rebel's association to the *kuhyang, sinhyang,* or *hyangoein.* Analysis of the social status of those rebels and counterrebels whose personal information is available suggests that the local yangban, along with other social status groups, had representatives in both groups. This simply reflects the divided state of the local elite. Whether to participate or not in the rebellion must have involved complex calculations having to do with kinship-group membership, social status, wealth, and personal networks, all of which are impossible to disentangle with available evidence.

2 Regional Discrimination and the Hong Kyŏngnae Rebellion

Local politics partly explains divided allegiances between the rebel sympathizers and the militia organizers at the time of the Hong Kyŏngnae Rebellion. Both groups, however, resented the exclusionary political culture of the center and resultant social and political discrimination against them. The issue of regional discrimination was the most critical tool for the rebels in provoking regional sentiment and promoting a degree of regional solidarity, although it also became a crucial weakness, for the rebels' appeal was inherently confined to a region whose ideological positions were not unified. Examining the nature of regional discrimination and the discourse of that region's identity therefore opens an avenue to understanding the rebels' ideology and strategy as well as their limitations.

P'YŎNGAN RESIDENTS IN THE CIVIL SERVICE EXAMINATIONS

In the first half of the Chosŏn dynasty, there were very few historically prominent personalities from the northern provinces (as discussed in chapter 1), and northerners did not perform well on the state examinations either. As table 2 shows, of about 1,814 *munkwa* graduates from 1392 to 1550 whose residences are known, only 22 are identified as residents of P'yŏngan Province. Particularly surprising is that no one from the Ch'ŏngbuk area was able to earn the degree in this period, largely because the area was militarily and territorially a frontier.

TABLE 2. *Munkwa* Degree-Holders from P'yŏngan Province by Half-Century Periods

	1392–1450	1451–1500	1501–1550	1551–1600	1601–1650	1651–1700	1701–1750	1751–1800	1801–1850	1851–1900	Total	% of 12,889	% of 14,607
Ch'ŏngbuk				2	3	26	57	160	147	202	597	4.63	4.09
Ch'ŏngnam	5	9	8	14	26	47	63	78	85	151	486	3.77	3.33
P'yŏngan Province Total	5	9	8	16	29	73	120	238	232	353	1083	8.40	7.41
Total[a]	376	568	870	982	1265	1424	1679	1987	1544	2194	12,889		
% with known residents in P'yŏngan	1.33%	1.58%	0.92%	1.63%	2.29%	5.13%	7.15%	11.98%	15.03%	16.09%	8.40%		
Total[b]	862	1051	1160	1242	1447	1438	1679	1987	1544	2197	14,607		
% from P'yŏngan	0.58%	0.86%	0.69%	1.29%	2.01%	5.08%	7.15%	11.98%	15.03%	16.07%	7.41%		

[a] Number of *munkwa* passers with known residences in Chosŏn.
[b] Total number of *munkwa* passers.

The political standing of northern residents in terms of passing the *munkwa* improved dramatically in the latter part of Chosŏn dynasty, as revealed in table 2 and in Edward Wagner's analysis of the local place of residence of successful candidates for the higher civil service examination degree. Indeed, northern candidates came to outperform their southern counterparts, especially considering the fact that residents of the capital city and its immediate environs accounted for about half the total number of successful candidates.[1] A close analysis of the distribution of successful candidates among the northern provinces reveals that P'yŏngan Province produced almost 70 percent of the north's successful candidates from about 50 percent of the total population of the north.[2] More interestingly, a few places within each northern province show a heavy concentration of successful passers. For example, Haeju and P'yŏngsan in Hwanghae Province, Hamhŭng and Anbyŏn in Hamgyŏng Province, and P'yŏngyang and Chŏngju in P'yŏngan Province boasted a remarkable concentration of successful candidates. The success of candidates from the town of Chŏngju, just north of the Ch'ŏngch'ŏn River, was most striking. Chŏngju, whose population was less than 4 percent of P'yŏngan and less than 2 percent of the total population of the northern provinces, produced 282 successful candidates—27 percent of the P'yŏngan total and 18.7 percent of the overall northern total.

Corresponding to the national trend, relatively few descent groups supplied a major portion of degree-holders in the northern provinces.[3] Among more than 300 descent group designations that identify northern candidates in the examination rosters, 182 descent groups (60 percent) produced one or two candidates, providing 14.5 percent of the degree-holders, while 19 percent, made up of the most successful descent groups, provided over 70 percent of the degree-holders. It is worth noting that most descent groups that accomplished illustrious success in the civil service examination in the northern provinces were branches of the main lineages residing in the southern provinces that produced many degree-holders and government officials. Wagner speculates that the forbears of the northerners whose original lineage domiciles were in southern provinces began to reside there from a very early date, even before the beginning of the Chosŏn dynasty, and that they held government positions there and remained there. The description of relocation cases of a number of northern descent groups given in chapter 1 supports Wagner's hypothesis.

The performance of northern residents on the lower civil service examinations coincided with the general trend revealed in the higher civil service

TABLE 3. *Saengwŏn* and *Chinsa* Degree-Holders by Province and Half-Century

	1392–1500	1501–1550	1551–1600	1601–1650	1651–1700	1701–1750	1751–1800	1801–1850	1851–1900	Total
Capital	253 (44.00)	1224 (46.15)	1319 (50.85)	2126 (49.09)	2487 (46.25)	2197 (42.47)	1605 (36.03)	1871 (34.65)	1256 (16.04)	14,338 ((37.35))
Kyŏnggi	51 (8.86)	163 (5.14)	154 (5.94)	187 (4.30)	429 (7.97)	449 (8.69)	593 (13.31)	679 (12.68)	1063 (13.59)	3768 ((9.82))
Ch'ungch'ŏng	40 (6.95)	175 (6.60)	217 (8.37)	533 (12.30)	690 (12.98)	789 (15.26)	658 (14.77)	717 (13.27)	1327 (16.95)	5154 ((13.44))
Chŏlla	81 (13.10)	428 (16.16)	324 (12.49)	547 (12.64)	556 (10.34)	479 (9.26)	331 (7.43)	394 (7.30)	854 (10.91)	3994 ((10.40))
Kyŏngsang	102 (17.91)	501 (18.89)	411 (15.85)	565 (13.05)	705 (13.12)	642 (12.41)	543 (12.19)	736 (13.63)	1193 (15.23)	5399 ((14.07))
Hwanghae	11 (1.91)	55 (2.08)	54 (2.08)	120 (2.77)	147 (2.73)	178 (3.44)	194 (4.34)	151 (4.34)	519 (6.62)	1512 ((3.94))

TABLE 3. (*continued*)

Kangwŏn	29	64	44	132	200	206	162	273	470	1580
	(5.05)	(2.41)	(1.71)	(3.05)	(3.73)	(3.99)	(3.64)	(5.06)	(6.00)	((4.11))
P'yŏngan	7	20	50	82	100	168	260	375	769	1831
	(1.22)	(0.76)	(1.93)	(1.89)	(1.86)	(3.25)	(4.84)	(6.94)	(9.82)	((4.75))
Hamgyŏng		21	21	37	54	54	109	117	378	799
		(0.80)	(0.80)	(0.86)	(1.01)	(1.24)	(2.45)	(2.15)	(4.82)	((2.08))
Miscellaneous		1		2	1	1		4	1	10
		(0.04)		(0.05)	(0.02)	(0.02)		(0.07)	(0.01)	((0.03))
Total	575	2652	2594	4331	5377	5173	4455	5399	7830	38,386
	[1.50]	[6.91]	[6.76]	[11.28]	[14.01]	[13.48]	[11.61]	[14.07]	[20.40]	[100.0]

SOURCE: Ch'oe Chinok, *Chosŏn sidae saengwŏn chinsa yŏn'gu*, p. 204.
() = percentage of total degree-holders per province for each time period
(()) = percentage of total degree-holders per province 1392–1900
[] = percentage of total degree-holders from all provinces for each time period

examinations. Throughout the Chosŏn period, P'yŏngan Province produced 1,831 *chinsa* or *saengwŏn* degree-holders, or 4.75 percent of the 38,386 degree-holders whose places of residence were identified.[4] As table 3 reveals, the representation of P'yŏngan Province in the lower examinations was meager until the late seventeenth century but increased noticeably after the early eighteenth century.

THE NATURE OF THE DISCRIMINATORY POLITICAL CULTURE

One might question the reality of the political discrimination against northern residents, given that in the late Chosŏn period the three northern provinces became proportionately more successful than their southern counterparts in passing the civil service examinations. There was, however, substantial political discrimination against northerners in office holding in the late Chosŏn, despite northerners' illustrious display of talent in the examination process.

In fact, the court discriminated against northern residents from the moment they passed the examination. As noted by Chŏng Yagyong (1762–1836), a renowned scholar of the late Chosŏn period, successful candidates from prestigious descent groups (*ch'ŏngjok*) were given apprenticeships in the Office of Diplomatic Correspondence (Sŭngmunwŏn), whereas northern residents were assigned to train at the Royal Academy (Sŏnggyun'gwan) and nothoi of yangban at the Office of Editorial Review (Kyosŏgwan). Military examination passers were also treated differently, in that their first jobs were assigned in accordance with their social backgrounds. Only those who were from prestigious yangban descent groups were given prestigious positions at the Office of Transmission (Sŏnjŏn'gwanch'ŏng), via which they could be promoted to higher offices. Those with less prestigious family backgrounds were given positions at the Office of Patrol (Pujangch'ŏng) or the Gatekeeper's Office (Sumunjangch'ŏng).[5] This differential treatment of successful examination candidates according to their family backgrounds did not emerge until sometime in the mid-Chosŏn. According to Yi Ik (1681–1763), another well-known scholar, in the early Chosŏn successful examination candidates were divided into groups according to their age and talent and then were placed in different offices (this initial assignment is known as *pun'gwan*). By Yi Ik's time, however, this initial assignment system had been transformed into a hierarchical one that gave preferential treatment to the members of prominent capital-based yangban families (*pŏryŏl*), because those who were assigned to the Office of Diplomatic Correspondence and the Office of Transmission had a much better chance of holding higher ranking offices.[6]

The initial assignment system was only the first of many obstacles for northerners seeking official careers. Their advancement toward the prestigious and reputable positions (*ch'ŏngyojik*) and toward positions of ministerial rank (*tangsanggwan* Sr. 1–Sr. 3) were blocked by the multiple layers of a formidable screening system. The prestigious positions (*ch'ŏngjik*) in the central government were more esteemed than others because they served in physical proximity to the king and also required great scholarship. The *ch'ŏngjik* included mid- to low-level positions both in the censorate offices and in offices in charge of recording and writing documents, such as the Office of the Censor General (Saganwŏn), the Office of the Inspector General (Sahŏnbu), the Office of the Special Counselors (Hongmun'gwan), and the Office of Royal Decrees (Yemun'gwan). The royal messenger of the Office of Transmission (Sŏnjŏn'gwan) in the military rank also belonged to this category. The reputable positions (*yojik*) were another category of prestigious positions in the court hierarchy. The positions of section chief (Chŏngnang) and assistant section chief (Chwarang) in the six ministries belonged to this class.[7] Most importantly, it was almost a prerequisite to hold those prestigious and reputable positions in order to have a ministerial rank.

One way to preserve the integrity of these prestigious offices was to control the process of selecting officials. For most offices, either the Ministry of Personnel (Yijo) or the Ministry of War (Pyŏngjo) submitted a list of three candidates to the king, who made the final decision by placing a dot beside the name of the candidate of his choice. In contrast, candidates for positions in the Office of the Special Counselors were selected by the officials currently holding positions in that office, who marked a circle by the chosen candidate's name (*kwŏnjŏm*). After the censorial offices reviewed this roster of successful candidates (Hongmullok), state councilors with second rank or higher, the director of the Office of the Special Counselors, and *tangsanggwan* of the Ministry of Personnel met to examine the qualifications of each candidate (*hoegwŏn*). The final roster (Todangnok) was presented to the king, who then appointed officials according to the grade that each candidate earned.[8] Similar steps were taken to select officials for the Office of Royal Decrees.[9]

These measures were originally designed to ensure that only talented and qualified people held prestigious positions in the government. However, they soon became an effective way to screen for family and factional backgrounds in the selection of candidates for prominent positions that guaranteed further advancement on the ladder of bureaucratic success.[10] For example, among 2,955 people listed in the Todangnok in the late Chosŏn, 78.4 percent earned *tangsanggwan* positions, whereas only 42.7 percent of *munkwa* passers obtained such positions. Not only did most of the Todangnok members live in the capital, but thirty-four of the forty top-performing descent groups represented in the Todangnok were those *pŏryŏl* identified by Ch'a Changsŏp.[11]

Such complicated screening procedures had a profound impact on the northerners' success in the central bureaucracy. An examination of the Todangnok, the roster from which members of the Office of the Special Counselors were selected, reveals no examination passers from P'yŏngan Province in the late Chosŏn.[12] This indicates that the opportunity for northern residents to acquire ministerial rank was extremely limited, because in late Chosŏn Korea the main path to *tangsanggwan* positions was through appointment to the Office of the Special Counselors.

Two social groups—nothoi of yangban and residents of the northern provinces—lodged repeated complaints against this discriminatory and exclusive appointment system. Relentless efforts to unlock this system by nothoi of yangban resulted in a series of reforms that gradually allowed them to take the civil service examinations, to hold *yojik* (beginning in 1625), and, finally, to hold *ch'ŏngjik* as well (beginning in 1772).[13] Northerners and their sympathizers also appealed to the court on numerous occasions for rectification of the unfair appointment and promotion systems. These appeals often received favorable orders from the king to resolve the issue in their favor.[14] For both nothoi and northerners, however, the reality of discriminatory practices continued until the end of the dynasty, despite legal revisions and royal efforts to undo the injustices of the appointment system.

DISCRIMINATION IN ACTION:
THE CASE OF PAEK KYŎNGHAE

The career of one man from P'yŏngan Province illuminates the discriminatory practices against residents of this region.[15] Paek Kyŏnghae (1765–1842), born to the Suwŏn Paek descent group residing in Chŏngju, began his studies at the age of five, when his father, Paek Sŏnyang, opened a village school on the sunny slopes of Kadŏk Mountain and invited the teacher Ch'oe Kyŏngnim (?–1805) to instruct his sons.[16] Paek Kyŏnghae's own talent was recognized early, for it is known that he was able to discuss the *Analects* at fourteen.[17] When he took the *munkwa* in 1786, at the age of twenty-one, the examiners assumed that he must be a man of Yŏngnam and a disciple of Yi Hwang (1501–70) or Yi Ŏnjŏk (1491–1553), the two most prominent Neo-Confucian scholars of the Chosŏn, because his scholarly performance at the examination was excellent.[18] The examiners were greatly disturbed after learning Paek's regional background—a reaction that proved to be an unfortunate prelude to the ups and downs of Paek's subsequent career.

Indeed, despite such an outstanding performance at the examination, Paek was assigned to the Royal Academy as a trainee, like other successful candidates from the northern provinces. In 1788, two years after he had earned the *munkwa* degree, Paek received his first position, as third proctor at the Royal Academy (Sŏnggyun'gwan Hagyu, Jr. 9), and concurrently served as administrator of the Bureau of Superannuation (Kiroso Sujik). As appendix B shows, his career looked quite promising in his early years at court, for he was appointed temporary recorder of the Royal Secretariat (Sŭngjŏngwŏn Ka-chusŏ), a senior seventh-rank position, almost immediately after he began his official career.

In 1789, while Paek was a recorder (Chusŏ), he encountered one of the many ordeals he endured in the course of his official career. On the twenty-second day of the second lunar month, though there was much business to take care of, Paek brilliantly carried out his job of recording court sessions and reading memorials aloud, which involved simultaneous translation and interpretation from Korean into literary Chinese and from literary Chinese into Korean. Impressed by this, King Chŏngjo (r. 1776–1800) asked which descent group the recorder came from. Not knowing the answer, Second State Councilor Yi Sŏngwŏn (1725–90) asked Paek. Paek answered, "I belong to the descent group of previous third inspector of the Office of Inspector General (Sahŏnbu Changnyŏng) Paek Inhwan."[19] After hearing this, the king said, "Then you are not the descendant of Paek Ingŏl." (Paek Ingŏl was also a member of the Suwŏn Paek descent group but belonged to a different branch that flourished in the south.) Third State Councilor Ch'ae Chegong (1720–99) then commented, "How could a person from a remote place know about Paek Ingŏl?" Upon the king's praise of Paek's outstanding literary talent, Ch'ae again remarked sarcastically, "That was not the real nature of a person from a remote place [*hat'o-chi-in*]." The king, however, not only repeatedly praised Paek's ability but also promoted him to assistant section chief of the Ministry of Rites, ignoring these pointed comments from high ministers.[20]

This promotion was a coup for Paek, both because this position was one of the *yojik* and one rarely bestowed on a person from P'yŏngan Province and because it meant that he had been promoted to the *ch'amsanggwan* (positions of rank six and above), a major hurdle for all members of the Chosŏn court in their advancement toward higher positions in the bureaucratic hierarchy. Yet he also had to face a censorate's rebuff of his promotion on grounds of the rarity of a person from the countryside (*hyanggok-chi-in*) holding such a prestigious position. Probably under special protection provided by the king, Paek did manage to assume the position of assistant section chief.[21]

Nonetheless, the king's favor was not consistent, as exemplified in two incidents in 1789 and 1790. The episodes had to do with King Chŏngjo's power game against court officials of the highest echelon over the treatment of a close royal family member, and the king expected Paek, who was a historian (Kyŏmsa) at the time, to side with him unconditionally. Paek's political orientation at the time is unknown, but he twice disobeyed royal orders because he considered them in violation of proper norms and values. On the first occasion, he received the rather demeaning royal admonition that the position of Kyŏmsa was not much different from that of a eunuch (implying that he must thus be subservient to the king). The second time, Paek was repeatedly scolded by the king and beaten for punishment. He not only lost his position but did not receive any appointments between 1790 and 1801, except for a few months in 1794–95 when he held the position of section chief of the Ministry of Rites (Yejo Chŏngnang).[22]

One can argue that Paek's demotion in these two cases had little to do with his regional background but was the result of court politics. Nonetheless, the court politics that the king tried to take advantage of at the time were closely tied to regional issues. According to Paek, the position of Kyŏmsa had originally been one of the *yojik*, but from 1776 on it had been given to men from the countryside, especially those from P'yŏngan Province.[23] This policy can itself be seen as one of the measures the king took to augment monarchical power and authority by hiring people previously marginalized from central political power. However, the original purpose did not seem to prevail, for the esteem in which a Kyŏmsa was held had declined ever since the policy was adopted. Paek argued that the degradation of the position had worsened because Kim Ponghyŏn (1732–?, *munkwa* in 1768) from Chŏngju had developed a submissive attitude toward court ministers and had accepted abusive treatment from them during his many years of service as a Kyŏmsa. This had resulted not only in the aforementioned perception that those holding the position of Kyŏmsa were little more than eunuchs, but also in the practice of deliberately humiliating people from P'yŏngan.²⁴ In Paek's two cases of disobedience, the king had apparently assumed that Paek would blindly follow orders because, being from P'yŏngan, his political fate by and large depended on the king's favor. Paek's defiant stance put a halt to his official career at the center, though it earned him the reputation of being an upright official and the respect of his fellow literati of P'yŏngan.²⁵

Paek's bitter experience of discriminatory politics did not prevent him from pursuing his official career; rather, he seems to have sought ways to recover his opportunity to earn a position at the central court. For one thing, Paek paid great attention to the grave sites of his deceased ancestors, for he, like many other people at the time, believed in geomantic blessings supposedly emanating from auspicious grave sites.²⁶ He relied on professional geomancers in selecting auspicious sites, though his teacher Ch'ŏe Kyŏngnim, who was proficient of geomancy, also made authoritative contributions.²⁷ Yet, reliance on geomantic benefit alone would not have brought practical consequences. In concert with looking for geomantic gain, Paek sought favors from high, powerful officials at the court by paying visits to them. For example, he traveled to Seoul late in the fourth lunar month of 1801 and stayed there for four months, until he finally received the appointment of fourth secretary at the Bureau of Royal Rituals (Pongsangsi Ch'ŏmjŏng, Sr. 4) with the assistance of Yi Ingmo, one of the ministers at the time.²⁸ In a section of his collected works entitled "Career History" (*hwanhae chingbi*), Paek recorded the names of certain officials (who probably supported his attainment of such appointments) immediately after the entry for each new position he held after 1801.²⁹

Paek Kyŏnghae's family had established itself as a renowned yangban family by the late eighteenth century, but it was because of the loyal death during the 1812 rebellion of Paek Kyŏnghan (1761–1812), Kyŏnghae's older brother, that the family earned the court's attention and began to enjoy substantial prestige.³⁰ The fact that seven of Paek's father's descendants passed the *munkwa* between 1831 and 1885 is indicative of this.³¹ On a personal level, Paek's own career began to shine, for he broke through another difficult barrier in court hierarchy and qualified for one of the prestigious positions (*ch'ŏngjik*) in 1816, when he was appointed third inspector of the Office of the Inspector General (Sahŏnbu Changnyŏng, Sr. 4).³² This was a moment of great honor for a man from P'yŏngan Province, whose residents were effectively screened out and not considered for such opportunities. Throughout Paek's diary, only a handful people are recorded as passing this bureaucratic barrier: Paek Inhwan in 1787, Yi Ŭnggŏ in 1799,[33] Kim Ch'osŏp in 1816,[34] Paek's nephew Yi Kijun in 1830,[35] and Paek's second son, Paek Chonggŏl, in 1835.[36] Paek tackled the final hurdle on the bureaucratic ladder when he received the honorary ministerial rank (a *tangsanggwan* rank) of T'ongjŏng taebu (Sr. 3) at the age of sixty-three, as a reward for his involvement in the revision of the royal genealogy. Finally, he obtained a *tangsanggwan* rank of Kasŏn taebu (Jr. 2) at the age of seventy-two, and a junior second-rank position of second magistrate of the Seoul Magistracy when he was seventy-five years old.

An episode in 1818, six years after the Hong Kyŏngnae Rebellion, at the height of Paek's official career, illustrates the discriminatory treatment that the men of P'yŏngan Province suffered and their responses to it, along with the position of Paek himself, who was a venerated senior official from the region by this time. The incident began with an altercation between Yi Hyŏngju, a historian (Kyŏmsa) from Chŏngju, and Kwŏn Tonin (1783–1859),[37] another historian (Hallim) of lesser rank from the capital region, over whether to prohibit all those with the rank of Kyŏmsa from smoking inside the residential hall where they stayed when at court.[38] The incident of 1818 involved two different types of historian positions—Kyŏmsa and Yemun'gwan Hallim, which was a lower rank than Kyŏmsa but a *ch'ŏngjik* envied by successful *munkwa* candidates nevertheless.[39] The contempt the Kyŏmsa from the north received from high-ranking officials has already been discussed. It apparently became progressively worse, and even young capital aristocrats who held prestigious offices at court came to emulate the practice of heaping scorn on Kyŏmsa from P'yŏngan Province, as this incident shows.

On the seventeenth day of the sixth lunar month of 1818, Hallim Kwŏn Tonin insulted Kyŏmsa Yi Hyŏngju by insisting that he refrain from smoking in the residential hall so as not to confuse the distinction between men from P'yŏngan and other areas.[40] Enraged by this direct insult, Yi left the office after some quarreling. This incident incited all the court officials from P'yŏngan Province, who discussed the possibility of resigning as a group. Paek objected to this idea, reminding them that the position of the Kwansŏ region (P'yŏngan Province) had become much more perilous ever since the 1812 rebellion. Thus he advised them to be cautious. Despite Paek's advice, all three Kyŏmsa from P'yŏngan Province decided to resign, and consequently three Kyŏmsa were arrested for improperly vacating the office. Soon after, three other senior northerners, including Paek himself, were accused of coaxing the Kyŏmsa and leading people from P'yŏngan Province to resign

their positions. After several days of investigation and flogging, Paek and
the others were sentenced to exile. However, in recognition of Paek's brother
Paek Kyŏnghan's loyal death during the 1812 rebellion, Paek was forgiven,
along with the others implicated in the incident. In his diary, Paek notes
that both Kyŏmsa and Hallim are positions of a historian, but the rank of
Kyŏmsa is higher than that of Hallim. Then, he deplores "the discussion
of making a distinction between this and that is nonsense."[41]

SOURCES OF DISCRIMINATION: AN EXPLANATION

When and how did such unjustifiable regional discrimination begin? On
what basis was the discrimination defended? We can find some answers in
a letter written in 1802 by Paek Kyŏnghae to the State Council on behalf
of P'yŏngan residents, in which he bitterly criticizes social political discrimination against P'yŏngan people and the prejudice harbored by the
central elite as pretexts of regional discrimination.[42] As a Confucian scholar
who was completely immersed in Confucian culture, Paek based his discussion on Confucian morality, which was quite persuasive and reasonable.
He opens his letter with very general remarks, pointing out that "When a
father and eight sons [representing the king and eight provinces] live
together, their nobleness and baseness or thinness and fatness must be the
same."[43] He then discloses the essence of the discrimination against P'yŏngan
people in the employment of court officials, a view that he shared with
Chŏng Yagyong: "Civil officials [from P'yŏngan Province] are assigned only
to the Royal Academy and military officials to the Gatekeeper's Office. Even
though one is a scholar who masters the Heavenly Principle and has an
unprecedented talent, one has no hope of advancement." Such political
discrimination stirred public contempt, to the extent that "even toddlers
who have just learned to speak already differentiate and insult people from
P'yŏngan Province, and people of base status, pushing carts, arrogantly
embrace such popular contempt toward P'yŏngan people. Everyone calls
us '*sŏin*.' Even worse, they call us '*sŏ-ji-han*.'"[44] Paek goes on to cry out,

[They scorn us] as though Heaven does not cover us, Earth does not
embrace us, the Sun and Moon do not shed their light upon us, and frost
does not fall on us. [They do so as though] we are not human, we are not
animal, either; they do not seem to know what kind of monster or ghost
we are. It seems that nothing can be compared to us. Alas! What crimes
have we *sŏin* committed? Are *sŏin* alone not endowed with the nature of

yin-yang and the five elements? Is our speech completely incomprehensible, given that it is likened to that of the western barbarians? Are our caps and dresses so different and strange compared to those of other provinces? Does the land become despicable because of people [living there], or people become despised because of the land? I have never heard, in the world under Heaven and Earth, that any [country] divides the land, looking down on a part of it and abandoning it for such a long time [and] to such a severe extent as this.[45]

Paek then seeks the origins of such regional contempt, which were all too bitterly humorous to him. Contrary to the conventional belief that political discrimination against P'yŏngan people had been prevalent from the beginning of the Chosŏn dynasty, Paek indicates that it began in the middle of the dynasty. He first acknowledges that, at the outset, the Chosŏn court did root out the coarseness of Silla and Koryŏ institutions and did not differentiate between remoteness and closeness, or between inner and outer regions, in the employment of officials. Therefore, he points out, in the early Chosŏn there were people from P'yŏngan Province whose appointments reached positions known as *ch'ŏngjik* and even ministerial levels. According to Paek, it was only from the mid-dynastic period that the P'yŏngan people were blocked from obtaining *ch'ŏngjik*. The story goes that one civil minister (*munjae*) who stayed in P'yŏngyang for a long time, as an escort of a Chinese envoy (Kwanbansa, Sr. 3), was bitterly criticized for his wild debauchery by a local Confucian scholar. His frustration and hatred against the people of the area allegedly led to the initiation of regional prejudice and discrimination. The offending civil minister was So Seyang (1486–1562, *munkwa* in 1509), a powerful and talented scholar-official of the sixteenth century. In 1633, this episode was cited by Minister of Personnel Ch'oe Myŏnggil as the origin of regional discrimination and was also recorded in a local gazetteer.[46]

Paek, however, does not blame any one person for triggering such political discrimination. He goes on to analyze three popular perceptions that were held by people at the time to justify political discrimination against people from P'yŏngan Province.

First, "there are no yangban there." Paek comments that this first point is illogical and groundless. After defining yangban as high civil and military officials (*yangbanja munmu kogwan chi ch'ing ya*), he argues that it is not true that there have been no high military and civil officials from P'yŏngan over the preceding two hundred years. He names as examples Special Capital Magistrate (Uyun, Jr. 2) Cho Ch'angnae (1686–?, *munkwa* in 1715),[47] Yangŭi-gong Kim Kyŏngsŏ (1564–1624),[48] and Yangmu-gong Chŏng Pongsu, resenting that their descendants have been unable to receive the same degree of honor given to people of similar family pedigrees from other provinces but have been discriminated against from the moment they entered the central bureaucracy. Paek concludes that, if people from P'yŏngan Province are employed in the future, they should not be scorned under the pretext that there are no yangban there.[49]

Although Paek did name a few renowned officials from P'yŏngan Province, even he could not deny that the number of scholars and officials from the region who had earned fame in the Chosŏn up until his own time was embarrassingly small. In addition, since the proper family background was crucial for being a yangban in the late Chosŏn, Paek and his colleagues from P'yŏngan were fighting a losing battle in terms of obtaining official recognition of their qualifications for *ch'ŏngjik*. There is no doubt that by Paek's time the elite in P'yŏngan had successfully adopted mature yangban culture based on Neo-Confucian prescriptions. Yet those cultural practices could not alter the family pedigrees of Paek and his fellow elite from P'yŏngan, and pedigree remained the most critical qualification for penetrating the thickly woven network of the central aristocracy, which almost monopolized high and prestigious positions in the central bureaucracy.

Second, "the province is close to the barbarian land." On this second point, Paek's argument is creative and appealing. After reminding his readers that the Chosŏn state is close to the Wae (Japanese) to the east and the Ho (northern barbarians, or Manchus) to the north, he questions whether there are any differences between the Wae and the Ho in terms of their uncivilized nature. He then points out the inconsistency of the popular perception that linked spatial proximity to "barbarians" to a coarse nature and unrefined culture. In other words, people scorned P'yŏngan Province because it was close to the Ho, yet they did not debase the Yŏngnam region (Kyŏngsang Province) despite its proximity to the Wae. Paek concludes that this discussion of proximity to the Ho is deceptive and unwarranted, a ploy to legitimize regional discrimination.

In arguing proximity to both the Wae and the Ho, Paek may have had more in mind than just physical and geographical space. Physical closeness entails material, cultural, and human contact, which can result in a mixture of blood and cultural influence.[50] Recent experiences of direct contact in the form of the Japanese and Manchu invasions—which to the Chosŏn people represented their barbaric nature in its most extreme form—must have had a similar effect. Paek regarded the Japanese and Manchus as sharing a similar uncivilized nature, so it must have seemed cogent to him to argue that physical proximity to the Manchus alone could not be used as proof of the north's cultural vulgarity.

Paek's worldview was fundamentally not much different from the China-centered culturalism (*chunghwa sasang*) that Confucian literati upheld in the Chosŏn period. The ancient Zhou dynasty had been a symbol of *chunghwa* culturalism and had thus been revered throughout history (*chonju* means "revering the Zhou"), although the legitimate holder of true Confucian civilization had changed successively over time. The essence of *chunghwa* theory was *hwa-yi-ron*, *hwa* here referring to *chunghwa*, the successor of Confucian civilization, and *yi* referring to those barbarians who had not reaped the benefits of Confucian transformation and who thus relied only on naked power and force. The Chosŏn elite took pride in having been blessed with the transformative effects of Confucianism and therefore promoted the Chosŏn state as eager participants in its civilized world. They developed this line of thinking into *so-chunghwa* thought, in which the Chosŏn dynasty was viewed as a lesser but legitimate center of Confucian civilization. After the demise of the Ming, this *sohwa* consciousness developed even further, so that some Chosŏn intellectuals believed that it was the Chosŏn that had inherited legitimate Confucian culture, and hence that it was their responsibility to defend that culture.[51] Naturally, Paek borrowed the language of his contemporary Neo-Confucian literati to position the Chosŏn dynasty at the center of cultural discourse. Furthermore, he defended the northwestern region as a participant in this civilized sphere, and one that should not be stigmatized simply for its physical proximity to the uncivilized Ho.

Finally, "there is no scholarship there." Paek constructs an elaborate argument against the third popularly held bias, that there was a lack of scholarship in P'yŏngan Province. He acknowledges that the people of P'yŏngan were ashamed of their less prominent scholarly achievements, but maintains that such shame only came from their own modesty. After pointing out that there was no special breed of people who were born to be great ministers or generals, he asks whether there can be no one who is endowed with "the right forces of Heaven and Earth" in the forty-two districts of P'yŏngan.[52] Paek adds what he had heard from elders: namely, that in the early Chosŏn the king at the court never discriminated against people from the periphery, nor did provincial and district administrators utter the word "*sŏt'o*" with contempt.[53] Instead, they established schools and encouraged proper decorum in order to lay the foundation for respecting one's superiors and being willing to die for one's elders. Moreover, people of the region had not considered themselves, as *sŏin*, to be the objects of contempt. Therefore, northern people had often exerted themselves, caught others' attention, and had been recommended to the court. Such people included Sŏnu Hyŏp,[54] Hwang Sunsŭng of P'yŏngyang,[55] Pak Hapkang of Sŏngch'ŏn, Han Chŏngan of Sunan, and Yun Kŏhyŏng[56] and Yun Chese,[57] a father and son from Yŏngbyŏn. All had been from P'yŏngan Province and had comprehended the truth, learned from their mentors, and achieved illustrious scholarship.[58]

Neo-Confucianism began to spread in P'yŏngan Province as early as the sixteenth century, as Paek tries to prove (and as discussed earlier). Inhyŏn Academy (*sŏwŏn*), the first private academy established in P'yŏngan Province, was founded in 1564, about twenty years after Paegundong Academy, the first private academy that unleashed the movement of founding private academies, was established by Chu Sebung in 1543 in P'unggi, Kyŏngsang Province.[59] A number of private academies and Confucian shrines were founded from the latter part of the sixteenth century on.[60] Furthermore, there is evidence that the P'yŏngan elite were operating smaller-scale private study halls from the sixteenth century on.[61] As was the case in many academies and shrines built in other provinces in the following centuries, literati in P'yŏngan Province busied themselves participating in this cultural movement of the time, as table 4 shows.

It is true that, in the absolute number of private academies and shrines established during the seventeenth and eighteenth centuries, P'yŏngan Province lagged behind the southern provinces, and Kyŏngsang Province in particular.[62] Even after the spread of Neo-Confucian studies, the depth of study in the region probably did not reach the level in the south, where philosophical debates and writings on Nature and Principle proliferated.[63] Although the number of private academies in P'yŏngan Province increased, these schools did not provide the organizational or political support needed for northern scholars to advance in the central government. A few northern scholars were known to be able to engage in debates with their southern contemporaries, but their scholarly accomplishments were reportedly modest and they failed to make political connections with any of the leading factions.

Nonetheless, it remains arguable whether the low level of scholarship in P'yŏngan Province accounts for the political and social discrimination levied against the people of that province.[64] Regional discrimination in the

TABLE 4. Academies and Shrines in Korea Established during the
Seventeenth and Eighteenth Centuries, by Province

Kyŏngsang	*Chŏlla*	*Ch'ungch'ŏng*	*Kyŏnggi*	*Hwanghae*
257 (55)	142 (38)	101 (39)	53 (42)	39 (21)

SOURCE: Chŏng Manjo, *Chosŏn sidae sŏwŏn yŏn'gu*, pp. 142–43. (#)=number
of chartered academies (*saaek sŏwŏn*).

advancement of official careers had developed as an integral part of a long
process of marginalization of some members of the yangban ruling class—
and as part of an accompanying concentration of central political power in
a relatively small number of yangban groups residing in Seoul and its vicinity. In short, competition for power at the center alienated scholar-officials
from the central bureaucracy beginning in the early days of the Chosŏn
dynasty. The first groups affected by this process were the nothoi of yangban
and local clerks (*hyangni*) who were disqualified from the civil service
examinations. Numerous literati purges and the subsequent development
of hereditary factional strife from the sixteenth century on effectively severed the losers in these power games from access to central power.

In this game of narrowing down the power-sharing pool, northerners
were easy prey because the far northern territory became a secure part of
the Chosŏn state only in the latter part of the fifteenth century. To develop
the area after incorporating it, the state forcefully relocated people to the
north from the south, including criminals and corrupt administrators. The
Confucian prejudice against any peripheral area that is physically distant
from the center of civilization, and is thus regarded as crude and barbaric
in nature, probably provided ideological justification for the political and
social discrimination subsequently endured by people from the northern
region.[65] Moreover, the political trend of sharing power among a limited
group of yangban aristocracy at the center was well established by the seventeenth century. Given these facts, it is remarkable that northerners' efforts
at emulating the dominant literati culture in the late Chosŏn succeeded in
producing a relatively large number of *munkwa* degree-holders—and hardly
surprising that their achievements did not extend to actually breaking down
institutional discrimination and ushering in a meritocracy.

Paek argues that the three bases for prejudice discussed above are only
excuses, and he advocates reform of discriminatory practices against
P'yŏngan residents in terms of official advancement at the central court.

Kangwŏn	P'yŏngan	Hamgyŏng	Total
43 (8)	56 (24)	33 (8)	724 (242)

He criticizes the court's extremely inflexible attitude, which held that the practice of prohibiting P'yŏngan people from obtaining prestigious positions (*ch'ŏngjik*) could not be altered because it was a long-held tradition. Indeed, Paek asserts, the court clung to this idea as though it had inherited some great principle that Heaven had bestowed and Earth embraced. Resorting to a Confucian dictum, he appeals to high officials at the court, writing:

> Not changing [things] for three years is the great rule of the human Way.[66] Yet Confucian scholars of the past still said, "Why should one wait for three years if that were not the Way?" Now, is blocking [people from P'yŏngan Province from having prestigious positions] the unchangeable law of the dynasty? Or is it an instruction of great sages and canons? It is nothing but mistaken discussion by a civil official which cannot even be verified. What kind of Way and Principle is it to still pick it up and tenaciously hold on to it? Suppose that *sŏin* indeed committed crimes that deserve to bring about the prohibition. Rewards reach down for five generations, whereas punishment does not impact the son of the criminal. Then, two hundred years [of prohibition] would be regarded as too long a time. Thus, for present-day discrimination, how is it not resentful? It is really so.[67]

Before Paek makes his final appeal, he goes over the efforts that previous kings had made to abolish such discriminatory practices. At the same time, he resents that no king's words have had any effect in rectifying the situation because each monarch's subjects have been unwilling to carry out his orders. Paek concludes by urging the State Council to take his words seriously, discuss the matter at court, and to follow the great benevolence of previous kings to clear away several hundred years of injustice, so that people from P'yŏngan Province can be treated the same as people of other provinces.[68]

Indeed, Chosŏn kings had received numerous written and oral appeals about this issue, submitted by northerners and non-northerners alike. Subscribing to the Confucian notion that hiring talented people was the most critical requirement of good government, they demanded that the practice of hereditary preference be mended. Korean kings wholeheartedly agreed with the complaints and issued orders to employ and promote people according to their ability and talent.[69] Obviously, these orders fell on deaf ears, as Paek laments, and were never fully realized until the late nineteenth century.

CULTURAL IDENTITY OF P'YŎNGAN RESIDENTS

How did the P'yŏngan elite respond to the popular prejudice against them, which gravely affected their social and political lives? In 1714, about a century before Paek Kyŏnghae wrote to the State Council, the P'yŏngan elite collectively participated in a series of movements to submit a memorial to the king in response to an accusatory report made by Secret Inspector to P'yŏngan Province Yŏ P'irhŭi (1679–1721) on non-Confucian cultural traits allegedly practiced in the province.[70] Yŏ had concluded in his report that the people of P'yŏngan were no better than barbarians (*ijŏk*) or birds and beasts (*kŭmsu*) and had recommended that they not be allowed to sit for the examinations for thirty years. King Sukchong (r. 1674–1720) acted on Yŏ's recommendation.

Because the essence of Yŏ's attack against the region revolved around cultural practices (*p'ungsok*) in regard to learning, funeral rites, marriage customs, and social mores, the memorialists focused on defending regional cultural practices as no different from those accepted by mainstream Chosŏn Neo-Confucians at the time.[71] The first step toward proving this was to locate the sources of right cultural tradition in regional history. Thus the memorial emphasizes that P'yŏngan Province's cultural genealogy goes back to the time of Kija (Ch.: Jizi, Viscount of Ji), the legendary transmitter of ancient civilization to Korea. The memorial reminds the reader that, as the founding place of Kija, the land of P'yŏngan Province earned the reputation of being a "small civilization" (*sohwa*).[72] It adds that Kija's legacy still exists in the region despite the thousands of years that have elapsed since then. On top of that, it claims, the transformative power disseminated for the preceding three hundred years by the current dynasty has further cultivated proper cultural qualities in the region.[73] Paek Kyŏnghae reiterates this historical consciousness in his letter to the State Council, although he adds that the cultural legacy of the region emanated from Tan'gun, another ancient cultural hero.[74]

Worship of Kija and Tan'gun had become an integral part of Korean cultural identity by the late Chosŏn period. As early as the Three Kingdoms period (?–668), Kija had been recognized as the transmitter of civilization to Korea, though it was during the Chosŏn period that his heritage was highlighted.[75] From the beginning of the Chosŏn dynasty, the court declared its intention to resume the indigenous transmission of the Way, originally implanted in Korea by Kija, as a measure to legitimize the founding of the new dynasty. Subsequently, Chosŏn intellectuals often regarded Kija as a great Confucian sage. It was in this early Chosŏn period that Tan'gun also came to be celebrated on a regular basis as the legendary progenitor of the Korean people. Concomitantly, the court established separate shrines for Tan'gun and Kija in P'yŏngyang and began offering memorial services to them.[76] Although the court was criticized for its negligence in the maintenance of these shrines, from this time on these two figures became tangible cultural symbols of the Chosŏn dynasty.[77] The P'yŏngan people embraced such cultural symbols as their own because they shared the same space as these two cultural heroes, who had presumably established their rules in the north where they themselves resided.[78]

In contrast to the P'yŏngan literati, who emphasized the permanence of Kija's influence over the north and who thus regionalized his cultural legacy as their own, others tended to detach Kija from a specific region. For example, Song Siyŏl, in his preface to the collected works of Sŏnu Hyŏp, an alleged descendant of Kija and a distinguished scholar from P'yŏngyang, comments that the civilization brought to the region by Kija waned and was overrun by militarism before being reintroduced by the current dynasty.[79] In this formula, the inheritors of Kija's legacy were the Chosŏn dynasty and its literati, not necessarily P'yŏngan Province or its people. Such "nationalization" of a cultural hero effectively denied the northern region's claim to the same source for its own cultural origin. This delicate tension between regional and national identification with Kija's heritage continued throughout the late Chosŏn period. Therefore, although both the memorialists in 1714 and Paek Kyŏnghae in 1802 cited Kija's regional cultural legacy, their arguments no doubt failed to impress most people from other provinces.

The next step the memorialists took to defend their regional culture was to identify themselves as rightful members of the ruling dynasty. Thus the memorial of 1714 points out that for the last three hundred years the people of P'yŏngan Province had received the transformative effects of Confucian learning that the kings of Chosŏn promoted. The memorial specifically mentions King Sukchong's efforts to institute special examinations in order to select talented people from the province and award them some of the prestigious positions that were strictly reserved for those of proper scholarly and familial background. As a result of such consideration and encouragement from the monarch, the memorial argues, the region's culture was elevated to the extent that literati increased their scholarship and even ordinary people living in the hinterlands came to honor benevolence and propriety.[80] Using a popular Confucian cliché, it opines, "The eight provinces are one family. [The king's] instructions reach them evenly. Your Royal Highness is our parent. The people of Kwansŏ [P'yŏngan Province] are children of Your Royal Highness. The cultural practices in Kwansŏ are the matter of Your Royal Highness's family (*kajŏng*)."[81] In a similar fashion, Paek in his 1802 letter also emphasizes that P'yŏngan is one of eight provinces of Chosŏn and argues that all people are the same regardless their place of origin, and thus should be treated as the same.

While the orientation of the 1714 memorial is fundamentally defensive and shows the strong centripetal force of Confucian ideology, Paek Kyŏnghae's regional identity contains a more particularistic thread. For example, Paek's 1821 thesis on the original, correct sound of the Korean colloquial language discusses a unique cultural asset that the northern region had preserved.[82] Paek points out that the sage King Sejong created the native alphabet and established the correct sound of the native language by gathering wise scholars and repeatedly consulting Ming Chinese scholars. He argues that King Sejong must have acknowledged that Kwansŏ was the birthplace of Korean civilization and must have adopted the sound of this region as the standard when he systemized the native language (*pangŏn*), although since King Sejong's reign the pronunciation of the native language had changed in other parts of the Chosŏn state. For example, the original sound *t'yŏn* (텬) became *ch'yŏn* (쳔), while *ti* (디) turned into *chi* (지). Thus the sound of *t'yŏn-ti* (텬디), Heaven and Earth, changed to *ch'yŏn-chi* (쳔지). Likewise, the sounds *ta* (다) and *t'a* (타) became *cha* (자) and *ch'a* (차). While wondering why seven regions (excluding Kwansŏ) followed the same path of transformation in pronunciation, Paek emphasizes that the people of Kwansŏ still preserve the original, correct sound of the native language. He also refers to other evidence that depicts Kwansŏ as the original source of the correct sound of the native Korean language. For example, King Sukchong evidently had the same question in mind when he asked his officials which dialect was correct. One renowned official replied that it was that of Kwansŏ. Therefore, Paek triumphantly concludes, "Under Heaven, the sound of *chunghwa* is correct; in our eastern country, the sound of Kwansŏ is correct. Kwansŏ provided the basis of our eastern country's language."[83]

Paek's 1821 essay thus posits the northwestern region as the cultural center of Chosŏn within the sphere of his China-centered culturalism. Yet this self-glorifying thesis also sheds light on how the P'yŏngan dialect—which Paek deemed to be original and correct, albeit different and distinct from others—may have provided non-P'yŏngan people with a foolproof way of distinguishing northern from southern Koreans. When Paek argues that even toddlers can distinguish P'yŏngan people from others probably on the basis of their speech, his point is well taken. It is ironic that the linguistic preservation that Paek felt compelled to advertise turned out to be an all too effective way to discern regional uniqueness.[84]

REGIONAL IDENTITY AND REBELLION

The regional identity that was part and parcel of the mindset of the 1812 rebels, as shown in their rebel manifesto, was almost identical to that advocated by the 1714 memorialists and, a century later, by Paek Kyŏnghae. The rebels stressed the significance of the province as the founding place of Kija and Tan'gun, boasted of its military contributions to saving the country during the Japanese and Manchu invasions, and highlighted the many talented scholars from the province, such as Sŏnu Hyŏp. Despite all these cultural, military, and scholarly accomplishments, prejudice against people from P'yŏngan Province for being militant, wild, and barbarous, and for lacking hereditary yangban traditions, permeated the perceptions of people of every social status. As a result, P'yŏngan residents were socially insulted and politically demeaned. To be sure, the regional elite who tried to infiltrate the central court must have experienced this most keenly. But such frustration must also have been transmitted to the general population of P'yŏngan Province, who eventually internalized it as their own resentment toward the central government. At the very least, feelings of a common fate must have provided a ground for solidarity when the rebels picked up regional discrimination as something that urgently needed to be rectified.

Interestingly, no higher examination degree-holders, including Paek Kyŏnghae, played a visible role in the rebellion, although a few names on rebel testimonies point to possible connections between some of the *munkwa* passers and rebels. In addition, a small number of active rebel leaders are identified as close relatives of *munkwa* passers, as table 5 shows.

It seems that *munkwa* passers' Neo-Confucian loyalty to the reigning dynasty kept them from participating in an antidynastic plot. Yet *munkwa* passers from P'yŏngan Province did not conspicuously oppose the rebellion either, especially in its early stages. Looking at the suspicious behavior surrounding esteemed *munkwa* degree-holders and their associates from Chŏngju during the rebellion, and their possible links to the top rebel leaders, might enrich our understanding of the social and political complexities facing these people, not to mention their final choices.

Persons of interest to us in this regard include Paek Kyŏnghae, his older brother Paek Kyŏnghan, Han Houn, and Kim Ikhwan (1753–1833), all of whom studied under Ch'ŏe Kyŏngnim, and the rebel leaders Hong Kyŏngnae (?–1812) and U Kunch'ik (?–1812). The loyal deaths of Paek Kyŏnghan and Han Houn have already been mentioned; interestingly, however, the government did not immediately recognize their deaths as loyal due to widespread suspicion over P'yŏngan residents' commitment to the rebels. Paek Kyŏnghan was caught and taken to the walled town of Chŏngju by the rebels on February 14 and was killed on February 28 because he allegedly tried to assemble a counterrebel group while there. Yet his loyal death was only reported to the central court by the provincial military commander on June 3, after the rebellion was suppressed. Only after gathering corroborating evidence and receiving letters of appeal from Paek's advocates did the government accept his loyalty as a fact.[85]

Han Houn, who was in Seoul when the rebellion broke out, arrived in Chŏngju in late April. He entered the walled town alone and reportedly tried to persuade Hong Kyŏngnae to surrender. In response, Hong asked Han what official positions and benevolent treatment Han had received since he had passed the *munkwa* and told him not to waste his life standing by the court. When Han continued to preach to the rebels about the Confucian norms of righteousness and loyalty, one of the rebel soldiers stabbed him in the leg with a spear. Hong eventually had U Kunch'ik kill Han because he could not bear killing him by himself, for Hong and Han had played together when young and Han was known to be a filial son. Again, Han's loyal death was not recognized for more than ten days after his death, when his colleague Ch'oe Taesik (1777–?, *munkwa* in 1807) from Chŏngju wrote a letter of appeal on his behalf and the provincial governor took it seriously.[86]

A number of questions arise, including why Paek Kyŏnghan was kept alive for many days and what made Han think he could win over Hong. Because they were killed by the rebels, the two have been recorded as loyalists ever since. But the case of Kim Ikhwan, who had been banished for his involvement in the sale of *hyangan* memberships in 1789, is more mysterious. The rebels forced Kim, who was famous for his literary skills, to compose a ritual oration when they offered a rite at the Chŏngju Confucian shrine, a symbolic act to prove their reception of the Mandate of Heaven. Kim supposedly refused to do so, writing that "the crime of presenting a false rite to the Confucian shrine is worse than becoming a rebel." He then cried out, "You won't take my brush away unless you cut off my hand." The rebels were allegedly overwhelmed by his valiant spirit and did not dare harm him.[87] This story, written down in the local gazetteer in 1931, may be true, though there is some room to review it critically. First of all, this episode does not appear in other records, especially the *Chinjung ilgi* (A Diary at the Military Camp), written by the Chŏngju yangban and militia leader Hyŏn Inbok, whereas the records related to Paek Kyŏnghan's death are abundant. In addition, Kim's name is not included in the list of rewardees whom the government recognized for their loyal contributions to the counterrebel campaign. Moreover, it is questionable how Kim survived and escaped from the Chŏngju rebel camp when his colleague Paek Kyŏnghan was imprisoned and eventually met death. The anecdotal note that Kim's valor won over the rebels' heart is too dramatic to believe.[88]

There are also suspicious aspects to Paek Kyŏnghae's attitude and whereabouts during the rebellion. According to his diary, he happened to be at the district office of Chŏngju the day after the rebels had occupied two nearby districts, Kasan and Kwaksan. While he was there the rebels, led by Ch'oe Iryun, broke into the jail to free a compatriot. Noticing that the magistrate of Chŏngju, Yi Yŏngsik, was unable to control the terrifying situation, Paek tried to persuade Kim Idae, the director of the local yangban bureau (Chwasu), to suppress the rebels and defend the district by beheading Ch'oe and his followers, not knowing that Kim himself had already joined the rebellion. Unsuccessful in convincing Kim, Paek returned home and reportedly began to gather like-minded people to counterattack the rebels. In his diary, he wrote that he spent several days amid chaos (even his aunt died on February 2). He left for P'yŏngyang on the evening of February 5, five days after the rebellion began, and arrived there on February 8.[89]

Like many other parts of Paek Kyŏnghae's diary, the entries about the 1812 rebellion must have been written after the fact, when he had had a chance to review the situation. In this diary and in other historical records, there is no clear evidence that Paek committed himself to the rebel cause in the beginning and changed his position later on. Nonetheless, several points are suspect. First, he justified his loyalist position by emphasizing that he had tried to persuade Kim Idae to turn back the clock and suppress the rebels. But it is equally possible that Kim for his own part tried to gain Paek's approval and cooperation. Kim's social standing was comparable to Paek's, for he was a lower civil service exam degree-holder (*chinsa*).[90] The Yŏnan Kim descent group, to which Kim belonged, was the most successful in Chŏngju at producing *munkwa* passers and had maintained many marriage ties with Paek's descent group. Some of Kim's fellow yangban in the area had already committed themselves to the rebels at the preparation stage, and the rebels continued to try to enlist powerful local yangban to support their cause. Moreover, the rebel manifesto stressed that the primary reason they revolted was their discontent over regional discrimination. As is evident in his writings, Paek shared resentment over unfair political practices with other members of the regional elite, so he may well have sympathized with the feelings of the rebel leaders.

Second, it is puzzling (as in the case of Kim Ikhwan) that Paek Kyŏnghae managed to leave the walled town of Chŏngju when it was already in rebel hands if he adamantly opposed the rebels. Third, his explanation for his delay in returning to his post in P'yŏngyang is unsatisfactory. Thus it is not unreasonable to suppose that Paek may have considered participating in the rebel leadership. At the very least, he and his colleagues probably monitored the progress of rebel activities closely before reaching a firm decision not to side with the rebels.

It is also important to investigate possible links between these yangban and two top leaders of the rebellion, Hong Kyŏngnae and U Kunch'ik, whose primary occupation was as geomancers. As mentioned earlier, Paek Kyŏnghae believed in geomancy, and his teacher Ch'oe Kyŏngnim was also an expert practitioner of geomancy. Under Ch'oe's direction, the Paek family had moved its homestead as well as its ancestors' tombs.[91] This shared interest in geomancy may have provided cultural space for these yangban "customers" and professional "providers" of geomantic services such as Hong and U to meet. And as already mentioned, Hong Kyŏngnae and Han Houn had been playmates. Finally, Ch'oe Kyŏngnim was originally from the Paengnyŏng subdistrict of Yŏngbyŏn, which U had visited about a year before the rebellion, most likely to gather rebel supporters and to establish a rebel base. Curiously enough, the Paengnyŏng subdistrict caught the court's attention as a very suspicious place where "wicked diviners and unorthodox practitioners" were said to have gathered in 1783.[92]

This is only circumstantial evidence for the possibility that this circle of

Chŏngju yangban was related to the rebellious plot. Nonetheless, History records these yangban as loyal subjects of the dynasty, and those who survived the rebellion actively claimed to be so, for obvious reasons. The outcome proved to be a huge blessing for them during their lifetimes, and for their descendants as well, as discussed earlier in this chapter (the case of Paek Kyŏnghae) and later in chapter 6 (the cases of Paek Kyŏnghan and Han Houn). Because their true political position cannot be known, my remaining discussion of their activities follows the information in the historical records available to us.

It was those local yangban elite who had not personally earned the *munkwa* degree, but whose family background and social standing in the local society were not far behind those of the *munkwa* degree-holders, who translated their resentment into action and provided critical support for the rebellion. Kim Idae, with a *chinsa* degree from 1805, is a case in point. He was a member of the established yangban (*kuhyang*) and of the rather prominent Yŏnan Kim of Chŏngju. His maternal great-grandfather, Cho Sudal of Paech'ŏn Cho, had passed the *munkwa* in 1708. His brother, Kim Sangdae, married a member of the P'ap'yŏng Yun whose great-great-grandfather, Yun Hungap, had passed the *munkwa* in 1679.[93] In addition to Kim Idae, Kim Ch'angsi of the Kwangju Kim, who also held the *chinsa* degree, joined the rebellion from the planning stage and composed the rebel manifesto.[94]

A number of people who had held centrally appointed offices also supported the rebellion, as table 6 summarizes. Chŏng Kyŏnghaeng and Chŏng Sŏnghan from the Ch'ŏlsan Hadong Chŏng descent group, whose ancestors had established illustrious merit during Manchu invasions several generations earlier, had previously served as a magistrate and a chief commander (Yŏngjang) respectively before participating in the rebellion. They were appointed commander-in-chief (Tojihwisa) and magistrate of Yongch'ŏn, respectively, by the rebels.[95] Pak Sŏngsin from Kwaksan, previously army second deputy commander (Ch'ŏmsa), was appointed Kwaksan magistrate by the rebels.[96] Furthermore, there were a number of military degree-holders who provided rebel leadership.[97] Although their individual motivations are unknown, they may have had a chance to interact with people of other regions, Seoul in particular, and to experience regional discrimination. Their resentment must have helped them decide in favor of the rebellion, expecting that they would fare better in the new government under Hong Kyŏngnae.

In sum, the transformation of northern P'yŏngan Province from the

TABLE 5. *Munkwa* and *Chinsa* Degree-Holders and Rebels

Name (Residence)	Relation to the degree-holder	Role played in the rebellion
Kim Idae (Chŏngju)	*Chinsa* in 1805	Magistrate of Chŏngju
Kim Ch'angsi (Kwaksan)	*Chinsa* in 1810	One of the core leaders
Kim Kukpŏm or Ch'angbae (Kwaksan)	His brother, Kim Ch'angje, passed the *munkwa* in 1810[a]	Strategist, and a member of the vanguard cavalry
Im Yong (Chŏngju)	His nephew and uncle were *chinsa*[b]	Chwasu under the rebel administration
Kim Sayong (T'aech'ŏn)	Kim Ch'ijŏng's (*munkwa* in 1783) eleven *ch'on*[c] relative. Kim Ch'ijŏng was a candidate for magistrate of T'aech'ŏn under the rebel administration[d]; Kim Sŏkt'ae of Kasan (*munkwa* in 1790) was the father-in-law of Kim Ch'ijŏng's daughter	One of the core leaders
Kim Iksu (Kasan)	Kim Sŏkt'ae's (*munkwa* in 1790) uncle and Kim Kŏnsu's (*munkwa* in 1762) younger brother[e]	Chief commander of Kasan
Kim Namch'o (Chŏngju)	His son, Kim Insu, passed the *munkwa* in 1819	Supervised military affairs under the rebels, but fled after four days
Kye Namsim (Sŏnch'ŏn)	His grandfather, Kye Tŏkhae, passed the *munkwa* in 1774[f]	As a master of occult arts, devised a strategy to occupy Ŭiju
Kye Hangdae (Sŏnch'ŏn)	His nephew, Kye Hyangbung, passed the *chinsa* in 1805[g]	Contributed grain to the rebel camp

TABLE 5. *(cont.)*

Name *(Residence)*	*Relation to the degree-holder*	*Role played in the rebellion*
Sŭng Ilsul (Chŏngju)	Sŭng Ido's (*munkwa* in1675) five *ch'on* relative, and Sŭng Kyŏnghang's (*munkwa* in 1786) eight *ch'on* relative[h]	Granary supervisor
Sŭng Chŏnghang (Chŏngju)	Sŭng Ryun's (*munkwa* in 1774) nine *ch'on* relative[i]	Rebel military officer

[a] The father's name (Hanik) for both Kim Kukpŏm and Kim Ch'angje is identical. Kim Kukpŏm (also known as Ch'angbae), Kim Ch'angje, and Kim Ch'angsi could be cousins because their ancestral seat is known to be Kwangsan (Kwangju) and one of the characters (Ch'ang) in their given names is identical (*tollimcha*). Most descent groups in the late Chosŏn (and even today) set a literary Chinese character (or a radical) as a part of a given name for the same generation. Kim Kukpŏm's nephew was reportedly engaged to Kim Sayong's niece. KP 3:318 and KP 5:90.

[b] KP 5:481. Im Yong was found guilty of high treason (*moban taeyŏk choe*). KP 5:506.

[c] "*Ch'on*" is a marker that shows the remoteness and closeness of relatives to oneself. For example, father and son are one *ch'on* while brothers and sisters are two *ch'on*. When the blood relation moves vertically from one generation to the next, one *ch'on* is added, while two *ch'on* are added when the blood relation moves horizontally. Thus, a cousin is four *ch'on* from oneself and an uncle is three *ch'on* from oneself.

[d] KP 3:122–23.

[e] *Sunch'ŏn Kim ssi Ch'ŏlwŏngong-p'a sebo*, 680–94. Kim Sŏkt'ae was a son of Kim Kŏnsu, whose six direct descendants passed the *munkwa*. According to the testimony of Kim Mongha of Ŭisŏng Kim in T'aech'ŏn, a son of Kim Ch'ijŏng (a *munkwa* degree-holder) and a relative of Kim Sayong, Kim Sŏkt'ae knew about the outbreak of the rebellion beforehand and sent his sister (Kim Sŏkt'ae's daughter-in-law) to her natal home to escape upcoming violence. KP 3:122. According to the genealogy, Kim Iksu died about a month before the end of the rebellion.

[f] *Suan Kye ssi inmaek po*, 351.

[g] Ibid., 53–54.

[h] KP 2:518; and *Yŏnil Sŭng ssi chokpo*, 116.

[i] *Yŏnil Sŭng ssi chokpo*, 430 and 427; and KP 2:516. Sŭng Ŭngjo had been indicated as one of the rebel commanders. It is unlikely that this is the same person who passed the *munkwa* in 1782 because it would be impossible for his grandson, Sŭng Chint'ae, to have been successful in the *munkwa* in 1846 if he had joined the rebels. SSP 22–23; and KP 4:114.

dynasty's territorial frontier and cultural periphery in the fifteenth century into a well-integrated part of the whole by the eighteenth century was a striking one. As the region became militarily and financially stable (as discussed in the next chapter), it quickly adopted the main cultural practices embraced by the dynastic ruling elite. The local elite of P'yŏngan Province made great efforts to be recognized as equal participants in the central political process—efforts that were met only with heightened status con-

TABLE 6. Former Court Officials in the Rebel Camp

Name (Residence)	Former office in Chosŏn court	Role played in the rebellion
Chŏng Kyŏnghaeng (Ch'ŏlsan)	Magistrate	Commander in chief
Chŏng Sŏnghan (Ch'ŏlsan)	Chief commander	Magistrate of Yongch'ŏn
Yi Sanghang[a] (Chŏngju)	Garrison commander; also passed the military exam[b]	Commander
Pak Sŏngsin (Kwaksan)	Army second deputy commander	Magistrate of Kwaksan
Yi Yangp'il[c] (Chŏngju)	Army second deputy commander	Recruited rebel troops
Kim Iguk[d] (Sŏnch'ŏn)	Garrison commander	Military officer
Ho Yunjo[e] (Ch'angsŏng)	Outpost officer[f]	Suspected as a rebel supporter
Hwang Chongdae[g] (Chŏngju)	Army second deputy commander; also passed the military exam	Commander, but later fled from the rebel camp
Kim Chŏnghan[h] (Yongch'ŏn)	Army second deputy commander	Contributed grain and money to the rebels

[a] CJI 232 and KP 1:490.

[b] Pyŏlchang (garrison commander) is a junior ninth rank military position appointed by the central government.

[c] SJ 42 and KP 3:127.

[d] KP 1:469.

[e] CJI 348–49.

[f] Kwŏn'gwan (outpost officer) is a junior ninth rank military position appointed by the central government.

[g] *Kwansŏ sinmirok*, 109–12.

[h] KP 3:71 and KP 4:203.

sciousness among the central aristocracy and with the strategies of exclusion adopted by them. The discrepancy between members of the local elite's aspirations, arising from their accumulated cultural capabilities, and the unfailing political and social discrimination they faced, fueled frustration among them. Frustration had traditionally been expressed in peaceful ways, such as submitting memorials and appeals seeking justice within the allowed parameters of court politics. The 1812 rebels resolved to take matters into their own hands by destroying the ruling dynasty and establishing a new one in which the regional elite would become the core ruling group. Once provoked, this regional sentiment was rather easily channeled into popular movements against the status quo. Yet we cannot overlook the internal division and competition among the local elite themselves, for it explains the polarized state of local elite society at the time of the rebellion, with one faction leading the revolt and the other putting it down.

3 The Economic Context of the Hong Kyŏngnae Rebellion

As noted in the last chapter, P'yŏngan residents performed dramatically better in the civil service examination in the late Chosŏn compared to the early Chosŏn period. Success in the examination required a long-term commitment, which was impossible without substantial material support from the candidate's family. Thus the sudden increase of *munkwa* passers from P'yŏngan Province in the late Chosŏn bespeaks relative material wealth present in the region. A regionwide rebellion whose preparation spanned more than a year and which involved mercenaries was also possible only with considerable material backing.[1] Furthermore, merchants' participation in the rebellion was particularly conspicuous and demands explanation. Hence this chapter explores economic conditions of P'yŏngan Province during the Chosŏn period, especially those economic changes in the late Chosŏn that enabled P'yŏngan elite to succeed at the examinations and that entailed the emergence of regional merchant groups. In addition, it discusses the economic conflicts that developed between the regional elite, merchants, and the general populace in their relations to the center.

THE NORTHERN ECONOMY AND THE TAX ADMINISTRATION

Geographically, the northern region was mountainous and infertile. There was only a small tract of flat land along the coast, and even it was not considered to be very productive compared to land in the southern provinces.

66

In general, it was understood that the wet fields in the southern provinces were the most fertile, followed by the wet fields of Kyŏnggi and Hwanghae provinces, while those of Hamgyŏng, Kangwŏn, and P'yŏngan were the least productive.[2] In 1404, the amount of land in P'yŏngan Province registered as under cultivation was 6,648 *kyŏl*, only 0.7 percent of the total cultivated land in the country (931,835 *kyŏl*).[3] This increased dramatically to 19 percent (308,751 *kyŏl*) in the reign of King Sejong (1418–50), and then stabilized at about 10 percent of the total registered land (150,000 to 170,000 *kyŏl*) until the late sixteenth century.[4] After the Japanese invasions (1592–98), cultivated land dropped to 90,000 *kyŏl* and decreased to 47,561 *kyŏl* by 1646, after the Manchu invasions (1627 and 1636), illustrating the truly devastating impact of wars in the region. By 1720 the amount of cultivated land had recovered to 90,804 *kyŏl*, or 6.5 percent of the total registered land, slowly increasing to more than 120,000 *kyŏl* by the mid-nineteenth century.[5]

Although most land under cultivation was dry-field in P'yŏngan Province, the wet cultivation grew steadily, from about 10 percent in the reign of King Sejong to around 17 percent just before the Japanese invasions.[6] The 1807 figure still registers 17 percent of the cultivated land as wet-field, which probably reflects the maximum possible land under wet cultivation given the environmental circumstances and the agricultural technologies available in the late Chosŏn.[7] It is uncertain when or if the northern region began to adopt the method of transplanting rice seedlings, which had been gradually employed since the late seventeenth century in the southern provinces and had contributed to the increase in productivity there.[8] Instances of transplanting in Kyŏnggi Province and Kaesŏng can be observed in historical records from about the mid-eighteenth century on.[9] Yet U Hayŏng (1741–1812), a late Chosŏn Confucian scholar, reports that of the three northern provinces, only the Kaesŏng area used transplanting. He also reveals that cotton, whose cultivation had been introduced to P'yŏngan Province in the mid-seventeenth century, was still less popular than mulberry and hemp as raw material for clothing and bedding.[10]

Although the amount of registered land in an agrarian society reflects the economic welfare of the people to a certain extent, a more discrete economic picture must also consider the level of taxation by the state and the management of tax revenue. Because P'yŏngan Province was located on the northern border, the early administrators of the dynasty set up its tax administration in certain special ways. First of all, the land tax rate was lower than in other provinces. In the early fifteenth century, the tax rate was 20 *mal* per *kyŏl*, which was two-thirds the rate of other provinces. The overall land tax rate had been reduced to 4 *mal* for wet fields by the sixteenth century, but landowners in P'yŏngan Province paid two-thirds the usual rate in the case of wet fields and 83 percent in the case of dry fields. The rice surtax to support three types of soldiers (the tax was called *samsumi*), instituted during the Japanese invasions, was not levied in P'yŏngan Province. And the rate of the tribute rice surtax (*taedongmi*) that replaced previous tribute tax in kind was about half that in the south.

P'yŏngan residents were, however, subject to heavier military and labor service obligations and ad hoc miscellaneous payments of goods than their southern counterparts. Revenues from the land tax as well as the tribute rice surtax were kept in P'yŏngan rather than being sent to the central government, as was required in other provinces. The rice tax was stored in the province for very practical purposes, namely for use as military provisions in emergencies and also to cover various expenses for regular as well as emergency diplomatic exchanges.[11]

From the very beginning of the dynasty, the northern region had been vulnerable to military incursions and raids by the Jurchen tribes along and beyond the northern borders. The court established various mechanisms and strategies to defend the area against such threats. Numerous walled defense stations (*po*) and garrisons (*chin*) were constructed and old ones repaired. Administrative towns along the possible invasion routes were often defended by firearms and walls to fend off invading armies. Soldiers conscripted from the indigenous population, as well as from the southern provinces, watched for small-scale raids and large-scale attacks. Military strategies were also devised to meet a major invasion force.[12] And along with military preparedness, the court adopted a policy of appeasement that entailed frequent diplomatic exchanges with small and large Jurchen tribes both in the border area and at the capital. Gifts bestowed on the "visitors"—and the expenses of their trips to and from the capital—were the responsibility of residents living along the roads. The financial burden on the population of P'yŏngan to meet all these military and diplomatic demands was thus an enormous one.[13]

In the early seventeenth century this burden increased, due to demands to reinforce the defense system along the northern borders against the rapidly emerging Manchus in southern Manchuria.[14] In addition, Mao Wen-long (a Ming general stationed on Ka Island off the coast of Ch'ŏlsan) and Chinese refugees from Liaodong (driven out by the expansion of Manchus into the region) requested a huge amount of military assistance, using the excuse of defending the region against a possible military clash with the Manchus. Military provisions and transportation expenses to meet Mao's demand added tremendously to the burden on the P'yŏngan population. To make matters worse, the Ming refugees often looted villages and even killed innocent residents, and Mao either condoned or even led such arbitrary incursions until the Ming court discovered his behavior and put him to death in 1629. Even after Mao was removed, the Ming army remained stationed on Ka Island and the financial burden of supporting Ming troops and refugees continued until the Manchu invasion of 1636.[15]

As the Manchus took over north China proper, diplomatic expenses replaced the financial need to build up a military defense system and support Ming military activities in the area. Immediately after the Manchus invaded Korea, diplomatic missions between the two countries occurred quite frequently. Between 1636 and 1649, Qing envoys visited Chosŏn an average of 3.6 times per year. The number of missions decreased to 2.8 per year from 1650 to 1659, and to 1.2 per year from 1660 to 1674, then fell to less than one visit per year.[16] As the number of visits from the Qing decreased, so did the corresponding missions dispatched by the Chosŏn court. For the same time periods, the average numbers of tributary missions sent to the Qing court were 5.85, 4.5, and 3.2, respectively. In the eighteenth century, an average 2.5 missions per year were dispatched to the Qing.[17]

The expenses of the exchange of diplomatic missions included food and housing roundtrip between the border and the capital, transportation, guards, and gifts. One study found that it required about 50,000 *yang* (equivalent to 17,000 *sŏm* of rice) from P'yŏngan Province to properly receive one Qing mission in the early eighteenth century—more than two-thirds the provincial revenue from the land tax and tribute rice surtax.[18] As relations between the Qing and Chosŏn stabilized and the number of diplomatic missions declined, this provided financial relief to the provincial government and residents alike. The gradual increase in the amount of cultivated land and size of the population (see table 7) in the late seventeenth and early eighteenth century marks the general economic recovery in the north.

The fact that elite cultural practices—which required expensive rituals and rites, an extensive education, and an elaborate lifestyle—began to flourish in this region in the late seventeenth century also testifies to the economic surplus gained by the northern elite. For example, Sŭng Taegi (1588–1659) of Yŏnil Sŭng, one of the renowned yangban descent groups of Chŏngju, found that his family finances could not support a scholarly career in the early seventeenth century, so he quit his studies and put his best efforts into

TABLE 7. Demographic Changes in P'yŏngan Province[a]

Year	P'yŏngan Province		Whole country		% P'yŏngan household	% P'yŏngan population
	Households	Population	Households	Population		
1404	27,788	52,872	153,403	322,746	18.1	16.3
1406	33,890	62,321	180,246	370,365	18.8	16.8
1454[b]	41,167	105,444	201,853	692,477	20.4	15.2
1648	39,927	145,813	441,321	1,531,365	9.0	9.5
1657	55,623	184,799	658,771	2,290,083	8.4	8.1
1669	177,912	720,391	1,313,453	5,018,644	13.5	14.4
1678	150,689	706,675	1,342,428	5,246,972	11.2	13.5
1717	167,749	763,340	1,560,561	6,846,568	10.7	11.1
1723	174,373	791,918	1,574,066	6,865,286	11.0	11.5
1726	172,720	734,944	1,576,598	7,032,425	11.0	10.5
1753	297,603	1,267,709	1,772,749	7,298,731	16.8	17.4
1776	296,433	1,274,405	1,715,371	7,238,522	17.3	17.6
1786	299,523	1,288,399	1,737,670	7,356,783	17.2	17.5
1807	302,005	1,305,969	1,764,504	7,561,403	17.1	17.3
1837	214,976	853,048	1,591,963	6,708,529	13.5	12.7
1852	217,141	868,906	1,588,875	6,810,206	13.7	12.8
1864	217,577	872,825	1,703,456	6,828,521	12.8	12.8
1904	194,866	812,997	1,419,899	5,928,802	13.7	13.7

SOURCE: *Chŭngbo Munhŏn pigo, kwŏn 161, hogu-go 1, yŏktae hogu.*

[a] The numbers of households and population figures recorded in various primary sources do no[t] represent the accurate numbers of households and people in P'yŏngan Province at the time. The number[s] are not consistent, either. That is, the number of households recorded in the *Sillok* for a certain yea[r] does not agree with the number listed in another source. This unreliability of population data has bee[n] a primary reason for the relative absence of demographic study on Chosŏn Korea. Despite such weak nesses inherent in the demographic data, the figures given are useful in understanding general popula tion changes during the Chosŏn dynasty. For more discussion of population changes in Chosŏn an[d] household registrations, see *Hogu ch'ongsu*; Kwŏn T'aehwan and Sin Yongha, "Chosŏn wangjo sida[e] in'gu ch'ujŏng e kwanhan ilsiron"; Michell, "Fact and Hypothesis in Yi Dynasty Economic History" and Son Pyŏnggyu et al., *Tansŏng hojŏk taejang yŏn'gu.*

[b] Data for 1454 are from *Sejong sillok chiriji.*

farming. Subsequently, his family became wealthy and his investment in his sons' education paid off when his son Sŭng Tŭg'un (1618–86) passed the *munkwa* in 1675, followed by four more *munkwa* passers among his direct descendants. Four other members of the Yŏnil Sŭng of Chŏngju also earned *munkwa* degrees in the late Chosŏn.[19]

As the reserve grain in provincial and district granaries swelled because of lower military and diplomatic expenses, the central court began to tap these funds for its own use. Beginning in the late seventeenth century, a part of the reserve grain in P'yŏngan Province was transferred to other regions struck by famine as relief funds. And in the early eighteenth century, the Ministry of Taxation (Hojo) began to regularly utilize a large part of the land tax and the emergency fund collected and stored in P'yŏngan Province to supplement the state's reduced tax revenue and to meet expanded state expenses. When a state faces financial trouble, it usually raises the tax rate or finds other means of increasing its tax revenues and thus meets expenses. However, because Confucian norms dictated that a good government maintain a low land tax rate, the Chosŏn state looked for other ways to make up the inadequate revenue, and the reserve grain in P'yŏngan Province provided a perfect source of the funds it needed.[20]

Land tax and tribute tax belonged fundamentally to the court in any case, and the military threats that had rationalized the storage of these tax revenues in the northern region had disappeared by the eighteenth century. The Ministry of Taxation's practice of withdrawing funds from P'yŏngan Province paved the way for other offices and military agencies in the central government to request the transfer of funds from that province to finance relief operations and procurement of military equipment.[21] Yet this new practice of appropriating previously independent funds for the use of the central government led to a conflict of interest between the center and the periphery, for it meant that the state was taking over the management of local resources.[22]

OPERATION OF PUBLIC LOANS AND DISCONTENT OF LOCAL RESIDENTS

Not only did the central government rely on reserve grain in P'yŏngan Province for its expenditures in the late Chosŏn period, but a number of central government offices and agencies operated public loans in the province under the umbrella institution of the grain loan system (*hwanja*) in order to raise funds. The provincial and local governments had also operated public loans (*kwanch'ŏng singni*) on a wide basis since the eighteenth century to supplement revenue. The various tax revenues held in reserve were often utilized as a principal fund that was distributed to the peasants in cash in the spring and repaid in grain in the autumn, when the price of grain was low.[23] As already discussed, the grain reserves from tax collection in P'yŏngan Province were growing because the financial demands of diplomatic missions had decreased as foreign relations with Qing China stabilized, so the government loaned out the tax reserves with interest, which was a fairly lucrative way for the government to meet its expenses—and for the local authorities to accumulate personal wealth.

The Grain Loan System

The original purpose of establishing the grain loan system at the beginning of the Chosŏn dynasty was to provide relief to people during the spring grain shortage. In addition, the grain storage system was used to supply military provisions, to stabilize prices, and to accommodate working-capital loans.[24] In the beginning, grain loans were given to peasants interest-free; then, to make up for incidental losses in handling and storage, 2 percent interest was charged on loans. Since relief grain and other reserves could not be replenished at this low rate of interest, interest rates were raised after the mid-fifteenth century and set at 10 percent by the end of that century, even though it was already clear that the peasants were incapable of repaying the principal, let alone the interest.

Additional changes to the original institution took place sometime in the early sixteenth century, when the government began to utilize interest as a part of state revenues by requiring that one-tenth of the interest be sent to the Ministry of Taxation as a recording fee. In 1650, three-tenths of the interest became a major part of the income of the Ever-Normal Bureau (Sangp'yŏngch'ŏng), a policy that led other government agencies to rely on grain loans to meet their expenses.[25] By the late eighteenth century, almost every government office, whether in the province or in the capital, was loaning out its grain reserves at interest in order to raise funds. The result was the increase of total grain loan reserves over time: 416,900 *sŏm* in 1725; 1,377,000 *sŏm* in 1776; and 9,995,599 *sŏm* in 1807.[26] In accord with the national trend, the total grain loan amount grew rapidly in P'yŏngan Province, from about 700,000 *sŏm* in the late seventeenth century to 1,000,000 *sŏm* in the early eighteenth century, and then to 1,900,000 in the late eighteenth century.[27]

Such increases resulted largely from new operations established by the central government offices. The Ministry of Taxation, the Border Defense Command (Pibyŏnsa), and the Ever-Normal Relief Bureau (Sangjinch'ŏng) were operating the grain loans by 1769.[28] Two more offices, the Ministry of Punishments (Hyŏngjo) and the Capital District Office (Hansŏngbu), participated in the operation in 1776, and the Ministry of War, the Equal Service Bureau (Kyunyŏkch'ŏng), and three central military agencies set up their own loan operations in 1797, for a total of ten central government offices raising funds in P'yŏngan Province through public loans. In 1797, the total grain reserve loaned out in P'yŏngan Province was about 1,530,000 *sŏm*, of which 1,220,000 *sŏm* was operated by central government offices.[29]

Considering the high default rate on loans and the difficulty in refunding reserves because of the peasants' inability to repay their debts, the state could not in fact maintain such a vast reserve of grain for loan purposes. As a result, the grain loan system became corrupt in many ways. Sometimes, fictional reserves were maintained on paper and the principal of the loan was never repaid, though it remained "on the books." While most of the principal was left outstanding, the annual 10 percent interest rate continued to be collected. By the late eighteenth century, the regulation to loan out only a portion of the grain reserve was largely ignored and all the reserve grain was utilized for distribution for earning interest, leaving no actual reserve in the granaries. In other words, the reserve system was almost bankrupted while the grain loan became a fixed tax charged on peasants. Thus, although the total grain reserve had decreased by the early nineteenth century, the financial burden on rural residents did not necessarily become lighter because the amount of principal they were loaned might have increased.[30]

Since the amount of grain loan reserves was fixed in each district and local administrators were responsible for managing the system, numerous problems emerged. First of all, given the high default rate on peasant debts, the only way to meet revenue and reserve requirements was to manipulate the grain stocks, falsify the granary ledgers, and extort grain from peasants. A widespread problem was the arbitrary and forced distribution of loans to peasants who did not need them in order to obtain interest payments. Magistrates often selected rich households for loans to ensure the collection of revenue, and this was a popular practice in P'yŏngan Province. When the grain loan was carried out to relieve hunger, as it was originally intended to do, it was naturally distributed to poor households. But when the grain loan was transformed into a way to raise administrative funds, rich households were targeted, whether they needed a loan or not. At times, wealthy households were forced to receive a share, often on paper only, and to pay the interest. Even though the whole tax system was moving toward a more egalitarian distribution of wealth—and toward a progressive tax structure that broke the traditional attachment of social status to the taxing mechanism—for the time being this arbitrary collection of interest from wealthy but powerless households became a critical element in their resentment of the state.[31]

In addition, local administrators took advantage of territorial price variations to line their own pockets by shifting grain reserves from areas of glut to areas of shortage, selling off grain at high prices and restocking at low prices. It was common for tax administrators to manipulate the measures used at the times of grain distribution and repayment to make profits for themselves. They also cashed in on loan transactions by controlling cash-grain conversion rates.[32] They used these methods not solely for personal gain but also out of necessity, to provide income for the sound maintenance of the grain reserves, which would otherwise have decreased over time as a result of the peasants' basic penury.

The 1811 peasant revolt in Koksan in Hwanghae Province, just months before the 1812 Hong Kyŏngnae Rebellion, reveals the complicated problems in the administration of the grain loan system and subsequent conflicts among the magistrate, the local authorities (such as local yangban officers and clerks), and the peasant taxpayers.[33] Chŏng Yagyong, who had served as magistrate of Koksan in 1797–98, observed that the tax administration in Koksan was run very smoothly by the local authorities, who presumably were local yangban. As a result, local finance was in fairly good shape and the grain storage showed no deficit. In late 1809 and early 1810, however, when Pak Chongsin had just become magistrate of the district, he found that most granaries were empty. After interrogating local officers, such as the supervisor of the granary, Pak discovered that all the grain reserves had been moved to wealthy households in the area, where they were being stored until they could be sold in P'yŏngan Province when river transportation became possible in the spring. Granary officers and the local rich households were planning to share the profits from this illegal expropriation and sale of public grain by taking advantage of price differences between harvest time and the spring grain shortage. The local yangban officers, clerks, and wealthy households had colluded in this whole operation.[34]

Being responsible for district finance, Pak Chongsin forced those involved in this illegal operation to replenish the fund, but his measures became so harsh that they caused enormous resentment among the local wealthy households, clerks, and officers of the local yangban bureau (*hyangim*). For example, Pak collected from local clerks more than 1,000 *sŏm* of grain reserves that were missing from the original fund during the fall and winter of 1810. He also imprisoned the granary supervisor of one of the granaries and other yangban officers who had reportedly stolen 2,000 *sŏm* of grain, and forced them to repay it. Although some Koksan residents praised Pak for doing the right thing, in his zeal for reform, Pak went too far. He threatened clerks and illegally collected money from the rich for his personal use. He received bribes when he judged criminal cases. He also abused the legal system and arbitrarily tortured prisoners. As a result, almost a hundred people died from torture and physical punishment after he took charge of the district in November 1809.

It sounds as though the local authorities in Koksan, together with the local rich households, had appropriated public grain reserves to make a private profit by manipulating regional and seasonal price differences. However, this commercial enterprise may have been designed not only for private profit but also to fund local government and thus lessen the tax burden on ordinary taxpayers. This would explain how the rich, clerks, and yangban officers dared to transport most of district's grain reserves again in the winter of 1811, almost a year after Pak Chongsin had launched a close investigation of overall local finance. It would also explain why diverse local status groups, such as local yangban, clerks, and even ordinary residents, joined the 1811 uprising to oppose Pak, the magistrate of the time. In short, Pak arbitrarily interrupted practices that the local authorities had devised to solve the problem of tax administration, which caused discontent among the local populace and led to open rebellion.

The Koksan rebellion, which had been prepared through many meetings among local leaders, was led by a local elite group that included the top yangban officers of the local yangban bureau and the military bureau. The rebels targeted the district administration office where the magistrate, Pak Chongsin, resided. They invaded the office on February 23, 1811, took the official seals (the symbol of power and authority bestowed on the magistrate by the court), put Pak in an empty straw sack, carried him off beyond the district perimeter, and left him there. These actions symbolized rejection of the ruler and were a traditional way for peasants to display their discontent, and one that was rationalized in Mencius's notion of the people's right to revolt when their ruler had lost the Mandate of Heaven. The rebels then freed the supervisors, clerks, and other officers in charge of granaries who were in custody for appropriating or expropriating grain loan reserves and resisted government pacification efforts led by the three nearby district magistrates, who employed a rather mild policy of persuasion. The rebellion was finally put down at the end of March with added military force dispatched by the regional military headquarters. The punishment meted out to the rebels was harsh. Thirty-seven people were beheaded and thirty-nine were banished. Many were officers of the yangban bureau and military bureau or were local clerks. Although a contemporary observer viewed Pak's corruption as the main cause of the uprising,[35] it is also true that his intervention in the financial adventures led by the district's local elite caused widespread discontent among local residents.

The People's Fund (Min'go)

The establishment of a people's fund was designed to facilitate the convenient expenditure of miscellaneous taxes (*chabyŏk*) for the purchase of goods and services. Instead of requiring labor service and the payment of local products as tribute in kind, the people paid a tax in cash or grain, and the government then hired labor and purchased necessary goods through agents by using the tax fund. In the beginning, the system operated on a small scale, but the local government increasingly relied on the people's fund as local expenses grew. At first the local residents benefited, since no more surcharges followed after they paid a certain amount of money each year. However, as the annual charge increased over the years and ad hoc charges were added to refund losses caused by embezzlement or to meet increasing expenditures, residents suffered growing burdens to replenish the people's fund.[36] For example, the annual income for the people's fund in Chŏngju "in the old times" had previously been about 3,000 (*yang*, presumably), and that was enough to cover all the expenses. By 1808, however, the income had increased to 6,000 but was insufficient to meet the financial demand. One clerk sarcastically commented that the people's fund would not be operative unless there was a hole producing gold.[37]

To meet increased expenses, the sources of income for the fund were diversified. Surcharges on land (*kyŏllyŏm*), a portion of grain loan interest and the military support tax, the household levy (*horyŏm*), and interest income from loaning out the fund (*singni*) became major sources of income. Loans were made not only to ease food shortages and to pay personal expenses, such as marriage ceremonies and funeral services, but also to provide commercial capital to merchants and businessmen. The official annual interest rate for such public loans was 10 percent, which was half the recommended interest rate for private loans. But the actual interest rate was as high as 50 percent per annum during the eighteenth and early nineteenth centuries. Not only was the rate high, but it was often changed arbitrarily, and in some cases the compound interest method was applied to maximize profit. In addition, the interest was often taken off the principal amount at the time the loan was contracted.[38]

Another serious problem in the operation of public loans was the loss of principal over the years due to corrupt administrators. An example is the financial situation of the military headquarters of P'yŏngan Province in Anju at the time of the 1812 rebellion. The newly appointed provincial military commander had launched an investigation of the financial condition of his office in early 1812. According to his report to the central government in May 1812, only less than one-tenth of the official fund was left in the treasury in the form of cash, although the account book indicated that the fund was intact. The two main reasons for the missing funds were official embezzlement and reckless management of the loans by previous military commanders for several decades. As a result, the military headquarters had great difficulty in funding the counterrebel campaign when the rebellion broke out.[39] Chŏng Yagyong made a cutting remark about the harmful effects of the people's fund and public loans on the peasantry. He criticized the people's fund because it had been created by local administrators on their own authority, without the approval of the central government. Thus, he maintained, its operation had been destined to become corrupt.[40]

The main responsibilities for tax administration and for the operation of public loans in P'yŏngan Province fell to the officers of the local yangban bureau rather than the local clerks of the district magistrate. According to the 1796 report of Third State Councilor Yun Sidong (1729–97), the director of the local yangban association and the supervisor of the granaries (whom the director chose from reliable members of the local elite) were in charge of tax administration in Yŏngbyŏn. Local clerks were strictly limited in administrative function and were under the direction of yangban officers. This system prevented corruption on the part of local clerks and embezzlement of local finances.[41] Chŏng Yagyong also pointed out that the local elite played a leading role in distributing tax burdens among villagers in the northern region. When Chŏng was the magistrate of Koksan, he observed that the local elite met in the fall to allocate the tax among villagers after weighing the output of each household. Chŏng thought that this practice was reasonable and most beneficial to the people, compared to that in the southern provinces, where the local clerks played various tricks to draw profits for themselves.[42]

The local yangban officers and wealthy people in P'yŏngan Province often suffered from public loans through the grain loan system and the people's fund. Not only were wealthy householders targeted for forced loans, but they were also appointed to supervise the people's fund to ensure its sound operation. The superintendent of the people's fund was even called the Pumin-dogam (literally, "the superintendent of well-to-do residents"). The Pumin-dogam was also chosen on an ad hoc basis for financing local expenses incurred by tribute missions, as well as frequent ceremonial expenses for incoming and retiring magistrates. The heavy burden borne by men holding this position often bankrupted their erstwhile wealthy households.[43]

Individual cases that loosely fit these circumstances can be found among those who supported the 1812 rebellion. Ko Yunbin from Kwaksan, one of the original conspirators, was in charge of the government fund, and as supervisor of government storage he had 500 *yang* to supply post-station horses. He loaned out the fund with interest and kept an account book to keep track of loans under his control. Somehow, Ko was imprisoned just before the rebellion for embezzlement of the fund. According to another government source, Ko allegedly stole 1,000 *yang* from the treasury and gave it to Kim Ch'angsi, one of the ringleaders of the rebellion, sometime before the rebellion.[44] It is unclear whether Ko was imprisoned for the money that he supplied to Kim or for some other matter. But we do know that Ko was liable for the management of the fund and that mismanagement resulted in his punishment.

In a similar case, Yi Inbae from Anju, a staff military officer who became a rebel sympathizer, was making usurious loans from a fund to supply military uniforms to people throughout northern P'yŏngan Province, including in Chasan and Yŏngbyŏn, some of whom had a familial relationship with Yi.[45] Again, it is unclear whether the management of this fund drove Yi to join the plot, though Yi may well have fallen into some trouble over this financial adventure. An official remark that some rebels left heavy debts behind them and ordered the local governments to sell their property to repay the debts indicates that the people in charge of public loan funds had financial troubles that may have motivated them to join the rebellion.[46]

TAXATION, PEASANT PAUPERIZATION, AND THE REBELLION

Did the Hong Kyŏngnae Rebellion have a dimension of a tax riot by impoverished peasants? This seems to be the case on the surface, but the answer is more complicated. P'yŏngan Province had been hard hit by bad harvests in the years preceding the rebellion, as one local resident testified. Paek Kyŏnghae reported on weather and harvest condition in the year of 1810 as follows: "This year . . . P'yŏngan Province suffered flooding. The flood damage in the areas such as Ŭiju and Anbyŏn was particularly severe, and a commissioner was sent to soothe people. There was no wind damage. Harvest from dry-field was very bad in general, but it was the worst in P'yŏngan Province." His assessment at the end of 1811 stated: "This year, P'yŏngan Province suffered greatly from drought. Natural disasters, from late rain to wind, hail, insects, and frost, made things worse, resulting in no output at all from any kind of cultivation. It was the worst famine in one hundred years."[47] Based on such observations, Paek advised Provincial Governor Yi Mansu a few months before the rebellion that relief measures should be put into effect immediately because people had suffered severely that year from an unprecedentedly poor harvest. He even predicted a popular revolt if the situation could not be improved.[48]

The government did not seem to take any action to relieve the region's economic distress.[49] On the contrary, the source material reveals cases of collecting taxes after the extraordinarily bad harvest. Wŏn Taech'ŏn, a staff military officer (Chipsa) of Sŏnch'ŏn and a military degree-holder (*ch'ulsin*), went out to the villages to enforce repayment of grain loans in the eleventh lunar month of 1811.[50] Hwang Sŏkchu, a military officer of Kasan, was also touring the countryside to collect the grain loan interest when he heard about the rebellion.[51] Yi Hyegap, a village head (Chonwi) of Chŏngju who supervised the repayment of grain loans just before the rebellion, reported that the villagers refused to repay their loans when the rumor of an imminent rebellion spread to the area.[52] Kim Ch'igwan from Kasan fled with his wife to his in-laws' house in Ch'angsŏng because he could not bear the pressure of repaying his grain loan, especially when the harvest had been so bleak.[53] Under such depressing economic conditions, the forced payment of grain loans must have weighed heavily on the people, and the collection officers were also under stress because the responsibility of meeting the quota fell on them.

Thus the rebels' claim that corrupt officials at the center had ushered in a series of natural disasters—proof of Heaven's dissatisfaction over the regime, according to Confucian discourse—and caused the people great economic distress fit well with the historical situation and might have been perceived as justifying the uprising. The rebel manifesto says:

Now, since the current king is a minor, the influence of cunning but powerful officials grows day by day. Thus, the authority of the court has been robbed and manipulated by people like Kim Chosun[54] and Pak Chonggyŏng.[55] Subsequently, humane Heaven has sent down disasters. Winter lightning and earthquakes have occurred every year.[56] Because of these natural disasters, great famines have occurred repeatedly. As a result, those stricken with hunger litter the roads, and the old and the weak are falling over into the ditches. At last, everyone alive has one foot in the grave.[57]

Several days into the rebellion, the rebels announced that they had executed Chŏng Si, the magistrate of Kasan (the only magistrate killed by the rebels during the rebellion), for the crime of arbitrary taxation and corruption, whereas they had imprisoned Kim Iksun, the magistrate of Sŏnch'ŏn, for extracting money from well-to-do families, and Im Sŏnggo, the magistrate of Pakch'ŏn, for embezzling public funds.[58] The rebels also proclaimed that the district magistrates of the Ch'ŏngbuk region had surrendered to the rebel force because they knew the people's desire and that the Mandate of Heaven had then been transferred to the rebels.[59]

Nonetheless, the rebels did not show much interest in uncovering administrative corruption by magistrates or propose any reform plans for the tax system in the course of the rebellion. Fraudulent operation of the grain loan system and the people's fund made people—wealthy ones in particular—unhappy with the local government but seemed to be only a circumstantial cause for the rebellion. The great famine provided the rebels with a good excuse for mobilizing the poverty-stricken, yet the lack of spontaneous, coherent peasant solidarity with the rebels reveals the uprising's weak link to poverty itself.[60]

EXPANSION OF THE COMMERCIAL ECONOMY AND MERCHANTS' PARTICIPATION IN THE REBELLION

Some important changes occurred in commerce during the late Chosŏn period, spearheaded by reforms in the taxation system. The Uniform Land Tax Law (*taedongpŏp*) of the seventeenth century replaced the previous tribute tax paid in kind by each household with an additional rice payment assessed on land. At first this tax reform lightened the overall tax burden on peasants, although its long-term effect is controversial. Peasants were freed from the fees and surcharges of illegal tribute contracting and some labor service, but the tax on land definitely became heavier. Yet the overall land tax rate was still very low in the province, as discussed earlier in this chapter. The heavier land tax meant an increased burden on landowners and landlords, unless they could evade it by under- or nonregistration of their lands.[61]

More importantly, the reform greatly boosted the commercial economy, since the government-designated merchants (*kongin*) who served as purchasing agents for government requirements supplied the goods previously collected from each individual household. Subsequently, these merchants began to accumulate commercial capital and stimulated the emergence of independent artisans. The expansion of domestic commerce promoted the emergence of unlicensed private merchants and posed a serious challenge to licensed monopoly shops in Seoul. Private merchants demanded the freedom to buy and sell goods in contradiction to licensed monopoly rights and asked the government to grant them licensed privileges in conformity with the licensing system. The licensed merchants pressured the government to execute the law and to protect their monopoly positions. This contest between private merchants and licensed monopoly merchants consumed much of the latter part of the eighteenth century and resulted in a policy of compromise, namely the joint-sale decree (*sinhae t'onggong*) of 1791. The decree approved monopoly privileges only to six shops (Yug'ŭijŏn) for the products they traditionally sold and allowed unlicensed merchants to sell any products not covered by the six shops.[62]

Foreign trade, which was illegal except when carried out under official supervision, also expanded. The legitimate trade with China was conducted under the umbrella of scheduled tribute missions there, in which the kinds of trading goods and volume of trade were regulated. Trade with Japan, through a designated Japanese settlement in Tongnae on the southern coast, was also strictly controlled by the government. Despite such regulations, a triangular trade among Korea, China, and Japan developed in the seventeenth century through the official interpreters on diplomatic missions, who had trading rights and access to government funds for purchasing goods from China. In addition, private merchants often joined the missions as footmen or porters and smuggled Chinese goods back over the border. In return for this, these merchants had to provide a certain portion of the mission's expenses and bribe diplomats as well as border patrol officials at Ŭiju, who examined the trading goods at the border.[63]

Beginning in the early eighteenth century, as Qing China and Japan established direct trade and the supply of Japanese silver—the most important import item from Japan—dramatically decreased, the role of interpreters as the middlemen of international trade declined, and private merchants emerged as their competitors in foreign trade. When trade activities led by interpreters no longer met diplomatic expenses, let alone commercial profit, the government devised a new measure in 1758 by which the interpreters used government funds in silver to purchase winter hats from China for resale in Korea. The import of winter hats was profitable enough to pay diplomatic expenses in the beginning, though the government soon realized the difficulty of supplying silver for buying a consumer item. In 1777, the right to trade winter hats was granted to private merchants such as the Ŭiju and Kaesŏng merchants (*mansang* and *songsang*), who paid a trading tax on the hats. Though import of winter hats by private merchants declined rather rapidly, Ŭiju and Kaesŏng merchants that emerged as regional commercial interest groups by the late eighteenth century with their organizational and financial resources successfully handled other items in foreign trade and even the domestic production process of certain products, such as red ginseng. By the nineteenth century, overall government control over foreign trade eventually had become obsolete.[64]

A similar trend can be seen at irregular trading posts called *husi*. Trade through the market in the palisade settlement (*ch'aengmun husi*), a point of entry into China located in southern Manchuria, had been quite active since 1700, when the earlier foreign trade market established on the Chinese side of the Amnok River (*chunggang husi*) was closed down. Government policy on this market swung back and forth during the eighteenth century. The government prohibited private foreign trade and banned the market in 1727 because of an excessive outflow of silver and an inflow of luxury goods. Nonetheless, it was almost inevitable that trade be allowed, for many reasons. First of all, interpreters and envoys could not prepare the silver and ginseng needed for tribute missions without assistance from private merchants, who paid part of the expenses for the missions in return for business transactions in China. The commercial tax levied on these trading goods at the border was also part of the expenses of the tribute mission. Moreover, demands that the market be reopened from Chinese officials and merchants, who lost profits when it was closed, could not be ignored. Thus trade was allowed again in 1755, although it was abolished once more in 1787 and reopened finally in 1795.[65]

When market activity in the palisade settlement was prohibited, private merchants smuggled goods through other border towns on the upper stream of the Amnok River. Smugglers (*chamsang*) took great risks to do business, for they were severely punished once discovered. In 1732, three smugglers were caught and beheaded in Wiwŏn along the Amnok River, and five others were apprehended and executed in Ŭiju a few days later. All were accused of crossing the border and trading with Qing merchants.[66] A year later, Yi Chiyŏng was beheaded for smuggling, and the subarea commander (Manho) of Pŏldŭng was punished.[67] Secret Inspector Ŏm Rin, who set out for the northern provinces to investigate the open markets (*kaesi*) in 1760, requested punishment for smugglers, for those who patronized smugglers, and for those who received bribes in exchange for conniving at illegal trade without prior permission from the central government.[68] This indicates that there were government officials who were involved in illegal foreign trade and may also explain why some district magistrates were punished for negligence in regulating illegal trade.[69]

Despite the government censure of foreign trade and luxurious consumption, commercial expansion could not be checked, and occasional tightening of various trade regulations was not effective. For example, the purchase of luxury items, such as embroidered silks, for resale on the Korean market by tribute merchants often elicited court criticism of the luxurious yangban lifestyle and prompted a ban on the trade of this type of merchandise. Yet the illegal import of embroidered silk continued, and finally a law stipulating capital punishment for the smugglers was enacted in 1747.[70] A year later, some merchants used a loophole in the law to import plain silks instead of embroidered ones. Noticing that the original purpose of the ban had been violated, the king prohibited the purchase of both embroidered and plain silks.[71] Despite repeated royal edicts deploring the extravagant tendencies of yangban aristocrats and prohibiting the import of luxury goods, private merchants continued to take risks and bring in such items, probably because of consumer demand and the prospect of high profits.[72]

The ginseng trade was one of most lucrative businesses in Chosŏn Korea because the demand for ginseng was very high, both for domestic consumption and as a tribute item, though its production was limited. Naturally, the government put the production and trade of ginseng under strict regulation, and the commercial tax on it was set at one-tenth of its value. For example, private merchants who wanted to purchase ginseng from Kanggye, the most famous ginseng-growing district, were required to obtain a written permit from the Ministry of Taxation.[73] Not only was their travel to Kanggye scrutinized by the authorities, but the details of ginseng transactions—such as the names of seller and buyer, the origin of the product, and the amount of the transaction—were recorded. Before merchants sold ginseng in the market in the capital, they had to report their transaction to the Ministry of Taxation again, so that it could be matched to the original trade document filed in Kanggye. In addition, if merchants sold ginseng to the Japanese, they were put under stricter supervision and were required to pay another 10 percent fee.[74]

It is questionable whether these regulations, which required close coordination among government offices at both the central and local levels, were efficiently enforced by the authorities. From 1686 to 1752, the court declared special regulations of the ginseng trade eight times, including conditions for legal trade, punishments for illegal traders and their accomplices, and punishments for officials who were corrupt or negligent in enforcing the regulations. Private merchants often found ways to evade these cumbersome rules and to maximize their profits, although violation of the law meant capital punishment. According to a study by O Sŏng, illegal trading of ginseng expanded as demand from Japan and China increased and the profits from illegal transactions outweighed the risks. To minimize risk, merchants created secret connections with peasant producers, village middlemen, local officials, and even diplomats, such as interpreters. Local military officers and magistrates often received bribes or kickbacks in exchange for ignoring illegal business.[75]

Although overall government control of foreign trade had become lax by the nineteenth century, the court remained concerned about illegal border crossings and trade during the early years of Sunjo's reign and took intermittent punitive as well as preventive action. In 1804, twenty-five Qing merchants used Changja Island, off the coast of Yongch'ŏn, for smuggling transactions.[76] A few years later, Korean merchants doing business with Qing merchants on the same island were caught. They had traded 150 *sŏm* of rice and 70 *sŏm* of millet for various goods, including silver coins, porcelain, brass, and copper cash.[77] Alarmed by these incidents, a garrison was set up in 1807 on Sin Island, another island off the Yongch'ŏn district's coast, to crack down on illegal trade.[78]

Not only was foreign trade restricted and regulated by the government, but certain domestic commercial activities were also put under close supervision. Mining was one of them. During the late Chosŏn period, government policies on mining had fluctuated between direct government operation, semiofficial operation under government-appointed agents, and private mines with government licenses and tax obligations. Competition among various military units and other government agencies for the right to levy taxes on mines kept the central government from controlling mining in a uniform and profitable way. Lack of a coherent, consistent system of overseeing the mining business caused a number of problems, such as overtaxation, collusion between the taxing agents and the managers of the mines, and illegal operations. Even after mining taxes and permits were placed in the hands of the Ministry of Taxation, some mines were operated privately without permission.[79]

All these forms of government intervention, the lack of standard, stable policies, and the unreasonable restriction on foreign trade and domestic commercial activities, plus the harsh punishment of smugglers, must have caused frustration among merchants of P'yŏngan Province. A number of merchants took part in the Hong Kyŏngnae Rebellion, perhaps motivated by the desire to remove government restrictions on commerce and realize material gain. Probably more important was their aspiration to higher social status, a status comparable to their economic success, for merchants were at the bottom of the social ladder in Chosŏn Korea. Although there are no extant documents in which merchants state their reasons for joining the rebellion, we know that merchants often held local military posts and that they were willing to do so because a military official's social standing was higher than that of a merchant. Having a government connection would also have facilitated a merchant's commercial activity in the area, since business was always under close government control and subject to commercial taxes.

Two fascinating cases of merchant participation are those of Yi Hŭijŏ, a rebel financier, and U Kunch'ik, a rebel strategist. Yi's status mobility was remarkable. Originally a post-station slave, he had passed a military examination before purchasing membership in the local yangban association of Kasan. He may have accumulated wealth through mining and other commercial activities.[80] During preparations for the rebellion, Yi patronized U Kunch'ik, who had once been arrested by the Police Bureau (P'odoch'ŏng) on the charge of illegal trading in red ginseng. U was rumored to be a director of a new gold mine in Unsan, with material support from a financier in Seoul, a few months before the rebellion. It is possible that U and Yi had operated illegal mines and carried out other commercial ventures to raise funds for the rebellion.[81] Na Taegon, a wealthy merchant living in Anju, may have been connected to the rebels through his family relationship with Yi Hŭijŏ, his distant relative by marriage. He moved to Yŏngbyŏn just before the rebellion to coordinate the activities of conspirators in the area.[82]

The participation of Kim Hyech'ŏl and his sons is another good example of merchant involvement in the rebellion. Kim had once been a chief military officer (Chunggun), the highest military position in a district. Yet he was running a medicinal herb shop at the ferry station in Pakch'ŏn at the time of the rebellion. He was known as a big merchant (*kŏsang*) in the area and owned the biggest house in town. As noted in a study of the mid-seventeenth-century English revolution, country inns and taverns used by itinerants were centers for news and discussion, because wayfarers such as peddlers, merchant middlemen, and carters helped spread radical views.[83] Kim's shop must have functioned the same way, for his house was often used as a meeting place for the rebels during the preparatory stage, since it was conveniently located in the market place.[84] It is possible that Kim persuaded other merchants who did business with him to join the rebellion. He not only provided military provisions, monetary support, and fabric for rebel uniforms, but also housed rebel leaders and their family members in his residence.[85] Several months before the rebellion, Kim sent three employees to the northern border areas to collect payments, and this whole mission was suspected of recruiting rebel sympathizers in the area.[86] His son Kim Yunji was also a merchant and acted as rebel chief military officer, while another son was a cavalryman in the rebel army.[87]

Although the government's later contention that all the wealthy merchants in Pakch'ŏn marketplace supported the rebels with money and grain exaggerated the real situation, a number of other merchants besides Kim and his sons did join the rebellion.[88] Ch'oe Yŏun, a merchant of Pakch'ŏn, joined the rebels at the preparatory stage and was appointed a chief military officer of the district by the rebels. Pak Kwangyu, a wealthy Kaesŏng merchant, provided monetary support, participated in preparatory meetings, and served as a staff commander (Paebijang) of the assistant supreme commander of the rebels (Puwŏnsu), although he denied voluntary participation. Kwŏn Kyŏngbaek and Im Sahang, chiefs of gatekeepers (Sumunjang) in the rebel army, were Kaesŏng merchants living in Pakch'ŏn.[89] Though the participation of some Kaesŏng merchants angered government officials, their participation did not represent the whole Kaesŏng merchant community, since their decision to join the rebels was their own.

The role played by Ŭiju merchants is intriguing. In the early days of the rebellion, the rebels captured thirteen horseloads of Chinese goods belonging to a Kaesŏng merchant, Hong Yongsŏ, although they returned most of goods—minus a portion that was given as a payoff to the rebels—later, with the mediation of Yang Chehong. Yang, who had passed the military examination, was a wealthy merchant doing business with both Ŭiju and Kaesŏng merchants. As a rebel staff military officer (Chipsa), Yang was supervising the collection and distribution of military supplies when the rebels snatched Hong's Chinese merchandise. The government was very suspicious of Hong, who was thought to have voluntarily given a portion of his trading goods to the rebels. Not only were Hong and Yang interrogated several times, but Im Sang'ok, an Ŭiju merchant who had bought the Chinese goods for Hong, was also arrested for investigation.[90] Im, however, was commanding a progovernment militia in Ŭiju at the time of his arrest and was soon released to help the government purchase goods from the Chinese in Ŭiju. In return for his service, Im was later made a magistrate.[91] Although there are some puzzling questions about the whole incident, such as how the rebels knew about the goods hidden in the warehouses of agents of the Ŭiju merchants and why they were returned, it is highly unlikely that the whole Ŭiju merchants group was deeply involved in the rebel conspiracy.

Later, during the 1862 rebellions in the southern provinces and the Tonghak rebellions of the 1890s, when commerce was presumably more developed, there was no noticeable merchant participation in the rebel leadership. Because of geographical proximity to China and the opportunity to participate in tribute trade as well as illegal trade, commercial development in P'yŏngan Province may have been more advanced in 1812 than it was in the southern provinces. Merchants of P'yŏngan Province were much distressed, however, because of the restrictive and erratic regulations on their trade and exploitation by corrupt officials. For some merchants, it may not have been a difficult choice to support rebellion since their lives were already in danger due to the nature of their business. In addition, some hoped to earn higher social standing by participating in the rebellion.

This discussion of the economic background of the Hong Kyŏngnae Rebellion shows the complex makeup of financial causes of the rebellion on the individual as well as institutional level. The local elite may have been offended by the integration of local tax reserves into the finances of the center, interpreting this as state intervention in the management of local resources that had previously been under local control. The increasing presence and involvement of the center in other fields that were also thought to be local matters, such as the sale of *hyangan* membership and the management of taxation and public loans, probably invoked ill feeling against the state as well. And the contradiction between merchants' growing material power and their lack of upward social mobility may have become linked in the rebels' minds with the fact that P'yŏngan residents' increasing success on the *munkwa* exams was not being reflected in bureaucratic success within the central government because of regional discrimination.

On the surface, however, the rebels took on the garb of Confucian discourse—namely, the stance that the state was not heeding the economic distress of the people. As other studies of popular rebellions have shown, economic hardship alone does not lead to agrarian conflict.[92] Nor is ecological vulnerability (caused by natural disasters such as frost, flood, drought, hail, insect damage, and epidemics) considered an independent cause of social contention. Yet a Confucian state's lack of responsiveness to natural crises would invoke popular resentment, for the beliefs that the state is morally responsible for relieving its people of such difficulties and that the people are to rise up when the state does not meet that expectation are ingrained in Confucian ideology. This was the exact discourse in which the rebels couched the Hong Kyŏngnae Rebellion.

4 Prophecy and Popular Rebellion

Geomancy and prophecy were important political tools in mobilizing mass support and legitimizing the rebellion. Not only were key leaders such as Hong Kyŏngnae and U Kunch'ik geomancers, but geomantic practices and prophetic beliefs in dynastic changes played a key role in recruiting sympathizers. The rebel manifesto clearly states that their political movement to thwart the existing dynasty has been ordained by the Mandate of Heaven as manifested in popular beliefs in dynastic changes. This chapter examines the development of geomancy and prophecy as a vital element of political culture in Korea and how the rebels appropriated these popular beliefs and practices as their own.

GEOMANCY: THEORY AND PRACTICE IN KOREA

Geomancy (Kor.: *p'ungsu*, Ch.: *feng-shui*; literally, "wind and water") has been one of the most enduring and popular belief systems in Korean history. It originated in China and was apparently much indebted to the yin-yang and the five elements schools in its theoretical contents. According to the doctrine of geomancy, as yin and yang forces interact in their creativity in the universe, they also fill the earth and circulate under its surface like the blood running through a human body. Just as damage to a blood vessel results in sickness, so the ill treatment of certain vital spots on the surface of the earth, such as the improper selection of a temple site, disturbs the subterranean circulation of the yin and yang, which can in turn disrupt the harmony of human society. Conversely, the construction of a temple, pagoda, or house or the founding of a town or palace on an auspicious site is believed to revitalize the subterranean forces and prolong the prosperity of a dynasty, family, lineage, or town.[1]

Maurice Freedman's study of geomancy in China, which is instrumental in understanding the same tradition in Korea, notes that there is no reliance on the will of a deity, and hence no gods to serve or placate, in geomancy. Geomancy is based on propositions and principles that regulate the cosmos, however vaguely they may be formulated, and that are known to experts who operate along well-articulated lines of thought. In a word, geomancy is a technique, and men can use it to their advantage. Two consequences follow from this view. One is that geomancers are held in an esteem not shared by other religious practitioners. They are educated and so attract the curiosity of the educated. The second consequence is that faith in geomancy may well survive a change in religion, since its theory is not antagonistic to any hegemonic religion but shares with religion some of its basic notions, such as that of maintaining harmony between men and nature.[2]

Although geomancy is a human response to forces working within nature, it is preoccupied with success. It is when a man begins to think of increased prosperity for himself and his offspring, some measure of affluence having already been achieved, that he becomes concerned with geomancy. Already prosperous, he cannot afford not to take any geomantic precautions that will ensure his continuing success. Thus there is a fundamental notion underlying geomancy—namely, that all men are in principle equal, and can legitimately strive to improve their station in life. In other words, all men are entitled to take steps to elevate themselves and their descendants through scholarship, through the accumulation of wealth, and through the religious pursuit of good fortune.[3]

The status of geomancy has been ambiguous; it has not been part of the state cult, and yet it has been used by the government for the siting and protection of important tombs and buildings.[4] Though it was officially attacked for its harmful effects on public behavior, the government often responded to rebellion by smashing the ancestral tombs of the rebels. And while an educated man might criticize geomancy for being superstitious and misleading ignorant people, when selecting the burial site for his ancestors, he would rely heavily on the advice of a geomancer. For example, An Chŏngbok (1712–91), a late Chosŏn scholar, reported the practice of locating auspicious spots in a greedy search for wealth, success, and long life and warned against the ill effects of excessive geomantic investment.[5]

The source of this ambiguity was the fact that geomancy and state ortho-doxy shared some fundamental principles of thought. The *Book of Changes* (*Yi jing*), a prime source of geomantic theory, was a link between geomancy and all other systems of thought in the East Asian tradition, including Neo-Confucianism. This classic provided generation after generation of scholars and social elite with a basis for moral and metaphysical speculation, as well as a means of deciding on a line of conduct within the framework of the conditions prevailing at any given time. Thus it has been the bridge between canonic metaphysics and divination, on the one hand, and the popular system of geomancy on the other.[6]

The status of geomancer was as indeterminate as geomancy itself. The professional geomancer was in one sense a member of the social elite, since he was the master of a body of learning, yet his paid services were available to the common people. The basic metaphysics on which he operated—a universe pulsing between yin and yang, permeated by *ki* (Ch.: *ch'i*), moved back and forth by the five elements (five phases; *o-haeng*)—was the meta-physics of scholarship, the joint intellectual property of the Confucian literati, yet the geomancer put his metaphysics to common use. He mediated, then, between the two main strata of society, the learned and the common. The true scholar, for whom the ideal was government service, might well join in respectable divining exercises with his close associates, but he would not sell his talents on the open market.[7] The geomancer was a kind of literary figure, and yet not entirely so. Balancing between the literati and the common people, he did not clearly belong to either camp. From the point of view of the elite, he was tainted by his attachment to the popular and the extrabu-reaucratic; that same attachment, however, was his strength with the com-mon people.[8] Therefore, he was raised above the common people but looked down on by the social elite, especially in the Chosŏn context, in which a geomancer's family background was the most critical factor in determining his social standing, despite his being linked to the elite sphere through his services.

The pseudoscientific idea of geomancy holds sway over the entire tradi-tional history of Korea. Geomancy was transmitted to the Korean peninsula during the Unified Silla period (668–935), when cultural exchange with Tang China (617–907) became very active.[9] It was in the latter part of the Unified Silla dynasty that geomancy became very popular among the populace. As local power holders built strongholds in their respective localities, they justi-fied their political control by claiming that their regions were blessed by geomantic forces, in an attempt to earn popular support during this politically and socially chaotic period. In a military sense, also, geomancy was useful for finding strategically well-suited sites. Thus all the political leaders of the Later Three Kingdoms period tended to rely on geomancy for both political and military reasons.[10]

With the founding of the Koryŏ dynasty in the tenth century, geomancy received strong royal support, and one historian even noted that the rise and fall of the Koryŏ dynasty was closely related to geomantic theory.[11] The founder of the Koryŏ dynasty, Wang Kŏn himself, believed in the power of geomantic forces and sought the advice of the monk Tosŏn (826–98), the greatest champion of the terrestrial "wind and water" theory.[12] In the process of unifying the Korean peninsula, Wang Kŏn consulted geomantic theory in selecting the sites of temples and pagodas, military outposts, and the capital city of Kaesŏng itself.[13]

Wang Kŏn's faith in geomancy is clear in his Ten Testamentary Instructions (Hunyo Sipcho), in which he notes that he has accomplished unification with the aid of the protective forces of the mountains and streams of the peninsula, and he advises his descendants, "All newly founded temples and monasteries were built on the sites chosen by Monk Tosŏn in accord with geomantic principles. Tosŏn said that the indiscriminate construction of temples and monasteries in places other than those of his selection would damage and enervate terrestrial forces and thus bring a dynastic decline. . . . Guard against this."[14] Wang Kŏn's primary concern, couched in this injunction, may have been to prevent the economic waste that was likely to result from "the indiscriminate construction of temples and monasteries." At any rate, his unequivocal expression of belief in geomancy made it an important element in official thinking on the business of government.[15]

There are numerous cases throughout the Koryŏ dynasty of state affairs being governed by geomantic thinking. For example, to prolong the rule of the royal Wang line when it was believed that the terrestrial force of the Kaesŏng area was spent, King Munjong (r. 1047–82) built subsidiary palaces on propitious sites for the reigning kings to visit, presumably to be replenished by the still-fresh terrestrial forces there.[16] And King Sukchong (r. 1095–1105), prompted by geomantic experts, reconstructed the southern capital, where the king was to spend the spring months, near the site of modern Seoul. He did this to stabilize an unsettled political situation after a bloody succession struggle, and he prayed for the prosperity of the country by relying on auspicious geomantic forces.[17] King Yejong (r. 1106–22) expanded the western capital, P'yŏngyang, by undertaking an ambitious building program, and he enhanced its administrative status by upgrading the organs of the city government to a level almost equal to that of Kaesŏng itself. P'yŏngyang's excellent geomantic location had already been asserted in Wang Kŏn's Ten Testamentary Instructions, and King Yejong attempted to exploit the city's geomantic forces for a military expedition to subjugate the Jurchen tribes in the northeast, whose consolidation threatened the Koryŏ state.[18]

Not only kings but rebels tried to galvanize geomantic forces. For example, Myoch'ŏng used them to his advantage in his uprising in 1135. The geomantic view that P'yŏngyang was a preferable site for the dynastic capital had been held from the beginning of the Koryŏ dynasty. Whenever a natural disaster hit the country or a political power struggle caused chaos in society, some officials and geomancers argued that the terrestrial forces of Kaesŏng were exhausted and that transfer of the capital to P'yŏngyang was needed. Many kings, subscribing to these arguments, rebuilt and expanded P'yŏngyang and made royal visits to the city to obtain the terrestrial benefits it held. During the reign of King Injong (1122–46), after the bloody power struggle led by Yi Chagyŏm and T'ak Chun'gyŏng, a group of high-ranking central officials from the P'yŏngyang area gained royal support for their efforts to move the dynastic capital there. The leader of this group, Myoch'ŏng a Buddhist monk, combined the theories of Buddhism, geomancy, and yin-yang thought to persuade the king to transfer the capital to P'yŏngyang. However, the plan met with strong opposition from a group of Confucian officials of the Kaesŏng faction, who claimed that Heaven supported the capital remaining where it was, and who backed this up by showing that the supposed mystical signs indicated by Myoch'ŏng were lies. In the end, Myoch'ŏng and his followers established their own empire in P'yŏngyang and revolted against the court in Kaesŏng, once they realized that any chance of the capital being relocated had disappeared.[19]

In the founding of the Chosŏn dynasty, Yi Sŏnggye also utilized geomancy to legitimize dynastic change. He used the great masters Naong and Muhak the same way that Wang Kŏn had used Tosŏn. Debates on selecting and moving the capital to Hanyang (modern Seoul), part of the process to strengthen the newly established royal authority, were closely related to the popularity of geomancy at the time. However, as soon as the power of the new dynasty was established and society was stabilized, yang geomancy (which included the belief that a great personality would emerge in close relation with terrestrial forces) was silenced and yin geomancy (which emphasized the wise selection of a burial site, since subterranean forces were believed to influence the well-being of posterity through the bones of the buried ancestor) was favored instead.[20] Yin geomancy was in harmony with the Neo-Confucian emphasis on ancestor worship (which was an extension of filial piety, one of the five norms of Neo-Confucian social relations), although such ancestor worship was practiced as a form of devotion toward one's parents even after their deaths, whereas geomancy utilized ancestors' burial sites for the sole benefit of their descendants.[21]

In any case, after completing a dynastic change and establishing a stable social and political structure, a ruler no longer needed to highlight geomantic forces. On the contrary, geomantic theory was blamed for misleading people because of its superstitious nature. Nevertheless, geomantic thought maintained its popularity because it provided people with the dream of earning prosperity and success by choosing an auspicious spot for their ancestors' graves. In particular, geomancy laid a foundation for the prophetic belief in dynastic change that was systemized in written form in texts such as the *Chŏnggamnok* (The Record of Chŏng Kam), to which the 1812 rebels heavily resorted.

The *Chŏnggamnok* is a collection of prophetic writings that prognosticate the future of the Chosŏn dynasty by relying on geomancy and other supernatural omens, such as earthquakes, eclipses, and comets. Although its exact time of compilation is unknown, similar prophetic thought existed even before the founding of the Chosŏn dynasty.[22] The main theme of the book is that a man with the surname of Chŏng will establish a new dynasty at Mount Kyeryong once Chosŏn rule ends with military revolts and catastrophic natural disasters. In addition, the book suggests ten auspicious places, based on geomancy, where one can escape these natural and manmade events. Though all versions of the prophetic writings collected in the *Chŏnggamnok* (there are many variations of the text) converge on the prophecy of the demise of the Yi royal house and the rise of a Chŏng royal house, the details of the prophecy differ. For example, one variant says that the Chosŏn dynasty will last three hundred years, and others, four or five hundred years.

Such eschatological and apocalyptical overtones in the different texts of the *Chŏnggamnok* suggest certain ideological components found in the millenarian tradition.[23] Nonetheless, they do not qualify this particular prophetic tradition as millenarianism, for as Richard Emmerson argues, not all eschatological beliefs or forms of apocalypticism are necessarily millenarian. Emmerson adopts Robert Lerner's definition of millenarianism as the hope for an impending, supernaturally inspired, marvelous betterment of life on Earth before the End. He also points out that to use the term to identify the goals of a predominantly secular social or political movement is to define the concept too broadly, for "millenarianism" must imply religious motivations and goals if it is to retain its usefulness as an analytical tool.[24] In the Korean context, not a single reference to a religious aspect can be isolated in the *Chŏnggamnok*, thus making it difficult to identify the 1812 rebellion, which cited its prophecies, as a millenarian movement.[25]

Indeed, most prophecies that popular movements and conspiracies appropriated, including those garnered from the *Chŏnggamnok*, were secular and political in nature. These movements did not entail the deity worship, sacred scriptures, prescribed rituals, charms or chants of potent phrases, or religious community observed in popular millenarian movements. The term *Chŏng chinin*, or just *chinin*, for the supreme leader who appeared in numerous rebellious plots, including the Hong Kyŏngnae Rebellion, was probably adopted from the prophecy recorded in the *Chŏnggamnok*. The use of the term *chinin*, referring to a person who has attained the true Way (*to* or *dao*) of Daoism or Buddhism, shows that the projected ruler of a new dynasty was pictured as a man of extraordinary qualities.[26] In his study of folk stories about *chinin*, Cho Tongil indicates that the *chinin* shares certain characteristics with a god, in that he would not fail in his struggle against evil; with a hero, in that his existence is for the struggle itself; and with a mystic, in that he lives a mysterious life.[27] As manifested in various plots, however, the *chinin* was clearly neither a religious leader, a reincarnated Buddha, nor Maitreya (the Future Buddha) himself, but a simple secular leader with supernatural power.

Nonetheless, prophecies of dynastic change could pose more threat to a ruling dynasty than religiously charged movements, because such prophecies were destructive in themselves, as foretold in the *Chŏnggamnok*, whereas those who held millenarian beliefs turned to violence only when they expected the turning of the kalpa (or aeon).[28] In addition, because the prophecies in such books were very complex, with many omissions and misprints, various interpretations and subsequent manipulations of the content were possible. Exactly because the contents of such prophetic texts were antidynastic and could serve the intentions of rebels, the state prohibited the possession and transmission of them and burned them to exterminate this heterodox tradition. However, the prophetic tradition and subversive books such as the *Chŏnggamnok* not only survived but gained popular support, reflecting the wishes of the people for a better life under new leadership.[29]

The element of the *Chŏnggamnok*-type tradition that was responsible for its tenacity and popularity was its link to the Confucian moralism embedded in the idea of the Mandate of Heaven. The idea was that the mandate to rule a country is given by Heaven, so Heaven can also deprive a morally corrupt ruler of that mandate. Heaven conveys its dissatisfaction with a ruler through natural disasters and supernatural omens. Popular rebellions represent Heaven's displeasure with the ruler and are a valid way to install a new, morally upright ruler. This long-held political idea had been utilized for popular rebellions and dynastic changes throughout Chinese as well as Korean history.[30] Although all the predictions for future change in the *Chŏnggamnok* borrowed geomantic discourses, its primary concepts of dynastic change originated in Confucianism.[31]

The most well-known incident in Korean history utilizing the prophetic belief was the conspiracy of Chŏng Yŏrip in the late sixteenth century. Although some scholars argued that false charges were brought against Chŏng Yŏrip and Easterners by the Westerner faction, it is clear that Chŏng Yŏrip himself had antidynastic plans in mind.[32] The whole incident was closely related to folk belief in prophecy. To earn popular support, Chŏng attempted to spread a folk song (*minyo*), composed in literary Chinese, that ran, "The tree character perishes, the *chŏng* town arises" (*mok cha mang, chŏng ŭp hŭng*). This was a play on words, for the first two characters of the first stanza, *mok* and *cha*, when put together top and bottom, make up the royal surname Yi, and the first two characters of the second stanza, *chŏng* and *ŭp*, together side by side become the surname Chŏng. Thus the song symbolically alluded to the fall of Chosŏn dynasty and the rise of a new dynasty founded by a Chŏng royal family. It was also said that Chŏng grafted a horse's mane onto a mulberry tree to make it look as though the well-known saying had come true about any owner of a house that has a mulberry tree bearing a horse's mane being destined to become king.[33] In fact, it was probably Chŏng Yŏrip and his followers who compiled the *Chŏnggamnok*, based on prophecies transmitted from the beginning of the Chosŏn dynasty, in order to legitimize their conspiracy.[34]

There were numerous political conspiracies, popular rebellious plots, and incidents of posting seditious letters in the public marketplace or on gates (*kwaesŏ sagŏn*) advertising the content of the *Chŏnggamnok* and other prophecies during the late Chosŏn period. One example was a conspiracy in 1688 mainly based on belief in Maitreya Buddha, the ruler of the next world, where there would be no crime and pain but only purity and brightness. In this conspiracy, the Maitreya belief, a kind of millenarian utopianism, was mixed with belief in the dragon spirit (*yong sinang*) and the prophetic tradition prescribed in the *Chŏnggamnok*. The monk Yŏhwan was the core leader of the conspiracy, and his followers were recruited from the Yangju area in Kyŏnggi Province. Followers of this conspiracy believed that Maitreya Buddha would descend to the world soon, and that dynastic change would follow soon after. They also believed that Yŏhwan's wife, a shaman called Madame Dragon (*yongnyŏ puin*), would give birth to a son who would rule the new dynasty. Another female shaman, Kyehwa, who claimed that she was the True and Genuine Chŏng (*Chŏng chinin*), also played an important role in the plot. The conspirators predicted that there would be disastrous rains during the seventh lunar month (July 27–August 25) of 1688, which would totally ruin Seoul. After the ruin of the capital, the rebels would move in to occupy it and establish a new dynasty. Relying on this prediction, the rebels went to Seoul on August 10 and waited for rain, but in vain. They returned to Yangju, resenting the lack of response from Heaven. Later, when their conspiracy was discovered, all the leaders and followers were arrested and punished.[35]

Another plot, in 1697, was mainly led by Buddhist monks who used the *Chŏnggamnok*. The chief leader was the Chinese monk Unbu, who had come to Korea and resided at Mount Kŭmgang after the demise of the Ming dynasty. Unbu, supposedly having supernatural power, made an alliance with many prominent monks and a famous bandit leader of the time, Chang Kilsan. According to their plan, after they conquered Chosŏn Korea and established the True and Genuine Chŏng (*Chŏng chinin*) as a Korean king, they would invade China to set up an imperial house under the True and Genuine Ch'oe (*Ch'oe chinin*). Their plot did not bear fruit because one of the conspirators reported it to the government.[36]

An increasing number of rebellious plots and postings of seditious letters heavily influenced by the prophetic tradition were reported during the eighteenth and nineteenth centuries. During the reign of King Yŏngjo (1724–76), more plots were discovered than in any other period.[37] The frequent occurrence of rebellious plots reflected the insecure livelihoods of the people due to periodic natural disasters (such as flood, famine, and epidemics) and also the political alienation of many yangban elite after the consolidation of power by the Patriarch's faction (Noron). People both ignorant and educated tended to be susceptible to superstitious but subversive ideologies when their livelihoods were threatened by uncertain natural disasters as well as by social and political chaos and change.

The conspiracy of Yun Chi in 1755 reflects the political atmosphere of the time.[38] While planning a rebellion, Yun Chi lived in Naju in Chŏlla Province, to which he had been banished (probably because of his involvement in the Yi Injwa Rebellion of 1728). In choosing a strategic base for the rebellion and the time of insurrection, he relied heavily on the prophetic tradition of the *Chŏnggamnok*. In particular, the predictions of a dynastic change and the omens for it, as described in the *Chŏnggamnok*, were quite useful in attracting coconspirators from different areas. In fact, prophetic beliefs were widespread at that time among the educated populace and ordinary peasants alike, since books like the *Chŏnggamnok* were available in vernacular Korean (*ŏnmun*) and were also transmitted orally among the populace. Therefore, the conspirators, regardless of their faith in the prophecies, relied on prophetic beliefs and manipulated the content of the prophetic books, as shown in numerous conspiracies during the late Chosŏn period.[39]

PROPHETIC BELIEFS
IN THE HONG KYŎNGNAE REBELLION

The influence of the prophetic tradition, especially that of the *Chŏnggamnok*, cannot be missed in the Hong Kyŏngnae Rebellion. Hong Kyŏngnae, the leader of the rebellion, was a geomancer. Selecting his father's burial site at the back of the village shrine in Yonggang in P'yŏngan Province, he proclaimed that the site was a great place that would provide extraordinary protection. This claim presumably meant that he himself was fated to be a king with the aid of the geomantic force of this particular burial site, which provided legitimacy for his rebellion.[40]

The coleader of the rebellion, U Kunch'ik, was also a geomancer whom Hong first met in a Buddhist temple in Kasan. It is obvious that their common interest in geomancy and the prophetic tradition served as a basis for the close friendship between the two. When they met for a second time, in 1801, they discussed recent natural disasters and supernatural omens, such as earthquakes and solar eclipses, and predicted an armed rebellion in 1812 (the *imsin* year) led by "a person who would save the world" (*chese chi in*).[41] It is clear that they made such a prediction by taking descriptions in the *Chŏnggamnok* into account, for it is foretold in the chapter of *Kamgyŏl* (Revelation by Kam) in the *Chŏnggamnok* that an armed rebellion will break out in the year of *imsin* in the sixty-year stems-and-branches system.[42]

The connection between the future rebel financier Yi Hŭijŏ and U Kunch'ik was made because U, as a geomancer, selected a burial site for Yi's father.[43] When doing so U told Yi, "You will attain indescribable blessings in your lifetime."[44] Yi's faith in U's prophecy moved him to sponsor U and eventually to assist U and Hong's plot.

U Kunch'ik in fact used his geomantic skills to make personal connections with other people in P'yŏngan Province and to enlist them in the rebellion. Kim Kukpŏm, a local yangban in Kwaksan, probably came to know U when he joined a meeting at Kim Ch'angsi's library for U's selection of a burial site for Kim Ch'angsi's uncle, four months before the rebellion. At this meeting, they discussed the imminent rebellion, and Kim Kukpŏm later joined the rebels as a strategist (*mosa*).[45] U also selected a burial site for Kang Tŭkhwang, U's maternal relative living in Pakch'ŏn, a man who played an important role in recruiting rebel troops.[46] Kim Yŏjŏng, who helped recruit rebel troops and became a rebel military officer, also met U when U selected his father's burial site.[47] It is important to note not only that the service of selecting auspicious burial sites was widely available from geomancers, but also that there was popular demand for this service from people of every status background. This shows that northern residents in the early nineteenth century enjoyed a certain financial surplus to patronize geomancers and also that they aspired to achieve better economic circumstances and higher social stations by investing in prophetic beliefs.

One rebel manifesto clearly shows the influence of the *Chŏnggamnok* and other popular beliefs in the making of the rebellion. After claiming that people are greatly distressed by government corruption and natural disaster, it says:

How blessed it is that a savior (*sŏngin*) who can save the world was born on Red Robe Island of Kaya village in the vicinity of King Port, beneath the Sun and Moon Peak of Sword Mountain in Sŏnch'ŏn, north of the Ch'ŏngch'ŏn River.[48] He was divine from his birth. He followed a holy monk to China when he was but five years old. Upon his maturity, he retired in Kanggye and Yŏyŏn, the areas where the four abolished districts had once been located.[49] In the five years since he lived there, he commanded the descendants of the hereditary subjects of the imperial Ming dynasty. He subsequently decided to pacify the Chosŏn dynasty with one hundred thousand iron cavalrymen. However, since P'yŏngan Province was his imperial birthplace, he himself could not bear to launch an attack on the region. Thus he first allowed brave and worthy men from P'yŏngan Province to raise an army to save the people. All the places where righteous banners of our army arrive will be greatly revived.[50]

The rebels attempted to legitimize their rebellion in the manifesto by claiming that the Mandate of Heaven for the Chosŏn dynasty was ending, as indicated by the frequent occurrence of natural disasters and cosmic changes. The "savior who can save the world" seems to refer to the True and Genuine Chŏng, more specifically a man named Chŏng Chemin, or Sisu, whom Hong Kyŏngnae introduced to U Kunch'ik in 1810, when the two met in a Buddhist temple.[51] According to U's testimony, Chŏng Sisu had a plan to rebel against the Chosŏn dynasty after rallying followers, and U was asked to join the rebellion. It seems that this Chŏng Sisu was a figurehead at best, since no trace of his participation is found during the rebellion, although some rebel troops vaguely referred to a man with the surname Chŏng (Chŏng-ga) as their chief leader.[52] Moreover, a rebel testified that the popular story of the birth of a general (*changgun*) about fifty years before had been manipulated by the rebels. The story goes that a monstrously ugly baby, born in a village called Koaegol in Sŏnch'ŏn, was buried by the mother. The neighbors, suspicious because there was no sound of a baby's crying, made up a rumor that the baby was not crying because he was born to be a general. The rumor spread quite widely among the people in the region, and it was believed that the rebel leaders borrowed the story and developed it into the theory that the baby general, now the True and Genuine Chŏng, was to rise up to save the people.[53]

This story, which partly fit the prediction made in the *Chŏnggamnok*, may have been powerful enough to agitate the people who were suffering from a disastrous famine in the year preceding the rebellion. At the outset of the first violent attack on the administrative office of Kasan, Hong Kyŏngnae made a speech to the rebel army, and one of the main ingredients that created belief in victory in the hearts of the troops was Hong's statement that they were the vanguard force of the True and Genuine Chŏng.[54] The rebels repeatedly referred to belief in the True and Genuine Chŏng to galvanize popular support as they extended their occupation in the region and also after they retreated to Chŏngju.[55] This ideological justification must have become widespread, for Kang Hŭiyŏng, a temporary resident in Hwanghae Province at the time, reports in his diary that the ringleader of the rebels was a certain Chŏng.[56] It seems that the prophetic belief embodied in the personage of the True and Genuine Chŏng also provided a strong basis for unity between rich and poor, as well as among people of various status backgrounds.[57]

Indeed, many participants in the rebellion, especially fifth columnists (*naeŭng*), those local elite who had committed themselves to the plot and took control of the district offices before the rebel army's arrival, were strongly moved by the theory of the True and Genuine Chŏng. A poor local yangban, Kim Taehun, who managed a medicine shop in Kwaksan, heard about the True and Genuine Chŏng, and about the imminent armed rebellion, from Kim Ch'angsi.[58] In fact, it was Kim Ch'angsi who promoted the story of the supernatural birth of *Chŏng chinin* and his preparation for armed rebellion to earn support for the 1812 rebellion. At a meeting in late October or early November 1811 with Kim Taehun and Ko Yunbin, another local yangban, Kim Ch'angsi, stated that Hong Kyŏngnae and U Uk (Kun ch'ik) had already met the True and Genuine Chŏng and received an order to raise troops for rebellion. After occupying P'yŏngan and Hwanghae provinces, the True and Genuine Chŏng would come down to lead the rebellion, which would take seven years in all.[59] When Kim Taehun worried about how he might survive during the seven years of armed struggle, Kim Ch'angsi even promised to protect him, since they were friends. Faithfully believing what he was told, Kim Taehun supervised rebel finances and logistics as a chief administrative officer (Chongsagwan) during the rebellion.[60]

Another neighbor in the district, Pak Sŏngsin, who had once served the central government as army second deputy commander (Ch'ŏmsa, Jr. 3), was also moved by prophetic belief.[61] His participation in the plot seems to have been closely related to his faith in the True and Genuine Chŏng, for he transmitted the story to his close relatives to persuade them.[62] Not only did he become a rebel-appointed magistrate of Kwaksan, but his two sons took part in the rebellion as military officers.[63]

Ch'oe Iryun, a high-ranking military officer from Chŏngju, first met Hong Kyŏngnae when Hong came to the village school (*sŏdang*) to study for several months seven or eight years before the rebellion. In late December 1811 and early January 1812, a month before the rebellion, Hong invited Ch'oe to Bountiful Blessings Village (Tabok-tong) in Kasan, where planning was taking place, and told him that the impending armed rebellion would be commanded by the True and Genuine Chŏng. From the time of this meeting or even before, Ch'oe began to become deeply involved in the conspiracy. As a rebel-appointed magistrate of Chŏngju, Ch'oe recruited troops by using the government military roster (*namjŏngan*), took care of the preparation and transportation of military provisions, and distributed grain loans to peasants in the early days of the rebellion. Along with his brother and son, he stayed at the rebel camp in Chŏngju until the town was taken by government troops after four months of resistance.[64]

The theory of the True and Genuine Chŏng and armed rebellion clearly called for a dynastic change, as foretold in the *Chŏnggamnok*. The rebels not only took over the existing state organization by appointing magistrates and other local officials, but also set up a quasidynastic bureaucracy. Hong Kyŏngnae sent a secret letter to a collaborator in the border area whom he designated "king" on the envelope.[65] In addition, Kim Uhak, the director of the local yangban bureau in Yŏngbyŏn, was promised not only the post of magistrate of Yŏngbyŏn but a further promotion to the post of chief state councilor later on. Nam Ikhyŏn of Yŏngbyŏn, who held the highest local military position, was to become chief of the Military Training Administration (Hunjang), and Yi Iksu of the same district, the minister of personnel.[66] Kim Uhak was approached by a local yangban, Kim Sayong, who was a rebel assistant supreme commander (Puwŏnsu). Kim Sayong attracted Kim Uhak's attention with his mastery of the occult arts (*pyŏnsinsul*) and other supernatural powers.[67] Although it is not known whether Kim Sayong told Kim Uhak about the True and Genuine Chŏng, it is quite plausible that Kim Uhak and other conspirators in Yŏngbyŏn were informed about him.

Not only did the theory of dynastic change based on geomancy, as predicted in *Chŏnggamnok*, play a critical role in legitimizing the rebellion and mobilizing support, but other popular beliefs in prognostication and the occult arts were also important elements in the rebels' ideology and were instrumental in augmenting the almost mythical power and authority of rebel leaders. Most pronounced are narratives surrounding the tricks of Hong Kyŏngnae. In the early days of the rebellion, Hong convinced his followers that his art of sword dancing enabled him to jump over a tree 10 *chang* (20.8 meters) tall.[68] Later, when the rebels were enclosed in the walled town of Chŏngju, Hong boasted that he could block twenty bullets with one stroke of his sword. To prove such extraordinary skill, he had his colleagues surround him and deceivingly fire blank shots at him while he mounted a horse and brandished his sword to pretend to fend off the bullets. Faithful but stupid followers called him a general who had truly mastered the Way (*chindo changgun*).[69]

The above case of Kim Uhak and Kim Sayong illustrates both belief in and reliance on the occult arts. Kim Sayong reportedly relied on his knowledge of physiognomy when he chose rebel military officers.[70] He also put his shoe on a long bamboo pole and marked a footprint on the snow on the rooftop of a gate to make his followers believe that he had leapt over the gate to enter the building. Believing in his extraordinary power, his band called him a flying general (*pi-changgun*).[71] Kye Namsim of Sŏnch'ŏn, popularly known as the master of heavenly signs (*ch'ŏnmun*) and other occult arts, was invited to be a strategist by the rebels. Although Kye denied any expertise and asked to be freed on the pretext of illness, he prognosticated the fortune of future military actions at the request of the gullible Kim Tae-hun.[72] And Kim Ch'angsi, the rebel strategist who had recruited Kim Taehun, as already described, divined his own future when he was running away from government pursuit.[73]

Divination was the occupation of Pak Chŏngyong from Sŏngch'ŏn in Hwanghae Province, who served the rebels as a document clerk (Sŏgigwan) or a chief administrative officer (Chongsagwan). He was accused of recruiting vagrants (who practiced divination or occult arts) to become rebels and was decapitated for treason.[74] In Kusŏng, the rebels asked the blind Pak Wŏnbo to foretell their future and perform a sacrificial rite to Heaven.[75]

Reliance on folk beliefs about prophecy and magical powers was not exclusive to the rebels. The government also performed a sacrificial rite to Heaven on top of a mountain to invoke its assistance when the annihilation of the rebels was delayed. The performance, which was headed by the deputy commander of the Circuit Pacification Army Headquarters (Sunmu Chung-gun), was obviously carried out to earn mass support by symbolically claiming that Heaven was on the government's side. One of the most honored loyalists, Im Chihwan, a military officer who was killed by the rebels on his way to Ŭiju to transmit an order from military headquarters in Anju, also divined his fate using branches that he picked from a tree when he was arrested by the rebels.[76]

More interestingly, both rebel and government sides interpreted one and the same "supernatural" phenomenon—a comet—to their own advantage. The rebels saw the appearance of a comet in 1811 as the sign of Heaven's disapproval of the existing dynasty. In contrast, the day before the final attack on the rebels, one of the top government commanders predicted great success because a comet had appeared in the sky for 119 days the previous year, and the number of days of the rebellion, from the first day of revolt to the next day, would be exactly 119 days. He assured other commanders that the fall of the rebels was not a human affair but a heavenly design.[77] The same comet was also observed in China in the spring of 1811 and throughout the summer. In her study of the Eight Trigrams Uprising of 1813, Susan Naquin comments that the imperial court declared the comet to be a sign of great glory for the dynasty, though it is likely that the sect leaders considered it to support predictions about the imminent arrival of the new kalpa and an auspicious blessing for their enterprise.[78]

All these cases indicate that, regardless of their social status and political orientation, people were strongly influenced by various folk beliefs in prophecy and the occult arts.[79] Especially when their lives were hit by natural disasters, famine, and epidemics, and their social and political fortunes were at risk, people were rather easily influenced by popular beliefs that promised better living conditions. Even local yangban subscribed to prophetic beliefs and joined the rebels because they were distressed about the intense competition for power in the community and the increasing state control over their institutions and wealth. The promise of becoming a main actor in the new dynasty was extremely appealing to those marginalized elite who had been unable to achieve their political aspirations. The rebel leaders, for their part—whether they strongly felt the injustice of court politics or were truly concerned about the general degradation of people's lives—needed to announce the coming of a new era, as predicted in the popular prophetic tradition of the *Chŏnggamnok*, in order to gain popular support. This almost sagacious aim not only fit the dominant Confucian political culture of dynastic change but also touched the distressed hearts of people on the verge of a subsistence crisis wrought by the greatest famine in memory.

PART II

The Hong Kyŏngnae Rebellion of 1812

5 Leadership and Preparation

Conventional accounts say that the 1812 rebellion had been in preparation for over ten years, and primary sources indicate that Hong Kyŏngnae and U Kunch'ik, the two best-known ringleaders, met for the first time in 1800.[1] Over the next decade or so, plots for a rebellion matured and networks among like-minded people formed. This chapter follows such tracks to identify the main actors of the rebellion and the ingredients for their dedication to it. It also describes the material preparations for the rebellion, which were telescoped into the few months before the uprising itself.

FORMATION OF THE CORE LEADERSHIP

Hong Kyŏngnae

Hong Kyŏngnae's social status is somewhat controversial. He was commonly regarded as a fallen yangban (*mollak yangban*), based on the popular story that he was educated by his uncle and took the triennial lower civil service examination (*samasi*).[2] This story is questionable. At least two reliable sources inform us that Hong was a commoner. One source indicates that he was a commoner duty soldier who belonged to the provincial military headquarters in P'yŏngyang;[3] the other simply states that he was a commoner (*sanghan*).[4] O Such'ang argues for Hong's commoner status by taking up the remark made by Kim Chosun, probably the most powerful court official at the time, that Hong was a man of meager lowly birth (*hanch'ŏn chi p'ilbu*).[5]

Hong was poor, possessing neither land nor private slaves, but he was educated to some degree, and the geomantic techniques he learned became the source of earning his livelihood.[6] After he buried his father behind the village shrine, Hong told himself that he had chosen the great burial site that would provide symbolic protection for him in his lifetime.[7] As a geomancer, Hong traveled extensively and became acquainted with people of various statuses, including yangban who supported his antidynastic venture.[8]

It was during Hong's travels that he recruited rebel conspirators throughout northern Korea. Hong relied on two ideological propositions when rallying supporters for the rebellion: (1) the common Confucian precept that the difficulty of people's lives and unusual heavenly disasters were signs of the withdrawal of the Mandate of Heaven from the existing dynasty, and (2) the popular tradition of the prophetic belief in dynastic change described in the *Chŏnggamnok*. His arguments based on Confucian teachings and the theory of the emergence of the True and Genuine Chŏng were very persuasive in recruiting discontented elements in the rural population, especially the marginalized elite in P'yŏngan Province. Hong's confident speech to his followers asserting that the True and Genuine Chŏng was coming to save the people from their troubles was also quite effective in mobilizing popular support during the rebellion.

Contrary to negative descriptions of Hong's appearance and characteristics contained in government reports, Hong seems to have been a well-qualified leader of the rebellion. His determination was strong when he moved fourteen family members, including his mother, wife, sons, brothers, and nephews, from their home district of Yonggang to Tabok village in Kasan, the rebel base, a few months before the rebellion.[9] In his farewell address to the villagers, he swore that his will would be achieved.[10] According to the testimony of his family members, he told them that there would be an armed rebellion soon, although he may not have revealed that he would be the one who would lead it.[11] He also showed that he was a benevolent leader who upheld Confucian moral teachings when he ordered a proper funeral service for Paek Kyŏnghan of Chŏngju, a victim of the rebels. Paek had resisted joining the early stage of the rebellion and was regarded as "righteous" for maintaining his loyalty to the existing dynasty.[12] And because Hong regretted the death of Han Houn, a well-known filial son who died at the hands of the rebels, he let Han's son take Han's body for a funeral service.[13]

Though Hong earned popular support by displaying benevolent leadership, it was his extraordinary physical power, mastery of the martial arts, and effective military strategy that made him a great rebel leader. Hong directed the preparations for the rebellion with the aid of collaborators, and he personally commanded the rebellion as the supreme commander (Taewŏnsu) until the walled town of Chŏngju, where the rebels were besieged by government troops, fell four months after the rebellion began. Hong was shot to death when the government troops took over Chŏngju. He was posthumously punished as a traitor and rebel commander (*kŏbyŏng yŏkkoe yul*).

U Kunch'ik

U Kunch'ik was a nothous.[14] Another source indicates that he was a cousin of U Owŏlgŭm, a post-station slave of Kasan.[15] His mother apparently had sexual relations with more than one partner because U had a brother by a different father.[16] He was also called U Yongmun and was thirty-seven years old at the time of his arrest in 1812.[17] His wife seems to have come from a military family because Chŏng Mongnyang, a patrol officer of a mountain pass who arrested U as he tried to escape from a government search in May 1812, was related to U's wife.[18] U also kept a mistress from a Paek family, whose father served the rebel force as a military provisions supervisor (Kullyang kamgwan).[19] U's stepbrother and two younger brothers also joined the rebellion.[20]

Like Hong Kyŏngnae, U was a professional geomancer.[21] The two men first met in 1800, at the Blue Dragon Temple (Ch'ŏngnyongsa) in Kasan, where they were studying geomancy texts. At their second encounter in 1801, they had already discussed the possibility of an armed rebellion led by a "true and genuine man" who would save the people from great distress by responding to supernatural omens that foretold a violent social change.[22] U's geomantic practice became an effective medium for recruiting sympathizers such as Yi Hŭijŏ, a rebel financier, and U played a critical role in providing ideological support for the rebellion. When the rebels launched their first attack against Kasan, U claimed to be a holy master (*sinsa*), wore a cranelike robe, held a white-feathered fan, and proclaimed that Heaven was helping the rebels because he had observed heavenly signs that confirmed this.[23]

U had been involved in various financial ventures. He had once been arrested by the Police Bureau on the charge of illegal trading in red ginseng. He was rumored to be a director of a new gold mine in Unsan, with material support from a financier in Seoul.[24] He had loaned money to Kang Tŭkhwang, a relative by marriage, who used the money for a private usury operation.[25] It is possible that U and his financier, Yi Hŭijŏ, had operated illegal mines and carried out other commercial activities to raise funds for the rebellion, though there is no clear indication that they were planning to open new mines or that their frustration over the mining operation caused the rebellion, as some have argued.[26]

U had also mastered the martial arts and had many facial scars as a result, and he personally commanded the rebel forces in several battles.[27] Although he denied his voluntary participation in the rebellion in his deposition, after he was caught in early June 1812, claiming that he had been forced to join when Hong Kyŏngnae threatened him in 1810 and when Kim Ch'angsi, another core leader, did the same in early 1811, there is no doubt that U was one of the most active masterminds of the rebellion.

Yi Hŭijŏ

Yi Hŭijŏ was a post-station slave who had been able to pass the military service examination.[28] He had even purchased membership in the local yangban association and remained in it until the magistrate of Kasan, Chŏng Si (the only magistrate killed by the rebels), canceled his membership. He may have been greatly frustrated that this attempt to enhance his political and social standing had been ruined.[29] His wealth provided the main material resources for the rebellion. Not only did he support the families of U Kunch'ik and Hong Kyŏngnae, he also housed most of the rebel vanguard forces during the preparatory period. It is not known how he accumulated his wealth, though he may have done so through mining and other commercial ventures.[30]

Yi had known U Kunch'ik for years, but it was only after U selected an auspicious burial site for Yi's deceased father and predicted that Yi would achieve great wealth and prestige that U really gained Yi's confidence.[31] In 1809, Yi moved to Tabok village, which was known for its strategic location between Kasan and Pakch'ŏn along the Taejŏng River, and built tile-roofed houses there. Many people who were educated, talented, and experts in various technical and martial arts in P'yŏngan Province flocked to Tabok village, which became the main rebel hideout.[32] Yi's family connections with military officers (*kyo*), local clerks, and wealthy merchants (*puho taego*) in the region were instrumental in recruiting followers and organizing rebel forces. For example, Yi Ch'im, a wealthy staff military officer (Chipsa) of Chŏngju who actively supported the rebellion as a military provisions supervisor, was a cousin by Yi's father's sister. Yi Ŭngjŏ, another of his cousins, was also an active participant in the rebellion. Yi was an in-law of the Anju merchant, Yi Yangsin, and a creditor of Na Taegon, who provided financial support to the rebellion and played a role as an undercover agent in Yŏngbyŏn.[33]

Yi does not seem to have commanded rebel troops. After the rebel force was defeated at Pine Grove in Pakch'ŏn, ten days after the rebellion broke out, his residence in Tabok village was burned to the ground. Yi escaped to the walled town of Chŏngju with his family and stayed there, with Hong Kyŏngnae and other rebels, until the last day of the rebellion. He was arrested and decapitated by a local militia force after the town fell to the government and was posthumously punished for high treason (*moban taeyŏk yul*).

Kim Ch'angsi

Kim Ch'angsi was a local yangban who passed the triennial lower civil service examination in 1810.[34] According to a government report, Kim was a frivolous man who joined the rebellion because he had no way to meet his heavy debts.[35] However, he did have two female slaves, who officially belonged to his father, and a manservant, Kyedong, who accompanied him.[36] It is unclear how Kim was connected to Hong Kyŏngnae or the other rebel leaders. U Kunch'ik testified that Kim visited U around April 1811 and coerced him into joining the rebellion. U's testimony that he had been forced to join the rebellion is unreliable, but it at least suggests that U, Kim, and Hong Kyŏngnae knew one another by this time and that the plan for rebellion was underway.[37]

It is understandable that Kim's family members joined the rebel plot, but Kim seems to have been on good terms with local yangban throughout P'yŏngan Province, which greatly facilitated his recruitment of supporters for the rebellion.[38] He did so by appealing to the *Chŏnggamnok*. Kim Taehun, Ko Yunbin, Pak Sŏngsin, Kim Chiuk, and Yang Chaehak were all Kim's local yangban friends in the area who played important roles as administrators and military officers in the rebel administration. Kim was quite cautious in recruiting rebel agents and approached only those local yangban who could wield substantial power over local affairs. For example, after detecting who held real power in Sŏnch'ŏn, Kim contacted and earned the support of Yu Munje and Ch'oe Ponggwan, high-level military officers.[39]

Kim acted as a strategist (*mosa*) during the rebellion. He spread a rumor, in the form of a folk song, that an armed rebellion would break out in 1812.[40] As is well known, he also composed the rebel manifesto that was sent to the local officials. After the defeat at Pine Grove, he joined the rebel troops encamped north of Chŏngju while Hong Kyŏngnae and other rebels defended Chŏngju. When the rebels were placed at a disadvantage in a battle in Kwaksan on February 21, 1812, Kim headed for the border region to mobilize support from Ho Yunjo, an outpost officer (Kwŏn'gwan, Jr. 9) in the Pyŏktong area, but was killed by his own follower.[41]

Kim Sayong

Kim Sayong was a very poor local yangban whose father had been the director of the yangban bureau.[42] One of his remote relatives, Kim Ch'ijŏng (1749–?), who had held the office of section chief (Chŏngnang, Sr. 5) in the Chosŏn court, was a candidate for the post of magistrate of T'aech'ŏn in the rebel administration, although the government found Kim Ch'ijŏng innocent of involvement in the rebellion.[43] Kim Sŏkt'ae of Kasan (*munkwa* in 1790) was the father-in-law of Kim Ch'ijŏng's daughter, and Kim Sŏkt'ae's uncle, Kim Iksu, was the rebel-appointed chief commander of Kasan. Kim Kukpŏm's nephew was to become engaged to Kim Sayong's niece.[44] Kim Kukpŏm was a brother of *munkwa* passer Kim Ch'angje and was a matrilateral cousin of Chang Ponggŏm of Kusŏng, who was beheaded for supporting the rebels.[45] All these intricate marriage networks surrounding Kim Sayong were mobilized in recruiting collaborators, although the choice of supporting the rebellion was obviously made individually.

About a month before the rebellion, Kim Sayong, a master of martial and occult arts, won the support of Kim Uhak, the director of the yangban bureau in Yŏngbyŏn, and soon moved his family to Kim Uhak's residence. His activity as assistant supreme commander (Puwŏnsu) of the rebels was illustrious. Most of the administrative towns occupied by the rebels were placed under his control. After rebel troops dispersed when the government army approached their camps in mid- to late February 1812, Kim fled to Chŏngju, where Hong Kyŏngnae and other rebels were besieged by government troops. He died from battle wounds incurred about a month before the rebellion was finally put down and was posthumously sentenced to the crime of high treason.[46]

BUILDING THE REBEL NETWORK: OUTSIDE THE REBEL-OCCUPIED REGION

The main conspirators tried to gather like-minded people from a broad geographical area. Some rebels mentioned coconspirators in Hamgyŏng and Ch'ungch'ŏng provinces, and even from Japan or Tsushima Island in the south, who would soon rise up in concert to support them.⁴⁷ Although none of these vaguely designated groups turned out to exist, some other supporters outside the Ch'ŏngbuk region can be identified.

During his travels around northern Korea, Hong Kyŏngnae himself made contact with a number of local elites, military men, and ordinary people who could support the rebellion. Hong traveled as far north as Hongwŏn, Hamgyŏng Province, and stayed in the residence of Subarea Commander (Manho) Kim, although it is not known whether Kim sympathized with the rebel cause.⁴⁸ The vagabond Kim Kyŏngdam from Ŭiju met Yi Yŏngch'un and Hong Yŏsuk from Kasan at Bright Moon Temple in Hŭich'ŏn in late July and early August 1811—so it seems that Yi Hŭijŏ and Hong Kyŏngnae were traveling around with aliases such as Yi Yŏngch'un and Hong Yŏsuk. Yi told Kim about the plan for the armed rebellion and promised him wealth and honor if he spied on conditions in the border towns for the rebels. Kim was paid 5 *yang* for this role in advance. Though Kim failed to accomplish his mission, this story shows how the rebel leaders tried to recruit sympathizers to gather information before the rebellion broke out.⁴⁹

In addition, there was rebel testimony that Kang Sŏngmo of Ch'angsŏng and Kim T'aengnyŏn of Kanggye, border towns along the Amnok River, had exchanged letters with rebel leaders, and that Kim Sŏngmo of Ch'osan, a Mr. Kim of Wiwŏn, and Yi P'aengnyŏn of Sakchu were all conspirators.⁵⁰ There is no specific government report about these cases to prove these men's active involvement in the rebellion, though Yi P'aengnyŏn was suspected of being an undercover agent in the border area and of recruiting rebel soldiers there. Yi's personal background is rather interesting. His father had passed the military examination and established a rich household. Yi himself did not achieve much success and used up all the family resources soon after his father died. He managed to live by selling cotton cloth and housewares. He also did some temporary work during the famine. He was so poor that he could not support his family and had to send his son off to a clerk's house in Sakchu as a domestic servant (*sahwan*). When interrogated by government authorities, he strongly denied participating in the plot and said that he had neither any power base in the area nor any funds to support the rebellion. The government investigator did not believe him, but there is no report of the government's final decision on him.⁵¹ Yi certainly could not have provided material support for the rebellion, but he might have had some influence in the area that enabled him to gather rebel sympathizers. Although Yi himself was not able to preserve the high reputation of his family or its status and wealth, his family had lived in the area for many generations and his father must have built a reputation as a military officer. In fact, Yi can be compared to the poor yangban Kim Sayong, whose father had been the director of the yangban bureau.

Hong Kyŏngnae also recruited rebels from Hwanghae Province, including a military officer, Mr. Yun from Hwangju, and more than ten others from Chunghwa, who composed a vanguard force (*changsa*), a group of people who demonstrated their physical strength and military leadership during the rebellion.[52] It is difficult to identify the social status of this group, though a few of its members held yangban titles or were engaged in military occupations. It is probably safe to assume that they were marginalized local elite, particularly those who belonged to the military branch, considering that they often took command positions as cavalrymen (*sŏn'gi*) and military officers (*kun'gwan*). Nonetheless, we cannot exclude the participation of poor, landless commoner peasants who had outstanding military skills.[53]

U Kunch'ik also traveled south to recruit rebel sympathizers. He persuaded Yu Chongnyŏl and Chang Chihan from Hwangju, Hwanghae Province, to join the rebels. U probably persuaded Kim Igon and several others from Chaeryŏng, Hwanghae Province, to become members of the rebel rank and file.[54] One rebel testified that it was U Kunch'ik who won over military officers and local yangban from various areas to the rebel side.[55]

There is indirect evidence that Kim Ch'angsi might have tried to gather sympathizers outside P'yŏngan Province. Several months before the rebellion broke out, Kim visited his maternal relatives from the Ch'angnyŏng Sŏng branch in Ŏnyang, Kyŏngsang Province. Sŏng Ch'anghun shared Kim's concerns over the corruption of officials, maladministration, and the difficulties people were suffering. It is not known whether or not the Sŏng family made a commitment to join the rebellion, though it later faced terrible government retaliation because of its relationship with Kim.[56]

Kim also had known Ho Yunjo from Ch'angsŏng, a descendant of a Ming loyalist, who had been appointed to a number of military positions in the border area. They had been acquainted with one another for a long time; when Ho met Kim a few months before the rebellion, he congratulated Kim on his success in the lower civil service examination a year before. At the time of this meeting, Ho was in trouble because he had misappropriated grain reserves under his administration. It is possible that Ho promised to collaborate with Kim and that Kim had Ho in mind when he indicated in the rebel manifesto that the rebels had support from the descendants of the hereditary subjects of the imperial Ming dynasty. Ho himself strongly denied any connection with the rebels and claimed that there were only few troops under his control in the area in any case.[57]

There were also rebel contacts in Seoul. Han Kijo, a yangban living in Seoul, was decapitated for writing a sympathetic letter to the rebels in which he called the rebel leader the Sun and Moon, the Sage Ruler, and the Supreme Ruler—terms reserved for the king.[58] Yu Hansun from Yŏngyu was a rebel spy who attempted to incite the residents of Seoul by posting subversive letters on the wall of the south gate and on the gate at the Office of the Robust and Brave Guards (Changyong'yŏng). He also kept the rebels informed of the situation in Seoul. He was persuaded by Kim Sayong to join the rebellion, and he traveled back and forth between Seoul and the rebel base in Pakch'ŏn to report on his espionage under Kim's supervision.[59]

The central government was very apprehensive of rebel sympathizers working in areas other than the Ch'ŏngbuk region, and in Seoul in particular. A plot led by Yi Chinch'ae and his associates to enthrone a remote royal relative was discovered at the end of March 1812. Yi claimed to have extraordinary power, and he gathered supporters, including current and previous officials at the court. Borrowing some language from the *Chŏnggamnok*, the conspirators predicted the emergence of three political entities—presumably the Yi royal house, one led by the rebels in P'yŏngan Province, and their own.[60] Expecting prolonged turmoil, the conspirators also prognosticated that certain places would escape disaster, as discussed in the *Chŏnggamnok*.[61] The court's investigation naturally focused on the connection between these conspirators and the rebels in the north, but failed to find any conclusive evidence of a close working relationship between the two groups.[62]

In sum, the leaders of the rebellion did not earn critical support from outside the Ch'ŏngbuk region, except from a handful of martially capable men from Hwanghae Province and a couple of agents from Seoul. Those rebel sympathizers who promised to assist the rebels' occupations of their districts from within (as happened in the rebel-occupied districts) simply changed their allegiance when the rebels never reached their areas. It seems that they ignored rebels' pleas for assistance, denied connections to the rebels when interrogated, and eventually sided with the counterrebel campaign.

RECRUITING FIFTH COLUMNISTS:
THE CH'ŎNGBUK REGION

As the government subsequently acknowledged, the support of fifth columnists (*naeŭng*) was critical to the rebels' successful occupation of the region north of the Ch'ŏngch'ŏn River after launching their first attack on Kasan.[63] The rebel leaders used their family relations and their circles of friends to establish a network of fifth columnists far ahead of the rebellion. As Charles Tilly argues, individual grievances alone would not have materialized into collective action; rather, some level of organization and mobilization was required.[64] Preexisting institutional structures and collectivities, such as those of marriage, kinship, and village, tended to provide sources of such mobilization.[65] In their search for fifth columnists, the rebel leaders made sure to find local power holders who could influence others to support the rebels.[66] They were successful in bringing over to their side previous and incumbent officers at the local yangban bureau and in the military administration bureau in charge of local affairs. The rebel leaders were able to win their support by arguing that natural disasters and unusual cosmic changes signified that the existing dynasty had lost the Mandate of Heaven and that an armed rebellion and subsequent dynastic change, led by the True and Genuine Chŏng, were impending, as foretold in the *Chŏnggamnok*.

Those who had received offices from the court probably enjoyed the most respect in the region, because holding court-appointed office added prestige to one's descent group as well as to oneself. The rebels were not so successful in persuading those who had passed the *munkwa* or who had served the court in the central government offices to join the rebellion, although they did recruit a handful of men who had held certain centrally appointed positions, such as Chŏng Kyŏnghaeng and Chŏng Sŏnghan, two members of the Hadong Chŏng of Ch'ŏlsan; Pak Sŏngsin from Kwaksan; and some others who held mid- to low-level military positions in the border area.[67]

Pak Sŏngsin had once been army second deputy commander (Ch'ŏmsa), reportedly the highest military post that a northerner could earn, and was chief military officer (Chunggun) at the time of the rebellion. Other yangban of the area called him "master" (*chuin*) and paid frequent visits to his house. Because Pak's household brewed and sold wine, many people dropped in there. According to the testimony of Pak's cousin, Kim Ch'angsi and other rebel supporters met frequently at Pak's house and talked about the impending armed rebellion that would supposedly be led by Chŏng Chemin and a hundred thousand Manchu followers. Pak supplied 500 *yang* and 15 *sŏm* of rice to the rebels and assumed the position of magistrate of Kwaksan when the rebellion broke out.[68]

Chŏng Kyŏnghaeng, who had served as a magistrate sometime before the rebellion, was the head of an affluent yangban household that possessed six slaves. He had at least two sons from his wife and two from his concubine. One of his sons was an outpost officer in Kabam at the time of the rebellion. The central government even appointed Chŏng Kyŏnghaeng magistrate of

Kwaksan a few days after the rebellion broke out, not knowing that Chŏng held the top commanding position of commander in chief (Ch'ŏngbuk toji-hwisa) in the rebel organization. The central government was shocked that a yangban who had once been a government official could defy the dynasty and view the government as an enemy.[69]

Chŏng Sŏnghan had also served the government as a chief commander (Yŏngjang) and became one of the court's candidates for Kwaksan magistrate, along with Chŏng Kyŏnghaeng, when the rebellion broke out.[70] As a rebel-appointed magistrate of Yongch'ŏn, he supplied the rebels with food by collecting grain from the wealthy households of the area and also took over the government seal from the military garrison at Sin Island—both heinous crimes against the state.[71]

Chŏng Pogil, a remote relative of Chŏng Kyŏnghaeng and Chŏng Sŏnghan, had been a top military officer of Ch'ŏlsan for years. He was accused not only of leading other members of his descent group into the conspiracy but also of organizing fifth columnists in the region.[72] He conspired with Kim Ch'angsi months before the rebellion, acted as magistrate of Ch'ŏlsan during the rebellion, recruited a rebel army from the villages, and provided food and weapons for the rebels.

It was probably through Hong Kyŏngnae that three men from the renowned yangban descent group, the Hadong Chŏng of Ch'ŏlsan, decided to support the rebellion.[73] As discussed in previous chapters, even though the Hadong Chŏng of Ch'ŏlsan had established itself as a great local yangban descent group, three of its members—Chŏng Kyŏnghaeng, Chŏng Pogil, and Chŏng Sŏnghan—temporarily put the fortunes of the whole lineage in jeopardy when they decided to provide leadership and material support to the rebellion.

Because of the deep involvement of these three Chŏngs from Ch'ŏlsan, the whole lineage suffered greatly. Family members and close relatives of the three men were arrested, tortured, decapitated, banished, or enslaved, and the villages where they lived were burned and ransacked. Some Ch'ŏlsan Hadong Chŏng, who had sailed down to Hwanghae Province to escape punishment, were suspected of being rebel sympathizers simply because they were members of this descent group.[74] Chŏng Tal, who was caught in one of mountain passes in the northern border area, was also suspected of being a member of the Ch'ŏlsan Hadong Chŏng, a "treacherous" descent group that produced rebel leaders.[75]

The most critical support came from officers at the local yangban bureau and the military administration bureau, who practically ran the local administration and who held power and authority in the countryside. Most of the Chwasu (directors of the yangban bureau) and Chunggun (chief military officers)—the highest offices in the local bureaus in the seven districts (Kasan, Pakch'ŏn, Ch'ŏlsan, Sŏnch'ŏn, Chŏngju, Kwaksan, and T'aech'ŏn) that the rebels occupied in the first ten days of the rebellion—committed themselves to the rebel cause. Thus they had already put each district under their control even before rebel troops arrived and pressured each district magistrate to surrender to the rebels. As table 8 reveals, they subsequently assumed the office of magistrate or chief commander of each district.

Two powerful yangban officers in Chŏngju participated in the plot and played an important role in taking over this important district. Seven to eight years before the rebellion, Hong Kyŏngnae had established a friendship with Ch'oe Iryun, a top military officer in Chŏngju, when Hong stayed at Ch'oe's house for months to use his private library.[76] Under interrogation, Ch'oe later insisted that he only found out there was a plan for the rebellion a month before it occurred, when Hong invited him to Tabok village and informed him of it. Another source proved, however, that Ch'oe and his sons had joined the plot by late October or early November 1811.[77] Ch'oe supplied wine and meat to the rebels ten days before the rebellion and greeted Kim Sayong and his army when they came to take over Chŏngju, waiting for them a couple of miles outside the town seat. As a magistrate of Chŏngju and then as a staff officer (Ch'ammo), Ch'oe recruited rebel troops and provided military supplies.[78]

Kim Idae was the director of the yangban bureau in Chŏngju at the time of the rebellion. He held a lower civil service examination degree (*chinsa*), as did Kim Ch'angsi.[79] Kim Idae also joined the rebel meetings in late October or early November 1811 and assumed the position of magistrate of Chŏngju, succeeding Ch'oe Iryun. In taking over the position, Kim had to force Ch'oe to give up the official seals, an episode that reveals a power struggle between Kim, a local yangban who supervised civil matters, and Ch'oe, another local yangban of a military branch. This indicates that political aspiration was one of the main motivations of those local yangban who joined the rebellion.[80]

Yi Chŏnghwan, a chief military officer, and his son Yi Ch'im, a military officer, were also rebel supporters in Chŏngju. Yi Ch'im was a rich man who became a supervisor of rebel military provisions and who housed the families of rebel leaders. Yi Ch'im and his father served the rebels as assistant field commanders.[81] Chŏng Chinhang, a chief military officer, was one of those who gathered at Tabok village to make preparations for the rebellion in late

October and early November 1811, and he helped the rebels occupy Chŏngju.[82] Yi Sanghang, a military degree-holder, and Paek Chonghoe, a chief military officer, joined the rebels during the preparatory stage and served the rebel army as military provision supervisors and commanders.[83]

Ch'oe Ponggwan from Sŏnch'ŏn, a previous chief military officer of the district, was persuaded to join the rebels by Kim Ch'angsi, who thought that Ch'oe wielded great authority over the area. Ch'oe prepared weapons for the rebels and appropriated government grain for rebel provisions. With a silver seal he received from the rebel leader, he acted as an assistant field commander. In written exchanges with Chŏng Pogil and Kim Ingnyŏng, fifth columnists from Ch'ŏlsan, he referred to the government troops as "the enemy." He indicated his hatred of regional discrimination on the part of the central government by calling the rebel base "the northern military camp" and referring to people from the capital as "the southerners."[84]

Yu Munje was another ringleader in Sŏnch'ŏn. As a wealthy chief military officer of the Defense Command (Pang'yŏng Chunggun), he provided weapons and food for the rebels, who appointed him the chief commander of Sŏnch'ŏn.[85] Wŏn Taech'ŏn from Sŏnch'ŏn, a military examination degree-holder, was another conspirator who played an active role in handing Sŏnch'ŏn over to the rebel army.[86]

Kim Iksu was the director of the yangban bureau in Kasan and an uncle of Kim Sŏkt'ae, previous section chief (Chŏngnang, Sr. 5). He prepared food and other things for the rebels under the command of Hong Kyŏngnae and assumed the position of chief commander during the rebellion.[87] The chief military officer of the district, Kang Yunhyŏk, supplied the rebel army with food and wine before they attacked Kasan.[88] In Pakch'ŏn also, the director of the yangban bureau, Kim Sŏnggak, and a top military officer, Han Ilhang, assumed the positions of magistrate and chief commander, respectively, and supplied the rebels with food and weapons.[89]

In T'aech'ŏn, those local yangban who wielded substantial power in the district administration joined the rebels. The rebels appointed Pyŏn Taeik, a granary supervisor, as magistrate of the district. He was the son-in-law of Kim Uhak, director of the yangban bureau in Yŏngbyŏn. His three cousins all joined the rebellion through their relative Han Sinhang from Pakch'ŏn, a man who was very close to Yi Hŭijŏ, and acted as assistant field commanders.[90] Pak Yunsik, a military officer, functioned as a chief military officer under the leadership of Pyŏn Taeik.[91] Kim Yunhae, director of the yangban bureau, was one of those who visited the rebel base at Tabok village and greeted the rebels coming to the district.[92]

It has already been mentioned that Kim Sayong made contact with Kim Uhak, director of a yangban bureau, who showed boundless hospitality to the rebels, probably because they had promised him the position of chief state councilor if they succeeded in establishing a new dynasty. Nam Ikhyŏn, chief military officer, and Yi Iksu, another local yangban, were to be the director of the military training agency (Hunjang) and the minister of the Ministry of Personnel (Yip'an), respectively. They and Pyŏn Taeik of T'aech'ŏn, son-in-law of Kim Uhak, supplied cotton cloth, money, and food to the rebels.

The following case illustrates how an interest group in rural society could provide a foundation for rebel networking. In late October and early November 1811, about twenty current and former military officers in Anju, on the southern bank of the Ch'ŏngch'ŏn River—the location of one of the government's military headquarters in P'yŏngan Province—organized a *kye* (mutual assistance association) under the pretext of funding funeral services for their households.[93] Some members were local yangban who had been directors of yangban bureaus; others were chief military officers, some of whom had passed the military examinations. Most of them later underwent extensive government interrogation because two members, Yi Inbae and Kim Taerin, joined the rebellion, and relatives and in-laws of some of them were also involved in the uprising. They all might have joined the rebels and held positions such as district magistrate if the rebels had been successful in taking over Anju as planned. But fate went against their wishes. They quickly burned the documents containing the rules of the *kye* before their arrest, and all denied their involvement in the plot when apprehended and interrogated by the government.[94]

In sum, the sympathizers who played a vital role in the rebels' initial success represented the local elite of the Ch'ŏngbuk region. In terms of the social status hierarchy, the top-ranking rebels were Kim Ch'angsi and Kim Idae, who held *chinsa* degrees; Pak Sŏngsin, who had held a junior third-rank military position; and previous magistrates Chŏng Kyŏnghaeng and Chŏng Sŏnghan. They were followed by local yangban officials who manned the local yangban bureau and military bureau. The social status of military degree-holders was probably lower than that of civil service degree-holders but was certainly close to the top elite stratum.[95] Adding complexity to the social composition of fifth columnists were the remote and close relatives of *munkwa* passers. Despite delicate differentiation of social and political standing, these local elite were interconnected by kinship, marriage, and other associations.

TABLE 8. Selected List of Fifth Columnists (*Naeŭng*) in the 1812 Hong Kyŏngnae
Rebellion

Name (Residence)	Occupation or social status	Position in the rebel organization
Chŏng Kyŏnghaeng (Ch'ŏlsan)	Previous magistrate	Commander in chief of the Ch'ŏngbuk region (Ch'ŏngbuk tojihwisa)
Chŏng Pogil (Ch'ŏlsan)	Chief military officer (Chunggun)	Magistrate of Ch'ŏlsan
Chŏng Sŏnghan (Ch'ŏlsan)	Previous chief commander (Yŏngjang)	Magistrate of Yongch'ŏn
Ch'oe Iryu (Chŏngju)	Military officer (*kyo*)	Magistrate of Chŏngju
Kim Idae (Chŏngju)	Director of yangban bureau (Chwasu) and *chinsa*	Magistrate of Chŏngju
Pak Sŏngsin (Kwaksan)	Previous army second deputy commander (Ch'ŏmsa)	Magistrate of Kwaksan
Pyŏn Taeik (T'aech'ŏn)	Granary supervisor (Ch'anggam)	Magistrate of T'aech'ŏn
Ch'oe Ponggwan (Sŏnch'ŏn)	Chief military officer	Magistrate of Sŏnch'ŏn
Yu Munje (Sŏnch'ŏn)	Chief military officer	Chief commander (Yujinjang) of Sŏnch'ŏn
Kim Iksu (Kasan)	Director of yangban bureau	Chief commander of Kasan
Yun Ŏnsŏp (Kasan)	Yangban	Magistrate of Kasan
Han Ilhaeng (Pakch'ŏn)	Military officer	Chief commander of Pakch'ŏn
Kim Sŏnggak (Pakch'ŏn)	Director of yangban bureau	Magistrate of Pakch'ŏn
Ch'oe Pongil (Sŏnch'ŏn)	Military officer	Commander of Sŏnsa Garrison (Ch'ŏmsa)
Ko Chunggi (Sŏnch'ŏn)	Military officer	Commander of Tongnim Garrison (Pyŏlchang)
Kim Ingmyŏng (Ch'ŏlsan)	Yangban	Commander of Sŏrim Garrison (Ch'ŏmsa)
Chang Hanu (Ch'ŏlsan)	Officer of yangban bureau (*hyangim*)	Commander of Sin Island Garrison (Ch'ŏmsa)

More critically, all active supporters, especially the local yangban in P'yŏngan Province, shared sharp frustration over regional discrimination and were largely moved to join the rebellion because they hoped to obtain high office in the central bureaucracy of the new dynasty. The local yangban in P'yŏngan Province were alienated from national politics, their privileged status in the local community was under constant threat because they had to compete for office with others who might be wealthier and more prominent than they were, and they were subject to increasing institutional intervention by the state. When they saw that the rebels were offering them a promising future, they were willing to risk their precarious positions within the existing social order. In fact, the fifth columnists who played a key role in occupying each administrative town were immediately rewarded with positions (see table 8), and some of them were promised prestigious offices in the central government as soon as the rebels succeeded in taking over the Chosŏn dynasty.

PREPARATIONS FOR THE REBELLION

The material preparations for the rebellion apparently began about a year in advance. When Hong Kyŏngnae and U Kunch'ik again met at the Blue Dragon Temple, in December 1810, Hong came with a man named Chŏng Chemin (or Sisu), who was supposedly the True and Genuine Chŏng who would rescue the people from this distressed world. At this meeting, Hong revealed to U that he had been planning a rebellion and had recruited tens of thousands of Chinese soldiers (*tanggun*) stationed on Sin Island, off the Yongch'ŏn district coast. Since a garrison had been established by the central government on Sin Island in 1807, he had moved the army to the area north of Kanggye, where four districts (*p'ye sa-gun*) had once been located but where government control no longer reached because the districts had been abolished in the early Chosŏn. Hong mentioned that the True and Genuine Chŏng also was in command of some Manchu soldiers (*hogun*) and was seeking supporters from P'yŏngan Province before undertaking an armed rebellion.[96] In the rebel manifesto, these same supporters were described as the descendants of the hereditary subjects of the imperial Ming dynasty.[97]

The rebels used a few different terms for the reserve army stationed in the area of the four abolished districts. The most frequently used term was *hogun*, which commonly meant Manchu soldiers when talking about a large contingent of supporting troops the rebels sought before and during the rebellion. The reason the rebels used a different term in the rebel manifesto, implying that their effort to overthrow the Chosŏn dynasty was supported by the Ming, was probably due to the manifesto being written in literary Chinese by an intellectual, Kim Ch'angsi, to invoke support from educated elite of the Chosŏn dynasty who still rejected the legitimacy of the Qing dynasty established by the Manchus.[98]

Despite such delicate appropriation of symbols to validate their actions, the rebels did not generally mind advertising that their cause was supported by the Manchus, probably because historically a number of rebellious plots had sought military backing from northern neighbors.[99] Nonetheless, there was almost no possibility that such a large reserve force actually existed along the border. Chŏng Sŏkchong, who has written several articles on the rebellion, speculates that there were such reinforcements. Relying on earlier sources from King Yŏngjo's reign, he points out that criminal runaways who caused disturbances along the border area must have committed themselves to the cause of the rebellion.[100] Before Kim Ch'angsi was murdered by his subordinate, he claimed that he was also on his way to get reinforcements in the border area after the defeat at Four Pine Field in late February. Kim was carrying a silver seal, a symbol of military mobilization, which was supposed to match the one possessed by the *hogun* leader.[101] The action of the rebel camp in dispatching messengers to the border region in early March 1812, to contact the reinforcements, seems to add further evidence to the existence of outside help.[102] Oda Shōgo argues that it is logical to believe that the rebels besieged inside the walled town expected some kind of outside help, since they stubbornly resisted the government campaign for more than three months.[103]

All these arguments, however, draw on only circumstantial evidence, and it is hardly convincing that there was a large contingent of reserve army. A more plausible explanation is that there were some people in the northern border area who knew Hong Kyŏngnae or other rebel leaders, who were aware of the impending rebellion, and who may have pledged their support. Had the rebellion succeeded, these sympathizers could have become ardent supporters of it. Ho Yunjo, an outpost officer in Pyŏktong; Song Chiryŏm, a yangban of Kanggye;[104] and Yi P'aengnyŏn, a man from a military family, were examples of such sympathizers. Even so, the number of soldiers that rebels could muster would have been limited to some local residents, and the propaganda that rebels were backed by five thousand *hogun* must have been exaggerated.

While the leaders contacted rebel sympathizers to build a support network, they also recruited and trained a vanguard unit. They set up a training ground, tested the physical strength of their recruits by having them dig trenches, and gave out rewards to those men who were the strongest and most courageous. After they finished training the men in the unit, they sent them out to recruit others.[105]

Preparations became more intense as the date for the rebellion drew near. The leaders and fifth columnists got together more regularly in Tabok village, evidently to discuss concrete plans.[106] Supporters from each district also had frequent meetings on their own to prepare for the rebellion. The rebel network in Kwaksan was firmly organized by Kim Ch'angsi, who came from this district, knew many local yangban of the area, and won them over to the rebel cause. According to the testimony of the wife of Kim Chiuk, who supervised rebel provisions, Kim Ch'angsi, Yang Chaehak, Ko Yunbin, and Kim Myŏngyu had known each other very well and met together at Kim Chiuk's house quite often before the rebellion.[107] Yang Chaehak frequently visited the Tabok village rebel base to help plan the rebellion.[108] Ko Yunbin, who became a rebel staff military officer, expropriated 1,000 *yang* of government money and handed it over to Kim Ch'angsi to fund preparations for the rebellion.[109] Kim Myŏngyu was an artisan whose specialty was to make wool and leather clothes. He supposedly made leather outfits for the rebel leaders at the request of Pak Sŏngsin, Ko Yunbin, and Kim Taehun. Sometime before the rebellion, Kim let the mother of Hong Ch'onggak, a chief field commander (Sŏnbongjang), stay at his home.[110]

Ko Yunbin's house was another place the conspirators met. Kim Taehun, from the same district, who ran a medicinal herb shop, came to know Kim Ch'angsi through their business dealings. At their meetings at Ko's house in late October and early November 1811, Kim Ch'angsi disclosed the plan for the armed rebellion headed by the True and Genuine Chŏng. During this conversation, Kim Ch'angsi bragged that the wisdom of U Kunch'ik was better than that of Zhuge Liang and that the talent of Hong Kyŏngnae surpassed that of Zhao Zilong—the two famous heroes from the Chinese historical novel, *Romance of the Three Kingdoms (San guo zhi yan yi)*, written by Luo Guanzhong in the fourteenth century. Since they were close friends, Kim Ch'angsi promised to protect Kim Taehun from the armed rebellion, which he expected to last seven years. Kim Taehun ended up taking care of various rebel business during the early stage of the rebellion, such as issuing appointment documents, supplying rebel uniforms, taking care of rebel finances, and dealing with merchants.[111]

Material preparations were also well underway. Yi Hŭijŏ smuggled leather, cotton cloth, weapons, and bows, and stored them in Tabok village.[112] Yu Munje and Ch'oe Ponggwan took charge of the supply and transportation of weapons such as swords, spears, and muskets, while Chŏng Chingyo pre-pared bullets and candles. Chŏng Pogil took care of banners, and the mer-chants from Ŭiju provided uniforms and other clothing.[113] Pak Sŏngsin and other supporters from Kwaksan arranged for leather uniforms to be ready, probably for the field commanders and vanguard force. Fifth columnists from Yŏngbyŏn sent 2,000 *yang* and sixteen saddles to the rebel base and stored weapons and grain for the rebels in their own residences.[114]

Besides obtaining support from local yangban and wealthy households, the rebels dug a secret tunnel on Ch'u Island in the middle of the Ch'ŏngch'ŏn River, and minted counterfeit coins there.[115] According to the testimony of Kang Suhŭng, who originally lived on Ch'u Island but moved to Yŏngbyŏn just before the rebellion, he joined the rebels because the authorities had discovered that he was counterfeiting copper cash. Perhaps he was counter-feiting coins on behalf of the rebels, however, and ran away to Yŏngbyŏn when his illegal business was about to be discovered by the government. There he attempted to help others get ready to welcome the rebels.[116]

A month before the rebellion, the rebels began to recruit people to fill the ranks under the pretext that they were hiring miners. It is unclear whether or not the rebels' advertisement that they would open up new gold mines in Unsan and Sakchu with government permission and funded by someone from Seoul was truthful.[117] What is clear is that they used people who responded to fill the ranks of the rebel army. The measures to induce people to "sign up" for the cause were simple but effective. In late January 1812, a rumor spread that gold mines in Unsan or Sakchu would be opened imme-diately and that miners were needed. There were many poor and hungry people hanging around a marketplace close to the ferry station in Pakch'ŏn, looking for food, shelter, or jobs. These were men who had worked as boatmen, tanners, peddlers, hired laborers, porters, and cultivators. The great famine the previous year had driven them from their homes to seek other ways to survive. They were eager to work when they heard the call for miners. The offer of an advance payment of 1 to 10 *yang*, or its equivalent in cotton cloth, and a meal with wine and meat, was quite lucrative. The number of people recruited in this way is unclear; one source notes seventy, the other says a few hundred.[118]

A number of agents engaged in the recruitment drive. Kang Tŭkhwang from Pakch'ŏn, an in-law of U Kunch'ik, was most active. For years Kang had conducted moneylending operations with funds that U provided. Kang's father thought that Kang had become a supervisor of the Unsan gold mine when it was presumably opened and operated by U in late November and early December 1811.[119] O Yongson from Pakch'ŏn, a close relative of Chŏng Kukcho who was appointed a garrison commander, was another rebel agent who, together with Kim Yŏjŏng and Yi Tori of the same district, recruited miners. The core rebel leaders, such as U Kunch'ik and Kim Hyech'ŏl, also played an active role in recruiting miners.[120]

Other rebel members scoured the countryside to lure people into the rebel camp, but the market at the Pakch'ŏn ferry station was the most frequently used recruitment location. Kim Maengch'ŏm of Chŏngju, a houseguest (*sorin*) of a local yangban, Kim Hwajung, brought his neighbors over to the rebels.[121] Included among them were four members of a local yangban Kim family from Chŏngju and two others from nearby villages. Kim Maengch'ŏm approached these poor villagers and paid them 10 *yang* and 1 *yang* of cash, respectively, in advance, to work in a gold mine. Kim Hwajung himself hid swords, spears, and banners in his house and acted as a rebel military officer, while his son Kim Hun made rebel banners and joined the cavalry that attacked Kasan.[122]

People from various status groups, ranging from local yangban to commoners and the low-born, responded to the appeal for miners. Local yangban who were bankrupt or destitute showed no hesitation in joining the ranks of miners, who were traditionally looked down upon for engaging in demeaning menial work. This simply reflects the fact that economic forces had been creating downward mobility among yangban, a process that must have gained momentum in 1811 due to the extremely bleak harvest. Indeed, all the people who were recruited in the Pakch'ŏn ferry station market and from other villages were driven by poverty.[123] Despite their dire economic straits, their participation in the rebellion was not voluntary, and they ran away from the rebel army as soon as they foresaw its defeat. In fact, they had been used only to serve the political interests of the local elite who planned and carried out the rebellion.

6 Rebels and Counterrebels

Just before the rebellion broke out in January 1812, the people in the Ch'ŏngbuk region were greatly agitated over rumors about an impending armed rebellion. It was not unusual for such rumors to fly through the countryside among people who were economically distressed by bad crops. As mentioned earlier, the rebels had deliberately disseminated a folk song about the decline and fall of the royal Yi family and its replacement by the Chŏng family. A more puzzling and provocative folk song also became popular around this time. In written form, it was composed of eighteen Chinese characters that did not make sense by themselves, but that actually connoted four Chinese characters meaning "an armed rebellion in the year of *imsin*." Almost identical verses can be found in the *Chŏnggamnok*.[1]

> A scholar wears his hat askance (*il sa hoeng kwan=im*)
> The ghost takes off his clothes (*kwi sin t'al ŭi=sin*)
> Add one *ch'ŏk* to ten *p'il* (*sip p'il ka il ch'ŏk=ki*)
> A small hill gets two legs (*so ku yu yang chok=pyŏng*)

Studies of popular movements in traditional China have noted that the circulation of rhymes was popularly adopted by rebel conspirators to propagate their ideologies and to mobilize popular support.[2] Cunning combinations of characters and words elicited strong curiosity among both the literate and illiterate about hidden messages in the rhymes. In the case of the 1812 rebellion, it was thought that the messages encoded in the folk rhymes were to be unveiled soon, and rumors of an impending armed rebellion spread from the marketplace to the countryside.[3] According to the testimony of Yi Hyegap, a village head (Chonwi) of Chŏngju, he first heard the rumor in late November 1811, and the villagers, expecting that a great social upheaval would take place, refused to repay their grain loan debts.[4]

THE EARLY STAGE OF THE REBELLION

The uprising was originally set for February 2, 1812. The rebels cast a fake silver military seal and circulated letters to the fifth columnists of each district to let them know the exact date of the rebellion.[5] For instance, Chŏng Pogil of Ch'ŏlsan received a secret letter containing that date from Kim Ch'angsi, personally delivered by Kim's brother.[6] For several days before the uprising, fifth columnists from various districts paid visits to the rebel base to deliver military supplies, grain, and money.[7] As it turned out, however, the rebels had to act before the set date because some of their leaders were arrested by local government officials who noticed the extraordinary activity in Tabok village. On January 31, 1812, the Kasan magistrate had ordered military officers to investigate Yi Hŭijŏ's residence because many suspicious people had visited his house. The magistrate of Sŏnch'ŏn had also arrested several key rebel supporters from Kwaksan, Sŏnch'ŏn, and Ch'ŏlsan, who disclosed the plot under torture. The more frequent meetings, the preparation of weapons and logistics, the mobilization of men to fill the rank and file, and the rumors of an imminent armed rebellion all made secrecy difficult and local officials apprehensive of subversive activities. The fear of further arrests and of aborting the uprising forced the rebels to put their plans into action without delay.[8]

Before the rebels attacked, they performed a formal ceremony to pledge their victory and set up a feast with wine and food for the rebel soldiers. Hong Kyŏngnae, the supreme commander of the rebel army, made a speech about the legitimacy of the rebellion and referred to the True and Genuine Chŏng who had vowed to save the people from their distress. U Kunch'ik, wearing a crane robe and holding a feather fan, observed the heavenly signs and predicted that Heaven was on the rebels' side. One captive later testified that the rebels decapitated two recruits who refused to join the rebel army, in order to prevent other rebel soldiers from breaching military discipline. In addition, the rebel soldiers had to lock arms with each other so that they could not run away.

About fifty rebels wore caps made of the skins of dogs, wildcats, or tigers,

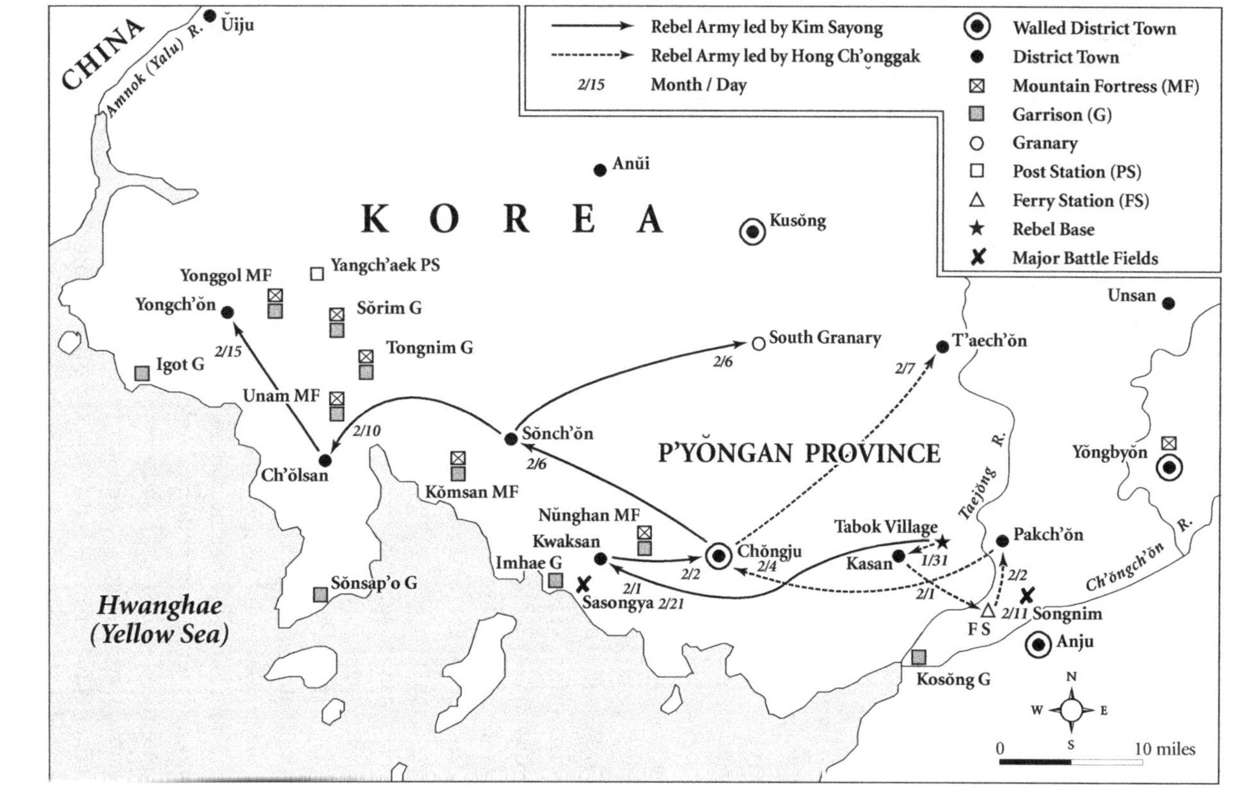

MAP 3. Map of Rebel Activities in the Ch'ŏngbuk Region

decorated with a piece of red cloth on top, and custom-made uniforms with colorful cotton cloth. Some wore leather vests with red ties, and some had green cloth winter caps. Five or six of them were equipped with complete leather armor and helmets. About fifty to sixty rebels were armed with swords and spears, while the rest held wooden clubs.[9] The military attire worn by the rebels was often referred in primary sources as a Manchu-style uniform (*hobok*). Perhaps the rebels intentionally adopted Manchu-style dress to strengthen their claim of support from Manchu soldiers (*hogun*).[10]

The rebel strategy at the outset was to divide their army in two. One unit was led by Kim Sayong, an assistant supreme commander, who set out to rescue those who had been arrested by the Sŏnch'ŏn magistrate and then moved north to the border. Another party, led by Hong Ch'onggak from Kwaksan, a poor peddler famous for his extraordinary physical strength and thus appointed as a field commander, attacked Kasan, planning to move south to take over Anju and, ultimately, Seoul.[11]

When Hong commanded the attack at Kasan on January 31, 1812, his force consisted of thirty to forty cavalrymen and about 150 foot soldiers.[12] Yi Maengŏk, a clerk of the Kasan district office, welcomed the rebels with band music, and the rebels, aided by other fifth columnists inside Kasan, occupied Kasan without much resistance. Just before the rebels arrived at the district office, the magistrate, Chŏng Si, found that the district office was empty and began to write an emergency report about the impending rebellion to military headquarters, located in Anju. Chŏng refused to submit to the rebel army, and the rebels killed him, along with his father, on the spot. Then Yun Ŏnsŏp, the director of the yangban bureau, who was appointed Kasan magistrate by the rebels, took over the administration of the district.[13]

The next day, the rebels set up their main camp at the Pakch'ŏn ferry station, and on February 2 they captured the magistrate's office there. A day before the rebellion, Im Sŏnggo, the magistrate of Pakch'ŏn, had caught a villager, Kang Nin, who had been recruited as a miner by the rebels but had run away after witnessing abnormal military activities in Tabok village. The magistrate secretly reported Kang's testimony about the suspected preparation of an armed rebellion to military headquarters in Anju.[14] Then he hid in a nearby temple when the rebels seized the district office. He was captured, but the rebels spared his life since he was known to be a benevolent official.[15] Im was imprisoned by the rebels and was freed only after government troops recovered Pakch'ŏn.[16]

Although the army of Hong Ch'onggak launched the rebellion successfully, his force and the main rebel camp did not take speedy military action because of a strategic split among leaders in the early days of the rebellion. Immediately after the rebels took over Pakch'ŏn on February 2, two military officers from Anju, Kim Taerin and Yi Inbae, insisted on attacking Anju as quickly as possible, while the government headquarters there was in disarray. They were opposed by U Kunch'ik who preferred to hit other districts to the north. When Kim and Yi realized that their plan would not be adopted, they felt that the rebellion was doomed to fail and decided that the only way they could survive was to kill Hong Kyŏngnae, so that their crime of participating in the rebellion would be forgiven. They tried to strike him with a sword, but Hong Kyŏngnae moved quickly to avoid the stroke. The spirit of the rebels was too high to be discouraged from continuing the rebellion, and their abortive attempt to assassinate Hong only resulted in their own deaths on the spot.[17] Nonetheless, the rebels had to delay an attack at Anju, giving the government time to establish its defense line and then strike back.[18] In a message from rebel headquarters to the provincial military commander Yi Haeu in Anju right after this incident, the rebels accused Yi of sending two assassins to kill Hong Kyŏngnae. Then they sarcastically advised Yi to hire non-P'yŏngan people next time and also not to have P'yŏngan residents in his defense lines because all the people of P'yŏngan Province would embrace the rebels' cause.[19]

Kim Sayong's force to the north was more successful and swiftly took over a number of district seats. In Sŏnch'ŏn, people in the town became restless and transported grain to the countryside to hide it after they heard about the impending armed rebellion. The magistrate of Sŏnch'ŏn, Kim Iksun, arrested Ch'oe Ponggwan on January 31, 1812, supposedly for circulating rumors. Ch'oe confessed that there was a plot and disclosed the names of those involved in the conspiracy. As a result, Chŏng Pogil from Ch'ŏlsan was arrested later that day and revealed the same thing. The magistrate also dispatched two officers to Kwaksan to take Kim Ch'angsi, Pak Sŏngsin, and Chang Hongik into custody.[20] The officers were returning to Sŏnch'ŏn with other officers and guards from Kwaksan when the rebels, led by Kim Sayong, ambushed them. This was several hours before another group of rebels, headed by Hong Ch'onggak, took over Kasan. The two officers from Sŏnch'ŏn were killed by the rebels, and nine of the twelve officers from Kwaksan (three ran away) were forced to join Kim Sayong and other rebels, who were launching an attack on Kwaksan on February 1. Many of the people in Kwaksan who had been mobilized by Ko Yunbin learned from Pak Sŏngsin that the rebels were approaching and greeted them.[21] The magistrate of Kwaksan, Yi Yŏngsik, was caught by the rebels in the beginning but was able to escape with the aid of a military officer, going first to Chŏngju and then to Anju, where he arrived on February 2, 1812. His two brothers and a son became victims of the outraged rebels.[22]

On the same day the rebels first took action, the Chŏngju magistrate, Yi Kŭnju, learned about the plot from a military officer, Paek Chonghoe, and subsequently arrested Chŏng Chingyo, who confessed.[23] The next morning, as Yi Kŭnju was trying to mobilize military officers and soldiers to defend the walled town, the wounded magistrate of Kwaksan, Yi Yŏngsik, arrived riding on the back of an ox. Then Ch'oe Iryun broke into the jail and set Chŏng Chingyo free, while Kim Idae, the director of the yangban bureau, and Yi Chŏnghwan, a chief military officer, strongly advised Yi Kŭnju to surrender to the rebels. When one of his clerks stole his official seals, the magistrate had no choice but to take flight, and he reportedly arrived at Anju the next day.[24] One report commented that the rebels spared his life because he had never pressed debtors hard to repay their official loans.[25]

On February 2, Kim Sayong led a rebel force into Chŏngju and named Ch'oe Iryun magistrate of the district. A few days later, however, the rebels replaced him with Kim Idae. Ch'oe protested while Kim showed off by requiring his underlings to bow to him before coming inside the office and by riding a sedan chair inside the courtyard.[26] Both Ch'oe and Kim were obviously ambitious to hold office, and both had great faith in geomancy and prophecy. When Ch'oe had been appointed to the post, his father had been very pleased for his family's good fortune and had attributed the blessing to his own selection of a fortunate grave site for his ancestors. Kim Idae, for his part, believed that a fortuneteller's prediction, made several years before, of good fortune in the year of *sinmi* meant that the appointment must go to him.[27]

The two rebel forces (one led by Hong Ch'onggak and the other by Kim Sayong) joined at Chŏngju on February 4. With added troops recruited from Chŏngju and Kwaksan, the combined force, led by Kim Sayong, marched northwest to Sŏnch'ŏn, which was already under the control of rebel sympathizers. Kim Iksun, the magistrate of Sŏnch'ŏn, first hid in Kŏmsan mountain fortress when he heard the fate of the two officers sent to Kwaksan. On the night of February 3, the rebel manifesto was delivered to the Sŏnch'ŏn magistrate's office, and the magistrate sent a letter of surrender to rebel headquarters. Kim was put in prison on February 4, and the rebels finally came to take over the district two days later.[28]

The district seat of Kusŏng was successfully defended by its magistrate,

Cho Ŭnsŏk,[29] although the rebels did take control of some areas under the jurisdiction of Kusŏng. On February 6, Kim Sayong's army of about a thousand men occupied the villages surrounding the Southern Granary (Namch'ang), with substantial local support led by a village head, Hŏ U, and his descent group. During their stay in the area, the rebels were fed meat and received a share of grain. They also recruited more soldiers from the villages and transported grain and firewood to the other rebel-occupied areas. When the rebel force heard of the defeat at Pine Grove, however, it broke up and departed.[30]

Rebel sympathizers also assumed power in Ch'ŏlsan before the rebel army, led by Kim Sayong, even set foot in the area. The magistrate Yi Changgyŏm had to surrender to the rebels because most of his aides from the yangban and military bureaus, and also his clerks, strongly pressured him to do so. Clerks copied and sent his letter of surrender to rebel headquarters, following the precedent established at Sŏnch'ŏn, and Yi turned over his official seals to the rebels.[31]

The rebel force led by Hong Ch'onggak was not as active as Kim Sayong's army. After replenishing in Chŏngju, Hong's force proceeded northeast to attack T'aech'ŏn, which fell under its control easily since the magistrate had run away to Yŏngbyŏn before the rebel army arrived. The rebels were greeted on February 7 with food and music prepared by coconspirators in the district, including the director of the yangban bureau and the grain storage supervisor. Pyŏn Taeik took charge of the district.[32] Yi Ch'wihwa and Yi Yunbang, a father and son from T'aech'ŏn, belonged to a leading local clerk family. They assumed the positions of military officers and took care of various matters under the rebel supervision.[33] Only a few local clerks provided leadership during the rebellion, although most incumbent clerks resumed their original posts and performed normal administrative work under the command of the rebel leaders.

During the early days of the rebellion, rebels occupied the area north of the Ch'ŏngch'ŏn River relatively easily and with little bloodshed. Magistrates of administrative districts either fled or surrendered to the rebels. In this relatively straightforward success, the fifth columnists from each district played a crucial role. Even the military commander of P'yŏngan Province acknowledged that these areas fell under rebel control so quickly solely because of the rebel sympathizers living in each district.

Despite such dramatic success in taking over most of the Ch'ŏngbuk area, the rebels failed to capture two very strategically important districts, Yŏngbyŏn and Ŭiju. Yŏngbyŏn, a gateway to Hamgyŏng Province, was famous as a natural stronghold and was equipped with substantial military supplies.[34] Several people from other districts moved to Yŏngbyŏn sometime before the rebellion to organize the rebel network there. Kang Suhŭng and his sons from Kasan, Yi Manbong from Pakch'ŏn, and Na Taegon, a wealthy merchant of Anju, bought houses in Yŏngbyŏn and worked together with Kim Uhak and other conspirators in the district. Yet Na Taegon was caught right before the arrival of the rebels in Yŏngbyŏn, and his disclosure of the plan resulted in the arrest of all the rebel sympathizers in the district. They were decapitated immediately, and so were many of their family members, as a warning to the people.[35] The magistrate of Yŏngbyŏn, with the aid of the magistrates and soldiers from Unsan and Kaech'ŏn, defended the walled town successfully.[36]

Ŭiju was almost taken by the rebels. Kim Kyŏnsin, a leading military officer there, was the brother-in-law of Yi Hŭijŏ and was involved in the plot at the outset.[37] Just after the rebellion broke out, Kim and a few dozen military officers gathered at his house and probably waited for the rebels to arrive in the area. At that critical moment, Kim changed his mind, after meeting the magistrate of Ŭiju, Cho Hŭngjin, who lectured him on the Confucian ethic of loyalty versus treason. Moved by the admonition, Kim displayed his loyalty to the dynasty by decapitating both his own wife, who was a sister of Yi Hŭijŏ, and his son. He became one of a few military officers who rendered distinguished service later on, in annihilating the rebel forces in Ch'ŏlsan, Yongch'ŏn, and Sŏnch'ŏn.[38]

By February 10, Kasan, Kwaksan, Chŏngju, Sŏnch'ŏn, Pakch'ŏn, T'aech'ŏn, and Ch'ŏlsan belonged to the rebels. The rebels simply took over the old administrative system and appointed new magistrates from among their own men. Those who took these prestigious positions had in fact been running the districts as officers of the local yangban or military bureaus before the rebellion. By replacing the government's magistrates with their own appointees, the rebel leaders took the first step in claiming the existing local government apparatus for themselves. As de facto administrators, the rebel magistrates and military officers ran the captured districts by making the best use they could of existing institutions. As soon as the rebels occupied a district, they opened up the government granaries and distributed grain, which was the most effective way to earn support from the hunger-stricken people. They also seized government funds to pay peasant soldiers or to earn popular support.[39] For example, Kim Idae, the director of the Chŏngju yangban bureau, was in charge of 27,000 *yang* of "contributions" made by those who had recently purchased new memberships in the local yangban association. Kim used some of the funds for rebel activities during the rebellion.[40] Ko Yunbin from Kwaksan also handed over more than 1,000 *yang* of tax money to Kim Ch'angsi.[41]

The rebels needed to strengthen their military force, so they recruited peasant soldiers using the existing military rosters. Village heads were responsible for recruiting these peasants, who were sent first to Chŏngju, then to the battle-front in Pakch'ŏn, to the south of Chŏngju, or to Yangch'aek and other military stations to the north. Some peasants volunteered to become soldiers because the rebels fed them and sometimes gave them monetary rewards. Although there were less than a hundred rebel soldiers when the rebels first occupied Chŏngju, their numbers grew to more than three hundred by February 10. The rebels also issued appointment letters to military officers in each district, inviting them to join the rebel force as officers. Most of the military officers who were later arrested by the government insisted that they had only joined the rebels because they were coerced. Nonetheless, it is clear that their loyalty toward the Chosŏn dynasty was not very firm.[42]

The rebels fully utilized the existing post-station system. They had the post-station chief (Palchang) or the post-station runner (Paeji) transmit rebel manifestos and other messages to the next targeted administrative town, both to let rebel sympathizers there know that they were on their way to take over the district and to discourage the magistrate from resisting.[43] Although the rebels secretly prepared weaponry such as spears and swords, their first priority was to get hold of government weapons for the rebel army. They collected bows, arrows, muskets, and bullets from the government armory in the Kosŏng Garrison and in T'aech'ŏn and sent them to Kasan.[44]

In addition to seizing grain, money, and cotton cloth from government warehouses, the rebels tapped private resources to acquire military supplies. Both ordinary and rich households were mobilized for these efforts. In the Sŏrim Garrison, they gathered firewood and fodder from villagers.[45] In Ch'ŏlsan, Chŏngju, and other places, they extorted money, clothes, and grain from the rich, some of whom resisted.[46] Yu Munje, rebel magistrate of Sŏnch'ŏn, mentioned that one or two rich people of this town should be decapitated to set an example. The testimony of Kye Hangdae, a rich local yangban in Sŏnch'ŏn, graphically illustrates how Kim Sayong threatened to kill Kye when Kye did not immediately provide money and grain. Enraged, Kim preached to him: "Do you have one head or two? We want the money and grain that you have. Why are you so stingy and unwilling to contribute? You must want to die!" Kye had to pay 11 *sŏm* of rice to save his life and promise a further 3,000 *yang* in cash and 100 *sŏm* of rice. Kye's own account contradicts the government's report, which states that it was very regrettable that Kye, a man from a yangban descent group who had received great favors from the government, had betrayed the dynasty. At any rate, Kye was quite opportunistic, for he provided 40 *sŏm* of grain to the government camp and promised to provide another 1,000 *yang* before his involvement in the rebellion was discovered.[47]

Several episodes found in primary sources indicate that local wealthy people were pressured to make material contributions to the rebel army for purely practical reasons rather than as an aspect of class struggle. An impoverished yangban himself, Kim Sayong's goal when intimidating Kye Hangdae was basically to fund the rebellion, not to persecute a presumably exploitative wealthy person in the countryside. Similarly, Yu Munje, who held high military positions for a long time and who was very rich himself, forced other affluent neighbors to contribute military supplies for the sake of the success of the rebellion, not necessarily to defend the class interests of the poor.[48] In Chŏngju, Ch'oe Iryun also pressed the well-to-do to donate material goods for the rebels and reportedly had a few of them killed when they did not obey.[49] In this case, also, Ch'oe's main motive was to get as much money from the rich as he could to finance the rebellion.

In fact, most local yangban, wealthy persons, and military officers who sided with the rebels testified that they had been forced to join to save their lives. It appears reasonable that their lives were in jeopardy, because on some occasions those who refused to join the rebel army were decapitated, as in the district of T'aech'ŏn.[50] Nonetheless, most of them probably concluded that they had more to gain by aiding the rebels than by opposing them. This may explain why the rebels were able to control so much territory in the first ten days of the rebellion. In other words, the yangban and wealthy people who supported the rebels were simply being opportunistic. The Confucian teachings of loyalty to the ruling dynasty did not prevail among these local elite, and only a very few chose to defy the rebels. Needless to say, the government later deplored the fact that so many prosperous households were supplying the rebels with money and grain while so few resisted the rebels at the beginning of the rebellion.[51]

THE REACTION OF THE CENTRAL GOVERNMENT AND THE BATTLE AT PINE GROVE

On the day after the rebellion started, a secret report from the magistrate of Pakch'ŏn, which said that there were unusual military activities going on in Tabok village, arrived at the office of the provincial military commander in

Anju. News also arrived of the rebels' capture of Kasan and the immediate desertion of the people living in the town. The magistrate of Anju, Cho Chongyŏng, realizing that the swift success of the rebels had been possible thanks to fifth columnists in each district, thoroughly investigated rebel supporters from Anju and arrested more than ten people in three days.[52] Although he believed that there were more supporters on the loose, these arrests must have helped prevent some subversive action. Cho also had to decapitate two soldiers who tried to avoid their duty upon hearing the disturbing news to warn others. The gates of the walled town were secured while the soldiers were called into town for defense of the area. Nonetheless, the provincial military commander, Yi Haeu, was quite concerned about the defense of Anju because there were very few soldiers available. Although the military headquarters sought additional troops from five districts under its command, only about sixty troops from Sukch'ŏn began to arrive two days after the conscription order was sent out. Yi was dismayed that he had not prevented the uprising from breaking out just across the river in the first place, and he was even more distressed that his army was not prepared for such a sudden military engagement. In his subsequent report to the court, he explained that Kasan had been captured precisely because things had been so peaceful for such a long time that the people just ran away from home at the first news of rebellion. He claimed that nine of every ten houses were empty when the government tried to recruit peasant soldiers.[53] Even though Yi wanted to fight back, he had no troops to command. And the rebels might indeed have invaded Anju if the aforementioned assassination attempt of Hong Kyŏngnae had not taken place.

News of the rebellion in the Ch'ŏngbuk area arrived in P'yŏngyang on February 2, two days after the rebellion had started.[54] The provincial governor, Yi Mansu, dispatched one company of soldiers from Sunan to Anju on February 4 and later sent five more companies led by Yi Chŏnghoe, the deputy commander of the Circuit Army Headquarters (Sunyŏng Chunggun) stationed in P'yŏngyang. Furthermore, Yi Mansu sent warnings to areas under his control to guard the main and arterial roads and other strategic points. Yi also recruited more soldiers and prepared military supplies. Keeping pace with government efforts to suppress the rebellion, the private sector—led by Confucian scholars, current and retired officials, and descendants of civil and military officials and merit subjects around the P'yŏngyang area—sent out a circular (*t'ongmun*; see fig. 1) to organize militia units, which either proceeded to the front lines in Chŏngju or stayed in P'yŏngyang to protect the area.[55]

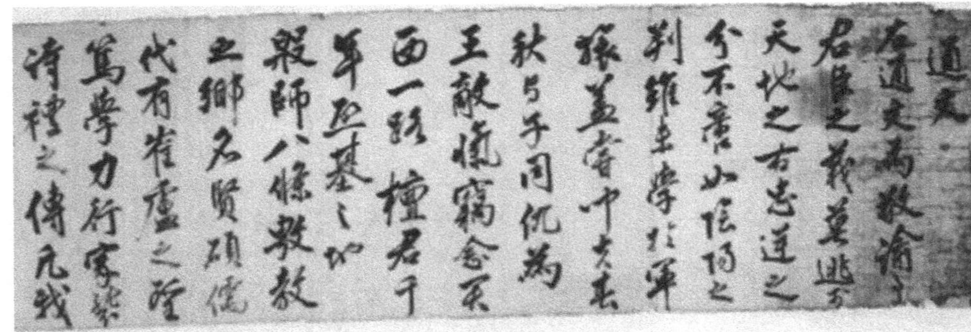

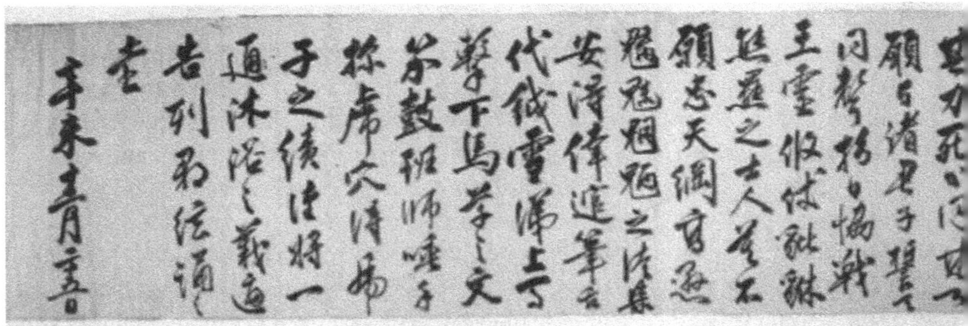

FIG. 1. Circular to the P'yŏngan People (*Kwansŏ t'ongmun*). This circular—only the first and last parts are shown here—was written on February 7, 1812. By permission of the National Institute of Korean History, Seoul, GF 3757 (28–279–03).

The central government learned about the rebellion four days after it had begun.[56] The government was obviously caught by surprise when it received the report submitted by the provincial governor and the provincial military commander of P'yŏngan Province. Two days later, Chŏng Mansŏk, a royal commissioner, was sent to the area to investigate the situation and show the king's solicitude for the people. In addition, the government immediately established the Circuit Pacification Army Headquarters (Sunmuyŏng) inside the Forbidden Guard Division (Kŭmwiyŏng), which was to supervise all the military activities directed to quell the rebellion. Yi Yohŏn, a member of the royal family, was appointed as chief of the headquarters. About eight hundred troops recruited from the capital area under the deputy commander

(Sunmu Chunggun), Pak Kip'ung, set out for the rebel-occupied region ten days after the rebellion broke out, arriving there another ten days later.[57]

The news of the rebellion certainly caused confusion among people both at the center and in the countryside. Seoul residents, including families of high-ranking officials, initiated a frantic exodus to the countryside, assuming that the rebels would soon approach the capital. Thieves and robbers took advantage of the chaos.[58] In Hwangju, Hwanghae Province, a few days after news of the rebellion arrived, looting by a group of boatmen invited violent revenge from the victims, which resulted in the loss of 336 houses by fire and the deaths of four people.[59] Around the same time, local disturbances in Chaeryŏng, Hwanghae Province, were so widespread that the magistrate could not put the district back in order quickly.[60] In mid-February, hundreds of people of Chunghwa refused a conscript order and pillaged the villages.[61] Kang Hŭiyŏng, who was living relatively close to the area affected by the rebels, reported the rumor that there were rebel sympathizers not only in P'yŏngan and Hwanghae provinces but also in Kyŏnggi, Hamgyŏng, and the southern provinces.[62] He also noted local disturbances in Kŭmhwa, Ch'ŏrwŏn, Ich'ŏn in Kangwŏn Province, and Kwangch'ŏn market in Ch'ungch'ŏng Province.[63] There is no evidence that any of this violence was directed by the rebels in northern P'yŏngan Province. Nonetheless, these simultaneous disturbances must have caused great concern to the central government.

The king's edict, promulgated on February 5, was aimed primarily at the rebel-affected area, to encourage loyalty toward the dynasty and to comfort the hunger-stricken refugees who were now fleeing from the rebels. It also sought to stabilize other areas by assuring the populace that the rebels were nothing but a band of thieves who were taking advantage of the terrible economic conditions in the countryside, which were due to the extraordinary famine the previous year and which would soon be put right.[64] This perspective, expressed in the edict, was fundamentally different from that of Yi Haeu, the provincial military commander of P'yŏngan Province, who pointed out on February 11 that this uprising was not a simple disturbance caused by a band of thieves but an act of treason supported by the whole province, including a broad range of people with different social and economic backgrounds.[65] Nevertheless, the court saw maladministration and crop failure as the fundamental reasons for the popular rebellion, so the first things it tried to do were to dispatch new local administrators and to punish the old ones, relieve the famine, and lessen the burden of tax payments temporarily, just as any traditional Confucian government would have done in such a situation.

By February 10, about two thousand local troops from five districts south of Anju gathered in Anju under the command of the military headquarters there. Because many peasant soldiers were not only old but weak from famine, nine hundred men were selected and organized into nine companies (*ch'o*) for the first battle with the rebels the next day. Extremely concerned about the quality of this army, Yi Haeu mentioned in a report that he felt the soldiers would run away like surprised animals or birds once they heard the thundering sound of the cannon. Because it had been a long time since the people of P'yŏngan Province had taken part in any military action, he feared defeat in the first battle and asked the central government to dispatch a central army in the best interests of the dynasty.[66] Indeed, a study of the late Chosŏn military system shows that the units in the countryside, called *sogo-gun*, rarely convened for training. Especially after the King Chŏngjo's reign (1776–1800), *sogo* units were recalled to provide labor services, such as repairing dikes, reservoirs, and defense walls, rather than to practice military skills and strategies.[67] If that was the case, Yi Haeu's concern was no exaggeration.

It was because the rebel army was hardly better than the government troops that the government troops were able to defeat the rebels at the battle of Pine Grove on February 11. In the beginning, the rebel army, led by Field Commander Hong Ch'onggak, seemed to have the upper hand. The provincial military commander, who was observing the fight from a watchtower on the wall of Anju, dispatched reinforcements led by Yi Yŏngsik, former magistrate of Kwaksan. Soon the rebel soldiers deserted the line of battle, frightened by the government gunfire and the deaths of a few of their commanders.[68] It turned out to be a great victory for the government and a turning point in the rebellion, because right after losing this battle the rebels had to retreat to the walled town of Chŏngju.

As the rebels retreated to Chŏngju, the regional army swept through the rebel base in Tabok village, set fire to it, and then recovered Pakch'ŏn the same day. The government's scorched-earth strategy was thorough. The government pacification army, sent by the central government, which passed through the area several days later, saw only ashes and corpses in the villages and fields. A large village of eight hundred households on Ch'u Island, in the middle of the Ch'ŏngch'ŏn River, whose residents were viewed as rebel sympathizers, was also burned to the ground.[69] Not only were the rebel soldiers killed, but countless innocent people lost their lives. Only two hundred of the one thousand rebels who fought at Pine Grove survived the massacre to escape to Chŏngju. Faced with the government's merciless killing, burning, and looting, many of the people living in the Kasan and Pakch'ŏn areas had no choice but to follow the rebel army and escape to Chŏngju.[70]

Pang Ujŏng, a lieutenant of the central government army, criticized the mistakes committed by Yi Haesŭng, the army inspector of Anju's military headquarters (Jr. 3), who commanded the government troops at Pine Grove. Above all, Yi's indiscriminate violence drove the people to follow the rebels and resist the government's pacification campaign to the death. According to Pang's report, Yi was initially scared and did not want to command the regional army when he was ordered to do so. Everyone laughed at him for wailing and calling out to his mother when he was driven out of the gate to take part in the battle. Ironically, upon the defeat of the rebels, he turned into a ruthless beast. He was also quite greedy. The goods he looted during the five days after the battle of Pine Grove took thirty horses to carry away. The greatest error Yi made was that it took five days for his army to reach Chŏngju, where the rebels had entrenched themselves. During those five days, while the regional troops were busy ransacking Kasan and Pakch'ŏn, the rebels prepared themselves for the upcoming siege by government troops by gathering all the material and human resources they could manage.[71]

THE REBELS NORTH OF CHŎNGJU AND THE CONTRIBUTIONS OF MILITIAS (*ŬIBYŎNG*)

The rebels who occupied the area north of Chŏngju were frustrated by the defeat at Pine Grove, but they succeeded in capturing Yongch'ŏn on February 15, 1812. The magistrate of Yongch'ŏn, Kwŏn Su, chose not to surrender despite his military officers' insistence that he do so. He was prepared to defend the district by setting up a base at the Yonggol mountain fortress, but his soldiers fled as soon as the rebels arrived, so he himself was forced to flee north to Ŭiju.[72] The rebels also took control of strategically important fortresses, such as Tongnim and Sŏrim, and the Yangch'aek post station.[73] They also intended to attack Ŭiju and devised a strategy to take it over with assistance of a number of locals, but the rebels never had a chance to carry out this plan.[74]

Of the fifteen people who proposed the plan, Kye Namsim of Sŏnch'ŏn had reportedly mastered the technique of metamorphosis.[75] Pak Chŏngyong from Sŏngch'ŏn, a staff officer of the rebel army, was a geomancer.[76] Pak

Ch'iyŏng from Sŏnch'ŏn was an herbal doctor and had been involved in the rebellion from the planning stage as a friend of Kim Ch'angsi.[77] Chŏng Chisang, a member of the Hadong Chŏng descent group in Ch'ŏlsan, was a rather renowned Confucian scholar in the area and was serving the rebels as a chief administrative officer (Chongsagwan) when he presented a proposal to take over Ŭiju.[78] Hong Sŏngjong, a longtime friend of Kim Ch'angsi, also devised a scheme to get hold of Ŭiju and personally wrote a letter to Kim Kyŏnsin to persuade Kim to surrender.[79]

Gaining the support of local power holders before military action took place had been critical in taking over district seats at the beginning of the rebellion, so serious efforts were made to gain the support of the local yangban in Ŭiju as well. First of all, the rebels kidnapped the family members of Kim Ch'wigyu, former army second deputy commander (Jr. 3), and Chang Mongyŏl, previous magistrate, to hold them as hostages. They also sent intimidating letters to Kim Kyŏnsin and to Kim T'aengmin, the son of Kim Ch'wigyu, demanding their support.[80] Yet, possibly due to the change of heart of Kim Kyŏnsin and his leadership, military officers of Ŭiju vowed to defend their home district. The rebels' success in earlier campaigns was consequently reversed when militias led by Ŭiju military officers played a decisive role in defeating the rebels north of Chŏngju.

Nonetheless, full-scale military action against the rebels on the part of militia units came only after the rebel force had been substantially weakened by its defeat at the battle of Four Pine Field near Kwaksan. Yi Yŏngsik, magistrate of Kwaksan at the time of the rebellion, had fled from the rebels, but led a successful battle at Pine Grove, then recovered his district on February 20. He launched a second major battle against the rebels the next day and defeated them. The rebels suffered several hundred causalities and the survivors ran away.

The arrest and subsequent death of Yi Chech'o from Kaech'ŏn, Hwanghae Province, the rebel field commander at the Four Pine Field battle, was a great loss to the rebels. Yi Chech'o and his brother, Yi Chesin, had joined the rebel leadership right before the rebellion. The government military officers were physically unable to capture Yi Chech'o because he was too tough and well built to subdue. But they were able to persuade him to surrender. After tying him up, they decided to kill him because they were afraid he might escape. Yi had been poor and had lived in a thatched house without land or slaves, but he did have a small collection of books. His participation in the rebellion brought great hardship on his family. His father died of torture, and other relatives were imprisoned.[81]

The rebel side also suffered the critical loss of Kim Ch'angsi right after the Four Pine Field battle. Kim was on the run northward in the hope of mobilizing rebel sympathizers in the border region along the Amnok River. Unexpectedly, his follower Cho Munhyŏng beheaded Kim while he was asleep, intending to present Kim's head to the government and receive the promised reward. Instead, Cho sold Kim's head to Kim Iksun, the Sŏnch'ŏn magistrate who had earlier surrendered to the rebels and who pledged to pay 1,000 *yang* for it. Yet Kim Iksun did not make payment but ran away with the head while Cho was drunk. He then pretended that he himself had killed Kim Ch'angsi when he presented the head to the government army. Kim's cunning scheme came to light when Cho appeared at the government camp and gave his version of the story, though it did not save his own life, not to mention that of Kim Iksun.[82]

Cho's betrayal reveals just one aspect of the rebels' troubles. The defeat at Four Pine Field, on top of the loss at Pine Grove ten days before, punctured the morale of the rebel troops. At this juncture, the militias from Ŭiju began an offense that scared the rebels to the bone. The rebels—stationed at strategic points around Yongch'ŏn, Ch'ŏlsan, and Sŏnch'ŏn—scattered when the militias came near to attack. Most rebel forces had been conscripted by fifth columnists and district administrators or had been chosen by the rebels from commoner peasants listed on the government's military rosters. Since the peasants suffered from famine and harsh taxation and the rebels appeared to be powerful and generous, the recruits initially supported the rebels. Nonetheless, the morale of these conscripted soldiers was not high, and they were not willing to risk their lives in fighting government forces by this time. Furthermore, the rebels did not make any serious efforts to win spontaneous support from the peasants by proposing substantial reforms in tax administration, land ownership, or the social status system, which would have directly improved the lot of the peasants. The prospects of eliminating political discrimination against P'yŏngan Province on the part of the central government and achieving a change of dynasties were not enough to satisfy the immediate interests of the peasants and to inspire them to risk their lives. As a result, the peasant soldiers did not have to think twice before running away when the government forces and the militias attacked them on both flanks.

The militia led by the local elite of Ŭiju recovered Yongch'ŏn on February 22, the Yangch'aek post station and Igot Garrison on February 23, the Yonggol fortress and Sŏrim Garrison on February 25, Sŏnch'ŏn on February 27, and Ch'ŏlsan and the Tongnim Garrison on February 28. Thus the government had recovered all the areas affected by the rebellion, except Chŏngju, by February 28, 1812, and the official communication line between Anju and Ŭiju was finally reestablished.

Three members of the Ŭiju elite played a prominent role in recovering the area north of Chŏngju. The aforementioned Kim Kyŏnsin's military actions were most illustrious and he was lavishly rewarded for his help in recovering rebel-occupied areas. The central government granted him the military post of garrison commander at the Kabam Garrison (Kabam Kwŏn'gwan), and later appointed him magistrate of T'aech'ŏn, then royal messenger (Sŏnjŏn'gwan, Sr. 3), and finally military commander of Ch'ungch'ŏng Province (Jr. 2), the highest position a military officer could obtain in the Chosŏn dynasty. He also received 20 *kyŏl* of land, twenty slaves, and other material rewards.[83]

Kim Kyŏnsin's success was unprecedented, since only a few people from P'yŏngan Province had been able to attain such a high position in the central government throughout the Chosŏn dynasty. Nonetheless, his success was made possible only because of his military contribution to the survival of the dynasty, rather than through normal channels of political advancement. Also, the fame he earned was a bitter one, because he had been insulted for being a northerner while he fought for the court—not to mention that, to prove his loyalty to the court, he had seen fit to kill his own wife and son. Pang Ujŏng reports in his diary that his associates from the capital became jealous of Kim Kyŏnsin's achievement and slandered him for being a person from a border region. Pang himself did not care about a person's regional background and admired Kim's valor and achievement.[84]

Hŏ Hang, a military officer, also played a central role in annihilating the rebels active in Yongch'ŏn and Ch'ŏlsan. He died during the rebels' surprise attack on the night of April 30, and thus was named one of six "loyal subjects" who sacrificed their lives for the sake of the dynasty during the Hong Kyŏngnae Rebellion. He was posthumously appointed regional naval commander (Samdo t'ongjesa, Jr. 2).[85] Ch'oe Sinyŏp, another military officer, also played an active role in restoring order. He was immediately rewarded with the position of garrison commander of Kabam and was then appointed magistrate of Ch'osan. However, he was later charged with obstructing the grant of merit to other officers and with looting property during the military campaign against the rebels.[86]

Military forces provided by local militias and material donations made by private individuals were also important in putting down the rebellion. The central government appealed repeatedly to the local yangban of P'yŏngan

Province to demonstrate their loyalty by joining the government effort to suppress the rebels. Historically, the government had always relied on the voluntary participation of the yangban in any serious military campaign, as clearly seen during the Japanese and Manchu invasions centuries earlier. For more than four hundred years before the Hong Kyŏngnae Rebellion, the regular military had not been able to defeat major enemies, domestic or foreign, except during the early years of the Chosŏn dynasty. Moreover, because the dynasty had been fairly peaceful for a long period prior to the Japanese and Manchu invasions, the military structure had gradually fallen apart. During and after those invasions, the government rearranged the military structure, but the whole system was not in a very effective, functional condition when the rebellion broke out.[87] Thus the government had to call for help from the local ruling stratum.

Moreover, it was even more important than usual for the government to maintain the support of the local yangban at the time of the Hong Kyŏngnae Rebellion because many of the local yangban had sided with and provided leadership to the rebels. In other words, those who volunteered to join the government forces, and who contributed military supplies to the government camp, could just as easily have joined the rebel camp. They shared the same concerns and discontents over government discrimination against appointing people from P'yŏngan Province to high office and over the center's intervention in local affairs to tap local resources. They were also likely to have heard and believed in the coming of the True and Genuine Chŏng and in his promise to overturn the dynasty. Therefore, it was critical that the government urge local yangban to support the dynasty by appealing to the Confucian cliché about the importance of loyalty and righteousness, norms that any Confucian scholar was supposed to uphold. The government also promised material rewards and career opportunities in the central bureaucracy for those who achieved military merit by killing or arresting rebels.[88]

Nonetheless, the response from the local elite was quite slow.[89] There was only one case of local yangban organizing a militia before the rebel troops retreated to Chŏngju after their first major defeat by the government army at Pine Grove. Hyŏn Inbok, a yangban from Chŏngju, got together with Ko Hansŏp and Paek Kyŏnghan when the rebellion broke out. First they sent a messenger to Anju military headquarters, then Hyŏn and Ko went to Anju while Paek recruited more like-minded people. When they arrived at the gate of Anju military headquarters on February 5, they were even suspected of being rebel spies and temporarily put in prison.[90]

It is interesting to note that government officials suspected almost all

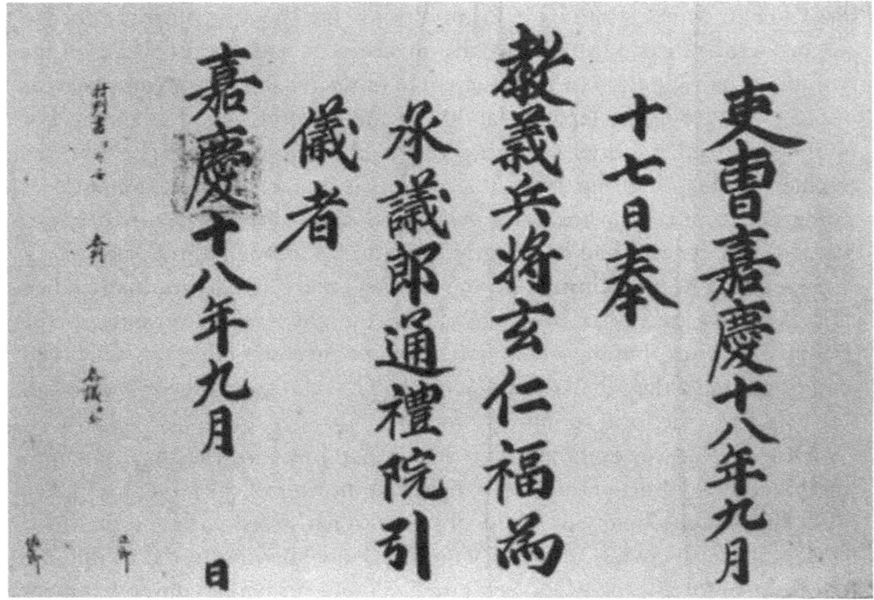

FIG. 2. Official Appointment Certificate for Hyŏn Inbok 1 (*Hyŏn Inbok kyoji*). A certificate to appoint Hyŏn Inbok to the ritual preceptor at the Office of Ceremonies (T'ongnyewŏn Inŭi) in 1813. 57×81.5 cm. By permission of the National Institute of Korean History, Seoul, GF 3759 (28–279–05).

P'yŏngan residents, regardless of their social status, at the outbreak of the rebellion. Paek Kyŏnghae, a younger brother of Paek Kyŏnghan, who was inspector of P'yŏngan Province (Tosa) at the time, hurried back to his post in P'yŏngyang after learning about the rebellion at his hometown of Chŏngju. However, Provincial Governor Yi Mansu, suspecting him of being a rebel supporter, had Paek surrender his official seals. Even when Paek arrived at Yŏngbyŏn to assume the position of magistrate of Unsan several days later (the previous Unsan magistrate, Han Sangmuk, had fled to Yŏngbyŏn right after the rebellion broke out), he was denied entrance to the fortress and had to wait outside it.[91]

Meanwhile, a plan for Hyŏn and his militia to join the government troops and make a concerted attack on the rebels on February 9 came to naught because the government commander was not ready for action by that date. At any rate, a circular sent out by Hyŏn and Paek to local yangban in the area

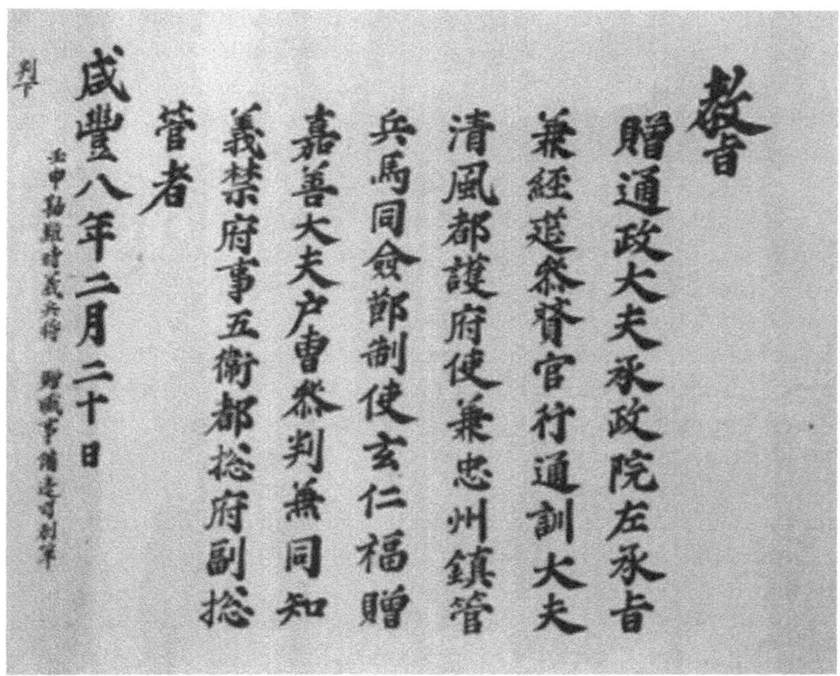

FIG. 3. Official Appointment Certificate for Hyŏn Inbok 2 (*Hyŏn Inbok kyoji*). A certificate to appoint Hyŏn Inbok posthumously to the junior second rank (Kasŏn taebu) and to the second minister of the Ministry of Taxation and equivalent military positions in 1858. 72.5×87 cm. By permission of the National Institute of Korean History, Seoul, GF 3766 (28–279–12).

on February 8, urging their participation in organizing militias, slowly garnered responses.[92] The militia, led by Hyŏn, was composed of five hundred local yangban (mainly from the Hyŏn, Paek, and Sŭng descent groups) and peasants. It joined the main government camp outside Chŏngju on February 16 and played an active role in several battles against the rebels.[93] Hyŏn also provided military supplies and rations for the government army. He was later appointed army second deputy commander (Jr. 3) of Sŏnsa Garrison, but politely refused to take the office since he was seeking a civil career, which he was soon able to pursue, as surviving documents testify (figs. 2 and 3).[94]

Paek Kyŏnghan's death has been discussed in earlier chapters. He was caught by the rebels on February 14 and was tortured to death. The government rewarded his loyalty and righteousness toward the Chosŏn dynasty by granting him a posthumous appointment as second minister of the Ministry of Taxation (Hojo Ch'amp'an, Jr. 2), though only after confirming that his death was indeed for a loyal cause. He was also named one of the six loyal subjects who lost their lives during the rebellion.[95]

The other four loyal subjects whose names and merits were inscribed on the Stele of Loyalty and Righteousness (Ch'ungŭi-dan) were Im Chihwan, Che Kyŏnguk, Kim Taet'aek, and Han Houn. All six had volunteered for service. Im Chihwan, a scholar from Anju, was a seventh-generation descendant of Im Ch'ungsŏ, who had died in the line of duty during the Manchu invasions and had been posthumously appointed second commander of the Military Training Command (Hullyŏnwŏn Chŏng, Sr. 3). Im volunteered to deliver a secret letter sent by the office of military headquarters in Anju to the magistrate of Ŭiju when the rebels still had control of the area north of Chŏngju. On his way, he was caught by the rebels and killed, furiously refusing the rebels' demand that he surrender. The posthumous office of second minister of the Ministry of War (Pyŏngjo Ch'amp'an, Jr. 2) was bestowed on him.[96]

Che Kyŏnguk from Seoul was the sixth-generation descendant of Che Mal, the Duke of Loyalty (Ch'ungjang-gong), who was the magistrate of Chinju, Kyŏngsang Province, and who had died at the time of the Japanese invasion. Che once held the office of army inspector (Jr. 3). He was shot to death only a few days after he joined the pacification army during the battle against the rebels inside the Chŏngju . He was posthumously named regional navy commander (Samdo t'ongjesa, Sr. 3).[97]

Kim Taet'aek from Kasan, former military commander at the Five Military Commands (Owijang), was staying in Seoul to seek an office at the time of the rebellion. He joined the army dispatched by the Circuit Pacification Army Headquarters but was also shot to death in the same battle at which Che Kyŏnguk lost his life. His death earned him the posthumous position of military commander of Hamgyŏng Province.[98]

Han Houn from Chŏngju had passed the civil service examination and later attained the office of director of loyal tombs (Jr. 5). On April 28, Han approached the rebel defense line by himself in an effort to persuade the rebels to give up. Reportedly, he was still scolding the rebels when he was put to death. The court bestowed on him the posthumous office of second minister of the Ministry of Rites (Yejo Ch'amp'an) to honor his courageous death.[99]

The social and political backgrounds of these loyal and righteous people were very similar to those of some of the rebel leaders. Im Chihwan and Che Kyŏnguk can be compared to three men from the Hadong Chŏng descent group of Ch'ŏlsan. All were descended from prominent ancestors who had established merit during the foreign invasions centuries earlier. The path chosen by Han Houn, a *munkwa* degree-holder, could have been that of Kim Ch'angsi, who successfully passed the lower-level examination and became the brains of the rebel forces. The three Chŏngs and Kim chose to upgrade their lot by joining the rebel leadership. In contrast, Han, Im, and Che's choice repaid them with great honor and privilege, not only for themselves but for their offspring, for the hundred years left in the life of the dynasty.

The participation of local yangban in the rebellion and the process of the government pacification campaign demonstrate the extreme divisions and tensions within this privileged status group in local society. At the same time, the process of individual decision making not to support the rebels but to aid the government reveals the opportunistic but rational political behavior of the local elite. For those loyal to the existing rule, the benefits promised by the rebels were not convincing enough. For *munkwa* passers and their immediate family members, who had already earned fame and privileges within the existing structure—albeit not comparable to those enjoyed by centrally based yangban—there was probably no benefit to be gained from joining the rebellion beyond the circumstances they already had. Because the promised gains would be realized only at the end of prolonged political and military struggle, and the risks involved outweighed the possible benefits, the choice was probably clear for them. And it must only have become clearer once the counterattacks organized by the government, with the assistance of local militia leaders, seemed destined to be effective in defeating the rebel army.

After the efforts of Hyŏn Inbok, many local militias were organized and continued to join the main government military camp in Chŏngju (see table 9 for examples). By April 29, the number of volunteers had swelled to about fourteen hundred.[100] Some militias remained in their hometowns to defend strategic passages, mountain fortresses, or post stations. The means that the loyal yangban used to recruit militia volunteers were almost identical to those that the rebels had pursued to earn local support. They mobilized family and marriage relations, influential figures in the village, and their networks of friends—the major social networks in the traditional peasant

Name (Residence)	Occupation or Social status	Reward
An Myŏngnyŏl (Anju)	Local yangban (*hyangin*)	Upgrade rank (*kaja*)
Kang Inhak (Ch'angsŏng)	Kwŏn'gwan (Outpost Officer, Jr. 9)	Sixth-rank office in Ministry of Military
Pak Taegwan (Ch'ŏlsan)	*Chinsa*	Upgrade rank
Kim Kukch'u (Ch'ŏlsan)	*Hallyang*[a]	Upgrade rank
Ham Ŭihyŏng (Hŭich'ŏn)	*Hallyang*	Upgrade rank / military office in border region (*pyŏnjang*)
Song Chiryŏm (Kanggye)	Yangban scholar (*sain*)	Magistrate of Samdŭng
Kye Unhae (Kanggye)	*Hallyang*	Military office in border region
Kim Chonguk (Kilchu)	*Hallyang*	Upgrade rank / office at the central court (*silchik*)
Kang Chip (Kwaksan)	Chwasu (director of the Bureau of Local Yangban)	Upgrade rank
Wŏn Yŏngjŏng (Kwaksan)	*Hallyang*	Entry-level office (*ch'osa*)
Kim Chihwan (Kusŏng)	Former Manho (subarea commander)	Upgrade rank
Kim Kyŏngno (Pyŏktong)	Yangban scholar	*Pondo chŏllang*[b]
Ch'a Kyŏngjin (Sŏnch'ŏn)	Former Changnyŏng (third inspector of the Office of the Inspector General)	Magistrate position
Yi Sibok (T'aech'ŏn)	Yangban scholar	*Pongdo chŏllang*
Ch'oe Sinyŏp (Ŭiju)	Military officer	Magistrate of Ch'osan
Hong Yŏil (Ŭiju)	Former Ch'ŏmsa (army second deputy commander)	Upgrade rank
Chŏng Naehong (Ŭiju)	Yŏngjang (chief commander)	Upgrade rank / office at the central court

SOURCE: *Sunjo sillok*, 16:6b–8a, Sunjo 12.6.9 (*kyŏngsul*); and *Sunmuyŏng tŭngnok*, 2: 49–100.

[a] *Hallyang* seems to refer to those who belonged to a military branch and who were unemployed and regarded as semi-yangban in the late Chosŏn. For more discussion of *hallyang*, see Yi Chun'gu, "Chosŏn hugi hallyang kwa kŭ chiwi."

[b] *Pondo chŏllang* seems to refer to the positions such as the superintendent (Ch'ambong, Jr. 9) at the Kija shrine (Sunginjŏn) and Tan'gun shrine (Sungnyŏngjŏn) located in P'yŏngyang. See Paek Siwŏn, *Nop'o sŏnsaeng munjip*, 4:3b and 4:5b; *Chŏngjo sillok*, 35:33b, Chŏngjo 16.7.15 (*imja*); *P'yŏngyang sokchi 1*, 552. For the history of these two shrines, see O Such'ang, "Chosŏn hugi P'yŏngyang kwa kŭ insik ŭi pyŏnhwa."

TABLE 10. Donors to the Government Camp

Name (Residence)	Social status	Amount	Reward
Hong Tŭkchu (Ŭiju)	Confucian scholar (*yuhak*)	1,218 *sŏm* of grain and 5,200 *yang*	Entry-level office
Ch'a Hyŏnggi (Sukch'ŏn)	Local yangban (*hyangin*)	2,000 *yang*	Military office in border region
Pak Kyŏng (Anju)	Local yangban	1,500 *yang* and 8 *sŏm* of grain	Military office in border region
Kim Kyŏngjung (Anju)		1,000 *yang*	*Pondo chŏllang*
Ch'a Hyŏnggyu (Sukch'ŏn)	*Chinsa*	30 *sŏm* of grain, 35 *yang*, and 7 cows	Provincial award as wished
An Sagwŏn (Pyŏktong)	Local yangban	100 *sŏm* of rice	Provincial award as wished
Kye Chinhŭng (Chŭngsan)	Military officer	20 cows	Provincial award as wished
Yi Hyŏnt'aek (Sakchu)	*Hallyang*	15 *sŏm* of rice and 10 cows	Provincial award as wished
Yu *choi* and Ch'oe *choi* (Kanggye)	Commoner housewives	15 and 5 *yang*, respectively	Tax exemption

SOURCE: *Sunjo sillok*, 16:9a–9b, Sunjo 12.6.9 (*kyŏngsul*).

society—in their search for the like-minded. To cite one case of many, Kang Inhak from Ch'angsŏng, the seventh-generation descendant of Kang Paengnyŏng, who had earned prominent military merit during the Manchu invasions, came to the battle line together with more than forty-two young descent group members in early April.[101]

Beginning with the first donation made by a resident of Chŏngju on February 14, 1812, material support in the form of money, grain, foodstuffs, and other goods with which to make weapons and machinery flowed in to aid government forces (see table 10 for examples).[102] The largest contribution was made by Hong Tŭkchu, a yangban scholar from Ŭiju, and amounted to 1,218 *sŏm* of grain and 5,200 *yang*.[103] This bought Hong an express ticket to a post in the central government. Support from people of various social status backgrounds increased as the final suppression of the rebels approached. All those who provided loyal support in any form were rewarded with offices in the central and provincial bureaucracy, with ranks, titles, or offices at the local bureaus, or with tax exemptions. As had happened in other military adventures during previous centuries, the counterrebel campaign of the Hong Kyŏngnae Rebellion provided a good opportunity for local elite to consolidate their privileged status in their communities by displaying leadership and loyalty.

7 Rebels on the Defense

The government troops led by Yi Haesŭng, army inspector of Anju military headquarters, finally arrived at the foot of Chŏngju on February 15, 1812, followed by seven army companies from P'yŏngyang under Yi Chŏnghoe, deputy commander of Circuit Army Headquarters (Sunyŏng), on the same day. They set up the main military camp near the east gate of the walled town of Chŏngju (see fig. 4). The pacification army dispatched by the central government joined the camp eight days later, and Pak Kip'ung, deputy commander of Circuit Pacification Army Headquarters, began to control all the military operations on the scene. The government force numbered more than 6,300 men on February 15, 1812. More than 800 men from the central army joined the camp a few days later, and reinforcements from all around P'yŏngan Province arrived throughout the counterrebel campaign. According to the March 22 report made by Yi Minsik, the royal messenger to the Ch'ŏngbuk region, the total force numbered 8,534 men (see fig. 5), and it numbered 8,355 men on May 1. During the three and a half months of the pacification campaign, the government maintained a force of more than 8,000.[1]

Although government forces outnumbered the rebel army that was besieged in Chŏngju, the morale and discipline of the government troops were extremely low. The excessive and indiscreet killing, burning, and looting by government troops just after the battle at Pine Grove was discussed in chapter 6. That was only the beginning; the reckless destruction of private property and life continued throughout the campaign. Those who were

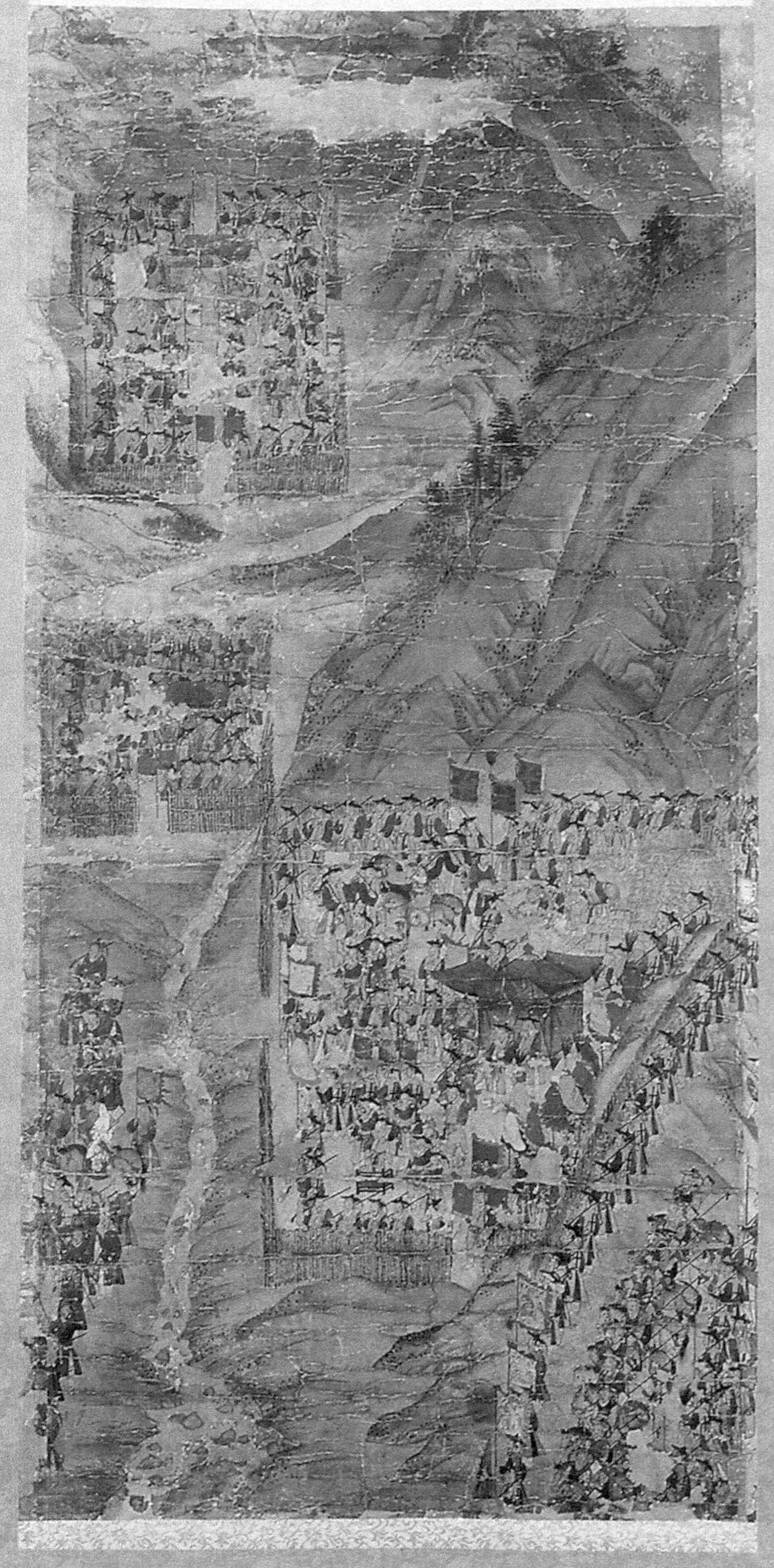

conscripted at the beginning of the rebellion pillaged private property on their way to join their government units.[2] Both officers and men sacked money, grain, and domestic animals and even assaulted people under the pretext of searching for rebels and maintaining security. Not only the immediate areas where the government camps were located, but most of P'yŏngan Province was affected. Government abuses were reported in Sunch'ŏn and T'aech'ŏn in particular.[3] In some cases, innocent travelers were killed without proper inquiry, under the naïve suspicion that they were rebel agents.[4] Repeated government warnings against such behavior did not seem to work, even though the government occasionally put a few violators to death.[5] In the early days of the rebellion, Paek Kyŏnghae commented on such ruthless behavior in a conversation with Provincial Governor Yi Mansu, saying, "The vicious rebels have already been able to restrain looting by beheading offenders. It is really a great concern that the people in the area south of Ch'ŏngch'ŏn River and north of P'yŏngyang, where the rebels have not set their feet, have been devastated by governmental abuses. This is something that the rebels would scorn and thus must be forbidden."[6]

Government officials were frustrated by the military officers' misuse of their power over innocent people, especially when they were searching for runaway rebels after the rebellion was over. According to one government report, the villages were in chaos because of the terror and pillaging carried out by the policing officers. Again, government orders failed to mitigate the situation immediately.[7] The behavior of some militias was hardly different from that of the government conscripts. There was one report that warned the Ŭiju militias not to invade villages on their way back home because the plunder they had practiced when they began military activities had caused

FIG. 4. *(facing page)* Illustration of the Circuit Pacification Army Camp *(Sunmu-yŏng chindo)*. A documentary painting that depicts various pacification army units surrounding the walled town of Chŏngju. This particular illustration must be a part of a larger painting or multiple screens because it shows only a few units that camped in the northeast of Chŏngju. The painting was probably done by a court painter who was dispatched to Chŏngju to record the situation by drawing it, and it reflects the situation circa April 10, 1812. The painting illustrates the wooden fence that each unit was protected by, commanders' tents, banners, military bands, and fully armed cavalry and foot soldiers, whose numbers are much smaller than the actual number. For example, the unit shown at the top of the painting commissioned by Kim Kyŏnsin was composed of three hundred soldiers according to the written description in the painting, but only a few were drawn there. 93×44 cm. By permission of the Kyujanggak, Seoul National University, koch'uk 4252. 4–23.

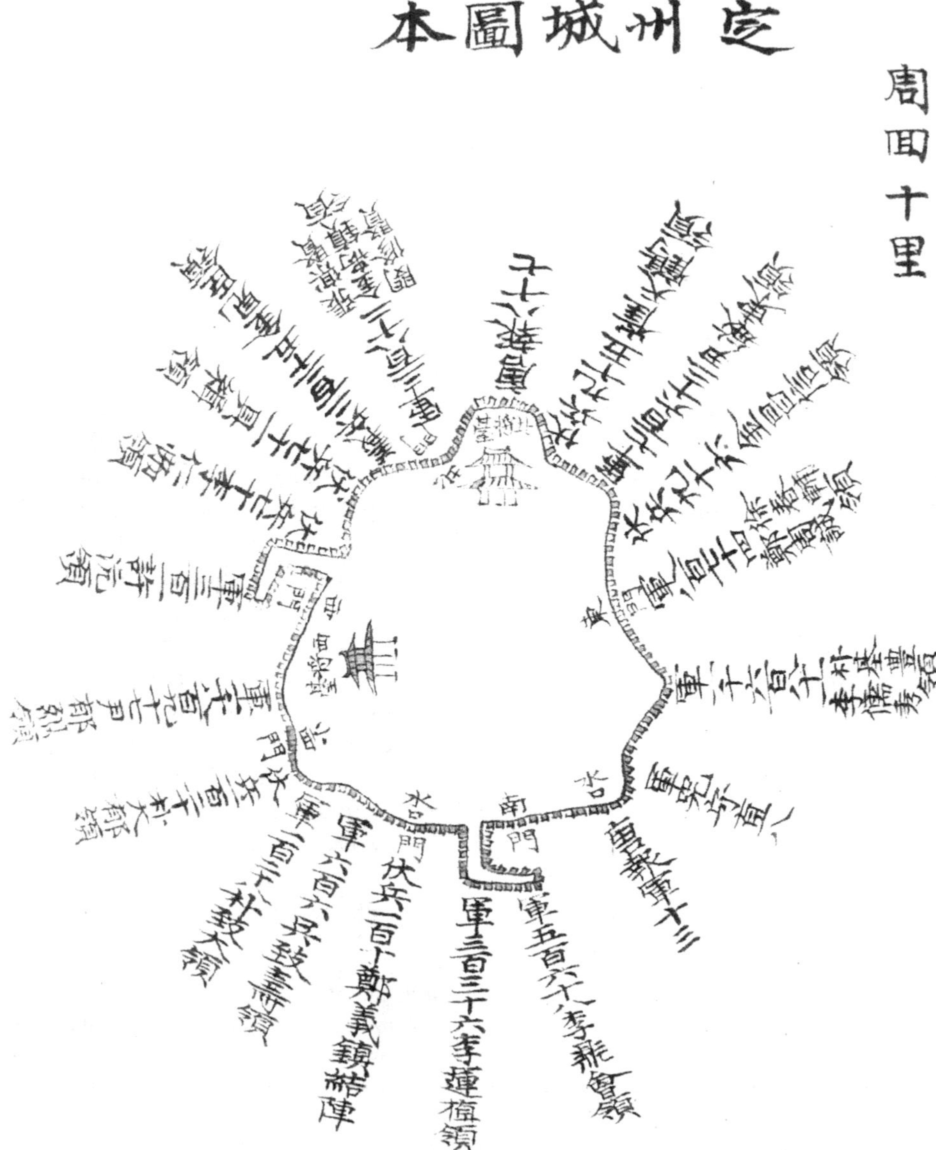

FIG. 5. Illustrated Map of Government Camps in Chŏngju (*Chŏngju sŏngdo pon*). From *P'yŏngsŏ ponmal* (The Essence and Branch of Pacifying P'yŏngan Province). An attachment to the report made by Yi Minsik, royal messenger to the Ch'ŏngbuk region, on March 22, 1812. Courtesy of the East Asian Library, Asami Collection, University of California, Berkeley, Asami 15.23.

a great disturbance in the countryside. Militias from Anju also looted private property in the Sunan and Sukch'ŏn areas.[8]

About two hundred rebel soldiers had been driven into Chŏngju after they were defeated in the battle of Pine Grove, and they had recruited about four hundred able-bodied men residing in Chŏngju to guard the walled town.[9] After the rebels north of Chŏngju had joined the defense of the town in early March, the number of people besieged (including children and the elderly) had reached almost four thousand. The rebel army was organized into companies (*ch'o*) of thirty soldiers, under the control of a company commander (Ch'ogwan). Two companies composed one battalion (*sa*), which was headed by a battalion commander (P'ach'ong). Although the trained rebel soldiers numbered only about 360, morale was high and discipline of the rebel army was very strict. They were trained every day and were not allowed to have idle conversations with each other. They were not permitted to leave their posts, and all the soldiers in the same unit were punished if any ran away.[10] Someone accused Hong Kyŏngnae of spreading the rumor that the government army would kill anyone who ran away from the rebel camp, so that rebel troops would be afraid to desert their units.[11] Yet a simple threat by the rebel leader might not have been sufficient to hold the rebels and peasants together for prolonged resistance against a government army, which was fed better and equipped with superior firearms.

In fact, the peasants who were driven into Chŏngju with the rebels were not the peasant soldiers who had been conscripted when the rebels took control of the Ch'ŏngbuk area. Most of them had lived in Pakch'ŏn and Kasan, which had been burned to the ground during a government reprisal. After witnessing the cruel and indiscriminate burning and killing by government troops, these people felt they had no choice but to join the rebels. Thus their resistance against the government campaign was tenacious and well organized during the siege. Interestingly, one runaway rebel reported in late February that the insurgents had arranged the units of the peasant army in a way that placed the peasants from Kasan and Pakch'ŏn in between the soldiers from Chŏngju, to prevent them from deserting.[12] Although a few peasants deserted and were arrested by the government troops, most stayed inside the wall for the four months of the siege with very few rations.

The government troops attempted to break through the rebel defense line on the wall many times with superior equipment and weapons, but to no avail. As soon as government forces arrived in Chŏngju, they began to make ladders to reach the top of the wall. Their first attempt, on February 17, was unsuccessful. Another attack on February 19, and subsequent

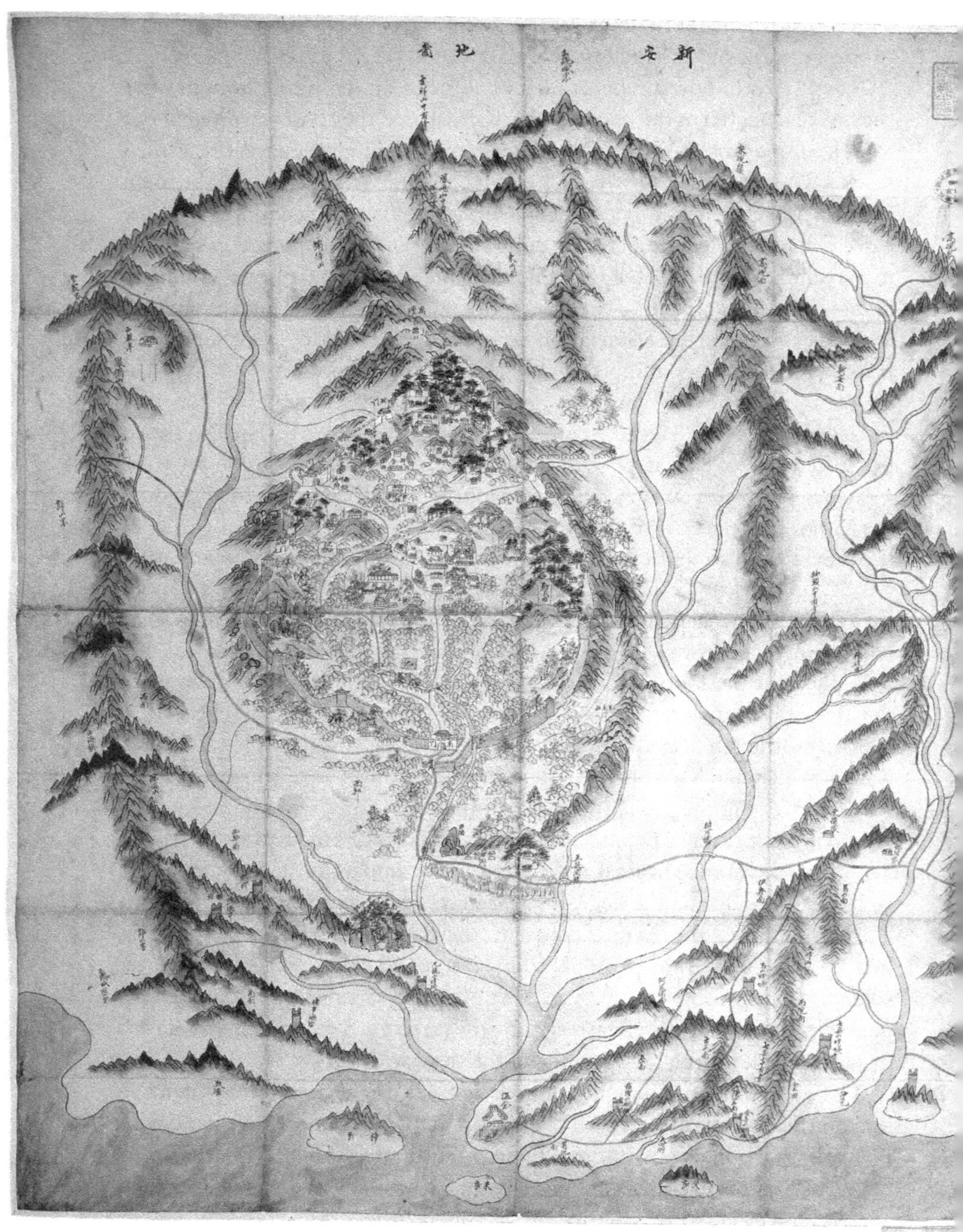

attempts to lure the rebels to venture outside the wall, also failed.[13] The joint government army, under the command of Pak Kip'ung, deputy commander of Circuit Pacification Army Headquarters, launched its first major attack on February 27, followed by another major attack four days later.

The government side had great difficulty in scaling the wall around Chŏngju and suppressing the rebels because of the topography of Chŏngju and the durability of the wall itself (see fig. 6). The wall had been rebuilt about a century before (in 1714), during the reign of King Sukchong. It was located on a rugged mountain slope. All three sides, except the southern wall, abutted the mountain, and two rivers that flowed from the northeast and northwest surrounded the wall and met at the southeast side. The wall was 5,585 *po* (about 6,981 meters) in circumference and 15 *ch'ŏk* (3.1 meters) tall. Inside the wall were the district offices, warehouses, temples, pavilions, and residential quarters. Double walls protected the west and south gates, which were exposed to open fields. Since the northern side, which was naturally shielded by precipitous hills, was higher than the other sides, the rebels could observe the government camp from the Northern Commander's Pavilion (Pukchang-dae).[14]

It was a great advantage for the rebels to occupy the walled town, and it required a tremendous effort for government forces to recover the town. In addition to the usual weapons and equipment used for battle, such as muskets, bows and arrows, and cannon, the government army had to devise new equipment for a successful attack. One of these innovations was a battle cart (*chŏnch'a*), which had four wheels and a wooden chamber on top in which dry wooden sticks and gunpowder were stored. The plan was to push the cart toward a gate in the wall and set it on fire to destroy the gate.[15] This specially built battle cart was used during the first all-out attack on February 27, although it did not function as it was designed to, because the wheels that had to support the heavy weight of the upper structure got stuck in the mud and broke apart before it reached the targeted gate.

FIG. 6. *(facing page)* Illustrated Map of Chŏngju (*Sinan chido*). A typical map painting, which focuses on the district seat, largely ignoring other territory of Chŏngju district. Certain cartographic features such as roads (red), bridges, some names of subdistricts, mountains, and streams (blue) are present, but it looks more a painting than a map. Inside the wall, the magistrate's office (*asa*) is at the center; the guesthouse of Chŏngju (Sinan'gwan) is just below it to the left; the local school (*hyanggyo*) is above it on the southern slope of the hill; and on top of the hill is the Northern Commander's Pavilion (Pukchang-dae). 115.7×94.8 cm. By permission of the National Library of Korea, Seoul, han-kojo 61–68.

The rebel defense strategy was quite effective in holding the walled town despite the rebels' insufficient military supplies. In the early days, the rebels placed wooden soldiers on top of the wall to deceive the government army.[16] In each guard station (*ch'ŏp*), a tent was set up for the soldiers patrolling the area. Bricks and stones were gathered to rain down on the enemy. The soldiers were ordered to shoot arrows when the enemy was farther than 100 *po* (about 125 meters) from the wall, and muskets when the enemy was within 100 *po*. When the enemy came within 30 *po* (37.5 meters), the rebels were to throw stones.[17] This strategy caused heavy casualties among the government troops. In the battle of February 27, the government lost two courageous volunteers, Che Kyŏnguk and Kim Taet'aek. In addition, on March 2, when the peasant soldiers of the government army were frightened and hesitated to engage in battle, the government lost another good opportunity to scale the wall and penetrate the rebel defenses.[18]

The next major attack came on March 16. By that time, the government force had been able to build better equipment. A revised battle cart called the Flying War Cart (*unjech'ungch'a*) looked like the one used before but had a chamber on top that was enclosed by wooden boards and iron. The cart was tall enough for three musketeers to hide in it, look down on the enemy inside the walls, and fire their guns at them. The cart was pushed by a couple of dozen soldiers hiding in the lower part of the cart, where they were protected by many layers of ox hides and cotton cloth. The cost of each cart was 400 to 500 *yang*.[19] Nevertheless, this clever machine did not help the government army penetrate the wall. The wheels were again too weak to sustain the heavy structure on top, and they were soon mired in the mud below. Of four carts used in this battle, two broke down before they got close to the battle line. The other two were successfully pushed near the wall but were not very useful in shielding the rain of arrows and bullets fired by the rebels. Despite several attempts to advance, the government army had to retreat, with many casualties, as darkness descended. The costly battle carts were burned to a crisp since they could not be wheeled back to the camp.[20]

On April 6, government forces attempted another attack using six battle carts. Despite a well-planned and -equipped strategy, the government troops again failed to scale the wall and lost all the carts in the process.[21] These repeated failures lowered the spirits of the government soldiers, even though the government held an advantage in terms of troop size, military provisions, and supplies. Moreover, the continuous arrival of militias reinforced the government's strength.

In the meantime, the central government fired Pak Kip'ung, the supreme field commander of the government pacification force, for his inability to put down the rebellion. Yu Hyowŏn was appointed to take over the position of deputy commander of the Circuit Pacification Army Headquarters, and he arrived in Chŏngju on April 9, 1812. At the same time, Sin Hongju, magistrate of Yŏngbyŏn, was named provincial military commander of P'yŏngan Province.[22] Meanwhile, the main government camp in Chŏngju had performed a sacrificial rite on March 27 at the Pavilion of the Great General (Wŏnsu-dae) near the walled town of Chŏngju, a historic place where Yi Sŏnggye, the founder of the Chosŏn dynasty, had defeated the Mongol army centuries earlier. The next day, another memorial service was carried out at the Altar of General Im (Im-changgun-dang) on a nearby mountain.[23] At these ceremonies, the officials in charge reported the treason of the rebels and prayed for help from various gods and spirits to win over the rebels and to cease all the hardships of the soldiers.

The rebels inside the walled town were effectively isolated, despite a few cases of secret communication with people on the outside, especially during the earlier stage of the government campaign. In the middle of March, there were reports that some people from Kwaksan and Kusŏng were clandestinely transporting food to the rebels at night.[24] Another report maintained that some residents of Chŏngju were spying on the government camp during the day and feeding the rebels at night.[25] The government was outraged at local residents for interfering with the thoroughness of the siege. But such outside help did not continue, and the rebels' situation deteriorated as time went on.

The rebels took over 2,500 *sŏm* of rice and 1,000 *sŏm* of other types of grain left in the district granaries to feed soldiers and seized 11,800 *yang* of cash from public funds to reward their soldiers and to purchase the goods they needed. According to the testimony of Yi Hyegap, who was captured on March 8 while fleeing the government round-up, having earlier assisted the rebels, there were 100 *sŏm* of salt and three hundred jars of soy sauce stored in various government storerooms in Chŏngju. There were also three hundred cows inside the walled town and six wells supplying water. Contributions from wealthy households in Chŏngju, made either voluntarily or forcibly, were also an important part of food supplies, as table 11 shows.[26]

The rebels inside the walled town tightly controlled their food reserves. In the beginning, every rebel soldier received 3 *toe* (1.8 liters) of either rice or hulled millet per day.[27] By mid-April, daily rations were reduced to 2 *toe* (1.2 liters) of millet, and runaway rebels began to report a serious shortage of food inside the town. A few days later, a captive testified that the rebels

TABLE 11. Material Contributions Made to the Rebel Camp in Chŏngju

Name	Amount of contribution
Hong Inch'ŏl (armory supervisor)	About 1,200–1,300 *sŏm* of rice
Yi Chonggi (merchant)	30 *sŏm* of beans
Yi Taech'ik (Yi Chonggi's brother)	Over 100 *sŏm* of rice
Kim Yŏhae	About 80 *sŏm* of rice
Yi Min (Kim Yŏhae's nephew)	About 80 *sŏm* of rice
Yi Yŏngdol	About 100 *sŏm* of rice and cows
Yi Komi	About 100 *sŏm* of rice and cows
Kim Ch'iyong	About 100 *sŏm* of rice and cows
Pak Munhyŏk	About 80 *sŏm* of rice and cows
Kim Naeyong	About 70 *sŏm* of rice
Sŏ Kyejo	About 70 *sŏm* of other types of grain

SOURCE: *Kwansŏ p'yŏngnallok*, 2: 514–19.

had consumed all the grain in the public granaries and had to beg for food from the local people. When the rich households could not supply food to the rebels any more, they had to look for food from even the poorest households. As a result, the poor hid what was left, and the price of foodstuffs skyrocketed.[28] Reflecting the pressing problem of food supplies, the rebels began to change their tactic from defense to offense. On the night of April 19, about five hundred rebels attacked the government camp under the command of the magistrate of Hamjong and inflicted more than eighty government casualties. The government was obviously unprepared for such a large-scale raid.[29]

The rebels launched many small- and large-scale attacks in order to break through the government encirclement. As time went on, however, the possibility of breaking out grew dim. On April 30, more than a thousand rebels attacked the government force commanded by Hŏ Hang, a militia commander from Ŭiju, who died in the battle. They attempted another major assault two days later, at the cost of hundreds of casualties. During this series of military engagements, hundreds of rebel soldiers were killed or captured. Some rebels simply fled during battle. Kim Sayong, the assistant supreme commander of the rebel army, died on May 2, and Hong Ch'onggak, a field commander, had been injured earlier. After the big loss at the May 2 battle, rebel morale evaporated.[30]

Interestingly, on May 3 and May 6, the rebels released 5 adult men, 45 children under ten years old, and 103 women who were residents of Chŏngju, Pakch'ŏn, and Kasan. These people reportedly had no relatives inside the town and took refuge inside the wall or accompanied the rebels when the rebels retreated to the town after the defeat at the battle of Pine Grove. The government was puzzled as to why the rebels drove these people outside the walls but concluded that they simply wanted to reduce the number of people they had to feed. Subsequently, the government commander released the women and children and had them return to their home villages.[31]

The shortage of food inside the walls became critical. By the middle of May, the rebels were peeling bark from the pine trees to eat.[32] Still, each person was given 2 *toe* (1.2 liters) of mixed rice and millet per day.[33] The ration was further reduced to 6 *hop* (0.36 liter) of rice mixed with malt for three days. According to another account, 5 *hop* (0.3 liter) of rice and malt was distributed at each meal, and all the livestock, such as chickens, pigs, and oxen, had been consumed.[34]

Rebel leaders tried to convince their troops that the Manchus were on the way to break up the government siege. The rebels brewed five jars of wine on February 26, reportedly for the purpose of greeting Manchu supporters.[35] On March 3, Hong Kyŏngnae showed an unconvinced rebel a letter from someone who was his superior—presumably the True and Genuine Chŏng— and told the rebel that Hong himself was only one of the commanders working for him.[36] On March 9, Hong dispatched secret messengers, Kim Samhong and Pak Chinbyŏk, to the border region to deliver his confidential letter to "the Manchu horse rider" (*ki homa ch'ullae in*), calling for urgent deployment of reinforcements.[37] In another record, the letter was addressed to "the military camp at Umo Pass," and Kim was instructed to locate "a general riding a white horse" (*paengma changgun*).[38] Such vague and ambiguous directions seem to corroborate the notion that a Manchu supporting force was nonexistent. At any rate, both agents were caught and the letter undelivered. Pak Chinbyŏk, one of the messengers, even testified that he had doubted the reality of Manchu reinforcements and had volunteered to become a messenger only to escape the rebel camp. In mid-May, the rebels stoutly declared that the Manchu force would arrive in Chŏngju on May 29.[39] Ironically, that was the day that the rebels were rounded up by the government.

THE REBELLION FAILS

Frustrated over its inability to take the rebel stronghold, the government finally devised a creative tactic to penetrate the wall—namely, to undermine it from below. Beginning May 13, the government dug tunnels, one beginning about 100 *po* (125 meters) from the Northern Commander's Pavilion inside the wall, and the other about 60 *po* (75 meters) away from the east gate of the wall, under the supervision of both government officials and militia leaders.[40] These were risky undertakings because the laboring soldiers were within shooting range of the rebel camps. A number of soldiers were indeed shot to death, and probably because of this the work from the east side was halted at least once and resumed later.[41]

Nonetheless, soldiers worked day and night on both tunnels, using long hoes to dig and willow baskets to transport the dirt. Each tunnel was about 4 *po* (5 meters) wide and 1 *chang* (2.08 meters) high. The dirt accumulated outside each tunnel like a mountain, and the government camp erected shields along the top of the manmade mountain to protect the laboring soldiers. By May 22, the northern tunnel reached 30 *po* (37.5 meters) from the wall, while the eastern one reached 50 *po* (62.5 meters) from the wall.

For their own protection, the rebels built a smaller-scale wall within the original wall.[42] They also discussed ways of interfering with the tunnel work by digging ground from their side. Then Hong Ch'onggak argued that the powder used for explosions, laid inside the tunnel, would not ignite, and that even if it did, the explosion would not carry its force forward but only backward, toward the government camp. He concluded that the government plan would only cause trouble to the government troops and that there was nothing to worry about. Persuaded by this theory, the rebels evidently gave up the idea, though they tried to deter the digging process by shooting arrows and muskets at the soldiers.[43] Approaching very close to the wall, the north tunnel hit a huge rock, while the east one met a coffin, but the diggers simply chose to go around them.[44]

By May 28, the north tunnel was finished, though the east one was still 6 to 7 *po* (7.5 to 8.75 meters) from the target spot. To prevent collapse, large wooden studs and thick, flat wood panels were knocked into place. At dawn the following day, a group of explosives experts, led by Kim Ch'iŏn, secretly entered the tunnel, placed five layers of straw mats under a reed mat, and positioned as much as 1,800 *kŭn* (about 1 ton) of gunpowder. One end of thick leather rope was buried in the middle of the gunpowder, and the other was placed right outside the tunnel. Then, to prevent the explosion from going toward the government side (as Hong Ch'onggak had predicted), the tunnel entrance was sealed with a combination of mud and rocks. The huge blast successfully demolished a part of the northern wall, letting more than eight thousand government troops march into the town. Thirsty for blood, they slaughtered the rebels at will. The rebel troops were frightened and overwhelmed by the government strike and succumbed to the raid quickly.[45]

Although a few rebels had escaped the town during the more than three months of resistance, most of them held together until the last day of the rebellion. Countless people were killed during the last battle, and among those captured, 1,917 of the 2,983 men in the town were decapitated, while 842 women and 224 boys less than ten years of age were spared. Hong Kyŏngnae himself was shot to death during the battle. His head was cut off and sent to the capital. Rebel leaders and commanders like Hong Ch'onggak, Yang Siwi, Kim Hyech'ŏl, Kim Idae, and Yun Ŏnsŏp were arrested and sent in carts to the capital for interrogation. Yi Hŭijŏ was reported missing, but later his head was presented by one of the militia commanders.[46] U Kunch'ik and Ch'oe Iryun managed to escape but were arrested a few days later.[47] Certainly more than three thousand stayed in the walled town until the last day of resistance, although we will never know the exact number. The number of those who held out testifies to the determination not only of the original rebels but of the peasants who joined the rebel army, whether voluntarily or by force.

It is clear that most rebel leaders either died in battle or were captured during the rebellion and put to death later. Charged with high treason (*moban taeyŏk*), their bodies were dismembered and displayed to the public to warn the people against any further commotion. Rebel leaders' families also suffered greatly. Usually their property was confiscated, their houses burned, and their close relatives either enslaved or banished to remote areas.[48] The investigation of all suspected participants and sympathizers lasted quite a while. By the end of August, there were about three hundred prisoners waiting to be sentenced. The number soon decreased to about a hundred, and the king ordered that all cases be resolved before October 24. The execution of eleven rebels on November 19 brought the investigation to an end.[49]

The government army also suffered great losses. Many soldiers died during the battles, but more were wounded or were victims of disease, cold, and hunger from exposure on the bare fields and hills under harsh weather conditions. According to the memorial stele erected in Chŏngju in 1814, the number of soldiers who died at the battles was either 348 or 425.[50] The number of deaths from other reasons is unknown. The relatives of those who died in battle were given compensation of 3 *yang* and 1 *p'il* of cotton cloth and an exemption from the military tax for one son for his lifetime. In addition, the miscellaneous household levy was waived for ten years, while all the debts incurred from official grain loans were written off. Those who died of illness during the campaign also received rewards, albeit to a lesser degree. For example, 1 *p'il* of cotton cloth as military tax and their annual household levy were waived. In some areas, their unpaid military taxes, grain loan, and loans from the people's fund were canceled.[51]

The commanders and military officers who earned merit during the campaign received material rewards as well as offices corresponding to their merit and status. The soldiers mobilized for the counterrebel campaign were also rewarded according to their merit. In Sunch'ŏn, those who stayed at the front and killed rebels received rice and cotton cloth, plus exemption from the military and other miscellaneous taxes for ten years. Others of lesser merit were given rice and cotton cloth or received a tax exemption for seven years.[52]

How did contemporaries view the 1812 rebellion in the northwestern region? The government concluded that the main causes of the rebellion were the corruption of officials and arbitrary taxation at a time when the peasants were stricken by disease and famine. For example, in the memorial presented by Im Pok, third censor of the Office of the Censor General (Saganwŏn Hŏn-nap, Sr. 5), on February 7, 1812, Im argued that the corruption and avarice of local magistrates and clerks had caused the rebellion. Thus a fair management of personnel affairs and employing upright persons in local administration were the most urgent things to be done to stabilize the countryside.[53] A few days later, An Sangmuk, fourth censor of the Office of the Censor General (Saganwŏn Chŏngŏn, Sr. 6), also mentioned that corruption and heavy taxation had driven the people into extreme difficulty, which had ultimately led them to rebel.[54] Yi Kwangmun, sixth counselor of the Office of Special Counselors (Hongmun'gwan Such'an, Sr. 6), seconded An's and Im's opinions by citing Zhu Xi's view that the only reason rebels could overthrow a country would be poverty. Consequently, Yi suggested that the government needed to take action to relieve the hunger even if it were short of funds.[55]

In response to such Confucian diagnosis of the rebellion, the king prohibited ad hoc taxes until there was a good harvest, canceled the accumulated interest on official grain loans, and reduced the military support tax rate during and after the rebellion. At the same time, he ordered relief grain distributed to sustain the peasants and to win peasant support after the rebellion was suppressed. In addition, some officials had been accused both of failure to detect the rebellion in advance and of corruption. The censorate in particular criticized the corruption of Yi Haesŭng, army inspector of Anju military headquarters, and Yi Haeu, provincial military commander of P'yŏngan Province. Yi Haeu had profited by making usurious loans and dunning people for the payment of debts and interest, by collecting bribes, and by taking advantage of his personal relationship with power holders in the central government.[56] Yi Haesŭng was a close relative of Yi Haeu and had been greedy from the beginning. When he had held a post in Hamgyŏng Province, he had lived off the poor and manipulated the grain loan documents. He continued to take bribes, sell offices, and practice usury when he held office in P'yŏngyang. He became worse after he took the office of army inspector.[57] These two people had held the highest offices at the military headquarters in Anju, just across from where the rebellion broke out, and had been responsible for maintaining public peace and order. Not only had they been unable to detect the rebels in advance, but they had been too busy enriching themselves while the people suffered from famine.

Meanwhile one particular court official had more critical insight into the cause of the rebellion. In a memorial submitted on March 24, 1812, O Yŏnsang, fourth deputy commander of Five Military Commands (Owi Puhogun), suggested holding a special provincial examination for the scholars of the northwestern province in order to assuage their discontent.[58] The special provincial examination was one of the exams that was held once only, at the king's special order. Those who passed could sit for the final stage of examination held in Seoul without taking other preliminary examinations. In P'yŏngan Province, the provincial examination had been first held in 1643, during the reign of King Injo, right after the Manchu invasions of 1636, and it had then become the custom to institute the provincial examination every ten years. According to O Yŏnsang, the provincial examination had not been held for a long time, which the scholars of the area deplored. Despite O's recommendation, the special provincial examination was not held until three years later, in 1815, showing court's insensitivity to the issue.[59] Much worse, the reforms in any of the court's discriminatory promotion screening system came very slowly. Only in 1831 was Paek Chŏnggŏl, second son of Paek Kyŏnghae, unprecedentedly assigned to the Office of Diplomatic Correspondence after passing the *munkwa*. Social contempt against people from P'yŏngan Province apparently continued into the early twentieth century.[60]

8 Nation, Class, and Region in the Study
of the Hong Kyŏngnae Rebellion

Divergent perspectives on the 1812 rebellion, and its leader Hong Kyŏngnae, have surfaced ever since the rebellion was put down, showing the immense impact that this event has had on Korean history and culture. Whether in the popular imagination or in scholarly analysis, the rebellion has been remembered and presented in ways that reveal historical and cultural conditions in Korea since 1812. The colonization, division, and democratization of Korea in the twentieth century cast a certain shadow on the scholarly interpretation as well as popular consumption of this episode—a shadow that has generally obscured the regional origin of the rebellion.

In the years immediately following the rebellion, rumors that Hong Kyŏngnae had not died—or that he was still living on an island, as historical heroes and mystics were pictured in popular imagery of the late Chosŏn period—were widespread and inspired subsequent antidynastic conspiracies, such as the one by Yi Inha and others that was aborted in 1817.[1] In contrast to popular deification of Hong, two *kasa* (a long vernacular verse form), composed immediately after the rebellion by someone who participated in the counterrebel campaign, viewed the rebellion as treason and emphasized its traumas.[2] And Cho Susam (1762–1849), a commoner poet who happened to witness the rebellion because he was in the area on his way back from China, wrote a series of poems about the rebellion in classical Chinese. His poems convey a mixed assessment. Though he saw the event as an unacceptable subversion, he was also critical of official corruption and arbitrary taxation and, more penetratingly, of regional discrimination.[3] The 1861 publication of *Sinmirok* (A Story of the *Sinmi* Year), a vernacular Korean fiction based on the rebellion, by a private publisher in Seoul, reveals the high profile this event occupied in people's minds, although it lacks structure and a coherent story line. Created for popular consumption, it simply highlights the main characters' bravery.[4]

THE INDIGENOUS PROGRESSIVE REVOLUTIONARY TRADITION VERSUS DYNASTIC DECLINE

A strikingly different perspective on Hong Kyŏngnae and the rebellion, which further separated the issue of regional discrimination from the incident, began to emerge in the twentieth century under colonial rule (1910–45). The first of these, the *Hong Kyŏngnae silgi* (A Tale of Hong Kyŏngnae), appeared in 1917 as a Korean publication. Its author, Nam'ak-chuin (Ch'oe Namsŏn? 1890–1957), regards the rebellion as a missed opportunity to destroy the corrupt dynasty, spread the "great principle" (*taeŭi*), and bring "public goods" (*kongni*) to the world, depicting Hong Kyŏngnae as an unusually endowed person although much of the narrative is devoted to describing battles from the government perspective.[5] Examples of Hong framed as a revolutionary leader became abundant in the 1920s and 1930s. A nationalist intellectual discourse to seek the cause of Chosŏn's decline and colonization, as well as to find "national" inspiration for resistance against colonial rule, must have motivated intellectuals to highlight a historical figure like Hong. One of the earliest cases is an article that appeared in the monthly journal *Kaebyŏk* (Creation) in 1920. Defining Chosŏn as an autocratic state, the author Yi Tonhwa (Paektu-sanin, 1884–?) argues that the rebellion was caused by regional discrimination in terms of official employment—a "political slavery" (*chŏngch'ijŏk noye saenghwal*). He states that he wants to introduce Hong to people because he admires Hong's heroic qualities and the "historical energy" (*yŏksajŏk hwalgi*) emanating from his movement.[6] This article was followed by a book by An Hwak (1886–1946), who proclaims that the rebellion was a revolutionary movement that advocated people's rights.[7] In a similar fashion, Mun Ilp'yŏng (1888–1936) declares that the rebellion was the herald of a people's revolution (*minjung hyŏngmyŏng ŭi sŏn'gu*) and that Hong Kyŏngnae took up armed struggle to demolish yangban society, root and branch.[8] Meanwhile, Hyŏn Sangyun's novel *Hong Kyŏngnae chŏn* (Story of Hong Kyŏngnae), serialized in the *Tonga ilbo* (Tonga Daily) in 1931, also adopts this line of nationalist discourse, narrates the whole event from the side of the rebels, and concludes that the rebellion was an antidynastic social movement.[9]

This attempt to write "a truly national history, the story of the origins and struggle for survival of the Korean nation" as an effort to create a new, modern national identity began to emerge as a part of broad intellectual movement known as the Korean enlightenment at the turn of the twentieth century.[10] Breaking away from traditional Confucian historiography in which sinification and Confucian morality were the primary yardsticks for measuring the level of civilization, historians such as Pak Ŭnsik (1859–1925), Sin Ch'aeho (1880–1936), and Ch'oe Namsŏn (1890–1957) stress unique, autonomous development of the Korean nation. During a period of colonial oppression, scholars and writers in this camp tried to appropriate historical events such as the Hong Kyŏngnae Rebellion to create an indigenous, modern "revolutionary tradition and spirit" that might be of use against the Japanese.[11]

While Korean colonial-period scholars were finding in the Hong Kyŏngnae Rebellion an indigenous and progressive revolutionary tradition, Japanese historians of Korea tended to find decline and stagnation that implicitly justified their takeover of Korea. The first scholarly analysis of the rebellion was written in the 1930s by a Japanese scholar, Oda Shōgo (1871–?). He sees the rebellion as a phenomenon of dynastic disintegration caused by longstanding political strife. He emphasizes the harmful impact of factional strife and Hong Kyŏngnae's personal failure to advance through the civil service examination as prime causes of the rebellion.[12] He explores the political frustration of the elite of P'yŏngan Province who did not have the opportunity to advance into the higher offices at court as a possible cause, but brushes away the issue because he thinks that regional discrimination was not an established court policy and that the major reason for the obstacle to bureaucratic advancement for P'yŏngan people was their lack of strong ties with dominant factions that would have supported their employment.[13]

CLASS STRUGGLE AS THE DRIVING FORCE OF REBELLION

Postwar studies in North and South Korea have conceptualized Korean history primarily in terms of progress and linear development, with class struggle as the main driving force of historical change. Eschewing the notion of an Asiatic mode of production, most studies adopt Stalinist application of Marx's theory of historical interpretation that takes the development of the West as universal. The research of Hong Hŭiyu from North Korea, who not only follows the official position of North Korean historiography but has inherited the spirit of popular nationalist discourse from the colonial period, is one example. He explains that the basic force that caused the rebellion was extreme class conflict between landlords and peasants, which was the result of economic changes during the late Chosŏn dynasty. He highlights the participation of the urban poor, day laborers, artisans, miners, and vagrants who were driven off their farmland by onerous taxation and landlord exploitation. According to Hong, the miners and artisans were the forerunner of the laboring class in an emerging capitalist society. Hong concludes that because they were exploited by both the "feudal" government and the "capitalist class," they were the most active participants in the struggle.[14]

Chŏng Sŏkchong, who has conducted the most representative study about the Hong Kyŏngnae Rebellion in South Korea, argues that the leaders of the rebellion were entrepreneurial peasants (*kyŏngyŏnghyŏng punong*) who bought offices in the local yangban and military bureaus with their accumulated wealth. Chŏng's entrepreneurial peasant replaces Hong Hŭiyu's poorest class as the leading actor in rural conflict. In other words, the rebellion was the armed struggle of the intermediate peasant class of entrepreneurial peasants against the "feudal" landlord class who maintained close connections with the government. Therefore, these peasants had to remove the central government in order to realize their class interests, according to Chŏng.[15]

Research on the Hong Kyŏngnae Rebellion and other nineteenth-century popular movements has expanded greatly since 1980. Antiauthoritarian government movements from below, under the rubric of the *minjung* (mass) movement in the 1980s in South Korea, have stimulated research in which historians have looked for historical experiences of collective movements from below, just as intellectuals under colonial rule tried to trace the same. Spurred by the *minjung* perspective, an avalanche of works has been published in the spirit of discovering and inheriting the tradition of resistance from below against the corrupt, authoritarian, and exploitative ruling class.[16] Relying on previous and contemporary research on late Chosŏn social and economic history, these works have certainly enhanced our understanding of the social structure, tax administration, and power relations at the local level. Most, however, are still based on modernist and teleological interpretations of history. In studying the Hong Kyŏngnae Rebellion in particular, scholars have continued to rely on the theory of the class struggle of the poor and landless peasant against the landlord, even though this rebellion was planned and led by members of the local elite to claim their legitimate social, economic, and political space—as illustrated by the rebels' prime goal of establishing a new dynasty. An example comes from O Such'ang's works on the 1812 rebellion and the regional history of P'yŏngan Province. Despite his meticulous investigation of the social, political, and economic history of the region, he aims to detect a new social group arising from the underprivileged that not only provided leadership in resistance movements but became the key force in transforming Korea into a modern society—a teleological position that sees history primarily in terms of progress and linear development.

It is clear that the Marxist perspective, which is based on the experience of the West, cannot and should not be directly applied to Korea, whose historical experience is quite different. The theory of class struggle is no longer the best framework for explaining the causes of revolution and rebellion even in world history. Recently, the classic argument about the English and French revolutions—namely, that a capitalist class rose up against feudal restrictions—has been discredited by many scholars. New research has revealed that some members of the commercial classes were on the side of the monarch and that some feudal noblemen actively joined the revolutionaries.[17] In Chinese historiography, the class struggle argument has been challenged by several scholars. A classic study of Chinese communists' ideology and their historiography by James P. Harrison sheds light on how the historiography of peasant movements has been reconstructed by party policies to stress the progressiveness of the class struggle as the primary force of historical evolution.[18] Susan Naquin, who has studied millenarian movements of the late eighteenth and early nineteenth century in China, argues that the composition of rebel leadership was very diverse and that class interests had little to do with causing rebellion.[19] Daniel Little has also pointed out that—though exploitation took place through rents, interest rates, taxation, and so on—in many cases of social conflict in rural China, nonclass factors such as religion, intervillage conflict, and horizontal social organization (such as kinship and secret societies) played important roles.[20]

It is difficult to rely solely on the idea of class struggle to explain the causes of the 1812 rebellion and the general direction of Korean history from premodern to modern capitalist society. Certainly some social and economic changes toward a more commercialized society had taken place during the late Chosŏn dynasty. Yet economic development in the late Chosŏn consisted basically of slow progress, not a major transformation of the economy. Class differentiation and subsequent class conflict were not acute enough to invite class struggle in traditional Korean peasant society. Furthermore, the mechanisms of social and economic control based on the traditional value system were still holding society fairly tightly.[21]

Empirically speaking, almost no primary sources indicate that members of the oppressed classes, including tenants and landless laborers, used violence against their superiors, such as landlords, in the course of the Hong Kyŏngnae Rebellion. In fact, it was not poor peasants but those who were in positions of local leadership who organized the rebellion. And these local elite were not entrepreneurial farmers who had obtained positions at the local yangban and military bureaus through social upward mobility, as Chŏng Sŏkchong schematizes. They were also different from O Such'ang's heroes—namely, "defiant intellectuals" (*chŏhang chisigin*) and "military mischiefs" (*changsa-ch'ŭng*)— who arguably emerged from economically deprived and socially low-status groups.[22] Although Hong Kyŏngnae, U Kunch'ik, Yi Hŭijŏ, and some of rebel commanders could be categorized as such, the main energy for the rebellion originated from marginalized local elite of the Ch'ŏngbuk region and the problems of regional discrimination.

As a few previous works propose, this study finds the participation of merchants in the Hong Kyŏngnae Rebellion to be a unique phenomenon in the history of rebellions in Korea.[23] Being located along the route to China, the region offered many trade opportunities, both domestic and foreign. Commercial and mining activities in the area greatly expanded in the late Chosŏn. This promoted the growth of the merchant class, whose members then sought to enhance their social standing by earning more prestigious positions, usually military posts in the local military administration bureau. This enhanced status in turn facilitated their trade activities and their links to the established local elite. Various regulations, often arbitrary, and government efforts to tighten its reign over commerce and industry were anathema to this growing group and probably motivated them to join the rebellion. Though some merchants in the area provided military services and material support to the rebels, they were subject to the rebel leadership and did not act as an interest group to improve their financial condition or social standing. Thus, it is hardly justifiable to see merchants as a vanguard revolutionary social force, although the burgeoning of merchant participation in any social and political process in Korean history requires further scholarly attention considering the important role that merchants played in the modern transformation of the West.[24]

REGIONAL DISCRIMINATION AND CENTER/PERIPHERY RELATIONS IN THE LATE CHOSŎN

Not class, but the social and political discrimination that the P'yŏngan residents faced in the late Chosŏn is the most persuasive explanation for the rebellion. It is true that political discrimination affected only those who passed the state examinations, those who were qualified to receive official appointments in the central bureaucracy by other means, and the members of their immediate families. Yet the prejudice against people from P'yŏngan Province for being militaristic and culturally backward was widespread, so that they were also socially demeaned in their everyday encounters with others. The rebels saw the issue of such social and political discrimination as a regional problem that stigmatized the whole population of the region. The popular imagery of a condemned region offered a strong motivation for its local elite to join the rebellion and also gave ideological justification to the mobilization of many people of different statuses under the same banner. Thus the rebels—both leaders and rank-and-file soldiers—identified themselves as northerners rather than as representatives of any one economic class or social status group. This collective identity, which crisscrossed class and social status boundaries, derived from the central government's discrimination against men from P'yŏngan Province in its recruitment of regular officials and from society's accompanying bias against them.

The reasons people of P'yŏngan Province felt so strongly about regional discrimination can be clearly understood when we consider the social and economic dynamics of this region and its relation to the center. Economic recovery and subsequent growth after the Manchu invasions, and the stabilization of diplomatic relations with the Qing from the late seventeenth century on, produced resources that enabled the local elite to practice Confucian culture and participate in the state examination system. The growth of these economic and cultural capabilities in the late Chosŏn is reflected in the local elite's increasingly articulate expressions of regional identity and their strong demands for proper space in central politics. The more affluent they became and the more successful they were in the *munkwa*, the more frustration they felt over the unfair social and political treatment they received from the center.

Another frustration in terms of state-society relations originated from escalating state intervention in previously autonomous local affairs and local finance. By the late eighteenth century, local control of local resources had become the crucial point of local politics as the state strove to integrate provincial funds into the center, which must have put extra pressure on local tax administrations and public loan operations. More directly, state interference in the management of previously autonomous local yangban associations, in the form of selling memberships in them as a means for fundraising, must have troubled established local elites. Here, I agree with Theda Skocpol, who views the state as an autonomous actor, and with Anders Karlsson, who emphasizes that changing relations between the center and the periphery, especially in terms of financial administration, often provoke political conflict.[25] Nonetheless, changes in resource extraction by the center were not the primary cause for the rebellion, even though they did aggravate the regional elite's discontent. According to Karlsson, social and economic developments in the eighteenth century brought changes in the character and role of central power and its relationship to local society. He argues that the stability of Chosŏn was based on the balance between centralization and local autonomy and that the stronger influence and heavier presence of central power in the late Chosŏn period over the provinces and their financial administration caused local discontent. He concludes that the rebellion was a reaction to this development and in that sense was a defensive protest claiming customary rights of local leaders to control both work at the district offices and management of the district's resources. However, Karlsson's "macro-level" finding of the conflict between central and local power as the source of the rebellion does not resonate with the extensive "micro-level" narratives. Simply put, participants of the rebellion did not leave clear evidence that the intensified presence of the state in local affairs and finance was the prime motivation for them to rise up against the existing rule.[26]

THE ROLE OF GEOMANCY AND THE MANDATE OF HEAVEN IN THE REBELLION

In her comparative study of social revolutions, Skocpol argues that ideology serves to unify people from diverse particularistic backgrounds against old regimes and to mobilize the masses for political struggles and activities.[27] Did ideology serve this function in the Hong Kyŏngnae Rebellion? The ideology of dynastic change based on geomancy was closely intertwined with the Confucian idea of challenging the Mandate of Heaven. In P'yŏngan Province these ideas were especially instrumental in mobilizing the rebel leadership, in enlisting mass support, in unifying people from diverse particularistic backgrounds, and in legitimizing their antidynastic venture.

Geomancy has long played an important role in Korean history, as both a beneficial and harmful force for the rulers and the ruled alike. During the Chosŏn dynasty, a prophetic belief in dynastic change, supported by geomantic theories, was widespread among the populace and was frequently used by recalcitrants and insurgents to legitimize their antidynastic movements. The same prophetic belief found fertile ground in which to flourish in P'yŏngan Province, where people were already aggrieved over their social and economic difficulties and over the regional discrimination they suffered at the hands of the central government.

The tradition of prophetic belief in Korea was different from the millenarianism found in China and Europe. In contrast to the White Lotus movements in contemporary China, in particular, there was no god to worship or any formation of a religious community in Korean prophetic belief. The utopia that Korean believers sought was to be realized in this world, by establishing a new dynasty under the rule of a new royal family. In addition, there was no concept of personal salvation or hope for eternal life, since the historical view among Koreans in the prophetic tradition was basically cyclical and worldly. This absence of any formation of a religious community meant that prophetic belief in Korea offered no concrete organizational foundation for the rebellion. Nevertheless, its message of saving people from all the misery of the world and bringing about harmony and order by establishing a new dynasty was powerful enough to earn the support of the rural population.

The spread within the north of prophetic ideology and practices (such as geomancy and the occult arts) among people of various social statuses (both elite and nonelite) tells us at least two things about the condition of P'yŏngan society. First, it is the instability of a society (and resulting uncertainty about the future) that makes people seek such unconventional resolutions. Second, financial conditions in the north were such that a certain group of people could afford geomantic services even while many others were dying of hunger and disease. When geomantic practices were not socially and politically restrained on a consistent basis, and when the state declined to soothe general grievances among the population, it is not surprising that disgruntled members of society relied on an alternative ideology as a way to vent their discontent and fulfill individual wishes that they could not accomplish by conventional means. And in fact, the gap between the Confucian idea of the Mandate of Heaven and the popular belief in dynastic change inscribed in prophetic texts was not too wide and rather easy to cross.

Yet prophetic belief in dynastic change, and even the issue of regional discrimination, did not hold all the people of the region together when rebellion broke out, especially after the rebels were on defensive. In the end, Confucian legitimation of popular revolt as a sign of the departure of the Mandate of Heaven was not very effective in attracting support from a broad spectrum of either the masses or the elite. The rebels were full of fighting spirit at the outset and believed that victory was assured because they had a determined leadership, a tangible goal that would relieve their suffering, and the promise from their leaders of material rewards. Their confidence in their cause and in their ultimate success fell apart, however, when their leaders split over strategy, when material resources in the rebel camp ran short, when the government got the upper hand in terms of military power, and when collaborators in the region breached their pledges of loyalty and deserted to the government's side.

Besides all this, the rebels erred by failing to put forward a grand vision of social reform that could have earned the support of marginalized elites and other elements of society in other regions. As Joseph W. Escherick has remarked, rebellious and even revolutionary activity in China tended to base itself, in its earliest stages, on the preexisting customs, loyalties, and networks of the old society. Yet it is equally clear that any movement that fails to transcend those parochial loyalties is doomed to failure.[28] In 1812, the ideology of rectification of the central government's regional discrimination against P'yŏngan Province mobilized enough support to garner initial success. At the same time, however, the local nature of this grievance gravely undermined the possibility of obtaining support from a wider circle of the discontented population beyond regional boundaries.

REBELLION AND ITS IMPLICATIONS

The marginalization of local elites was a nationwide trend that went hand in hand with the compartmentalization of regions in the Chosŏn period. Each region formed its own almost exclusive cultural enclave, separated by marriage networks, academic tradition, political orientation, regional history, and so forth. Interregional networks and organizations, especially ones that crossed the invisible boundaries between north and south, did not form. Thus, when one region rebelled because of resentments felt only by the residents of that region, other regions naturally supported the cause of the center, from which their status and privilege emanated and to which their loyalty belonged, rather than a fellow region that they had almost nothing to do with. Although each region (except Seoul and its vicinity) had become a victim of political marginalization through various exclusionary political processes by the early nineteenth century, a united front against the ruling dynasty and its allies at the center did not emerge. This demonstrates the high degree of ideological and cultural integration of Chosŏn social and political structure with its central elite, whose authority and legitimacy remained, not surprisingly, at the center itself.

Indeed, the north's regional resentment did not even bond all the elements within the region itself. The political choice of the *munkwa* passers and other members of the local elite who owed their status to the center (and who were hence supposed to be bastions of the state ideology of loyalty to the throne) graphically testifies to the strength and durability of the state structure and ideology. For a successful collective movement, ideological and social justification that would surpass regional divisions and unify people across the narrow regional spatial boundaries was necessary. The rebellion's failure to attract members of the highest social stratum (i.e., the *munkwa* passers and other successful members of the local elite), who were the key to unlocking the tight social networks in local society, meant that this group threw its support to the government, consequently dealing the rebel camp a mortal blow.[29]

In responding to the rebellion, state officials downplayed its structural and institutional causes and presented it as nothing but a revolt of poor and ignorant peasants who had been deceived by a few treacherous ne'er-do-wells. Yet it was not because the central court underestimated the scope of the rebellion but because of the incompetence of the local and provincial military system that the rebels sustained their struggle longer than the court officials wished. Indeed, the military exigencies created by the rebellion inadvertently revealed the debility of the Chosŏn military system in terms of mobilization, logistics, and command structure. The fact that a small band of a few hundred men took over a number of district offices in a few days without any military opposition—and that the provincial government took ten days to put together the first major military engagement—shows that the local and provincial military system could not defend the area against local armed disturbances. The rebel army grew rapidly in size while the government had difficulty assembling troops based on outdated peasant military rosters. The system of periodic military training had become loose, and thus soldiers were not properly trained. There were neither permanent separate military establishments in the local area nor professional commanders who were conversant with military affairs. This inherent weakness in the military system cost the government a great deal in suppressing the rebellion, which could otherwise have been put down at the time of its initial attacks, since it was quite small in scale in the beginning.

These shortcomings made the state greatly dependent on voluntary assistance from the local area that was in trouble. The government solicited local yangban to provide leadership in defeating the rebels and praised the role played by militia leaders in the counterrebel campaign. Responses to the court's appeal were diverse. A few acted promptly to join the militias, while others changed sides; many others remained undecided until the later stage of the rebellion. The opportunism of local yangban was revealed in the increasing numbers of militias and increasingly frequent material contributions to government troops as the rebellion drew to an end. This, too, reflected the complex social and political conditions of local society, in which preexisting internal competition, division, and conflict marked the behavior of the marginalized local yangban.

In nineteenth-century China, the White Lotus and Taiping rebellions were destroyed not by centrally controlled imperial forces but by locally recruited irregular forces led by the local elite, as well as by provincial armies organized by governors-general and governors of provinces. Similarly, the government pacification campaign during the Hong Kyŏngnae Rebellion relied heavily on the militias and material support organized by the local elite. In China, the realignment of military power from the center to the provinces was accompanied by devolution of power to the local elite in other spheres of local administration, such as tax collection and local police. The militarization of the 1840s and 1850s then eventually caused the disintegration of the traditional elite, which, by virtue of its undiminished community influence, its tradition of orthodox learning, and its ethic of administrative service, had made possible the long-term stability of Chinese society.[30] In Korea, militarization of the local elite played an important role in the pacification campaign but was put under the control of government commanders both formally and practically. Furthermore, the local elite in Korea did not hold onto their military function after the rebellion was put down, nor did they take over any power from the court in a way that would have contributed to the disintegration of the state structure. Rather, they remained within the status quo, albeit with enhanced social and political standing, for the court's award of titles and offices confirmed their power and prestige in local society. In the end, however, the state's practice of mobilizing the private sector and its resultant success in ending such domestic disturbances did not motivate the central government to reform its military system, which remained ineffective in coping with both domestic and external military challenges in the latter half of the nineteenth century.

The 1812 rebellion had a number of consequences for elites in the Ch'ŏngbuk region. Above all, the failure of the rebellion meant the disappearance of those regional elite who had supported the rebellion, and thus (temporary) removal of intra-elite competition. At the same time, it meant the rise of the progovernment elite after the rebellion. After the fighting was over, the court bestowed handsome material and political rewards on those who had made politically correct decisions by volunteering for military service and/or making financial contributions to the government pacification campaign. Thus the institution of rewards and punishments (a legalistic tactic adopted by the bureaucratic model of state that Confucians had chosen to serve since the Chinese Han dynasty) not only enabled the Chosŏn dynasty to continue without carrying out major reforms but also functioned to confirm the privileged status of local yangban in their own communities. As a result, the progovernment regional elite came to prosper both financially (because of the tax exemptions they received as rewards for their contributions to the government campaign) and socially (because of the privileges and enhanced prestige that accompanied their new offices, ranks, and titles). The increasing numbers of regional elite who passed the *munkwa* exams after the rebellion up until the *munkwa* was abolished in 1894 are also evidence of this group's well-being.[31] The court's "humane policies" of giving out generous tax breaks apparently prevented further serious challenges to the dynasty from the P'yŏngan population, which remained rather silent during the 1862 rebellions and the Tonghak rebellions of 1894–95.[32]

As Daniel Little points out, one grand theory may not capture the complexity involved in the making of popular rebellion; rather, we must recognize the multiple causes at work in such phenomena.[33] From multidimensional investigation of the event of 1812, the present study finds that the rebellion was an explosion of accumulated discontent harbored by the upper layers of rural population against the state rather than a class struggle launched by the bottom layers of society. It also identifies the importance of subversiveness imbedded in popular beliefs in geomancy and the Mandate of Heaven. Although I emphasize the regional factor greatly, I do not intend to single it out as the only cause of this rebellion. As we have seen, a number of other ingredients shaped the unique history of the northern region and of the people living there, its culture, its relation to the center, and the consequent development of this popular movement at that moment in time. Above all, I have tried to present views from the local level rather than those from the center, in the hope of rescuing local history from nation- and class-dominated historiography and because regional history, culture, and identity are critical elements in making history.[34]

Primary Sources and Methodology

All information vis-à-vis civil service examination degree-holders (*munkwa, saengwŏn,* and *chinsa*) and their immediate family members (such as their fathers, grandfathers, maternal grandfathers, and brothers) comes from the following online resources: *The Wagner and Song Munkwa Roster of the Chosŏn Dynasty,* compiled and annotated by Edward W. Wagner and Song Chunho, made available by Dongbang Media at http://www.koreaa2z.com/munkwa/; and *Sama pangmok,* compiled by Chŏngsin munhwa yŏn'guwŏn, made available by Dongbang Media at http://www.koreaa2z.com/sama1/.

The 1812 rebellion is well documented. The voices of participants were preserved in criminal depositions recorded by interrogating local officials, whose investigations were reported to upper-level government offices and subsequently filed in government archives. These voluminous depositions, along with daily reports of battlefield and military camp proceedings, were photocopied and reprinted as multivolume sets, which makes access to the material very easy. Two such sets of five volumes each are available, entitled *Kwansŏ p'yŏngnallok* (The Record of the Pacification Campaign of the Hong Kyŏngnae Rebellion) and *Han'guk minjung undongsa charyo taegye; 1811–1812 nyŏn ŭi nongmin chŏnjaeng p'yŏn* (A Collection of Primary Sources in the History of the People's Movement in Korea; the Peasant War of 1811–1812). These interrogations took place in the military camps in Chŏngju and nearby district offices as soon as rebel sympathizers were captured during the four-month-long campaign. A number of rebel leaders were sent to the capital for further investigations and a final verdict. Their testimonies are invaluable in reconstructing the rebellion in detail. Individual depositions also supply unintended information on the lives of ordinary people—information unrelated to the rebellion itself—because people often talked about their occupations, economic conditions, family relations, and their concerns in their daily lives.

One source of this type of official compilation that has been newly discovered and incorporated in this study is the *P'yŏngsŏ ponmal* (The Essence and Branch of Pacifying P'yŏngan Province), one volume in manuscript form from the Asami Collection at the University of California at Berkeley, thanks to the assistance of Korean librarian Mr. Chang Jaeyong. Although the compiler(s) are unknown, they must have had a position of record keeping at the court, for the manuscript contains many records concerning the court's daily business that are not necessarily related to the rebellion at all. In this sense, this material is distinctive from other similar compilations, such as the *Kwansŏ p'yŏngnallok* and *Sunmuyŏng tŭngnok* (The Records of the Circuit Pacification Army Headquarters), which do not usually include items unrelated to the rebellion. This surviving volume of almost 275 double-leaved pages, however, is only a part of the whole. Because this volume ends with the entry of the twenty-ninth day of the second lunar month of 1812 (1812.2.29), covering a little more than one-half of the whole length of the rebellion, it is reasonable to suppose that the original compilation may have comprised at least two volumes.[1]

In addition to these records collected and compiled by the various levels of government offices, personal accounts in the forms of diaries by men who were directly involved in the rebellion or who happened to be in the area provide further views of the event. An example of the former is the *Chinjung ilgi* (A Diary at the Military Camp), probably written by Hyŏn Inbok, one of the militia leaders from Chŏngju.[2] The *Sŏjŏng ilgi* (Records of the Pacification Campaign in P'yŏngan Province), written by Pang Ujŏng, a lieutenant (Ch'ogwan) of the army dispatched by the central government to put down the rebellion, is another example. A third-person perspective appears in the diary *Ilsŭng* (A Daily Record), left by Kang Hŭiyŏng (1796–?), who was residing in Suan, Hwanghae Province, where his father was district magistrate at the time of the rebellion, and who recorded what he heard about the uprising.[3] Although he was not in the area directly affected by the event, his diary describes the local conditions of an area close to the rebel-occupied region, especially recruitment of local troops to shore up defenses and the disarray of local order. Paek Kyŏnghae (1765–1842), a member of the yangban elite from Chŏngju and the inspector of P'yŏngan Province at the time of the rebellion, kept a diary throughout his life; the portion during the rebellion is separately named *Ch'angsang ilgi* (Diary in the Vortex of Chaos) and is preserved in his collected works. His record does not convey anything particularly different from information found in other sources, except that he criticizes the undisciplined behavior of the government troops.

Genealogies and gazetteers, mostly compiled and published after the late nineteenth century, are helpful in reconstructing the social and cultural history of P'yŏngan Province during the Chosŏn dynasty. The reliability of genealogies has been questioned by a number of scholars because of what is presumed to have been increasingly widespread fabrication of genealogical records, especially from the nineteenth century. The authenticity of genealogies compiled by families of northern origin has been totally discredited, probably because contemporary scholars assume that there were no yangban in the northern region.[4] In this work, I argue that the lifestyle, culture, and values that the northern elite upheld in the late Chosŏn were no different from those of the southern yangban. The compilation of genealogies was a part of yangban culture that tried to illuminate the social origins of yangban and preserve their privileges as members of the ruling elite; and the northern elite did compile their genealogies with the same purpose and extreme care. Thus I regard northern genealogies as highly usable primary sources, relying on Song Chunho's argument that the fabrication of genealogy did not and could not take place widely, both because each descent group must have been very apprehensive about preserving its reputation and because any forgery would be disclosed in the tightly knit yangban society.[5]

Indeed, northern yangban descent groups put extra effort into authenticating their entries. For example, the prologue of the 1827 edition genealogy of the Hadong Chŏng of Ch'ŏlsan comments that the genealogy begins with Chŏng Lim, the early Chosŏn ancestor who first established his residence in Ch'ŏlsan, even though one of their relatives had found evidence in 1798 that could connect Chŏng Lim with the southern branch of the Hadong Chŏng. The author of the prologue remarks that he would rather not take advantage of that piece of evidence because it did not come from authentic published records. This comment testifies to how prudent the compilers were in terms of cross-examining the evidence, despite their strong wish to be hooked up with the southern branches.[6] In addition, the prominent ancestors (*hyŏnjo*) that each northern yangban descent group claimed had first resided in the area were not really major figures in Chosŏn history but had only held mid- to low-level posts in the central bureaucracy, nor did the early Chosŏn figures recorded in the northern genealogies hold any significant positions in the central bureaucracy. It was probably true that the northern elite were not regarded as equal in social status to their southern counterparts in the late Chosŏn, but they did think of themselves as equal participants in yangban culture and practices. Thus they must have tried to make a clear distinction between their origin and that of other status groups and no doubt wanted to preserve their integrity in their own regional sphere as well.[7]

One popular source, the *Hong Kyŏngnae*, often used by scholars (beginning with Oda Shōgo) in discussing Hong Kyŏngnae's personal history and qualities, requires critical evaluation. Written in classical Chinese, the *Hong Kyŏngnae* is more like a fiction based on this particular historical event. Yi Usŏng and Im Hyŏngt'aek speculate that this novel was written during the period of the patriotic enlightenment movement (*aeguk kyemong-ki*, 1900s), considering its wording and grammatical style.[8] However, the content of this novel is almost identical to the *Hong Kyŏngnae imsin saryak* (A Short History of Hong Kyŏngnae in 1812). The *Hong Kyŏngnae imsin saryak* is an addendum to the *Sok choya chipyo* (The Recapitulated History in and out of the Court, Supplementary Edition), *kwŏn* 12, compiled by Chang Suyŏng, with a preface by Yi Chŏnggu and handwritten copy in 1932. Hyŏn Sangyun (1893–?), a descendant of the militia leader Hyŏn Inbok, wrote in vernacular Korean (*han'gŭl*) the *Hong Kyŏngnae chŏn* (Story of Hong Kyŏngnae), which was serialized in *Tonga ilbo* in 1931. The content of Hyŏn's novel is again identical to that of the *Hong Kyŏngnae* in classical Chinese. Thus it seems likely that Hyŏn is the author of both the *Hong Kyŏngnae* and the *Hong Kyŏngnae chŏn*. And a copy of it in classical Chinese may have been inserted as an addendum to the *Sok choya chipyo* when a copy was made in 1932.

As for the reliability of the *Hong Kyŏngnae imsin saryak*, Oda Shōgo gives it most of the credit for the information about the rebellion in his book, *Shinbi Kō Keirai ran no kenkyu* (A Comprehensive Study of the Hong Kyŏngnae Rebellion of 1811). In contrast, O Such'ang points out that both the novel entitled *Hong Kyŏngnae* and the history entitled *Hong Kyŏngnae imsin saryak* are unreliable, since they were written in a later period and include some additional facts whose validity is questionable.[9] At this point, it remains difficult for me to determine the value of the *Hong Kyŏngnae imsin saryak*. Its author quotes some information from other sources, such as the *Chinjung ilgi*, which I, too, have heavily relied on. On the one hand, the *han'gŭl* version includes author's notes, which the author claims to have heard from elderly people from his hometown, Chŏngju. On the other hand, some information (for example, an episode that describes Hong Kyŏngnae luring Kim Ch'angsi into a deep mountain hideout to persuade Kim to join in the plot) is too dramatized and hard to believe as fact. Therefore, I have always sought to verify this source against other sources when making judgments about the reliability of the information in various materials.

Paek Kyŏnghae's Career History

Date (age)	Office and position	Rank
1786 (22)	Passed the civil service examination, assigned to the Royal Academy (Kukcha pun'gwan)	
1788.3.1 (24)	Third proctor of the Royal Academy (Sŏnggyun'gwan Hagyu) / administrator of the Bureau of Superannuation (Kiroso Sujik)	Jr. 9
1788.4.17	Temporary recorder of the Royal Secretariat (Sŭngjŏngwŏn Ka-chusŏ)	Sr. 7
1789.6.20 (25)	Librarian at the Royal Academy (Chŏnjŏk) / assistant section chief of the Ministry of Rites (Yejo Chwarang)	Sr. 6
1789.7.1	Section chief of the Ministry of Works (Kongjo Chŏngnang) / drafter of the Bureau of State Records (Ch'unch'ugwan Kijugwan)	Sr. 5
1790.4.17 (26)	Section chief of the Ministry of Rites	Sr. 5
1790.5.6	Section chief of the Ministry of Works / recorder (Ch'unch'u)	Sr. 5

Date (age)	Office and position	Rank
1794.12.1 (30)	Section chief of the Ministry of Rites / recorder	Sr. 5
1801.8.23 (37)	Fourth secretary of the Bureau of Royal Rituals (Pongsangsi Ch'ŏmjŏng)	Jr. 4
1803.3.20 (39)	Section chief of the Ministry of Rites	Sr. 5
1803.4.10	Drafter of the Bureau of State Records—concurrently held with the section chief of the Ministry of Rites position	Sr. 5
1804.2.13 (40)	Section chief of the Ministry of Taxation (Hojo Chŏngnang)	Sr. 5
1804.7.10	Superintendent of Yugok Post Station (Yugok Ch'albang)	Jr. 6
1810.1.15 (46)	Superintendent of Chogyŏng Shrine (Chogyŏngmyo Yŏng)	Jr. 5
1811.8.10 (47)	Inspector of P'yŏngan Province (P'yŏngan Tosa)	Jr. 5
1812.5.8 (48)	Magistrate of T'aech'ŏn (T'aech'ŏn Hyŏng'am)	Sr. 6
1816.10.17 (52)	Third inspector of the Office of the Inspector General (Sahŏnbu Changnyŏng)	Sr. 4
1817.6.11 (53)	Secretary of the Military Procurement Administration (Kunjagam Chŏng)	Sr. 3
1819.12.25 (55)	Magistrate of Changyŏn (Changyŏn Hyŏng'am)	Sr. 6
1821.12.6 (57)	Third inspector of the Office of the Inspector General	Sr. 4
1827.5.19 (63)	Secretary of the Bureau of Royal Records (Chongbusi Chŏng)	Sr. 3
1827.12.7	Special promotion of a rank as a reward	

Date (age)	Office and position	Rank
1827.12.13	Fourth deputy commander of the Five Military Commands (Owi Puhogun)	Jr. 4
1828.9.3 (64)	Fifth minister at the Office of Ministers-without-Portfolio (Chungch'ubu—Ch'ŏmjisa), an honorary position	Sr. 3 (*tangsang-guan*)
1829.12.19 (65)	First secretary of the Royal House Administration (Tollyŏngbu)	Sr. 3 (*tangsang-guan*)
1836.1.3 (72)	Promoted to Kasŏn taebu (Jr. 2) / third deputy commander of the Five Military Commands (Owi Hogun)	Sr. 4
1836.3.7	Fourth minister at the Office of Ministers-without-Portfolio (Tongjisa)	Jr. 2
1836.10.18	Third deputy commander of the Five Military Commands	Sr. 4
1839.5.25 (75)	Second magistrate of the Seoul Magistracy (Hansŏngbu Chwayun)	Jr. 2

SOURCE: SWJ, *hwanhae chingbi*, 8:1a–15b, and SWI.

NOTE: The dates indicate the appointment. The termination date for each position is not usually recorded. Paek did not necessarily keep a position from the date of appointment to the next appointment date.

Fates of the Key Rebel Leaders

Name	Date and mode of death (all dates in 1812)
Hong Kyŏngnae	Shot to death on 5/29; decapitated and dismembered later
U Kunch'ik	Captured on 6/1 and dismembered on 6/14
Yi Hŭijŏ	Killed and decapitated on 6/2
Kim Ch'angsi	Killed and decapitated on 2/28 by his own follower
Kim Sayong	Shot to death at the battle of 5/2
Hong Ch'onggak	Decapitated and dismembered on 6/14
Yi Chech'o	Killed and decapitated at the battle of 2/21
Chŏng Kyŏnghaeng	Captured on 2/27 and dismembered on 3/18
Chŏng Pogil	Captured on 2/27 and dismembered on 3/18
Chŏng Sŏnghan	Captured on 2/23 and dismembered on 3/18
Ch'oe Ponggwan	Dismembered on 3/18
Ch'oe Iryun	Captured on 6/1 and dismembered on 6/14
Yu Munje	Decapitated on 2/28

Name	*Date and mode of death (all dates in 1812)*
Pak Sŏngsin	Captured on 2/27 and decapitated on 2/28
Kim Idae	Captured on 5/29 and dismembered on 6/14
Pyŏn Taeik	Captured and decapitated on 2/14
Han Ilhaeng	Dismembered on 11/19
Yun Ŏnsŏp	Captured on 5/29 and dismembered on 6/14

SOURCE: Based on information found in the *Chinjung ilgi* and *Kwansŏ p'yongnallok*. Also see *Sunjo sillok*, 15:39a–39b, Sunjo.12.4.21 (*kyehae*) for a summary of the rebels' fates.

Kings of the Chosŏn Dynasty

T'aejo	太祖	1392–98
Chŏngjong	定宗	1398–1400
T'aejong	太宗	1400–18
Sejong	世宗	1418–50
Munjong	文宗	1450–52
Tanjong	端宗	1452–55
Sejo	世祖	1455–68
Yejong	睿宗	1468–69
Sŏngjong	成宗	1469–94
Yŏnsan-gun	燕山君	1494–1506
Chungjong	中宗	1506–44
Injong	仁宗	1544–45
Myŏngjong	明宗	1545–67
Sŏnjo	宣祖	1567–1608
Kwanghae-gun	光海君	1608–23

Injo	仁祖	1623–49
Hyojong	孝宗	1649–59
Hyŏnjong	顯宗	1659–74
Sukchong	肅宗	1674–1720
Kyŏngjong	景宗	1720–24
Yŏngjo	英祖	1724–76
Chŏngjo	正祖	1776–1800
Sunjo	純祖	1800–34
Hŏnjong	憲宗	1834–49
Ch'ŏlchong	哲宗	1849–63
Kojong	高宗	1863–1907
Sunjong	純宗	1907–10

Notes

INTRODUCTION

1. For the Confucian political idea of challenging the Mandate of Heaven and its relation to Chinese rebellions, see Perry, *Challenging the Mandate of Heaven*, ix–xxxii.

2. All the districts mentioned in the text were located in P'yŏngan Province unless indicated otherwise.

3. This area north of the Ch'ŏngch'ŏn River in P'yŏngan Province was often called "Ch'ŏngbuk," and the area south of Ch'ŏngch'ŏn River called "Ch'ŏngnam," in the late Chosŏn period. The area that was directly affected by the Hong Kyŏngnae Rebellion was the Ch'ŏngbuk region. "Kwansŏ" refers to P'yŏngan Province; "Kwanbuk" refers to Hamgyŏng Province. "Sŏbuk" refers to both P'yŏngan and Hamgyŏng provinces. In this book, "the northern region" refers to both P'yŏngan and Hamgyŏng provinces as a single unit, an area that was a target of social and political discrimination by the rest of the country in the late Chosŏn period. "The northwestern region" refers to the whole of P'yŏngan Province.

4. One of the most recent examples of popular fascination with the 1812 rebellion is found in the popular novel *Sangdo* (The Way of the Merchant), by Ch'oe Inho. Originally serialized in a newspaper for three years beginning in 1997, it was published as a five-volume set in 2001. More than one million sets have sold, and the novel was also broadcast as a TV drama.

5. For a summary of English-language literature in peasant rebellions, see Shin, *Peasant Protest and Social Change in Colonial Korea*, 9–21. For a comprehensive

review of peasants, peasant rebellions, and Chinese revolution, see Pepper, "The Political Odyssey of an Intellectual Construct."

6. How to label popular rebellions is a controversial subject in Korea because the label reflects one's perspective on how to interpret the rebellions. For example, in a collection of articles on popular movements in 1862, published as a book entitled *1862 nyŏn nongmin hangjaeng* (Peasant Resistance Movements in 1862), scholars criticized using the term "peasant rebellion" (*nongmin pallan*) because it reflected only the position of the ruling elite. They instead adopted the term "peasant resistance movement" (*nongmin hangjaeng*) to emphasize the position of the peasant. See Mangwŏn han'guksa yŏn'gusil 19 segi nongmin hangjaeng punkwa, *1862 nyŏn nongmin hangjaeng.*

7. For a general survey of popular movements during the Chosŏn dynasty, see Ko Sŏnghun et al., *Millan ŭi sidae.* The authors of this book differentiate various forms of popular movements, in particular the *millan* (popular rebellions), as economically charged resistance movements usually led by peasants, and the *pyŏllan* (politically charged rebellions) as more politically oriented antidynastic movements plotted by discontented intellectuals. At the same time they acknowledge that certain movements like the Hong Kyŏngnae Rebellion show the mixed nature of *millan* and *pyŏllan,* and that others, such as bandits and secret societies, do not fall into either category. Scholars of historical sociology and political science find various patterns of popular movements to enhance our understanding. For example, Elizabeth Perry divides agrarian movements in China into predatory and protective forms. See Perry, *Challenging the Mandate of Heaven.* Nonetheless, I do not see any analytical benefit to categorizing popular movements in the Chosŏn into *millan* and the *pyŏllan* because none of them clearly falls into one particular pattern. I also prefer terms such as "popular rebellions" and "popular resistance movements" to "peasant rebellions" or "peasant movements," because the word "popular" seems more inclusive of wider rural populations than does the word "peasant." This is helpful in understanding the Hong Kyŏngnae Rebellion because this particular rebellion was led primarily by the rural elite, though it attracted and was sustained by people of different statuses and class attachments. For the concept of "peasant" as developed by modern scholarship, see Sorensen, "National Identity and the Creation of the Category 'Peasant' in Colonial Korea."

8. See chapter 8 for more detailed historiographical discussion of the 1812 rebellion.

9. According to Song Chunho, the definition or boundary of "yangban" is subjective and relative because there was no legal definition of it. Yet, he argues, the most important qualification for yangban status was prominent ancestors

(*hyŏnjo*) in one's lineage (*kamun*). Although "prominent ancestors" meant those whose prestige might have been based on literary talent and outstanding ethical behavior as well as success in examinations or holding office, emphasis was put on the inheritance of status. The descendants of prominent officials were believed to practice proper scholarly and moral behavior even if they were not successful in passing examinations or holding office—they were regarded as yangban regardless. Thus, having a prominent ancestor in one's lineage was the most important and basic qualification for yangban status. The distance between a prominent ancestor and oneself did not matter, but descendents were supposed to make consistent efforts to maintain their yangban status by arranging marriage relations prudently, by passing examinations, and by holding office. Also, they were expected to have a semipermanent residence (*segŏji*) and to accumulate their own unique lineage tradition (*kap'ung*) as a yangban lineage. Song Chunho, *Chosŏn sahoesa yŏn'gu*, 242–59.

10. For more discussion of the *pŏryŏl*, see Ch'a Changsŏp, *Chosŏn hugi pŏryŏl yŏn'gu*. According to Ch'a, the term *pŏryŏl* refers to the capital-based families (*kamun*) who produced officials whose rank reached higher than senior third rank (*tangsanggwan*) for three generations in a row. The range of family members who could produce *tangsanggwan* was limited to the second cousin of each generation for three generations before oneself. Ch'a identifies fifty-seven *pŏryŏl* who had dominated political power and prestige since the reign of King Sŏnjo (1567–1608) by manipulating civil service examinations, creating marriage ties with the royal family as well as among themselves, using protection privileges, and employing the institution of "merit subject" to maintain and perpetuate their privileged status, even though the strength of each family fluctuated over time.

11. For the marginalization of Chosŏn elite, see Sun Joo Kim, "Negotiating Cultural Identities in Conflict"; and idem, "Marginalized Elite."

12. Goldstone, *Revolution and Rebellion in the Early Modern World*, 33.

13. For demographic studies based on statistics found in official records, see Kwŏn T'aehwan and Sin Yongha, "Chosŏn wangjo sidae in'gu ch'ujŏng e kwanhan ilsiron"; and Tony Michell, "Fact and Hypothesis in Yi Dynasty Economic History." For case studies founded on a more reliable source of genealogy, see Pak Hŭijin and Ch'a Myŏngsu, "Chosŏn hugi wa ilche sidae ŭi in'gu pyŏndong"; Yi Kisun, "Pongsan Yi ssi chokpo rŭl t'onghaesŏ pon Chosŏn sidae kajok kyumo"; and idem, "Chosŏn hugi Koryŏng Sin ssi ŭi kajok kyumo."

14. The number of successful examination passers increased from fifteen per year in the early years of the dynasty to over thirty during the centuries after the Japanese invasions. Especially during the period from 1753 to 1783, there were

on average forty-five annual examination passers. This is calculated from Wagner, *Yi Dynasty Munkwa Examination Passers.*

15. This perspective from the center that there were no yangban in P'yŏngan Province has been uncritically taken up by recent studies. See Kyung Moon Hwang, "From the Dirt to Heaven"; and O Such'ang, *Chosŏn hugi P'yŏngan-do sahoe palchŏn yŏn'gu.*

16. Most previous studies relegate regional discrimination to a secondary place. For the most recent examples, see O Such'ang, *P'yŏngan-do sahoe palchŏn yŏn'gu*; and Karlsson, "The Hong Kyŏngnae Rebellion 1811–1812."

17. Christopher Hill argues in his monumental study of radical ideas in mid-seventeenth-century England that "it is only from our modern vantage point that we can separate what is 'rational' in seventeenth-century science from what is not." Hill, *The World Turned Upside Down*, 89.

18. In Chinese historiography, regional approaches and analyses have long been advocated and practiced, beginning with G. William Skinner's regional systems approach to Chinese society. Little and Esherick, "Testing the Testers." For application of a regional approach in the study of peasant rebellions, see Perry, *Rebels and Revolutionaries in North China, 1845–1945.*

19. Prasenjit Duara notes the legitimacy of regional approaches that have been obliterated by the nationalist rendering of history. Duara, *Rescuing History from the Nation.* Criticizing postcolonial, nationalist historiography, Henry Em also emphasizes the history of the oppressed and excluded groups as the proper subject of historical research. Em, "Nationalism, Post-Nationalism, and Shin Ch'ae-ho."

20. The tendency for the last several decades to focus historical research on the southern provinces may have been related to governmental and institutional efforts to build a nationalist history that would legitimize the southern regimes by emphasizing certain aspects of Korean history, such as the unification of the Silla kingdom (?–935) in 668, and downplaying Korea's historical and spatial linkage to Manchuria and Koguryŏ. Schmid, "Rediscovering Manchuria"; and Moon, "Begetting the Nation."

21. For discussion of the primary sources used in the present study, see appendix A.

1   HISTORICAL DEVELOPMENT OF THE CH'ŎNGBUK REGION
    AND THE REGIONAL ELITE

1. Oda Shōgo denies that there was any discriminatory policy against the residents of P'yŏngan Province in the recruitment of government officials. As for

the reasons people from this northwestern region were not able to reach prestigious positions in the central government, Oda suggests that because the region was culturally behind, it produced no outstanding person before the reign of King Sŏnjo, nor any leading figure who could represent the interests of the region when factional strife became prevalent after King Sŏnjo's reign. He concludes that the rebellion was not the result of discrimination on the part of the central government, but does concede that the disappointment and frustration of the people from this region became a remote and general cause of the rebellion. Oda discusses the direct causes of the rebellion by examining factional politics during the late Chosŏn dynasty, Hong Kyŏngnae's personal relationship to the factions, and his frustration over the failure of northwesterners to advance politically. Oda, "Kō Keirai ran no gairyaku to sono dōki ni tsuite"; and idem, *Shinbi Kō Keirai ran no kenkyū.*

2. The rebel manifesto is preserved in a few different historical records, such as *Hong Kyŏngnae pallangi* (The Record of the Hong Kyŏngnae Rebellion), *Hong ssi ilgi* (A Diary about Mr. Hong), *P'yŏngsŏ ponmal* (The Essence and Branch of Pacifying P'yŏngan Province), and *Ilsŭng* (A Daily Record). Although there are some differences in wording, the contents are very similar. This book uses a copy found in the *Hong Kyŏngnae pallangi*, 3–4.

3. According to *Samguk yusa* (Memorabilia of the Three Kingdoms) and other later historical records, Tan'gun was the founding father of the Old Chosŏn (Ko-Chosŏn). The ancient Chinese classics recorded a story that Kija was enfeoffed as the king of Chosŏn around 1100–1000 B.C.E. There is no consensus among historians as to whether or not these are historical facts or as to where these states were located if they ever existed. See Iryŏn, *Samguk yusa*, 33–35.

4. For more discussion of the location of Old Chosŏn, see No T'aedon, *Tan'gun kwa Ko-Chosŏn sa*, 41–96.

5. Hyung Il Pai offers a critical study of Lelang in her book, *Constructing "Korean" Origins.*

6. Korean scholars believe that Parhae was a Korean kingdom, founded by a Koguryŏ people, and that Koguryŏ's people occupied most ruling positions. According to scholars, the Mohe ethnic group that composed the majority of the Parhae population held some offices but constituted a subject people. See Lee Ki-baik (Yi Kibaek), *A New History of Korea*, 88–91. Furthermore, Yi Usŏng argues that the period from the late seventh century to the early tenth century, in which the Unified Silla (668–935) in the south confronted Parhae in the north, must be called the period of the Northern and Southern States, fully incorporating the history of Parhae into Korean history. Yi Usŏng, "A Study of the Period of the Northern and Southern States." In contrast, Chinese scholars consider Tae Choyŏng (Ch.:

Da Zuorong), the founder of Parhae, as a Mohe and define Parhae as a political regime established by the Mohe, downplaying the contribution of the Koguryŏ people in the founding of the state. Subsequently, Chinese scholars treat Parhae history as a part of Chinese history. The perspective of Russian scholars is quite different from that of both Chinese and Korean scholars. They see Parhae as an independent state with its separate history among the various Siberian people, which makes it a part of Russian history. See Song Kiho, "Current Trends in the Research of Palhae History"; and idem, "Several Questions in Studies of the History of Palhae." As Song Kiho comments, because the territory of Parhae was spread over areas of the modern states of China, Russia, and Korea, the research of its history has been dictated by the nationalism of each country. In addition, scarcity of source materials and the unclear nature of written and archeological evidence have led to complex and contradictory interpretations. Scholarly exchange among researchers and a more objective research attitude would make for a better understanding of the nature of the Parhae state.

7. For discussion of Koryŏ's northern expansion policy and the rise of the Silla successionism among Koryŏ officials and scholars, see Rogers, "*P'yŏnnyŏn T'ongnok.*"

8. One thousand *ri* is approximately 449 kilometers. The number does not necessarily indicate exact length of the wall but rather symbolic meaning of a long defensive wall.

9. For examples of the relocation of population, see *Koryŏsa*, 1:16b, 58:29a–30a, and 58:33b–34a.

10. For Koryŏ's foreign relations, see Henthorn, *A History of Korea*; Lee Ki-baik, *A New History of Korea*; and Ledyard, "Yin and Yang in the China-Manchuria-Korea Triangle."

11. *Koryŏsa*, 127:26b–36a.

12. For more details on the military revolt, see Shultz, *Generals and Scholars*.

13. Koryŏ territory was divided into five circuits (Kyoju, Yanggwang, Kyŏngsang, Chŏlla, and Sŏhae) and two border regions (Pukkye and Tonggye). The northern border region (Pukkye) was reorganized as P'yŏngan Province in Chosŏn. The eastern border region (Tonggye) encompassed a part of Hamgyŏng and Kangwŏn provinces in Chosŏn.

14. *Koryŏsa*, 100:7b–11a. There was another revolt led by Kim Podang in 1173 in the northeastern region. Edward Shultz argues that these two incidents reflected a disdain that had built up in the north toward the central government. Shultz, *Generals and Scholars*, 34–35.

15. *Koryŏsa*, 58:30b and 58:15b.

16. Robinson, "From Raiders to Traders"; and Yi Sanghyŏp, *Chosŏn chŏn'gi pukpang samin yŏn'gu*, 17–32. For discussion of the nature of the border between China and Korea during the Chosŏn period, see Eggert, "A Borderline Case."

17. Yi Sanghyŏp, *Chosŏn chŏn'gi pukpang samin yŏn'gu*; Yi Kyŏngsik, "Chosŏn ch'ogi ŭi pukpang kaech'ŏk kwa nongŏp kaebal"; Yi Inyŏng, "Yi ssi Chosŏn sejo ttae ŭi pukpang imin chŏngch'aek"; Kim Sŏkhŭi, "Sejojo ŭi samin e kwanhan koch'al"; and Yi Sugŏn, "Chosŏn Sŏngjongjo ŭi pukpang imin chŏngch'aek."

18. For the relocation of criminals, see Yi Sugŏn, "Chosŏn Sŏngjongjo ŭi pukpang imin chŏngch'aek, ha," 96–100; and Yi Sanghyŏp, *Chosŏn chŏn'gi pukpang samin yŏn'gu*, 75–84. In my dissertation I suggested that the relocation of criminals to northern provinces might have contributed to the formation of prejudice against northerners. Pak Honggap proposes the same hypothesis in his work. In a similar vein, Kyung Moon Hwang argues that the bias against the northern population was rooted in "the aristocracy's (correct) perception of the northern population as descended from various low status groups of the early Chosŏn," such as Jurchen and "low-level" migrants. I disagree with Hwang's thesis that there was no *sajok* (aristocracy) in the north and with the view that the migrants were all members of a low-level social group. See Sun Joo Kim, "Marginalized Elite," 45–46; Pak Honggap, "Chosŏn chŏn'gi yanggye chŏngch'angmin"; and Kyung Moon Hwang, "From the Dirt to Heaven."

19. For discussion of early Chosŏn efforts toward centralization of government, see Duncan, *The Origins of the Chosŏn Dynasty*; Yi Sugŏn, *Han'guk chungse sahoesa yŏn'gu*; idem, *Chosŏn sidae chibang haengjŏngsa*; Yi Sŏngmu, *Chosŏn ch'ogi yangban yŏn'gu*; and Yi Chonhwi, *Chosŏn sidae chibang haengjŏng chedo yŏn'gu*.

20. Yi Sŏngmu, *Chosŏn ch'ogi yangban yŏn'gu*, 31–34; and Yi Sugŏn, *Chosŏn sidae chibang haengjŏngsa*, 100–109.

21. The origin of the ancestral seat system goes back as far as the late Silla period, when locally dominant descent groups, which created their own local enclaves of influence by taking advantage of disarray at the center, began to identify themselves by their locales by adopting Chinese-style surnames and the ancestral seat system. The new dynasty, Koryŏ, encouraged the system by granting surnames to locally prominent men as it reorganized the local administrative structure into the prefecture and county system (*kunhyŏn*, Ch.: *jun-xian*). Duncan, *The Origins of the Chosŏn Dynasty*, 30–35; Yi Sugŏn, *Han'guk chungse sahoesa yŏn'gu*, 34–69; and Pak Kyŏngja, *Koryŏ sidae hyangni yŏn'gu*.

22. For examples of the relocation of population during the Koryŏ period, see *Koryŏsa*, 1:16b, 58:29a–30a, and 58:33b–34a.

23. Yi Sugŏn, *Han'guk chungse sahoesa yŏn'gu*, 101–6 and 328–36.

24. The contrast between northern and southern provinces is striking. Kyŏng-sang Province in particular produced 401 prominent people during the Koryŏ and Chosŏn dynasties (35.73 percent of the total). This conflated figure for Kyŏngsang Province may represent the strength of Silla successionism in late Koryŏ and early Chosŏn historiography.

25. Yi Chaeryong, "Chosŏn ch'ogi ŭi t'ogwan e taehayŏ." The *t'ogwan* system was codified in *Kyŏngguk taejŏn* (Great Code of Administration) and still appeared in *Taejŏn hoet'ong* (Comprehensive Collection of Dynastic Code), but it is unclear whether this system had been functioning throughout the Chosŏn dynasty. *Taejŏn hoet'ong, ijŏn t'ogwanjik*, 1:51a–51b.

26. Ch'oe Chongt'aek, "Chosŏn ch'o P'yŏngan Hamgil-do ŭi chibang seryŏk."

27. SWJ, "Tae kwansŏ chein chŏng chŏngbu sŏ," 4:14b–19a.

28. For more discussion of the marriage and inheritance practices during the Koryŏ and early Chosŏn, see Deuchler, *The Confucian Transformation of Korea*; Peterson, *Korean Adoption and Inheritance*; and Yi Sun'gu, "Chosŏn ch'ogi chong-pŏp ŭi suyong." Uxorilocal marriage was a common strategy among important lineages in the lower Yangzi at least from Song China (960–1279) on. For example, the son of a family with higher social status could establish a new segment of the lineage by moving to another community and marrying the daughter of a family with no heir. But rather than carrying on the family line for the heirless, the son continued to use his own surname in a new community. Elman, *Classicism, Politics, and Kinship*, 37. For discussion of elite diasporas in the early Chosŏn, see Yi Sugŏn, *Yŏngnam hakp'a ŭi hyŏngsŏng kwa chŏn'gae*; Kim Chunhyŏng, *Chosŏn hugi Tansŏng sajokch'ŭng yŏn'gu*, 33–48; and Song Chunho, *Chosŏn sahoesa yŏn'gu*, 277–306.

29. *Sejong sillok*, 96:9a–9b, Sejong 24.5.13 (*imsin*).

30. *Chungjong sillok*, 54:40a, Chungjong 20.6.9 (*chŏngyu*).

31. *T'oegye sŏ chipsŏng*, 2:416. The concern for military duty matters not only for Yi's own sons but also for his slaves. See also ibid., 2:14, 2:238, 2:239, 2:242, 2:244–46, 2:320, 2:322–23, and 2:327.

32. Most scholars conveniently assume that voluntary as well as forced migrants from southern provinces were commoners because the scholars accept without criticism the late Chosŏn elite prejudice that there were no *sajok* in the north. Kyung Moon Hwang, "From the Dirt to Heaven," 135–50; and Ch'oe Chongt'aek, "Chosŏn ch'o P'yŏngan Hamgil-do ŭi chibang seryŏk," 157–59.

33. Zenshō, *Chōsen no shūraku*, 928–44.

34. A number of genealogies compiled by other yangban descent groups resid-

ing in the Ch'ŏngbuk region in the late Chosŏn period inform us that their ancestors had moved and settled in the area sometime in the early Chosŏn period. But they do not record specific reasons for relocation. See *Suwŏn Paek ssi Chŏngju chokpo*; *Yŏnil Sŭng ssi chokpo*; and *Paech'ŏn Cho ssi sebo*.

35. According to the *Sejong sillok chiriji*, compiled in 1454, there were eight moved-in descent groups (Paekchu Yu, Poryŏng Chŏng, Ch'unju Ch'oe, Sinju Kim, Hoeryŏng Yi, Ansan Kang, Haeju No, Hwangju Paek) in Chŏngju, P'yŏngan Province. See *Sejong sillok chiriji*, 314. Eight more descent groups (Hwasun Ch'oe, Paekchu Cho, Hamjong Sŭng, Ch'ungju Sŏk, Yonggang Kim, Yonggang Kang, Haeju Chang, Haeju O) were added to the surname section of the same district in the *Sinjŭng tongguk yŏji sŭngnam*, compiled in 1530. See *Sinjŭng tongguk yŏji sŭngnam*, 951. Sinju Kim in the former record and Yonggang Kim in the latter seem to refer to Yŏnan Kim.

36. The following discussion relies on the *Kwangju No ssi chokpo* (Genealogy of Kwangju No), compiled and published in 1898. In the *munkwa* roster, the ancestral seat of this particular branch of surname No residing in Chŏngju is recorded as Haeju rather than Kwangju. It is not known when or why this particular lineage began to designate its clan seat as Kwangju. According to Paek Kyŏnghae, his maternal family was Haeju No, a renowned descent group of the area, which was different from a commoner descent group of Kwangju No (SWI 1813.1.1). I refer to this lineage as "Haeju No" because earlier records agree on Haeju being its ancestral seat. I made a copy of all three volumes of the *Kwangju No ssi chokpo* from the photocopied edition in the private collection of No Unhŭi, a seventeenth-generation descendant of No Segŏl living in Seoul, Korea, when I interviewed him in summer 2003. No Unhŭi informed me that he had made his own copy from what is probably the only one surviving from the original publication in 1898, which one of his relatives had carried from his hometown of Chŏngju when fleeing to the south sometime between 1945 and 1950.

37. Yi Kŭngik, *Yŏllyŏsil kisul, Chungjong-jo kosa ponmal, sinsa An Ch'ŏgyŏm chi ok*, vol. 2, 154. According to Yi Kŭngik (1736–1806), many yangban officials implicated in this literati purge of 1521 were exiled to northern provinces, but only a few returned home alive. No Segŏl himself died in exile in 1529 and his family members certainly stayed in Chŏngju. Likewise, other yangban exiled to the north may have established their new residences there. For the purge of 1521 and how No Segŏl was implicated in the incident, see *Chungjong sillok*, 43:9a–11a, Chungjong 16.10.14 (*imjin*) and 43:22b–23a, Chungjong 16.10.20 (*musul*).

38. This is the reason the place of origin for this descent group was recorded as Haeju in *Sejong sillok chiriji* and the *munkwa* roster. However, the *Chungjong sillok* records that No Segŏl was exiled to Kyŏnghŭng in Hamgyŏng Province. It

is possible that his place of exile was later changed to Haeju but not recorded in the *sillok*. *Chungjong sillok*, 43:25a, Chungjong 16.10.21 (*kihae*).

39. *Kwangju No ssi chokpo, sŏ*: 2a and *Inŭi-gong chisŏngmun*: 5b. According to the *Chungjong sillok*, No Segŏl's case was considered for pardon in 1538, but the result of the court discussion is not recorded. *Chungjong sillok*, 88:19a, Chungjong 33.8.25 (*ŭlch'uk*).

40. *Hadong Chŏng ssi sebo*, introduction to the 1776 revised edition written by Chŏng Chŏn, 4. The introduction to the 1827 edition says that it was during the reigns of Kings Sejo (1455–68) and Sŏngjong (1469–94) that Chŏng Lim was exiled. Ibid., 9.

41. The Hadong Chŏng had been a prominent yangban descent group since the Koryŏ dynasty. It produced many famous scholars and officials during the Koryŏ and Chosŏn dynasties, including the famous scholar-official Chŏng Inji (1396–1478).

42. *Kwansŏ ŭpchi Chŏngju, kwanwŏn*, 17:193; and *Sinanji sokp'yŏn, hwanjŏk*, 63:119. The preceptor position was abolished sometime in the mid-dynastic period and documented as an abolished position in the *Taejŏn t'ongpy'ŏn* (Comprehensive Code) compiled in 1785. *Taejŏn hoet'ong, ijŏn oegwanjik*, 1:38b.

43. *Chŏngju ŭpchi, kwanjŏk*, 337; and *Sinanji sokp'yŏn, hwanjŏk*, 63:119.

44. *Yŏngbyŏnji*, 279–80.

45. Somerville, "Stability in Eighteenth Century Ulsan," 9; Nam Yŏnsuk, "Chosŏn hugi hyangban ŭi kŏjuji idong kwa sahoe chiwi ŭi chisoksŏng, II," 47–57; Kawashima, "The Local Gentry Association in Mid-Yi Dynasty Korea"; Yi Sugŏn, *Yŏngnam hakp'a ŭi hyŏngsŏng kwa chŏn'gae*; Yi Haejun, *Chosŏn sigi ch'ollak sahoesa*; Paek Sŭngjong, *Han'guk sahoesa yŏn'gu*; and Kim Hyŏnyŏng, *Chosŏn sidae ŭi yangban kwa hyangch'on sahoe*.

46. The loyal deeds displayed by Chŏng Pongsu and Chŏng Kisu had been repeatedly remembered by their descendants and fellow local yangban as well as the central court. Chŏng Sŏnghak, one of their descendants, finally compiled a book called *Yongsŏng Ssangŭirok* (Record of Two Loyal Subjects from Yongsŏng), a collection of biographies, their writings, eulogies, and so on, in 1794. Loaded with prefaces and prologues by renowned scholars and officials of the time, the book was published by the Office of Editorial Review.

47. Wagner, "The Civil Examination Process as Social Leaven," 25.

48. For close marriage ties formed among the three prominent descent groups of Chŏngju, Yŏnan Kim, Anŭi Im, and Haeju No, see Sun Joo Kim, "Chosŏn hugi P'yŏngan-do Chŏngju ŭi hyangan." Also see *Yŏnan Kim ssi Kaesŏng Puyun-gong p'abo*, vol. 1; *Anŭi Im ssi sebo*; and *Kwangju No ssi chokpo*.

49. *Kwangju No ssi chokpo, Kasŏn taebu Tongji-gong haengjang*, written by

Pak Munil in 1898. The Yŏnan Kim descent group produced three "loyal subjects" during the Manchu invasion of 1627. *Yŏnan Kim ssi Kaesŏng Puyun-gong p'abo*, vol. 1, 13 and 54.

50. *Sinanji sokp'yŏn, inmul*, 64:4–5; *Kwansŏ ŭpchi Chŏngju, inmul*, 17: 201–2; and *Tongguk wŏnsarok*.

51. *Sinanji sokp'yŏn*, 63:238–46. For the history of Chŏngju's local yangban association, see Sun Joo Kim, "Chosŏn hugi P'yŏngan-do Chŏngju ŭi hyangan."

52. *Hyangan* means literally "the local roster." Those whose names were listed in the *hyangan* formed an association, with governing rules and rituals, and held meetings to make decisions on local affairs. The *hyangan* often refers to such a local yangban association.

53. The Hyangch'ŏng was often called Hyangso. It was called Yuhyangso particularly in the early Chosŏn. Kawashima, "The Local Gentry Association in Mid-Yi Dynasty Korea," 115–16.

54. Kawashima, "A Study of *Hyangan*."

55. Song Chunho, *Chosŏn sahoesa yŏn'gu*, 147–48; and Kim Hyŏnyŏng, *Chosŏn sidae ŭi yangban kwa hyangch'on sahoe*, 65–73.

56. Deuchler, "Heaven Does Not Discriminate"; Yi T'aejin, "Sŏŏl ch'adae ko"; and Kyung Moon Hwang, *Beyond Birth*, 208–32.

57. Kim Ingŏl, "Chosŏn hugi hyangan ŭi sŏnggyŏk."

58. In some districts, such as Namwŏn, Chŏlla Province, the division between *yu* and *hyang* was very prominent. *Yu* refers to established yangban occupying the upper layers of the yangban status group, while *hyang* refers to yangban officials (*hyangim*) at the local yangban bureau and their families, who provided administrative services for the local government. Song Chunho, *Chosŏn sahoesa yŏn'gu*, 277–306; Ko Sŏkkyu, *19–segi Chosŏn ŭi hyangch'on sahoe yon'gu*; and Kim Ingŏl, "Chosŏn hugi hyangch'on sahoe pyŏndong e kwanhan yŏn'gu."

59. For the case of local strife in Yŏngyang, Kyŏngsang Province, see Ko Sŏkkyu, "19 segi chŏnban hyangch'on sahoe seryŏkkan ŭi taerip ŭi ch'ui."

60. For the history of the Chŏngju yangban association roster, see *Sinanji sokp'yŏn*, 63:238–68; *Chŏngju kunji*, 183–90 and 316–18; and *Kwangju No ssi chokpo, Kasŏn taebu Tongji-gong haengjang*.

61. *Sinanji sokp'yŏn*, 63:265.

62. *Chŏngju kunji*, 316–20.

63. Sun Joo Kim, "Chosŏn hugi P'yŏngan-do Chŏngju ŭi hyangan," 73–87.

64. The following discussion of the Chŏngju yangban association and the 1789 incident relies on Sun Joo Kim, "Chosŏn hugi P'yŏngan-do Chŏngju ŭi hyangan"; and Ko Sŏkkyu, "18 segimal 19 segich'o P'yŏngan-do chiyŏk hyangwŏn ŭi ch'ui."

65. It is difficult to estimate the value of 1 *yang* at this time. The commutation rate most generally used in government transactions in the eighteenth and early nineteenth centuries was that 1 *sŏm* of rice equaled 4 *yang* or that one bolt of cotton cloth was equivalent to 2 *yang*. The commutation rates, however, fluctuated greatly depending on the supply and demand of rice and cotton cloth throughout the late Chosŏn period. Pak It'aek, "Sŏul ŭi sungnyŏn mit misungnyŏn nodongja ŭi imgŭm, 1600–1909," 54.

66. It seems clear that there was no division between *yu* or *sajok* and *hyang* or *hyangin* in the Ch'ŏngbuk region. See Secret Inspector (Amhaeng ŏsa) Yi Myŏn'ŭng's report on the P'yŏngan elite in 1790 in *Chŏngjo sillok*, 29:55a–55b, Chŏngjo 14.3.24 *(kapchin)*. Although the court differentiated the *sajok* from *hyangjok* when they discussed each person who made material or military contributions to the pacification of the Hong Kyŏngnae Rebellion, in practice the distinction between the two was not so apparent. Kim Idae, the Chwasu of Chŏngju at the time of the rebellion, was a *chinsa*, and his maternal great-grandfather had been a *munkwa* degree-holder. *Yŏnan Kim ssi Kaesŏng Puyun-gong p'abo*, vol. 1, 180. Hyŏn Inbok, one of the militia leaders, was sometimes called *sajok* and other times called *hyangin*. KP 1:25; and *Allŭng ilgi*, 630–32 and 412.

67. A similar trend to draw lines between original yangban and "new" yangban members by keeping separate rosters can be found in Chinju, Kyŏngsang Province. An analysis of yangban households (*yuho*) in the school repair records of Chinju in 1832 reveals that there were two types of yangban households: *wŏn-yuho* and *pyŏl-yuho*. The *wŏn-yuho* (11.5 percent) are proved to be true yangban households that had resided in the area at least from the early sixteenth century, while the *pyŏl-yuho* (12.3 percent) are quasi-yangban households that moved into the area later or those whose social status had been upgraded by certain means. What is important from this investigation is that these two groups were clearly perceived as socially different status groups at the time. Yi Haejun, "Chosŏn hugi Chinju chibang ŭi yuho ŭi silt'ae." See also Yi T'aejin, "Chosŏn hugi yangban sahoe ŭi pyŏnhwa."

68. Paek Siwŏn, *Nop'o sŏnsaeng munjip*, 5:1b–3a.

69. SJ 11.

70. The sale of *hyangan* memberships reportedly became prevalent in all provinces in the nineteenth century. Ko Sŏkkyu, *19–segi Chosŏn ŭi hyangch'on sahoe yon'gu*, 146–58; and Kim Ingŏl, "Chosŏn hugi hyangan ŭi sŏnggyŏk," 553.

71. KP 3:351.

72. *Kwansŏ sinmirok*, 81–83; and KP 5:110 and 3:342.

73. KP 5:110; and *Kwansŏ sinmirok*, 81–83.

74. KP 1:442.

75. KP 1:441, 2:518, and 5:482; and *Allŭng ilgi*, 479.

76. KP 4:497 and 5:482.

2 REGIONAL DISCRIMINATION AND THE HONG KYŎNGNAE REBELLION

1. Wagner, "The Civil Examination Process as Social Leaven," 22–27. In the present study, "northern residents" refers to people residing in the three northern provinces of Hwanghae, P'yŏngan, and Hamgyŏng.

2. In contrast, Hwanghae Province produced 11.5 percent of the successful candidates from 22.2 percent of the population, while Hamgyŏng Province produced 19.3 percent of the passers with 27.2 percent of the population. Wagner, "The Civil Examination Process as Social Leaven," 24.

3. For the national trend, see Wagner, "The Ladder of Success in Yi Dynasty Korea."

4. Ch'oe Chinok, *Chosŏn sidae saengwŏn chinsa yŏn'gu*, 19–30. Ch'oe estimates that the total number of degree-holders produced during the Chosŏn dynasty was 47,997. Of these, 40,649 are identifiable through various examination rosters. Residential information on 9,611 degree-holders (20 percent) is missing, most of whom lived before the seventeenth century.

5. Chŏng Yagyong, *Kyŏngse yup'yo*, 1:51.

6. Yi Sŏngmu, *Chosŏn ch'ogi yangban yŏn'gu*, 71. In the early Chosŏn, those who were young and smart were assigned to the Office of Diplomatic Correspondence, those who were rather aged and virtuous to the Royal Academy, those who were broadly learned in the past and present to the Office of Editorial Review, and those who were fluent in classics and principles to the Office of the Special Counselors.

7. Song Chunho, *Chosŏn sahoesa yŏn'gu*, 12.

8. Yi Chongil, *Taejŏn hoet'ong yŏn'gu, kwŏnsu ijŏn p'yŏn*, 262–85.

9. *Taejŏn hoet'ong, ijŏn kyŏnggwanjik*, 1:2a–5b. See also Yi Chongil, *Taejŏn hoet'ong yŏn'gu, kwŏnsu ijŏn p'yŏn*, 297–319.

10. Late Chosŏn kings tried to counterbalance the domination of political power by the capital-based prominent families by altering selection processes and by exercising direct appointment without using recommendations by offices in charge of personnel matters. Their efforts did not succeed in suppressing yangban power. Ch'a Changsŏp, *Chosŏn hugi pŏryŏl yŏn'gu*, 218–34.

11. Ch'a Changsŏp, *Chosŏn hugi pŏryŏl yŏn'gu*, 148–59.

12. Nam Chidae, "Chungang chŏngch'i seryŏk," 129–65.

13. Deuchler, "Heaven Does Not Discriminate."

14. O Such'ang, *Chosŏn hugi P'yŏngan-do sahoe palchŏn yŏn'gu*, 187–204.

15. The subsequent sections in this chapter include excerpts from Sun Joo Kim, "Negotiating Cultural Identities in Conflict."

16. For the history of this school, see SWI 1814. About Ch'ŏe Kyŏngnim, see SWI 1794 and 1806; and *Sinanji sokp'yŏn*, 64:21.

17. SWI 1770 and 1779.

18. Yŏngnam refers to Kyŏngsang Province, where Yi Hwang and Yi Ŏnjŏk lived. SWI 1786.2.24.

19. Paek Inhwan (1722–1805) was Paek's remote relative but the leading figure of his descent group because of his success in the 1756 *munkwa* and subsequent official career, particularly earning *ch'ŏngjik* (prestigious offices) beginning in 1787. Paek's teacher Ch'ŏe Kyŏngnim and Paek Inhwan became the most esteemed role models in Paek's life. When Paek Kyŏnghae first assumed a position at the central court, it was Paek Inhwan who admonished him in detail to maintain good health, study diligently, avoid wanton drinking and womanizing, guard against greediness, and to cultivate his mind. SWI 1788.

20. SWJ, *hwanhae chingbi*, 8:1a–4a, and *purok, kajang*, 1a–3b.

21. SWJ, *hwanhae chingbi*, 8:1a–4a, and *purok, kajang*, 1a–3b.

22. SWI 1789.9.27 and 1790.11.15; and SWJ, *hwanhae chingbi*, 8:2a–3b.

23. SWI 1795.3.3.

24. SWI 1795.3.3.

25. *Suwŏn Paek ssi Chŏngju chokpo*, 1:78.

26. Graves also had an economic dimension in the late Chosŏn. The descendants of the occupant of a grave site came to have exclusive rights to the land surrounding the tomb and also to the resources, such as firewood, that were produced there. For more discussion of this subject, see Kim Sŏngyŏng, "Chosŏn hugi sansong."

27. SWI 1799.4.13.

28. SWI 1801.4.1–1801.8.23.

29. SWJ, *hwanhae chingbi*, 8:1a–15b.

30. For more detailed discussion of the death of Paek Kyŏnghan, see chapter 6.

31. *Suwŏn Paek-ssi Chŏngju chokpo*.

32. SWI 1816.10.17.

33. Yi Ŭnggŏ was appointed the chief magistrate of Hansŏng (Hansŏngbu P'anyun, Sr. 2) in 1799.

34. Paek refers to Kim Ch'osŏp only by his pen name, Chahwa. I discovered his given name by conducting a search at the online *Wagner-Song mun-*

kwa pangmok provided by Dongbang Media, http://www.koreaa2z.com/munkwa).

35. Paek refers to Yi Kijun by his pen name, Yunji. The online *munkwa pangmok* again was helpful in discovering his name.

36. Paek Chonggŏl received the appointment of fourth inspector of the Office of the Inspector General (Chip'yŏng). In addition, three men, Chŏng Chonghyŏn, Yi Ch'angsim, and Paek Ch'irak, are mentioned in the diary as candidates for the *ch'ŏngjik* in 1820.

37. Kwŏn Tonin was the fifth-generation descendant of Kwŏn Sangha (1641–1721), one of the most prominent scholar-officials in the late Chosŏn period. His father, Kwŏn Chungjip, was a magistrate. He passed the *munkwa* exam in 1813 and was appointed the Yŏngŭijŏng in 1845. As a member of the Andong Kwŏn descent group residing in the capital, he enjoyed a brilliant career. In his youth, as a member of the privileged ruling elite, he seems to have been arrogant, as this episode reveals. As an experienced official later, however, he advocated the employment of northerners. *Hŏnjong sillok*, 4:14b, Hŏnjong 3.12.10 (*kyech'uk*).

38. This incident is well recorded in Paek's diary and collected works. SWI 1818.6.17 and 1818.7.3; and SWJ, *hwanhae chingbi*, 8:10b–13b.

39. Hallim refers to Kŏmyŏl (Sr. 9) in a narrow definition. It sometimes refers to all the offices of Ponggyo (Sr. 7), Taegyo (Sr. 8), and Kŏmyŏl at the Yemun'gwan. Yemun'gwan itself is also called Hallim. For more discussion on the Hallim, see Yi Chongil, *Taejŏn hoet'ong yŏn'gu, kw'ŏnsu ijŏn p'yŏn*, 297–319.

40. Ever since the introduction of the tobacco plant to Chosŏn in the late sixteenth or early seventeenth century, and because of its popularity in the late Chosŏn period, a certain tobacco culture, in line with other social norms, had emerged. According to a late Chosŏn scholar, Yu Tŭkkong (1749–?), younger people were advised to refrain from smoking with the elderly, and someone of low status was not to smoke tobacco in front of someone of noble status. Yu Tŭkkong, *Kyŏngdo chapchi, p'ungsok tayŏn*, 3; and Yi Yŏnghak, "Tambae ŭi sahoesa," 125. Paek was against smoking, for he believed that smoking tobacco was extremely poisonous, fetid, and addictive, without one single benefit. Furthermore, planting tobacco decreased space available for other, necessary plants, which subsequently contributed to famine. SWI 1814; and SWJ, *so*, 2:9b–10a and *chapchŏ*, 6:14b–15a.

41. SWI 1818.7.3.

42. SWJ, "Tae kwansŏ chein chŏng chŏngbu sŏ," 4:14b–19a.

43. SWJ, "Tae kwansŏ chein chŏng chŏngbu sŏ," 4:15a.

44. SWJ, "Tae kwansŏ chein chŏng chŏngbu sŏ," 4:15a. *Sŏ-chi-han* might be equivalent to derogatory Korean colloquial words such as *p'yŏngan-do nom* or

sŏtchok-nom or *sŏch'i*. In the rebel manifesto at the time of the Hong Kyŏngnae Rebellion, *p'yŏng-han* was used instead of *sŏ-chi-han*, to mean something like "the common rabble of P'yŏngan." *Hong Kyŏngnae pallangi*, 3–4.

45. SWJ, "Tae kwansŏ chein chŏng chŏngbu sŏ," 4:15b.

46. *Injo sillok*, 28:47a–47b, Injo 11.10.10 (*kapsul*); *P'yŏngyang sokchi, mundam*, 243; and O Such'ang, *Chosŏn hugi P'yŏngan-do sahoe palchŏn yŏn'gu*, 21.

47. Cho Ch'angnae (1686–?) passed the *munkwa* in 1715, earned a *ch'ŏngjik*, and was appointed the special capital magistrate in 1756. O Such'ang, *Chosŏn hugi P'yŏngan-do sahoe palchŏn yŏn'gu*, 203.

48. Kim Kyŏngsŏ (1564–1624) is famous for his military merit during the Japanese invasions (1592–98). He earned the junior second rank of provincial military commander, the highest position that a military official could reach in the Chosŏn bureaucratic hierarchy. For the most complete coverage of his achievements, see Yi Sihang, *Kim changgun yusa*.

49. SWJ, "Tae kwansŏ chein chŏng chŏngbu sŏ," 4:16b.

50. In my dissertation I suggested that the relocation of criminals to northern provinces, and the blood and cultural mixture with northern tribal people, may have contributed to the formation of prejudice against the northerners. In a similar vein, Kyung Moon Hwang argues that the bias against the northern population was rooted in "the aristocracy's (correct) perception of the northern population as descended from various low status groups of the early Chosŏn," such as Jurchen and "low-level" migrants. Sun Joo Kim, "Marginalized Elite," 45–46; and Kyung Moon Hwang, "From the Dirt to Heaven," 150.

51. Chŏng Okcha has recently highlighted the emergence of one extreme "nationalistic" view among Chosŏn intellectuals that placed Chosŏn in the center of civilization, as the sole successor of Confucian civilization after the demise of Ming China in the mid-seventeenth century. Chŏng Okcha, *Chosŏn hugi Chosŏn chunghwa sasang yŏn'gu*. JaHyun Kim Haboush concurs that Chosŏn intellectuals viewed the Manchu conquest of China in 1644 and the fall of the Ming as a barbarian conquest of the center of the civilized world—the world order of which Koreans were a part—and that they felt it was imperative to reconstruct the epistemological framework in which an imaginary map of self and other could be redrawn. Haboush, "Constructing the Center." One example of placing Chosŏn as the center of civilization is the *Kija p'alchoji* (Eight laws of Kija), written sometime in the late eighteenth century and now preserved at Gakushuin University, Japan. See Yamauchi, "Chōsen o motte tenka ni ō tarashimu."

52. SWJ 4:166.

53. *Sŏt'o* literally refers to P'yŏngan Province.

54. Sŏnu Hyŏp (1588–1653) from T'aech'ŏn was remembered as "the Confucius of P'yŏngan Province" by the people of P'yŏngan. Rather than pursuing an official career, he devoted himself to improving his scholarship through scholarly discussions with contemporary scholars and to teaching students. His works were compiled and preserved as the *Tunamjip* (Collected works of Sŏnu Hyŏp). *Kwansŏ ŭpchi P'yŏngyang sokchi, inmul,* 14:362.

55. Hwang Sunsŭng was known to be a filial son and was recommended for a position at the central court. His great-grandfather, Hwang Yunhu (1587–1648), passed the *munkwa* in 1625 and held such prestigious positions as royal secretary (Sŭngji). *P'yŏngyang sokchi, hyoyŏl,* 116–17. Hwang Sunwŏn, a distinguished writer of the twentieth century, is a direct descendant of these renowned scholars.

56. Yun Kŏhyŏng (1654–1715), a renowned Confucian scholar, was recommended for a central government position but did not take it. *P'yŏngan-pukto chi,* 556.

57. Paek Inhwan, the relative whom Paek Kyŏnghae respected the most, learned from Yun Chese. SWI 1797.4.

58. Paek Kyŏnghae often deplored the fact that P'yŏngan literati had abandoned scholarship and that they blamed the court for not employing them; instead, he himself encouraged them to make their best efforts in learning in case the court did search for talented scholars from P'yŏngan Province. SWI 1810.2.5; and SWJ, *yŏ Pak Yŏjung sŏ,* 4:25a–25b.

59. *Kwansŏ ŭpchi P'yŏngyang sokchi, hakkyo,* 14:351; and Chŏng Manjo, *Chosŏn sidae sŏwŏn yŏn'gu,* 23–32.

60. Other private academies and shrines established in the sixteenth century in P'yŏngan Province are Ssangch'ungsa (founded in 1572, chartered in 1670) in Ch'ŏlsan; Sanghyŏn *sŏwŏn* (1576, 1694) in Hŭich'ŏn; Sagyo *sŏwŏn* (1583) in Sŏnch'ŏn; Muyŏlsa (1593) in P'yŏngyang; Osan *sŏwŏn* (1595?, 1671) in Yonggang; and Ssangch'ungsa (1599, 1646) in Sŏngch'ŏn. *Kwansŏ ŭpchi; P'yŏngan-namdo chi,* 654–55; *P'yŏngan-pukto chi,* 434–36; and *Tongguk wŏnsarok.*

61. Sŭng Taegi (1588–1659), a member of Yŏnil Sŭng descent group in Chŏngju, "graduated" from the family study hall (*ch'ulsuk*) at the age of ten in 1598. *Yŏnil Sŭng ssi chokpo,* 16. According to the 1915 statistics compiled by Chōsen sōtokufu, there were 1,015 study halls, or village schools (*sŏdang*) in northern P'yŏngan Province alone. *P'yŏngan-pukto chi,* 439.

62. O Such'ang, who has done extensive studies on the history of P'yŏngan Province, argues that the study of Neo-Confucianism began to spread to the northern region only in the early seventeenth century, almost a century after its dissemination in the south. He also states that, among 101 private academies

established by the end of Kwanghae-gun's reign (1608–23), only one, Inhyŏn Academy, was located in P'yŏngan Province. This discussion on the delay of the spread of Neo-Confucianism to the north and of the absence of private academies there requires reconsideration. O Such'ang, "17, 18 segi P'yŏngan-do yusaengch'ŭng."

63. The relative lack of surviving literary works by northerners makes it difficult to prove the level of their scholarship. Although an analysis of Paek Kyŏnghae's understanding of Neo-Confucianism is beyond the scope of this book, his collected works do include extensive discussions of the Confucian classics.

64. I question whether the regional discrimination and prejudice that prevailed in the late Chosŏn period compel us to judge the absence of scholarly achievement by P'yŏngan literati in this manner. Yi Ik, now regarded as one of the most renowned scholars of Chosŏn, belonged to the Southerner faction (Namin), which had not fared well since the late seventeenth century. His writings were only published in 1917 but are now widely available. Yu T'agil, *Sŏngho hangmaek ŭi munjip kanhaeng yŏn'gu.*

65. For more discussion on this topic, see Sun Joo Kim, "Marginalized Elite," 57–70.

66. "Three years" refers to the three-year mourning period for one's father or one's king.

67. SWJ, "Tae kwansŏ chein chŏng chŏngbu sŏ," 4:17b–18a.

68. SWJ, "Tae kwansŏ chein chŏng chŏngbu sŏ," 4:19b.

69. For detailed information about the efforts made by various kings, beginning with King Injo (r. 1623–49), to end discriminatory practices against northerners, see O Such'ang, *Chosŏn hugi P'yŏngan-do sahoe palchŏn yŏn'gu,* 53–64.

70. For detailed discussion of the 1714 incident, see Sun Joo Kim, "In Defense of Regional Elite Identity and Culture."

71. The memorial from the P'yŏngan elite protesting Yŏ P'irhŭi's report was composed primarily by Yi Sihang (1672–1736), who was known to excel at writing in classical Chinese. Yi was originally from Unsan, but his family had established a secondary residence in P'yŏngyang from the time of his father, Yi Chŏnghan. Yi Sihang had been recognized as unusually intelligent from childhood and had become a protégé of Yu Sangun (1636–1707), who was provincial governor of P'yŏngan Province when Yi was young and who went on to become the highest state councilor (Yŏngŭijŏng) at the peak of his career in 1696. *P'yŏngyang sokchi,* 427–28.

72. It seems that the earliest document that records the Chosŏn as "sochunghwa," as referred to by civilized people (*hwain*), is the *Chewang un'gi* (An Epic of Emperors and Kings), written in 1287 by Yi Sŭnghyu, *kwŏn ha*: 1b.

73. Yi Sihang, *Hwaŭn sŏnsaeng munjip*, 267.

74. SWJ, "Tae kwansŏ chein chŏng chŏngbu sŏ," 4:14b.

75. For discussion of early Chinese texts dealing with Kija and his self-exile to Chosŏn (Ch.: Chaoxian), and the lack of archeological support for such claims, see Byington, "A History of the Puyŏ State."

76. Sŏ Yŏngdae, "Chŏnt'ong sidae ŭi Tan'gun ŭisik"; Han Young-woo, "Kija Worship in the Koryŏ and Early Yi Dynasties"; and Chai-sik Chung, "Chŏng Tojŏn: 'Architect' of Yi Dynasty Government and Ideology."

77. One episode is worth citing. The Sŏnu lineage, which claimed to be one of the descendants of Kija, was given a hereditary office of the superintendent (Ch'ambong) of the Kija shrine according to the *Taejŏn hoet'ong, ijŏn oegwan* (provincial offices), P'yŏngan-do, 1:51a. When the father of Sŏnu Hyŏp (1588–1653), who was known to northerners as Zhu Xi of P'yŏngan, was appointed the superintendent of the Kija shrine, Kija appeared to the twelve-year-old Sŏnu Hyŏp in a dream and gave him a poem deploring the ill treatment of the court toward the shrine. Sŏnu Hyŏp, *Tunam chŏnsŏ, yŏnbo* and *haengjang*.

78. Tan'gun and Kija were solidly upgraded to national rather than regional symbols by the enlightenment thinkers at the turn of the twentieth century. Schmid, *Korea Between Empires*.

79. Sŏnu Hyŏp, *Tunam chŏnsŏ, Tunam sŏnsaeng chŏnsŏ sŏ*, 3.

80. Yi Sihang, *Hwaŭn sŏnsaeng munjip*, 267–68.

81. Yi Sihang, *Hwaŭn sŏnsaeng munjip*, 283–84.

82. SWJ, "Adong pangŏn chŏngbyŏn sŏl," *chapchŏ*, 6:27a–28a.

83. Adopting a sociohistorical linguistic approach, Paek Tuhyŏn argues that the social and political discrimination toward the people of P'yŏngan Province and the consequent feeling of inferiority they harbored motivated speakers of the P'yŏngan dialect to keep their dialect distinct from others. This meant that the dialect did not go through t-palatalization (*kugae ŭmhwa*) until well into the twentieth century. Paek Tuhyŏn, "On the Correlation between Non-realization of T-palatalization and Regional Identity in P'yŏngan Province."

84. I owe this point to a businessman I met when I presented a part of this research at the Korea International Forum held in New York in November 2002. This businessman, of Korean heritage from China, expressed his frustration at how Korean Chinese (Yŏnbyŏn-jok) who migrate to South Korea to seek employment are effectively singled out as Yŏnbyŏn-jok due to their distinct dialect and are discriminated against in the workplace as a result.

85. SWI 1812.1.4 to 1.16 and 1812.3.27; SWJ 4:26b–28b; and CJI 165, 195, 205, 322, 329, 424, and 614–16.

86. SJ 88 and 90; and CJI 301–2 and 331.

87. *Sinanji sokp'yŏn*, 64:21–22.

88. Kim Ikhwan, a scholar-in-training from a provincial area (*oebang yusaeng*), was punished with exile for leading a strike of students at the Royal Academy in 1788. It is not clear whether this is the same person as the one from Chŏngju discussed here. *Sŭngjŏngwŏn ilgi*, 1642, Chŏngjo 12.5.29, 87:522–23; and *Ilsŏngnok*, Chŏngjo 12.5.29, 13:524–25.

89. SWI 1811.12.18.

90. KP 1:444; and *Allŭng ilgi*, 363. Kim Idae was forty-two years old, while Paek Kyŏnghae was forty-eight at the time.

91. In 1769 Ch'ŏe Kyŏngnim had the Paek family move to another place because, although he regarded the homestead as a place for wealth, he believed that it was causing harm to people living there. Paek Kyŏnghan, *Puhojip*, *puho nyŏn'gi*, 1769 (*kich'uk*); SWI 1792, 1799.4.13, 1806.5.1, 1807, and 1809; and SWJ 6:7a–9a.

92. Paek Kyŏnghan, *Puhojip*, *puho nyŏn'gi*, 1770 (*kyŏngin*); and CJI 693. Direct quote is from O Such'ang, *Chosŏn hugi P'yŏngan-do sahoe palchŏn yŏn'gu*, 247–48.

93. *Yŏnan Kim ssi Kaesŏng Puyun-gong p'abo*, 1:180–81.

94. KP 2:596; and CJI 136.

95. CJI 134, 334–36, and 372.

96. CJI 134 and 308; and SJ 23.

97. Wŏn Taech'ŏn, Yi Hyŏngt'ae, Yang Chehong, and Yang Ch'ije from Sŏnch'ŏn; Yi Sanghang, Hwang Chongdae, Yi Inyŏng, and Yi Sanghang from Chŏngju; Chŏng Ch'anghyŏn and Kim Hyŏn from Ch'ŏlsan; Kim Taeso from Kwaksan; Ch'oe Taewŏn from Pakch'ŏn; Yi Namjae from Yŏngbyŏn; and Yi P'aengnyŏn's father from Sakchu were identified as successful military exam candidates.

3 THE ECONOMIC CONTEXT OF THE HONG KYŎNGNAE REBELLION

1. For the recruitment of the rebel army and the rebels' material resources, see chapter 5.

2. Chŏng Yagyong, *Kyŏngse yup'yo*, 1:324; *Sejong sillok*, 102:17a–b, Sejong, 25.11.2 (*kyech'uk*). For more discussion on the quality of land, see O Such'ang, *P'yŏngan-do sahoe palchŏn yŏn'gu*, 135–38.

3. *Kyŏl* is a constant measure of crop yield produced by an area that varied from 2.2 to 9.0 acres depending on the fertility of the land.

4. The unusually high figure of more than 300,000 *kyŏl* recorded in the *Sejong*

sillok chiriji does not seem to reflect the true amount of land under cultivation during Sejong's reign. Kwŏn Naehyŏn notes that this may have been exaggerated or may have included land to be reclaimed. Kwŏn Naehyŏn, "P'yŏngan-do chaejŏng unyŏng," 44.

5. Kwŏn Naehyŏn, "P'yŏngan-do chaejŏng unyŏng," 44, 60, 90, and 173.

6. Kwŏn Naehyŏn, "P'yŏngan-do chaejŏng unyŏng," 45.

7. *Man'gi yoram chaeyongp'yŏn 2, chŏn'gyŏl, p'alto sado wŏnjangbu chŏndap*, 202–10.

8. Yŏm Chŏngsŏp, *Chosŏn sidae nongbŏp paltal yŏn'gu*, 155–74.

9. Yŏm Chŏngsŏp, *Chosŏn sidae nongbŏp paltal yŏn'gu*, 175.

10. U Hayŏng, *Ch'onillok*, 160–65.

11. *Taejŏn hoet'ong, hojŏn, suse*, 2:21b–25a; Yi Chunghwan, *T'aengniji*, 242 (p. 131 in the translation); Ko Sŏkkyu, "18 segimal 19 segich'o P'yŏngan-do chiyŏk hyanggwŏn ŭi ch'ui"; and Kwŏn Naehyŏn, "P'yŏngan-do chaejŏng unyŏng," 44–64 and 89–98.

12. Yi Ch'ŏlsŏng, "17 segi P'yŏngan-do kangbyŏn 7 ŭp ŭi pangŏ ch'eje"; and Palais, *Confucian Statecraft and Korean Institutions*, 394–441.

13. Kenneth R. Robinson, "From Raiders to Traders."

14. The origin of the term "Manchu" as ethnonym is not very clear. Mark Elliott notes that the name was adopted in 1635 for the diverse Jurchen tribes grouped under Hong Taiji (1592–1643). For further discussion of what Elliot calls "the transformation from undifferentiated frontier to geographic region of that part of northeast Asia controversially referred to as Manchuria," see Elliott, "The Limits of Tartary."

15. The number of Ming troops and refugees must have fluctuated. In 1628, the number was 26,000 and they consumed more than 100,000 *sŏm* of grain. At the height of Mao's activities in the area, he demanded as many as 140,000 *sŏm* of grain from the Chosŏn court, most of which was locally supplied. *Injo sillok*, 19:32b, Injo 6.9.29 (*pyŏngsul*) and13:43b–44a, Injo 4.7.13 (*kyemi*). For more discussion on the financial drain caused by the Ming military camp at Ka Island, see Kwŏn Naehyŏn, "P'yŏngan-do chaejŏng unyŏng," 72–78.

16. Kwŏn Naehyŏn, "P'yŏngan-do chaejŏng unyŏng," 98–102; and O Such'ang, "Chosŏn hugi P'yŏngan-domin e taehan insa chŏngch'aek," 125–28.

17. Kwŏn Naehyŏn, "P'yŏngan-do chaejŏng unyŏng," 122–27.

18. Kwŏn Naehyŏn, "P'yŏngan-do chaejŏng unyŏng," 112–16. The central court itself spent approximately 80,000 *yang* for one Qing mission. According to another study of the economic burden incurred by tribute relations with the Qing, the total expense, including tribute goods and gifts, amounted to more than 810,000 *yang* per year in the period of 1637–44. After the Qing took over the

Ming, the Qing reduced the tribute amount dramatically, and the annual average expense decreased to around 400,000 *yang* in the period of 1645–1735. The expense decreased further, to about 200,000 *yang* per year, after 1736. Chŏn Haejong, "Ch'ŏngdae han-jung kwan'gye ŭi ilgoch'al."

19. *Yŏnil Sŭng ssi chokpo*, 16–18, 76–78, 224, and 236–37. For other examples, see chapter 2 in the present volume. For the wealth accumulated by Kye Wŏnsu of Sŏnch'ŏn in the early eighteenth century, see *Suan Kye ssi inmaek po*, 43.

20. O Such'ang, *P'yŏngan-do sahoe palchŏn yŏn'gu*, 151–57; and Kwŏn Naehyŏn, "P'yŏngan-do chaejŏng unyŏng," 203–13.

21. Kwŏn Naehyŏn, "P'yŏngan-do chaejŏng unyŏng," 213–34.

22. Anders Karlsson concludes that the Hong Kyŏngnae Rebellion "was a conflict between local society in P'yŏngan Province and central power." He argues that the most conspicuous development in the relationship between the center and the local level during the late Chosŏn dynasty was "a stronger influence and heavier presence of central power" and that the rebellion was "a reaction to this development and in that sense was a 'defensive' protest protecting the customary rights of local leaders to control work at the county offices and the management of its resources." Karlsson, "The Hong Kyŏngnae Rebellion 1811–1812," 275. For further discussion of Karlsson's work, see chapter 8.

23. The scale of damage to debtors in such transactions is well described in Third State Councilor Ch'oe Sŏkchŏng's attack on the role of cash in exacerbating the interest rate and the debt burdens imposed on poor peasants. If someone borrowed 1 *yang* in the springtime when rice was in short supply and its price was high, the borrower could only purchase 2 *mal* of it on the market. After the harvest in the fall the borrower would have to repay 1.5 *yang* of principal and interest combined. But since by then the temporary market price on grain was down to 5 *mal* per *yang*, it would cost the borrower 7.5 *mal* to obtain the 1.5 *yang* to repay the debt—3.75 times the grain value of the original loan in cash borrowed in the spring, or 375 percent. Palais, *Confucian Statecraft and Korean Institutions*, 930.

24. Palais, *Politics and Policy in Traditional Korea*, 132–34.

25. Mun Yongsik, *Chosŏn hugi chinjŏng kwa hwan'gok unyŏng*, 18–44.

26. Palais, *Politics and Policy in Traditional Korea*, 138.

27. Mun Yongsik, *Chosŏn hugi chinjŏng kwa hwan'gok unyŏng*, 142–62.

28. The Ever-Normal Bureau (Sangp'yŏngch'ŏng) and the Relief Bureau (Chinhyulch'ŏng) were independent offices that had been established on ad hoc basis. From about the mid- to the late seventeenth century, they remained as permanent institutions within the Office for Dispensing Benevolence (Sŏnhyech'ŏng),

in order to meet the frequent relief needs caused by natural disasters and famine. By the early eighteenth century, these two offices were often together called the Sangjinch'ŏng, and their funds the *sangjin'gok*, after the first letters of each bureau, for their functions largely overlapped. Mun Yongsik, *Chosŏn hugi chinjŏng kwa hwan'gok unyŏng*, 107–15.

29. Kwŏn Naehyŏn, "P'yŏngan-do chaejŏng unyŏng," 234–45.

30. Palais, *Politics and Policy in Traditional Korea*, 141–42; and Song Ch'ansŏp, *Chosŏn hugi hwan'gok chedo kaehyŏk yŏn'gu*, 9–19. In principle, only a half of the total reserve grain was to be loaned out. However, most of the new grain loans established by various offices and agencies in the late eighteenth century were operated under the policy of loaning out all the reserve grain to maximize interest income.

31. Ko Sŏkkyu, "18 segimal 19 segich'o P'yŏngan-do chiyŏk hyanggwŏn ŭi ch'ui," 368–71.

32. Mun Yongsik, *Chosŏn hugi chinjŏng kwa hwan'gok unyŏng*, 181–216; and Chang Tongp'yo, *Chosŏn hugi chibang chaejŏng yŏn'gu*, 43–67.

33. Only one study by Han Sanggwŏn has made a full investigation of the Koksan rebellion in 1811. A short section in a multivolume history of Korea commissioned by North Korea briefly deals with the rebellion. Han Sanggwŏn, "1811 nyŏn Hwanghae-do Koksan chibang ŭi nongmin hangjaeng"; and Sahoe kwahagwŏn yŏksa yŏn'guwŏn, "1811–1812 nyŏn P'yŏngan-do nongmin chŏn-jaeng," 13–15. This section on the Koksan rebellion was reconstructed from *Sŭngjŏngwŏn ilgi*, 1998–2000, Sunjo 11.4.1–11.5.6, 105:212–308; and *Ilsŏngnok*, Sunjo 11.3.1–11.3.14, 37:370–407.

34. The social status of local wealthy households, called *puho* in *Sŭngjŏngwŏn ilgi* (Records of the Royal Secretariat), is unknown, but they were most likely local yangban elite, although it is undeniable that non-yangban members of local society may also have been able to amass some wealth. *Sŭngjŏngwŏn ilgi*, 1998, Sunjo 11.4.13, 105:247.

35. SWI 1810. *yun* 3.5.

36. Chang Tongp'yo, *Chosŏn hugi chibang chaejŏng yŏn'gu*, 153–88.

37. SWI 1808.3.22.

38. O Yŏnggyo, "Chosŏn hugi chibang kwanch'ŏng kwa singni hwaltong"; and Kim Tŏkchin, "Chosŏn hugi chibang kwanch'ŏng ŭi min'go sŏllip kwa unyŏng."

39. KP 1:269–71.

40. Chŏng Yagyong, *Kyŏngse yup'yo chigwan suje*, *pugongje* 6 and 7, 3:1041, 1037, 1069, and 1073.

41. *Chŏngjo sillok*, 44:20a, Chŏngjo 20.2.25 (*sinch'uk*).

42. Chŏng Yagyong, *Yŏkchu mongmin simsŏ, hojŏn, sebŏp,* 2:355; Chŏng Yagyong, *Kyŏngse yup'yo, chigwan suje, chŏnje* 6, 2:586. For studies dealing with various aspects of local clerks in the late Chosŏn, see Yi Hunsang, *Chosŏn hugi ŭi hyangni*; Yŏnse taehakkyo kukhak yŏn'guwŏn, *Han'guk kŭndae ihaenggi chungin yŏn'gu*; and Hwang, *Beyond Birth,* 161–81.

43. *Chŏngjo sillok,* 20:14a–b, Chŏngjo 9.7.5 (*imja*) and 23:48a, Chŏngjo 11.4.16 (*kyech'uk*); and Ko Sŏkkyu, *19 segi Chosŏn ŭi hyangch'on sahoe yŏn'gu,* 197–202. In traditional China, well-to-do families were also appointed as the heads of local administration units and put in charge of tax collection. See Bernhardt, *Rents, Taxes, and Peasant Resistance,* 37–42.

44. KP 5:163, 5:468, and 3:343.

45. KP 1:656–59.

46. KP 3:143. Ho Yunjo, an outpost officer in the Pyŏktong area who was accused of collaborating with Kim Ch'angsi, was also in financial trouble because he had appropriated grain reserves under his administrative care. KP 1:600 and 3:233.

47. Entries at the end of SWI 1810 and 1811.

48. SWJ, *purok, kajang,* 5a–5b; and SWI 1812.7.

49. Indeed, after about a month after the rebellion broke out, an official criticized that if the court had taken relief measures, which would have cost less than one-third of counterrebel campaign expenses incurred by that time, it might have prevented people from revolting from the beginning. *P'yŏngsŏ ponmal,* 1812.1.24.

50. KP 4:409.

51. KP 3:79.

52. KP 2:512.

53. KP 5:51–54. The testimony of Kim Ch'igwan's wife and Kim Taeun (Ch'igwan's father in-law) about the activities and whereabouts of Kim Ch'igwan are unreliable. According to them, Kim and his wife left Kasan Tabok village, the rebel base, in late October or early November 1811 to avoid official pressure to pay back their debts, and stayed in the Ch'angsŏng and Wiwŏn area during the rebellion. However, Kim's own testimony reveals that he witnessed the military preparations for the rebellion in late January 1812 and joined the rank and file of the rebel army in the early stage of the rebellion. He escaped from the rebel camp at Chŏngju sometime in late February and was arrested by the government army in Ch'angsŏng while on his way back home. Regardless of whether or not they were pressed hard for the repayment of their debts, it is reasonable to assume that the difficulty of repayment became a logical excuse for running away from their original residence. SSP 61.

54. Kim Chosun (1765–1831) of the Andong Kim passed the civil service examination in 1785, and the highest office he attained was director of the Office of Special Counselors. When King Chŏngjo (r. 1776–1800) died and King Sunjo (r. 1800–34) succeeded to the throne as a young boy of eleven, Queen Dowager Chŏngsun, the regent until 1804, appointed Kim to assist her in governing state affairs. Later, as a member of the Andong Kim clan, he was able to marry his daughter to King Sunjo. This opened the way for politics to be controlled by consort family members of the Andong Kim clan for the next several decades. Yi Hongjik, *Han'guksa taesajŏn*, 1:331.

55. Pak Chonggyŏng (1765–1817), King Sunjo's maternal uncle and a member of Pannam Pak lineage, passed the civil service examination in 1801. He served in various government offices, including as minister of various ministries and commanding general of the military training administration. Although he was once accused by Inspector General Cho Tŭgyŏng of rapacious behavior, relying on his status as a close in-law of the current king, he enjoyed the great confidence of the king for most of his lifetime. Yi Hongjik, *Han'guksa taesajŏn*, 1:601. For Cho Tŭgyŏng's memorial to impeach Pak, see *Sunjo sillok*, 16:25a–27a, Sunjo 12.11.7 (*pyŏngja*). For Pak Chonggyŏng's response to Cho's criticism, see *Sunjo sillok*, 16:32a–33a, Sunjo 12.11.15 (*kapsin*).

56. In another text, comets and natural disasters caused by floods, insects, and frost were mentioned. Kang Hŭiyŏng, *Ilsŭng*, 32.

57. *Hong Kyŏngnae pallangi*, 4.

58. *P'yŏngsŏ ponmal*, 1811.12.24; and *Hong Kyŏngnae pallangi*, 4. The information about Im Sŏnggo is somewhat contradictory since other sources show that the rebels spared Im's life, along with that of Yi Kŭnju, the magistrate of Chŏngju, because they were lenient in financial administration and the people begged that their lives be spared. See SJ 11; KP 5:375; and *Hong ssi ilgi*, 17.

59. *P'yŏngsŏ ponmal*, 1811.12.24.

60. For the studies linking climatic changes to agricultural crisis and then to peasant uprisings, see Yi Hoch'ŏl, "19 segi nonŏp munje ŭi sŏnggyŏk"; and Yi Hoch'ŏl and Pak Kŭnp'il, "19 segi ch'o Chosŏn ŭi kihu pyŏndong kwa nongŏp wigi."

61. Palais, *Confucian Statecraft and Korean Institutions*, 771–814. Yi Hŏnch'ang's recent study on Kim Yuk (1580–1650), the master designer of the *taedongpŏp*, is the most up-to-date investigation of this law's conception and institution. Yi Hŏnch'ang, "Kim Yuk ŭi kyŏngje sasang kwa kyŏngje chŏngch'aek."

62. For details on the financial reform and commercial development, see Palais, *Confucian Statecraft and Korean Institution*, 771–814 and 964–98. For more specific studies on the emergence of private merchants and their struggles

with licensed merchants, see Pyŏn Kwangsŏk, *Chosŏn hugi sijŏn sangin yŏn'gu.* Ko Tonghwan investigates the growth of Seoul as a commercial hub, the development of domestic trade routes, and the formation of a market network in the late Chosŏn in his study, *Chosŏn hugi Sŏul sangŏp paltalsa yŏn'gu* (A Study of the Development of Commerce in Seoul in Late Chosŏn). In contrast, Kim Taegil explores the development of local markets in the late Chosŏn in his book *Chosŏn hugi changsi yŏn'gu* (A Study of Markets in Late Chosŏn). Paek Sŭngch'ŏl provides a comprehensive study of court debates concerning the policies on commerce, as well as Neo-Confucian perspectives on commerce, in *Chosŏn hugi sangŏpsa yŏn'gu* (A Study of the History of Commerce in Late Chosŏn).

63. Kim Chongwŏn, "Chosŏn hugi taech'ŏng muyŏk e taehan ilkoch'al."

64. Yu Sŭngju and Yi Ch'ŏlsŏng, *Chosŏn hugi chungguk kwa ŭi muyŏksa*; and Yi Ch'ŏlsŏng, *Chosŏn hugi taech'ŏng muyŏksa yŏn'gu.*

65. Yi Ch'ŏlsŏng, *Chosŏn hugi taech'ŏng muyŏksa yŏn'gu*, 43–50; and *Yŏngjo sillok*, 68:16a, Yŏngjo 24.9.14 (*ŭlch'uk*).

66. *Yŏngjo sillok*, 31:28a, Yŏngjo 8.*yun* 5.22 (*chŏngmi*) and 31:28b, Yŏngjo 8.*yun* 5.25 (*kyŏngsul*).

67. *Yŏngjo sillok*, 32:2a, Yŏngjo 8.7.4 (*muja*). In addition to these incidents, a number of reports on the arrest and punishment of smugglers are found in *sillok* (veritable record) entries during the eighteenth century. A wealthy merchant of Seoul was banished for illegal trading. Ibid., 58:37a, Yŏngjo 19.12.21 (*kyŏngo*). In 1764, a smuggler residing in Ŭiju killed a Qing national. Ibid., 103:21, Yŏngjo 40.1.9 (*sinyu*). Illegal traders who followed government envoys to the Qing capital were caught and banished to remote regions in the same year. Ibid., 103:24b, Yŏngjo 40.5.16 (*chŏngmyo*).

68. *Yŏngjo sillok*, 96:25b, Yŏngjo 36.11.29 (*kisa*).

69. The magistrate of Ŭiju was banished to a remote area south of the Amnok River because he failed to enforce the ban on foreign trade in 1763. *Yŏngjo sillok*, 102:5a, Yŏngjo 39.6.24 (*kyŏngsul*). A few years later, another magistrate of Ŭiju was dismissed from his office because he did not duly investigate smugglers. Ibid., 113:1a, Yŏngjo 45.7.4 (*kapsin*).

70. *Yŏngjo sillok*, 64:28b–29a, Yŏngjo 23.12.20 (*pyŏngja*) and 65:3a, Yŏngjo 23.1.12 (*imin*).

71. *Yŏngjo sillok*, 68:27a–27b, Yŏngjo 24.11.5 (*ŭlmyo*).

72. *Yŏngjo sillok*, 72:29a, Yŏngjo 26.12.25 (*kabo*). In 1749, the king repeated the ban on embroidered silk as well as on plain silk without embroidery and ordered a reduction in the amount of other trading items. Offenders were to be subject to the law pertinent to smugglers. In 1752, two officials were investigated and punished in relation to their involvement in silk trading. Ibid., 79:1b, Yŏngjo

29.1.5 (*sinyu*). About twenty years later, the king was still concerned about the outflow of silver to pay for luxurious goods and ordered that the law be strictly enforced. Ibid., 116:22a–22b, Yŏngjo 47.4.19 (*kich'uk*).

73. *Taejŏn hoet'ong, hojŏn, chapse,* 2:33a.

74. O Sŏng, "Insam sangin kwa kŭmsam chŏngch'aek," 23–30.

75. O Sŏng, "Insam sangin kwa kŭmsam chŏngch'aek," 51–52.

76. *Sunjo sillok,* 6:26b, Sunjo 4.8.1 (*chŏngsa*).

77. *Sunjo sillok,* 10:37b, Sunjo 7.9.21 (*kimi*). Kim Kunil was one of the owners of the boat involved in these illegal transactions. The same name appears once (on p. 260) in *Chinjung ilgi* (A Diary at the Military Camp) as that of a rebel soldier guarding the gate of Chŏngju. There is no other record that can confirm that these two people were in fact one individual.

78. *Sunjo sillok,* 10:51a–b, Sunjo 7.12.22 (*kich'uk*) and 11:1a, Sunjo 8.1.4 (*sinch'uk*).

79. The regulation of silver mining was codified in the *Soktaejŏn* (Supplement to the Dynastic Code). Basically, the Ministry of Taxation, various military units, and government agencies were allowed to draw tax revenues from silver mines after receiving permits from the central government. This regulation was revised in the *Taejŏn hoet'ong* (Comprehensive Collection of Dynastic Code) so that only the Ministry of Taxation was granted a permit for all the silver and copper mines. *Taejŏn hoet'ong, hojŏn, chapse,* 2:32b. For more detailed discussion of mining in the late Chosŏn, see Tsurusono, "Heian-dō nōmin sensō ni okeru sankasō," 64–66; and Yu Sŭngju, "Chosŏn hugi kwangŏpsa ŭi sidae kubun e kwanhan ilsiron."

80. *Sunjo sillok,* 14:59b, Sunjo 11.12. 20 (*kapcha*). See chapter 5 in the present volume for more details on Yi Hŭijo.

81. KP 3:604. See chapter 5 in the present volume for more details on U Kunch'ik.

82. SJ 13; SSP 21; and KP 2:495 and 2:502.

83. Hill, *The World Turned Upside Down,* 44–45.

84. Pak Sŏngsin's wine shop in Kwaksan also provided space for the spread of subversion. See chapter 5 for the role played by Pak in the rebellion.

85. On Kim Hyech'ŏl's participation in the rebellion, see SSP 77, 82, and 121; CJI 159; and KP 1:450, 3:167, 3:208, and 4:229.

86. KP 1:423 and 3:208.

87. SSP 77–78; and CJI 134.

88. KP 3:21–25.

89. SSP 77–78; and KP 3:21.

90. Yang Chehong was an opportunist. When the rebels were defeated and retreated to Chŏngju, he joined one of the progovernment militias (*ŭibyŏng*) and

made every effort to arrest the rebels to atone for his earlier participation in the rebel camp. When finally caught by the government and interrogated, he denied any voluntary participation in the rebellion. For Yang Chehong's activities, see *Kwansŏ sinmirok*, 49–52; and KP 2:10–16, 4:235, 5:18, 5:137, and 5:190.

91. KP 2:11, 5:144, 5:158, and 5:496; and Inaba, *Heian hokudō shi, ge*, 903.

92. White, *Ikki, Social Conflict and Political Protest in Early Modern Japan*, 77; and Little, *Understanding Peasant China*, 159–68.

4 PROPHECY AND POPULAR REBELLION

1. Joe, *Traditional Korea*, 165; Yi Pyŏngdo, *Koryŏ sidae ŭi yŏn'gu*, 21–30; and Yoon Hong-key, "The Image of Nature in Geomancy."

2. Freedman, *Chinese Lineage and Society*, 124.

3. Freedman, *Chinese Lineage and Society*, 125.

4. Freedman, *Chinese Lineage and Society*, 316.

5. An Chŏngbok, *Sunam sŏnsaeng munjip*, *yŏ-ssi hyangyak pujo*, 15:22a–22b.

6. Freedman, *Chinese Lineage and Society*, 322.

7. For example, Paek Kyŏnghae's teacher, Ch'oe Kyŏngnim, practiced geomancy and played a critical role in selecting proper burial sites for Paek's dead ancestors. SWI 1799.4.13.

8. Freedman, *Chinese Lineage and Society*, 323–29.

9. Yi Pyŏngdo, *Koryŏ sidae ŭi yŏn'gu*, 28.

10. Ch'oe Kilsŏng, "Koryŏ Chosŏn ŭi p'ungsu sasang."

11. Yi Pyŏngdo, *Koryŏ sidae ŭi yŏn'gu*.

12. Murayama, *Chōsen no senboku to yogen*, 29–36. For the ideological foundation of the Koryŏ royal house, see Rogers, "*P'yŏnnyŏn T'ongnok*."

13. Yi Pyŏngdo, *Koryŏ sidae ŭi yŏn'gu*, 41–55.

14. *Koryŏsa*, 2:15a.

15. Joe, *Traditional Korea*, 193.

16. Yi Pyŏngdo, *Koryŏ sidae ŭi yŏn'gu*, 138–56.

17. Yi Pyŏngdo, *Koryŏ sidae ŭi yŏn'gu*, 157–70.

18. Yi Pyŏngdo, *Koryŏ sidae ŭi yŏn'gu*, 175–89.

19. Yi Pyŏngdo, *Koryŏ sidae ŭi yŏn'gu*, 190–244.

20. Yi Pyŏngdo, *Koryŏ sidae ŭi yŏn'gu*, 23–24. Yoon Hong-key argues that yang geomancy preceded yin geomancy in its emergence. Yoon Hong-key, "P'ungsu chirisŏl ŭi ponjil kwa kiwŏn mit kŭ chayŏn'gwan."

21. According to Martina Deuchler, Confucians believed that the body was buried in order to preserve the person's mind-matter, or force (*ki*), which was

thought to circulate between the living and the dead. If the ancestors found peace in the ground, their descendants would find peace in this world. For the Confucians, the importance of burial lay in preserving the link between the dead and the living, and a properly prepared grave was security for the well-being of both. Therefore, its selection and construction were matters of the greatest importance in the funerary arrangements, and the siting of graves was increasingly based on geomancy from the fifteenth century on. Deuchler, *The Confucian Transformation of Korea*, 197–200.

22. Pae Hyesuk, "Yŏngjo nyŏn'gan ŭi sahoe tonghyang kwa min'gan sasang."

23. For example, in the period of the Northern and Southern States, Daoism contained many prophecies of cyclical world renewal, the end of the present cycle being marked by disasters and mysterious beings that would intervene to judge and save humankind. Upon its arrival in China, Buddhism also adopted a variety of apocalyptic currents. Ownby, "Chinese Millenarian Traditions." For later manifestations of millenarianism in Chinese popular belief system, the White Lotus in particular, see Naquin, *Millenarian Rebellion in China*.

24. Emmerson, "The Secret."

25. Anders Karlsson agrees that the ideas in the *Chŏnggamnok* are not to be interpreted as millenarianism, for the concept of eschatology in the *Chŏnggamnok* is deeply steeped in the cyclical view of history, and the perceived alternative to the existing social order was to establish a new dynasty. Karlsson, "Challenging the Dynasty." It seems that the cyclical view of history within divinatory texts does not necessarily disqualify them as millenarian because certain Daoist and Buddhist millenarian traditions conceive of time and history as cyclical. Ownby, "Chinese Millenarian Traditions," 1518–19 and 1524.

26. Morohashi, *Dai Kan-Wa jiten*, 8:201. Eclecticism is prevalent in many folk religious traditions. Tai, *Millenarianism and Peasant Politics in Vietnam*, 33.

27. Cho Tongil, *Minjung yŏngung iyagi*, 86–107.

28. For the cosmology and history of White Lotus sects of the Ming and Qing dynasties, see Naquin, *Millenarian Rebellion in China*, 9–18. For the similarities between the White Lotus and the Buu Son Ky Huong, a Vietnamese millenarian tradition, see Tai, *Millenarianism and Peasant Politics in Vietnam*, 27–33. Eric Hobsbawm shows in his study of millenarianism that a shared vision of a future, better world, no matter how vague and impractical it is, can provide powerful motivation for members of millenarian movements. Hobsbawm, *Primitive Rebels*, 57–107.

29. For the discussion of various prophetic records utilized by the conspirators, see Paek Sŭngjong, "18–19 segi *Chŏnggamnok* ŭl pirokhan kakchong yeŏnsŏ."

30. Official historiography of dynastic changes from the Unified Silla to the

Koryŏ and from the Koryŏ to the Chosŏn clearly borrows such moralistic Confucian notions of the Mandate of Heaven. See *Samguk sagi* and *Koryŏsa*. Also see Hurst, "The Good, the Bad and the Ugly."

31. Perry, *Challenging the Mandate of Heaven*, ix.

32. Yi Hŭigwŏn, "Chŏng Yŏrip moban sakŏn e kwanhan koch'al"; and Kim Yongdŏk, "Chŏng Yŏrip yŏn'gu."

33. For details, see Murayama, *Chōsen no senboku to yogen*, 570–71.

34. Murayama, *Chōsen no senboku to yogen*, 645–48. In contrast, Paek Sŭngjong argues that there is a strong possibility that the *Chŏnggamnok* was written in vernacular Korean first by a person from P'yŏngan Province no earlier than the early eighteenth century, based on the first record on the *Chŏnggamnok* in the *Chosŏn wangjo sillok* (The Veritable Records of the Kings of the Chosŏn Dynasty) in 1739, which reports the popularity of the book in the northern provinces. He then points out that by the late eighteenth century, the book was found throughout the peninsula. Paek Sŭngjong, "18 segi chŏnban sŏbuk chibang esŏ ch'ulhyŏnhan *Chŏnggamnok*."

35. For more details of the plot of 1688, see Chŏng Sŏkchong, "Chosŏn hugi Sukchong nyŏn'gan ŭi mirŭk sinang kwa sahoe undong."

36. For more details, see Chŏng Sŏkchong, "Sukchong nyŏn'gan sŭngnyŏ seryŏk ŭi kŏbyŏn kyehoek kwa Chang Kilsan."

37. According to Pae Hyesuk's study on rebellious plots during Yŏngjo's reign, plots were discovered on average once in three years. Pae Hyesuk, "Yŏngjo nyŏn'gan ŭi sahoe tonghyang kwa min'gan sasang," 89–91.

38. Pae Hyesuk, "Yŏngjo nyŏn'gan ŭi sahoe tonghyang kwa min'gan sasang"; and Yi Sangbae, "Yŏngjojo Yun Chi kwaesŏ sakŏn kwa chŏngguk ŭi tonghyang."

39. Yi Sangbae, "Chosŏn hugi Hansŏngbu kwaesŏ e kwanhan yŏn'gu"; idem, *Chosŏn hugi chŏngch'i wa kwaesŏ*; and Cho Kwang, "19 segi millan ŭi sahoejŏk paegyŏng."

40. CJI 131.

41. CJI 691.

42. See *Sinyŏk Chŏnggamnok, Kamgyŏl,* 14.

43. CJI 132.

44. CJI 132.

45. KP 3:321–33.

46. KP 4:225 and 3:619. Kang and his father were low-level military officers and engaged in commercial activities for a living.

47. KP 3:604–7 and 3:621–22. Because Kim Yŏjŏng was selling food to boatmen in the market of the Pakch'ŏn ferry station at the time of the rebellion, he had

many chances to meet poor people who could be easily persuaded by his offer of jobs at the mine. In addition he provided them with money, food, and wine.

48. It is most likely that the Red Robe Island did not exist. Various geographical names such as "Sun and Moon Peak" and "King Port" were apparently used to augment holy status of the savior supposedly born there.

49. During the reign of King Sejong, the four districts were established in the upper reaches of the Amnok River in order to secure the northern borders against the Jurchen tribes that often attacked the area. However, since it was very difficult to maintain these districts as administrative units due to a sparse population, unproductive terrain, and continuous conflicts with the Jurchen people, all four districts were abolished by 1459.

50. *Hong Kyŏngnae pallangi*, 4. According to this manifesto, the savior—*Chŏng chinin*—commanded the descendants of the Chinese Ming dynasty, which contradicts other sources that designated his army as Manchus (*hogun*). The whole story of *Chŏng chinin* and his army seemed to be propaganda from the outset, devised to earn popular support for the rebellion.

51. CJI 692.

52. KP 3:167.

53. KP 4:335–40.

54. KP 3: 606–7.

55. KP 4:494; and CJI 698–702.

56. Kang Hŭiyŏng, *Ilsŭng*, 30.

57. In his study of peasant protest during the Tokugawa period, Herbert P. Bix concludes that folk belief provided a new basis for class unity in peasant uprisings as the economy grew complex in eighteenth-century Japan. Bix, *Peasant Protest in Japan*, 215–28.

58. KP 5:86–89.

59. The *Chŏnggamnok* usually predicts a long-term bloody struggle for a dynastic transition. For example, *Kamgyŏl* expects twelve years of chaos. *Sinyŏk Chŏnggamnok*, 21 and 27.

60. For Kim Taehun's role in the rebellion, see KP 5:90–91 and 4:450. Kim Taehun was one of the rebels who was decapitated for treason (*moban taeyŏk choe*).

61. SJ 23.

62. KP 5:110–14 and 3:302; and *Kwansŏ sinmirok*, 81–83.

63. CJI 158 and 308; and KP 1:515. Pak Sŏngsin and his sons were all decapitated.

64. In addition to all these cases, there is much evidence of the widespread belief in the True and Genuine Chŏng and the role that belief played in recruiting the rebels. KP 1:19 and 2:503.

65. *Sunjo kisa,* 10:35b.

66. CJI 229–30.

67. KP 4:129.

68. CJI 142. One *chang*=10 *chu-ch'ŏk*=2.08 meters. Thus, 10 *chang* is about 20.8 meters.

69. CJI 241.

70. KP 1:470.

71. CJI 142.

72. KP 4:332–37.

73. KP 1:67.

74. Records about Pak Chŏngyong's involvement in the rebellion are too numerous to list. The most representative ones are in KP 5:89, 5:486, and 1:466; and *Sunjo sillok,* 16:19a, Sunjo 12.9.20 (*kich'uk*).

75. KP 4:32.

76. KP 4:358 and 4:388.

77. CJI 643.

78. Naquin, *Millenarian Rebellion in China,* 89.

79. The diary and child-rearing journal written by Yi Mungŏn (1494–1567) reveal how deeply the everyday life of this literatus living in the countryside depended on the blessings and curses of magical powers. Yi and Yi's family patronized a number of shamans and diviners on a regular basis, not only for the cure of diseases but also to prevent harmful forces from penetrating the household and to usher in good fortune. Yi Mungŏn, *Yangarok*; Yi Pokkyu, "Chosŏn chŏn'gi sadaebuga ŭi musok"; idem, "Chosŏn chŏn'gi sadaebuga ŭi chŏmbok kwa tokkyŏng"; and Kim Hyŏnyŏng, "Ŭi, chŏm, mu." During the late Chosŏn period, yangban literati did not prohibit their wives from patronizing shamans and fortunetellers. Walraven, "Popular Religion in a Confucianized Society," 160–98.

5   LEADERSHIP AND PREPARATION

1. CJI 691.

2. *Hong Kyŏngnae,* 118–61 (Korean translation) and 366–84. For an evaluation of *Hong Kyŏngnae,* which is almost identical to *Hong Kyŏngnae imsin saryak,* see appendix A.

3. Kang Hŭiyŏng, *Ilsŭng,* 29.

4. SWJ, *purok, kajang,* 6a.

5. O Such'ang, *P'yŏngan-do sahoe palchŏn yŏn'gu,* 262.

6. KP 2:214.

7. CJI 131.

8. KP 3:711 ff.

9. CJI 131 and 412; and KP 2:214.

10. CJI 131.

11. KP 2:198.

12. KP 4:479; and CJI 306–7 and 614–16.

13. CJI 619–21. For the government's suspicion about the loyal deaths of both Han Houn and Paek Kyŏnghan, see chapter 2 in the present volume.

14. CJI 132.

15. *Sunmuyŏng tŭngnok*, 2: 227.

16. KP 3:153 and 4:127.

17. CJI 691.

18. *Hong ssi ilgi*, 135; CJI 695; and KP 4:490.

19. KP 1:583 and 4:89.

20. KP 5:613 and 4:127.

21. KP 3:607.

22. CJI 691–92.

23. CJI 136.

24. KP 3:604 ff.

25. KP 4:225.

26. Tsurusono, "Heian-dō nōmin sensō ni okeru sankasō"; and Chŏng Sŏk-chong, "Hong Kyŏngnae nan ŭi sŏnggyŏk."

27. KP 1:607.

28. CJI 132.

29. SJ 11.

30. *Sunjo sillok*, 14:59b, Sunjo 11.12.20 (*kapcha*).

31. CJI 132 and 691.

32. Kang Hŭiyŏng, *Ilsŭng*, 67.

33. KP 2:502.

34. KP 2:596.

35. CJI 133.

36. *Allŭng ilgi*, 479; SSP 94; and KP 3:361.

37. CJI 693.

38. Kim Ch'angsi's younger brother Kim Ch'angjae, his cousin Kim Ch'anggŭn, and Ch'anggŭn's maternal uncle, Kye Ŭngnyŏl, were identified as participants in the rebellion and were decapitated. *P'yŏngsŏ ponmal*, 1812.1.25; and SSP 94.

39. KP 5:466.

40. CJI 135.

41. CJI 348–89.

42. KP 3:322.

43. KP 3:123 and 4:117–18. Kim Ch'ijŏng was a member of the Ŭisŏng Kim descent group residing in T'aech'ŏn. He passed the *munkwa* in 1783.

44. KP 5:90.

45. KP 4:90, 4:135, and 2:662.

46. KP 4:500; CJI 654 and 656; and SJ 78.

47. SSP 23 and 76; *Allŭng ilgi*, 399; KP 4:114; and *Sunmuyŏng tŭngnok*, 2:257.

48. CJI 698; and KP 3:712.

49. KP 3:218.

50. CJI 260.

51. KP 4:106, 4:406, and 5:125.

52. KP 3:712.

53. KP 3:335. O Such'ang argues that a social force called the *changsa* had emerged in P'yŏngan Province by the time of the rebellion. He names Hong Ch'onggak, Yi Chech'o, Yang Siwi, and Kim Ullyong as the most representative cases of this particular group. According to O, the *changsa* was a group of masters of martial arts who were usually impoverished members of the society engaged in various occupations. They played a key role in numerous battles and proved to be most rebellious. O Such'ang, *P'yŏngan-do sahoe palchŏn yŏn'gu*, 291–305. It is certain that a number of men called *changsa* in the sources provided military leadership, but it is questionable that this group of people formed a distinguishable antidynastic social and political force in P'yŏngan Province.

54. *Sunmuyŏng tŭngnok*, 2:112; and CJI 768. There were reports of widespread local disturbances from Hwangju, Chaeryŏng, and Chunghwa in the early days of the rebellion. It is unclear whether these were directly related to the Hong Kyŏngnae plot. See *P'yŏngsŏ ponmal*, 1811.12.28.

55. CJI 261.

56. Nam Yŏnsuk, "Chosŏn hugi hyangban ŭi kŏjuji idong kwa sahoe chiwi ŭi chisoksŏng, II," 71.

57. KP 3:234 and 1:600; and CJI 348–89 and 427. For the policy on the Ming refugees after the Ming fell, see Duncan, "Hyanghwain."

58. SSP 289.

59. *Allŭng ilgi*, 548; *Hong ssi ilgi*, 65; and *Sunjo sillok*, 15:24a, Sunjo 12.2.21 (*kapcha*).

60. *Sinyŏk Chŏnggamnok*, *Samhan sallim pigi*, 56 and 66.

61. *Sinyŏk Chŏnggamnok*, *Kamgyŏl*, 21–23 and 27–28.

62. For the details of this incident, see *Sunjo sillok*, 15:24a, Sunjo 12.2.21 (*kapcha*), 15:26b, Sunjo 12.3.3 (*ŭlhae*), and 16:15a–16a Sunjo 12.8.8 (*musin*); and *Ch'uan kŭp kugan*, *Choein Chinch'ae tŭng ch'uan*, 1–182.

63. CJI 186.

64. Tilly, *From Mobilization to Revolution*, 7–8.

65. For an analysis of the rebel network and type of associations, see Yoshikawa, "Kō Kei-rai no ran ni okeru hanran shudobu no senryaku to ishiki "

66. KP 5:125 and 5:466.

67. See chapter 2 for more discussion of those military officials who earlier held centrally appointed positions and who participated in the rebellion.

68. CJI 158; KP 5:462 and 5:111–13; SJ 23; and *Allŭng ilgi*, 427. Pak Sŏngsin and his two sons, who were also actively involved in the rebellion, were all killed by Kim Chihwan from Kusŏng, a previous subarea commander, as they fled government forces.

69. KP 3:229–39 and 3:396–420; CJI 168, 225, 279–80, and 336; and *Sunjo sillok*, 15:20a–b, Sunjo 12.2.6 (*kiyu*).

70. The appointment of the chief commander as the highest field commanding officer of the *sog o* army (*sog o-gun*) started at the time of Japanese invasions. As military officers, the Yŏngjang were to take over all the military affairs from the magistrate's office at the outset in order to enhance military readiness for foreign invasions. As the military threat from the north declined substantially after the establishment of the Qing in China, the main function of the Yŏngjang leaned toward maintaining local security in the eighteenth century. Also, magistrates served concurrently as the Yŏngjang in provinces other than the three southern provinces of Kyŏngsang, Chŏlla, and Ch'ungch'ŏng. This system was abolished in 1895. Sŏ T'aewŏn, *Chosŏn hugi chibang kunje yŏn'gu*; and Kim Uch'ŏl, *Chosŏn hugi chibang kunje sa*, 87–110.

71. CJI 370–72; SSP 137–38; *Allŭng ilgi*, 491; and *Hong ssi ilgi*, 3 and 17.

72. KP 1:65; SSP 59; and CJI 334–35.

73. CJI 698; and KP 4:494.

74. KP 2:162–79.

75. KP 5:171–74. Nonetheless, the fame of the descent group was soon partly recovered, at least at the local level, for a number of lineage members participated in the pacification campaign as leaders of volunteer armies. One example is Chŏng Hyŏnbak, who later passed the *munkwa* in 1822. *Hadong Chŏng ssi sebo*, 589; and *Sunjo sillok*, 17:38a, Sunjo 14.6.20 (*kimyo*) and 16:8b, Sunjo 12.6.9 (*kyŏngsul*).

76. KP 4:494; and CJI 698–702.

77. *Sunmuyŏng tŭngnok*, 2:227.

78. KP 5:470 and 2:514. Ch'oe Iryun was caught while trying to escape after the rebels were defeated at Chŏngju and was punished for high treason.

79. KP 1:444; and *Allŭng ilgi*, 363.

80. KP 2:514; CJI 181; and *Sunmuyŏng tŭngnok*, 2:227.

81. *Sunjo sillok*, 16:18b–19a, Sunjo 12.9.20 (*kich'uk*); KP 2:133; and CJI 134 and 141. Yi Ch'im changed his allegiance a few times in the course of the rebellion. He was known to be one of the core supporters or was even designated as one of the ringleaders. He and his father joined other rebels in Chŏngju to resist government encirclement. In mid-March, however, he secretly tried to collaborate with his relatives in the government forces to inflict decisive damage to the rebel defense line. This was discovered by the rebels and he barely escaped decapitation. On the day the rebels were defeated, he and his father attempted to commit suicide by jumping into a well. His father and brother were killed by the government troops and he was arrested and found guilty of high treason. KP 5:469 and 5:506; SJ 11 and 69; and CJI 434 and 662.

82. KP 2:133; and *Sunmuyŏng tŭngnok*, 2:227.

83. KP 2:515–18; KP 4:220; and *Sunmuyŏng tŭngnok*, 2:227.

84. *Allŭng ilgi*, 491 and 521; KP 5:466 and 2:516; and CJI 371. Ch'oe Ponggwan was punished for high treason.

85. CJI 138, 694; SSP 126; and KP 4:409 and 5:303. Yu Munje was captured while running away and was decapitated. Hong Tŭkchŏng from Ch'ŏlsan, a close in-law of Yu, was wealthy and promised to provide grain for the rebels. When Yu was caught, he was hiding in Hong's mountain cottage. KP 3:85.

86. KP 4:409 and 5:506. Wŏn Taech'ŏn was punished for high treason.

87. SJ 42 and 153; and KP 3:123.

88. SJ 11; KP 3:123 and 1:552; and CJI 138.

89. KP 4:509–10.

90. SSP 81 and 21; *Allŭng ilgi*, 411; and KP 2:607 and 3:120.

91. KP 2:498 and 2:507.

92. CJI 172; and *Sunmuyŏng tŭngnok*, 2:245 and 2:292. Most of these rebel sympathizers of T'aech'ŏn committed suicide or were decapitated when the district was recovered by government troops in late February 1812.

93. Kang Hŭiyŏng, *Ilsŭng*, 69. On the popularity and nature of *kye*, see Kim Chaeho, "Nongch'on sahoe ŭi sinyong kwa kye"; and Yi Yŏnghun, "18.19 segi Taejŏ-ri ŭi sinbun kusŏng kwa chach'i chilsŏ."

94. KP 1:424–39.

95. See chapter 2, note 97 for the names of fourteen men who held military degrees.

96. CJI 692–93. The identity of alleged supporters under the control of the True and Genuine Chŏng is unclear. The term *hogun* referred to Manchu soldiers in general.

97. *Hong Kyŏngnae pallangi*, 4.

98. Tsurusono, "Heian-dō nōmin sensō ni okeru sankasō," 74; Oda, *Shinbi Kō Keirai ran no kenkyū*, 39–40; and CJI 201.

99. The most recent example is the insurrection in 1624 by Yi Kwal and his followers, who reportedly urged the Manchus to invade Korea to redress the injustice of Kwanghaegun's removal from the throne. Kim Ungho, "Uri puja rŭl yŏkchŏk ŭiro moltani, Yi Kwal." For the case of a group of people rebelling against the Koryŏ court with the backing of Mongols, see Sun Joo Kim, "Marginalized Elite," 27–28.

100. Chŏng Sŏkchong, "Hong Kyŏngnae nan kwa kŭ naeŭng seryŏk," 383.

101. CJI 346–47; KP 1:569; and *Allŭng ilgi*, 484.

102. CJI 401 and 468; SSP 183–85; and SJ 44–45.

103. Oda, *Shinbi Kō Keirai ran no kenkyū*, 126–29. Oda assumes that *hogun* refers to horse-riding bandits in Manchuria.

104. According to *Hong Kyŏngnae imsin saryak* (A Short History of Hong Kyŏngnae in 1812), Song Chiryŏm, an officer of the yangban bureau in Kanggye, embezzled quite a large sum from public funds and was afraid of being discovered. When he heard that preparations for a rebellion were in progress, he joined the rebel leadership. After the rebels were defeated at the battle of Pine Grove on February 11, 1812, Song proposed to Hong Kyŏngnae that he go and get the *hogun* to join the rebel cause. Hong furnished Song with cash from the military funds to do this. Unfortunately for the rebels, Song changed his mind. He repaid what he owed the government and switched sides, recruiting volunteers for the government campaign using the money left over from the sum he had received from Hong. Song led ninety-four musketeers equipped with military provisions and arrived in the main government camp in early April 1812. Song's collaboration with Hong Kyŏngnae is not corroborated by any other sources.

105. CJI 132.

106. CJI 259.

107. KP 3:315.

108. KP 3:345.

109. KP 5:468 and 3:343.

110. KP 3:278.

111. KP 5:86–94. Other fifth columnists from the Kwaksan area included Yi Sŏngjong, who prepared uniforms and distributed food and money. He and Kim Taehun issued documents as chief administrative officers (Chongsagwan) when the rebel army took over Kwaksan. KP 4:235 and 5:89–91. Kim Kukpŏm, who knew Kim Ch'angsi and U Kunch'ik well enough to spend a night with them, played an active role in the rebel vanguard force and also served as a strategist. He shipped his books to the private library of Military Officer Yi (Yi Hŭijŏ) in

Kasan sometime before the rebellion. His nephew and Kim Sayong's niece were betrothed to marry, and Kim Taehun bought some goods from merchants for the wedding ceremony, at the instruction of Kim Sayong himself. KP 3:318 and 5:90; and CJI 133. Chang Hongik, another military officer from Kwaksan, was one of Pak Sŏngsin's group. A wealthy man, Chang promised to supply rebel provisions and took care of daily affairs for the rebels as a military supervisor. His brother, Chang Hoik, a staff military officer of a garrison, and other close relatives of his had all joined the rebels. CJI 694; and KP 3:48, 3:285, 5:466, 5:484, and 5:506. Both Chang Hongik and Hoik were punished for high treason.

112. CJI 134.

113. CJI 135.

114. CJI 151 and 229.

115. CJI 134.

116. KP 2:502.

117. One rebel testified that he had heard that Cho Sŏngsil had been sent down from Seoul as the supervisor for the newly opened gold mine in Sakchu. KP 5:12. In another record, Cho Sŏngsil commanded a rebel army that attacked Pakch'ŏn. KP 2:666. It seems that the recruiters faked the status of the supervisor of new mines to attract poor peasants. KP 5:331.

118. CJI 452; KP 3:620 ff.; and SSP 78–79.

119. KP 4:224–26.

120. For O Yongson's activity, see SSP 122; and KP 4:541 and 5:489. For Kim Yŏjŏng, see KP 3:19 and 3:604–622. For Yi Tori, see KP 2:665. For U Kunch'ik, see KP 5:331. For Kim Hyech'ŏl, see KP 1:20 and chapter 3 in the present volume.

121. KP 2:54–66.

122. KP 1:444; CJI 140 and 216; and SJ 42.

123. In his groundbreaking study of the English revolution of the mid-seventeenth century, Christopher Hill states that masterless men such as rogues, vagabonds, and beggars, roaming the countryside and belonging to no organized social group, sometimes in search of employment, were never a serious menace to the social order, though their existence was always a potential threat, especially in times of economic crisis, because they were susceptible to subversive ideas and could be recruited by various revolutionary armies. Hill, *The World Turned Upside Down*, 39–50.

6 REBELS AND COUNTERREBELS

1. CJI 135; and *Sinyŏk Chŏnggamnok*, 14 and 25.

2. Naquin, *Millenarian Rebellion in China*, 93 and 111.

3. CJI 525.

4. KP 2:512.

5. CJI 136.

6. KP 5:612.

7. *Sunmuyŏng tŭngnok*, 2:234.

8. CJI 695. Susan Naquin finds that government discovery in the last stages of mobilization was common, but argues that official investigations were a factor in the timing of an uprising, not in its conception and planning. Naquin, *Shantung Rebellion*, 66; and idem, *Millenarian Rebellion in China*, 121–46.

9. *Sunmuyŏng tŭngnok*, 2:235.

10. CJI 181 and 231; KP 5:89 and 5:560; and SJ 17.

11. CJI 167; SSP 10; and KP 3:729. "Ch'onggak" may have been a common colloquial designation for an unmarried male. One report shows that his name was Hong Pongŭi. KP 3:280.

12. CJI 143 and 136; and KP 3:604 and 3:54–64.

13. *P'yŏngsŏ ponmal, sinmi sŏjŏk kŏju*. Yun Ŏnsŏp was very likely a member of the P'ap'yŏng Yun of Kasan, who produced eight *munkwa* passers. The details about the situation at the time of Chŏng Si's death were recorded by Chŏng Si's cousin in the *Sunjŏllok* (The Record of the Loyal Deaths).

14. CJI 143.

15. SJ 11; and *Sunmuyŏng tŭngnok*, 2:237.

16. Im Sŏnggo was taken into government custody and transported to Seoul for investigation. It seems that he submitted his short memoir that recorded his activities during those days right before and after the rebellion, and a copy is found in the *P'yŏngsŏ ponmal* (The Essence and Branch of Pacifying P'yŏngan Province). See *P'yŏngsŏ ponmal*, 1812.1.16.

17. *Kwansŏ sinmirok*, 20–22 and 117; and CJI 145–46.

18. During that time, Kim Myŏngŭi from Anju, a *chinsa* degree-holder and secret participant in the rebel plot who had promised to open the town gates to welcome the rebels when they arrived, had a change of heart after observing that government defenses in the town had become too strong. The other rebel leaders got angry and threatened to kill him for changing his position. The rebel army never attacked Anju, and Kim denied his involvement when interrogated by the government. He was set free after a prolonged investigation. CJI 259; and *Kwansŏ sinmirok*, 113–14.

19. *P'yŏngsŏ ponmal*, 1811.12.24. Hyŏn Sangyun in his work *Hong Kyŏngnae chŏn* (Story of Hong Kyŏngnae), serialized in *Tonga ilbo* (Tonga Daily) in 1931, records hearsay from his hometown that Yi Haeu colluded with Hong Kyŏngnae in the beginning but later had a change of heart. Hyŏn Sangyun, *Hong Kyŏngnae*

chŏn, Tonga ilbo, 1931.8.3. Maybe that is why, in the same message to Yi Haeu, the rebels stated that Yi would be severely judged for his crime of siding with the central yangban once the rebels had taken over Anju.

20. KP 5:479 and 4:409–10.

21. KP 5:484 and 5:280–296.

22. CJI 139 and 161.

23. There is some confusing information about Paek Chonghoe, a former chief military officer of Chŏngju. It was said that Paek informed the magistrate about the plot, while several witnesses repeatedly pointed him out as one of the core conspirators. Perhaps Paek, an opportunist like many of the other participants, was constantly but rationally weighing the benefits and losses as the incident unfolded. In the end, his final choice to join the rebels cost him his life. KP 5:469–83. Paek Chonghoe was a member of the Suwŏn Paek of Chŏngju. *Suwŏn Paek ssi Chŏngju chokpo*, 2:107.

24. CJI 140–41 and 148–49.

25. SJ 11.

26. CJI 181.

27. CJI 145. The rebellion broke out in the lunar year of *sinmi*.

28. KP 5:34 and 4:410; and CJI 478. Kim Iksun was a member of the Andong Kim and was probably remotely related to the very powerful segment of the Andong Kim at the time, represented by Kim Chosun, father-in-law of King Sunjo. The power of his descent group could not spare his life, however, for he was decapitated for his disloyal behavior before the rebellion was suppressed. His family line suffered misfortune for generations because of his treason. His grandson, the famous Kim Sakkat (Kim Pyŏngyŏn), was prevented from ever holding office and from a young age took to the road as a wandering poet, gaining fame from his many satirical poems about nineteenth-century life. About Kim Pyŏngyŏn, see Yi Hongjik, *Han'guksa taesajŏn*, 1:295.

29. CJI 151.

30. *Kwansŏ sinmirok*, 99; and KP 4:32, 4:88, and 4:188–90.

31. KP 5:611; and *Kwansŏ sinmirok*, 77–79.

32. KP 3:115.

33. KP 4:87; KP 3:116–17; and CJI 173.

34. KP 2:495.

35. KP 4:7, 4:102, 4:129, 2:493–504, and 2:532–82; CJI 229–30; and SSP 21.

36. CJI 151.

37. According to a folk tale, Kim Kyŏnsin was born from his mother's second marriage to a wealthy person. This means that he was legally disqualified to take the civil service examination. The story says that it was Kim's mother who strongly

encouraged him to fight against the rebels. Kim Hyŏllyong, *Han'guk munhŏn sŏrhwa 3*, 182–83. This tale is found in "Ch'ang ŭibyŏng hyŏnmo ukcha" (The wise mother who encouraged her son to lead a volunteer army), in *Ch'ŏnggu yadam* (Folk Tales of Korea).

38. *Sunjŏllok*, 182–84; and CJI 172.

39. CJI 164, 186, and 193.

40. KP 5:482.

41. KP 5:468 and 3:343.

42. *Kwansŏ sinmirok*, 59 and 53; CJI 159, 491, 494, and 498; and KP 5:30 and 5:61–67.

43. KP 5:32, 5:95, and 5:128; and CJI 156, 161, and 184.

44. KP 4:14, 4:26, 1:32, and 5:13.

45. KP 5:23 and 5:123.

46. KP 5:55; and CJI 164 and 184.

47. KP 5:300–6 and 4:408. Kye Hangdae's family must have enjoyed great wealth even before his time. The father of Kye Hangdae, Kye Wŏnsu, fed all the hungry people of the district at the time of great famines in 1721 and 1725. *Suan Kye ssi inmaek po*, 43. The court probably granted a series of titles in reward for these relief efforts, for a number of his close ancestors and descendants held relatively high-ranking titles, although none seems to have served at the central court. In addition to Kye Hangdae, a number of his relatives joined the rebel army, but only one, Kye Namsim, who supposedly mastered various occult arts and devised a strategy to occupy Ŭiju for the rebels, is found in the genealogy (see p. 351). His grandfather, Kye Tŏkhae, passed the *munkwa* in 1774. A single-surname village of Suan Kye was located by Zenshō Eisuke in his field survey in the early 1930s. The villagers reported that the village had been established by Kye Imnyang about three hundred years before. One of the descendants of Kye Imnyang, Kye Yonghyŏk, passed the *munkwa* in 1891. Zenshō, *Chōsen no shūraku*, 3:937.

48. KP 3:32 and 5:303.

49. CJI 164.

50. KP 3:116.

51. CJI 193–94.

52. *P'yŏngsŏ ponmal*, 1811.12.30.

53. CJI 140, 143, 150, 152, and 162.

54. CJI 145.

55. *P'yŏngyang sokchi*, 235–36; *Hong Kyŏngnae kwan'gye t'ongmun*; and *Kwansŏ t'ongmun*.

56. CJI 158. The *P'yŏngsŏ ponmal*, a central government record on the rebellion, thus begins with the entry of February 4 (1811.12.22).

57. For the central government's immediate response to the news of the rebellion, see *Sunmuyŏng tŭngnok*, 1:3–10; and *P'yŏngsŏ ponmal*. For the details of military organization of the government army, sent by both the central government and P'yŏngan Province, and the names of military officers and servicemen, see *Sunmuyŏng tŭngnok*, 2:50–99, 1:11–36, and 1:49.

58. Kang Hŭiyŏng, *Ilsŭng*, 85; SSP 99; and *P'yŏngsŏ ponmal*, 1812.1.15 and 1812.1.23.

59. SSP 127–32, 147–48, and 207–9; KP 2:189; and *Hong ssi ilgi*, 11.

60. *P'yŏngsŏ ponmal*, 1811.12.29.

61. KP 4:23.

62. Kang Hŭiyŏng, *Ilsŭng*, 69.

63. Kang Hŭiyŏng, *Ilsŭng*, 57, 85, 86, 93, 95, 97, 102, and 111.

64. CJI 178; *Sunmuyŏng tŭngnok*, 1:6–8; and *Sunjo sillok*, 14:59b–65a, Sunjo 11.12.23 (*chŏngmyo*) and 11.12. 24 (*mujin*).

65. *Sunmuyŏng tŭngnok*, 2:248.

66. CJI 187–89.

67. Kim Uch'ŏl, *Chosŏn hugi chibang kunje sa*, 215–22.

68. CJI 190–91.

69. SJ 10 and 173.

70. CJI 197.

71. SJ 13. After the rebellion was over, Yi Haesŭng was punished with banishment to a border area for his crimes, which included excessive killing, losing the chance to annihilate the rebels by not pursuing the retreating rebels right away, and displaying greediness in administration. Yi had profited by appropriating the public fund of the military headquarters before the rebellion broke out. KP 5:507 and 5:575; and *Sunmuyŏng tŭngnok*, 2:138–41.

72. *Kwansŏ sinmirok*, 59; and SJ 12.

73. Those commanders in charge of Sin Island and the Sŏrim and Imhae garrisons surrendered to the rebels, while two other garrison commanders of Tongnim and Sŏnsa could not defend the areas in their charge. Those first three were decapitated; the other two were demoted to foot soldiers after the rebellion. SSP 151–52 and 346; KP 1:386–98, 2:381, and 5:426–39; and *Allŭng ilgi*, 612.

74. CJI 208; and KP 5:487.

75. KP 4:332. For Kye Namsim's family background, see chapter 2 in the present volume.

76. KP 5:89 and 5:486.

77. KP 4:326.

78. *Sunjo sillok*, 16:18b, Sunjo 12.9.20 (*kich'uk*); and KP 3:447 and 5:485.

79. CJI 534–37; and KP 3:560–62 and 5:118–20.

80. KP 5:117. Kim Ch'wigyu and Chang Mongyŏl reportedly did not submit to such intimidation by the rebels but devoted themselves to defending Ŭiju against rebel encroachment. The court awarded Kim the position of commander at the Five Military Commands (Owijang) and Chang an upgraded rank. *Sunjo sillok*, 16:8b, Sunjo 12.6.9 (*kyŏngsul*).

81. KP 3:694 and 2:275–86; and CJI 249.

82. *Allŭng ilgi*, 484 and 564; KP 1:363, 1:373, and 1:569; and CJI 329–30 and 542.

83. *Allŭng ilgi*, 453, 468, 525, 637, and 668; *Sunjŏllok*, 182–84; and KP 5:367–70.

84. SJ 31–33.

85. *Allŭng ilgi*, 430, 467, 571, and 576. The six loyal subjects whose names and merits were inscribed on the Stele of Loyalty and Righteousness were Hŏ Hang, Han Houn, Paek Kyŏnghan, Che Kyŏnguk, Kim Taet'aek, and Im Chihwan. The stele was erected on March 25, 1814, in Chŏngju, to memorialize the death of these men during the Hong Kyŏngnae Rebellion. More discussion of this appears below. *Sunmuyŏng tŭngnok*, 2:182; and *Sunjŏllok*, 353.

86. *Allŭng ilgi*, 441, 443, 480, and 639; CJI 315; and KP 5:517.

87. For the degeneration of the military system, see Kim Uch'ŏl, *Chosŏn hugi chibang kunje sa*; Sŏ T'aewŏn, *Chosŏn hugi chibang kunje yŏn'gu*; and Palais, *Confucian Statecraft and Korean Institutions*, 391–578.

88. See, for example, the royal edict published on February 5, 1812. CJI 251–54.

89. According to Chŏng Yagyong, the reason northern yangban could not organize militias quickly was because they did not have slaves to mobilize, in stark contrast to the events at the time of the Japanese invasions, when yangban were able to fill their militias with their own slaves. Chŏng Yagyong, *Yŏkchu mongmin simsŏ, yejŏn, pyŏndŭng*, 4:85.

90. CJI 165.

91. SWI 1811.12.29 and 1812.1.3.

92. CJI 173–77.

93. The list of volunteers is found in CJI 177–78.

94. The activities of Hyŏn Inbok are recorded in the *Chinjung ilgi* (A Diary at the Military Camp) in a great detail. See also *Allŭng ilgi*, 412, 422, 487, 605, and 630; KP 5:369 and 5:399; and *Sunmuyŏng tŭngnok*, 2:279.

95. *Sunjŏllok*, 353 and 357; and CJI 208, 306, and 614–16.

96. *Allŭng ilgi*, 428; and KP 4:355, 5:5, 5:183, and 5:198.

97. *Allŭng ilgi*, 409, 458, and 482; and CJI 304.

98. *Allŭng ilgi*, 482 and 506; and KP 2:372.

99. SSP 298; KP 1:113 and 5:371; and CJI 544 and 619–21.

100. CJI 549.

101. *Sunjo sillok*, 15:25b, Sunjo 12.2.27 (*kyŏngo*).

102. The first report of private contribution appears in CJI 209.

103. *Sunjo sillok*, 15:38b, Sunjo 12.4.21 (*kyehae*).

7   REBELS ON THE DEFENSE

1. CJI 218 and 554. According to a map showing government army deployment in Chŏngju around March 22, 1812 (fig. 5), there were 8,534 men surrounding the walled town. See *P'yŏngsŏ ponmal*, 1812.2.10. Another map of Chŏngju that was supposedly drawn around May 1, 1812, also shows the government force of 8,355. Yi Pyŏngdo, "Hong Kyŏngnae nan kwa Chŏngju sŏngdo," 381–33. For more detailed information on the constituents of the pacification army, see *Sunjo sillok*, 15:37b–38a, Sunjo 12.4.21 (*kyehae*).

2. KP 2:343.

3. KP 4:107, 4:119, 4:287–88, 1:150, 1:159, 1:177, 1:206, and 1:216.

4. Kang Hŭiyŏng, *Ilsŭng*, 55.

5. KP 1:168, 1:192, 1:201, 1:495, and 1:501; CJI 383; and *Sunmuyŏng tŭngnok*, 2:262.

6. SWI 1812.1.3.

7. KP 1:495, 1:501, 1:506, 1:588, and 1:592.

8. KP 3:570, 3:610, and 3:612.

9. CJI 700–1.

10. KP 5:614. This rebel army organization is a little different from that of the government under the *sog o* system, in which one company was composed of ninety-nine men in principle, although the organizational rule was not strictly observed because the number of soldiers available in each administrative unit varied. Kim Uch'ŏl, *Chosŏn hugi chibang kunje sa*, 44.

11. KP 5:610.

12. CJI 283.

13. CJI 220–93.

14. SJ 16; and Yi Pyŏngdo, "Hong Kyŏngnae nan kwa Chŏngju Sŏngdo," 379–400. The map inserted in the *P'yŏngsŏ ponmal* informs us that the circumference of the wall was 10 *ri* (about 4,500 meters). *P'yŏngsŏ ponmal*, 1812.2.10.

15. CJI 290. More details about this battle cart are found in Oda, *Shinbi Kō Keirai ran no kenkyū*, 90.

16. CJI 283.

17. CJI 290–306.

18. CJI 339.

19. CJI 388.

20. CJI 392–95.

21. CJI 428–31.

22. CJI 416.

23. CJI 412–15. General Im is Im Kyŏngŏp (1594–1646), who was famous for his loyalty to the Ming.

24. KP 1:190–91.

25. KP 1:193.

26. CJI 701; and KP 2:518–19.

27. KP 3:729.

28. KP 3:294; CJI 515–18 and 541. The price of 1 *mal* of grain went up to 3 *yang*. One *sŏm* of rice cost the same amount of money outside of the wall around the same time. *Sunmuyŏng tŭngnok*, 1:359. Right before the rebellion, one family could live for one month on 3 *yang*. KP 3:209.

29. CJI 518–19.

30. CJI 547–57.

31. CJI 602–5.

32. CJI 612.

33. KP 3:729.

34. KP 4:401–5 and 1:546.

35. CJI 296.

36. CJI 345.

37. CJI 401–2; KP 1:248; SSP 183–84; and SJ 44–45. Pak Chinbyŏk is variably recorded as Pak Chinyŏng or Pak Chinsŏk.

38. CJI 468.

39. CJI 628; KP 4: 497; and SJ 108.

40. CJI 623.

41. CJI 627, 628, and 631.

42. CJI 635.

43. CJI 636.

44. CJI 641.

45. CJI 643–47. The Qing army employed strikingly similar measures to demolish the defense wall of Hwa city, where the Eight Trigram rebels resisted for about a month in 1813. Naquin, *Millenarian Rebellion in China*, 259–64.

46. CJI 647–58; and KP 4:401.

47. CJI 678.

48. KP 1:381. Hong Kyŏngnae was the only one who was posthumously sentenced to the crime of leading the armed rebellion (*kŏbyŏng yŏkkoe yul*), one step more severe than the crime of high treason (*moban taeyŏk*). CJI 709.

49 KP 5:454 and 5:497–506. See appendix C for the fate of the key rebel leaders.

50. *Sunmuyŏng tŭngnok*, 2:191.

51. KP 5:411, 5:419, 3:215, and 3:571.

52. KP 3:257–58 and 3:750.

53. *Sŭngjŏngwŏn ilgi*, 2010, Sunjo 11.12.25, 105:646–47; and *P'yŏngsŏ ponmal*, 1811.12.24.

54. KP 5:557–58; *Sŭngjŏngwŏn ilgi*, 2010, Sunjo 11.12.29, 105:655; and *P'yŏngsŏ ponmal*, 1811.12.29.

55. *Sunjo sillok*, 15:15b, Sunjo 12.1.24 (*musul*).

56. *Sunjo sillok*, 15:10b–11a, Sunjo 12.1.19 (*kyesa*).

57. *Sunjo sillok*, 15:21b–22a, Sunjo 12.2.10 (*kyech'uk*). Yi Haesŭng's corruption was repeatedly criticized during and after the rebellion. KP 1:343; KP 5:507 and 5:575; and *Sunmuyŏng tŭngnok*, 1:172.

58. SSP 176–77; and *Sunjo sillok*, 15:19a–19b, Sunjo 12.2.4 (*chŏngmi*).

59. *Sunjo sillok*, 18:13b, Sunjo 15.7.20 (*kyemyo*), and 18:14b, Sunjo 15.8.6 (*muo*).

60. Yi Sŭnghun, "Sŏbugin ŭi sugwŏn sint'ong."

8 NATION, CLASS, AND REGION IN THE STUDY OF THE HONG KYŎNGNAE REBELLION

1. Chŏng Sŏkchong, "Hong Kyŏngnae nan," 355; *Ilsŏngnok*, Sunjo 17.3.17, 41:292; and *Sŭngjŏngwŏn ilgi*, 2081, Sunjo 17.3.17, 108:238.

2. Hwang P'aegang, "Hanmun sosŏl *Hong Kyŏngnae chŏn* yŏn'gu," 113–14.

3. Cho Susam, *Ch'ujaejip*, *Sŏgu tool* and *Nongsŏng chabyŏng 22 su*, 2:25a-29b.

4. *Sinmirok*; and Chŏng Yŏnghun, "*Sinmirok* yŏn'gu."

5. Hwang P'aegang, "Hanmun sosŏl *Hong Kyŏngnae chŏn* yŏn'gu," 3–4.

6. Yi Tonhwa (Paektu-sanin), "Hong Kyŏngnae wa Chŏn Pongjun."

7. An Hwak, *Chosŏn munmyŏngsa*, 325.

8. Mun Ilp'yŏng, "Sasang ŭi kiin."

9. Hyŏn Sangyun, *Hong Kyŏngnae chŏn*. Also see appendix A in the present volume.

10. Robinson, *Cultural Nationalism in Colonial Korea*, 34.

11. For more discussion of intellectuals inventing a national history and cul-

tural identity during the colonial period, see Robinson, *Cultural Nationalism in Colonial Korea*; and Schmid, *Korea Between Empires*.

12. Oda, *Shinbi Kō Keirai ran no kenkyū*.

13. Oda, *Shinbi Kō Keirai ran no kenkyū*, 6–8.

14. Hong Hŭiyu, "1811–1812 nyŏn P'yŏngan-do nongmin chŏnjaeng kwa kŭ sŏnggyŏk." Kawarabayashi Shizumi also believes that the conflict between landlords and poor peasants was the main driving force for this rebellion. Kawarabayashi, "1811 nyŏn ŭi P'yŏngan-do e issŏsŏ ŭi nongmin chŏnjaeng."

15. Chŏng Sŏkchong, "Hong Kyŏngnae nan kwa kŭ naeŭng seryŏk"; and idem, "Hong Kyŏngnae nan ŭi sŏnggyŏk." The thesis of entrepreneurial peasants originally came from Kim Yongsŏp, who constructed a nationalist perspective in the study of Korean history through his meticulous study of agricultural history in traditional Korea. Kim Yongsŏp, "Chosŏn hugi ŭi kyŏngyŏnghyŏng punong kwa sangŏpchŏk nongŏp."

16. For more discussion of the *minjung* historiography, see Abelmann, *Echoes of the Past, Epics of Dissent*; and Wells, *South Korea's Minjung Movement*.

17. Goldstone, *Revolution and Rebellion in the Early Modern World*, 12–17; and Tilly, *The Vendée*.

18. Harrison, *The Communists and Chinese Peasant Rebellions*.

19. Naquin, *Millenarian Rebellion in China*; and idem, *Shantung Rebellion*.

20. Little, *Understanding Peasant China*.

21. For the moral economy view, see Scott, *Moral Economy of the Peasant*. For the discussion of the nature of moral economy in Chosŏn, see Sun Joo Kim, "Marginalized Elite," 106–7; and Nam Yŏnsuk, "Chosŏn hugi hyangban ŭi kŏjuji idong kwa sahoe chiwi ŭi chisoksŏng, II," 62–71.

22. O Such'ang, *Chosŏn hugi P'yŏngan-do sahoe palchŏn yŏn'gu*, 252–305.

23. Merchant participation in the 1812 rebellion is the main focus of Tsurusono Hiroshi's study. Tsurusono Hiroshi, "Heian-dō nōmin sensō ni okeru sankasō." Hong Hŭiyu also emphasizes the role played by the merchant class in the rebellion. Hong Hŭiyu, "1811–1812 nyŏn P'yŏngan-do nongmin chŏnjaeng kwa kŭ sŏnggyŏk."

24. The role of merchants in the early transformation of Korean society in the late nineteenth and early twentieth centuries turned out to be minimal because the state and external forces led the modern transformation.

25. Skocpol, *States and Social Revolution*; and Karlsson, "The Hong Kyŏngnae Rebellion 1811–1812."

26. Karlsson, "The Hong Kyŏngnae Rebellion 1811–1812." Karlsson's dissertation deserves credit for its methodological divorce from previous ideological constraints and for throwing new light on the study of popular movements. How-

ever, not only does his two-level (macro and micro) theoretical framework fail to serve the goal of the study, he also misses a number of the rebellion's important aspects because his detailed investigation ends in the early stage of the rebellion. A full exploration of this popular movement and the government pacification campaign reveals a much more complex picture of local conditions.

27. Skocpol, *States and Social Revolution*, 169–71. Skocpol emphasizes, "Any line of reasoning that treats revolutionary ideologies as blueprints for revolutionaries' activities and for revolutionary outcomes cannot sustain scrutiny in the light of historical evidence about how Jacobinism and Marxism-Leninism actually did develop and function within the unfolding social-revolutionary situations in France, Russia, and China."

28. Esherick, "Symposium on Peasant Rebellions."

29. The localistic nature of popular movements is keenly recognized in Elizabeth Perry's study of the Nien rebellion. Perry, *Rebels and Revolutionaries in North China 1845–1945*, 96. A number of studies indeed make clear that effective organization and leadership are essential if local unrest is to be successfully aggregated into an effective political movement. Daniel Little further argues that the problems of coordination and assurance must be dealt with for local activism to be transformed into a national movement. In addition, for a successful movement, a high level of political education must be present to raise the political awareness of local activists from local concerns to regional or national interests. Little, *Understanding Peasant China*, 180.

30. Kuhn, *Rebellion and Its Enemies in Late Imperial China*.

31. See table 2 in chapter 2.

32. Government rewards for the dead and injured, conscripts, and their close kin, in terms of granting various tax breaks as well as the general distribution of a temporary tax reduction, are reflected in the population data for the late Chosŏn period, which show a lower (taxable) population than was actually the case. Thus a population survey completed in 1816 shows a sudden decrease of the total population in P'yŏngan Province compared to the previous survey of 1807; the total number of households decreased from 302,005 to 190,047, and the total population fell from 1,305,969 to 766,456—over a half million people. *Sunjo sillok*, 10:51b, Sunjo 7.12.30 (*chŏngyu*) and 19:36b, Sunjo 16.12.30 (*kapchin*).

33. Little, *Understanding Peasant China*, 24–26; and Shin, *Peasant Protest and Social Change in Colonial Korea*, 9–21.

34. For the illustrious role that the northerners played in adopting modern identity and leading the modern transformation of Korea from the turn of the twentieth century, see Hwang, *Beyond Birth*, 273–89. For the emphasis on region

in historical studies, see Wigen, "Culture, Power, and Place"; idem, *The Making of a Japanese Periphery*; and Silberman, *Ministers of Modernization*.

APPENDIXES

1. This book contains three unusual inserts. One is a short memoir written by Pakch'ŏn magistrate Im Sŏnggo that describes his actions during the first few days of the rebellion. Im might have submitted this to the State Tribunal (Ŭigŭmbu) that was in charge of investigating his crimes of not defending his district when it was invaded by the rebels. *P'yŏngsŏ ponmal*, 1812.1.16. The second insert is an illustrated map of government camps in Chŏngju (see fig. 5 in chapter 7) and the list of government armies, both attachments to the report made by Royal Messenger Yi Minsik on March 22, 1812. *P'yŏngsŏ ponmal*, 1812.2.10. The last insert, a one-day entry (1812.3.8) of a diary written by an official at the provincial military commander's office, is completely out of place because it is inserted between the entries of 1812.2.11 and 2.10.

2. Oda Shōgo identifies the author of the *Chinjung ilgi* as Hyŏn Inbok Oda, *Shinbi Kō Keirai ran no kenkyū*, 157. In the bibliographical essay on this diary, Chŏng Sŏkchong questions authorship by Hyŏn Inbok because the diary contains records that a nonofficial might not have been able to access. The compiler of the *Hong Kyŏngnae imsin saryak* (A Short History of Hong Kyŏngnae in 1812) notes that the *Chinjung ilgi* was written by Hyŏn Inbok when he cites the book. For the *Hong Kyŏngnae imsin saryak*, see the following discussion.

3. Kang Hŭiyŏng's father, Kang Chunhŭm, passed the *munkwa* in 1794 Two of his brothers also earned the *munkwa* degree, in 1820 and 1835, respectively. He himself passed the lower civil service exam (*chinsa*) in 1843. His son and his two nephews were also *munkwa* graduates.

4. Yi Sugŏn, "Chokpo wa yangban ŭisik," 29; and idem, "Chosŏn hugi sŏng-gwan ŭisik kwa p'yŏnbo ch'eje ŭi pyŏnhwa." Yi Sugŏn argues that the tendency in the late Chosŏn period to put a greater value on having prominent ancestors in one's descent group drove people to locate their apical ancestors farther back in history, such as in the Silla period or in ancient China. He insists that people in northern provinces who were given a new clan seat (*pon'gwan*) after being relocated there in the early Chosŏn period discarded them and adopted other prominent *pon'gwan* as theirs. His argument, however, is not supported by any evidence. In addition, he says that the tendency of changing one's *pon'gwan* into a famous one was not the monopoly of P'yŏngan residents, but a fashion practiced by many in the late Chosŏn period. There is no doubt that a lineage's claim to have originated from a

famous figure of ancient Korea or China might have been forged; nevertheless, a majority of information recorded in the genealogies still seems to be credible, and often invaluable, when used with other historical sources.

5. Song Chunho, *Chosŏn sahoesa yŏn'gu*, 41-45.

6. *Hadong Chŏng ssi sebo*, 8–9.

7. See chapter 2 for a detailed discussion of northern yangban and their genealogies.

8. *Yijo hanmun tanp'yŏn chip, ha*, 118.

9. O Such'ang, "Hong Kyŏngnae nan ponggigun ŭi ch'oego chihwibu," 233.

Glossary

aeguk kyemong-ki 애국계몽기 the period of the patriotic enlightenment movement

asa 衙舍 magistrate's office

chabyŏk 雜役 miscellaneous taxes

ch'aengmun husi 柵門後市 a market in the palisade settlement

Chakch'ŏng 作廳 Public Administration Bureau

Ch'ambong 參奉 superintendent at the Sunginjŏn and Sungnyŏngjŏn in P'yŏngyang, Jr. 9

Ch'ammo 參謀 staff officer

Ch'amp'an 參判 second minister of any of the six ministries, Jr. 2

chamsang 潛商 smugglers

ch'amsanggwan 參上官 positions of rank six and above

chang 丈 a measuring unit of approximately 2.08 meters

Ch'anggam 倉監 granary supervisor

changgun 將軍 general

Changgwan 將官 commander

Changnyŏng 掌令 third inspector of the Office of the Inspector General, Sr. 4

changsa 壯士 vanguard force

changsa-ch'ŭng 壯士層 military mischief

Changyongyŏng 壯勇營 Office of the Robust and Brave Guards

chese chi in 濟世之人 a person who will save the world

chin 鎭 garrison

chindo changgun 眞道將軍 a general who truly mastered the Way

Chinhyulch'ŏng 賑恤廳 Relief Bureau

chinin 眞人 a true and genuine person

chinsa 進士 a lower civil service examination degree or degree-holder

Chiphyŏnjŏn Haksa 集賢殿 學士 proctor of the Hall of Worthies

Chipsa 執事 staff military officer

Chip'yŏng 持平 fourth inspector of the Office of the Inspector General

ch'o 哨 a military company

Ch'oe chinin 崔眞人 True and Genuine Ch'oe

Ch'ogwan 哨官 company commander

chŏhang chisigin 저항지식인 defiant intellectuals

choi 召史 married commoner woman

ch'ŏllyu 賤類 people of low status

Ch'ŏmsa 僉使 army second deputy commander or garrison commander, Jr. 3

ch'on 寸 a marker that shows the remoteness and closeness of relatives to oneself

chŏnch'a 戰車 battle cart

Chŏng chinin 鄭眞人 True and Genuine Chŏng

chŏn'ga sabyŏn yul 全家徙邊律 punishment of relocating whole household to the border region

Ch'ŏngbuk 清北 area north of the Ch'ŏngch'ŏn River

Ch'ŏngbuk tojihwisa 清北都指揮使 commander in chief of the Ch'ŏngbuk Region

chŏngch'ijŏk noye saenghwal 정치적 노예 생활 political slavery

Chŏng-ga 鄭哥 a person with the surname Chŏng

Chŏnggamnok 鄭鑑錄 The Record of Chŏng Kam

ch'ŏngjik 清職 prestigious positions

ch'ŏngjok 清族 prestigious lineages

Chŏngju sŏngdo pon 定州城圖本 Illustrated Map of Government Camps in Chŏngju

Chŏngnang 正郎 section chief of any of the six ministries, Sr. 5

Ch'ŏngnyongsa 青龍寺 Blue Dragon Temple

Chŏngŏn 正言 fourth censor of the Office of the Censor General, Sr. 6

Chongsagwan 從事官 chief administrative officer

chŏnhwang 錢荒 shortage of copper cash

chonju 尊周 revering the Zhou

ch'ŏnmun 天文 heavenly signs

Chonwi 尊位 village head

ch'ŏp 疊 guard station

ch'osa 初仕 entry-level office

chu-ch'ŏk 周尺 a Zhou measurement unit

chuin 主人 master

ch'ulsin 出身 military degree-holder

ch'ulsuk 出塾 graduate from the family study hall

Ch'unch'u 春秋 recorder

chunggang husi 中江後市 a foreign-trade market established on the Chinese side of the Amnok River

Chunggun 中軍 chief military officer

chunghwa sasang 中華思想 China-centered culturalism

Ch'ungjang-gong 忠壯公 Duke of Loyalty

Ch'ungŭi-dan 忠義壇 Stele of Loyalty and Righteousness

Chusŏ 注書 recorder of the Royal Secretariat, Sr. 7

Chwarang 佐郎 assistant section chief in any of the six ministries, Sr. 6

Chwasu 座首 director of the Bureau of Local Yangban

Hagyu 學諭 third proctor at the Royal Academy Jr. 9

Hallim 翰林 historian

hallyang 閑良 unemployed military officer

hanch'ŏn chi p'ilbu 寒賤之匹夫 a man of meager lowly birth

han'gŭl 한글 vernacular Korean script invented in 1446

Hansŏngbu 漢城府 Capital District Office

hat'o-chi-in 遐土之人 a person from a remote area

Ho 胡 Manchus or barbarians

hobok 胡服 Manchu-style dress

hoegwŏn 會圈 an official selection process in which incumbent officials mark a circle by the chosen candidate's name after considering the candidate's qualifications

hogun 胡軍 Manchu soldiers

Hojo 戶曹 Ministry of Taxation

Hong Kyŏngnae chŏn 홍경래전 Story of Hong Kyŏngnae

Hongmullok 弘文錄 a preliminary candidate roster for the Hongmun'gwan

Hongmun'gwan 弘文館 Office of the Special Counselors

Hŏnnap 獻納 third censor of the Office of the Censor General, Sr. 5

hop 合 1 *hop*=0.1596 liter

horyŏm 戶斂 household levy

Hullyŏn tojŏng 訓練都正 a senior third-rank position in the Military Training Command

Hullyŏnwŏn Chŏng 訓練院正 second commander of the Military Training Command

Hunjang 訓將 chief of the Military Training Administration

Hunyo Sipcho 訓要十條 Ten Testamentary Instructions

husi 後市 irregular trading posts

hwabŏl 華閥 established descent groups

hwain 華人 civilized people

hwanhae chingbi 宦海懲毖 career history

hwanja or *hwan'gok* 還穀 grain loan system

hwa-i-ron 華夷論 a theory differentiating those who received the benefit of Confucian transformation and those who did not

hyangan 鄉案 local yangban association or its roster

Hyangch'ŏng 鄉廳 Bureau of Local Yangban

hyanggok hou yup'um chaje 鄉曲豪右流品子弟 sons and brothers of powerful local elite and previous officials

hyanggok-chi-in 鄉曲之人 a person from the countryside

hyanggyo 鄉校 local school

hyangim 鄉任 officers at the Bureau of Local Yangban

hyangin 鄉人 local yangban

hyangjŏn 鄉戰 local strife

hyangni 鄉吏 local strongmen in the Koryŏ and early Chosŏn periods; clerks in the district magistrate's administration office from the early Chosŏn on

hyangoein 鄉外人 nonmembers of a local yangban association

Hyangso 鄉所 supervisor of the local yangban bureau

Hyŏn'gam 縣監 magistrate sent to a lesser county

Hyŏngjo 刑曹 Ministry of Punishments

hyŏnjo 顯祖 prominent ancestor

Ijo 吏曹 Ministry of Personnel

ijŏk 夷狄 barbarians

il sa hoeng kwan=im / kwi sin t'al ŭi=sin / sip p'il ka il ch'ŏk=ki / so ku yu yang chok=pyŏng 一士橫冠=壬 / 鬼神脫衣=申 / 十疋加一尺=起 / 小丘有兩足=兵

Im-changgun-tang 林將軍堂 Altar of General Im

imsin 壬申 the year of *imsin*

inmul 人物 prominent personalities

Inŭi 引儀 ritual preceptor at the Office of Ceremonies, Jr. 6

Ip'an 吏判 minister of the Ministry of Personnel, Sr. 2

ipchinsŏng 入鎮姓 moved-in surname groups also known as *ipsŏng* and *naesŏng*

ipsŏng 入姓 moved-in surname groups also known as *ipchinsŏng* and *naesŏng*

Ka-chusŏ 假注書 temporary recorder of the Royal Secretariat

Kaebyŏk 개벽 Creation

kaesi 開市 open markets

kaja 加資 upgrade rank

kajŏng 家政 family

Kamgyŏl 鑑訣 Revelation by Kam

kamun 家門 lineage

kap'ung 家風 lineage tradition

kasa 가사 a long vernacular verse form

Kasŏn taebu 嘉善大夫 a junior second-rank title

ki 氣 force

ki homa ch'ullae in 騎胡馬出來人 the Manchu horse rider

Kiroso Sujik 耆老所 守直 administrator of the Bureau of Superannuation

kŏbyŏng yŏkkoe yul 擧兵逆魁律 punishment for a traitor and rebel commander

Kŏmyŏl 檢閱 a senior ninth-rank position at the Yemun'gwan

kongin 貢人 tribute middlemen or merchants

kongni 공리 public goods

kŏsang 巨商 big merchant

kuhyang 舊鄉 established yangban or original members of a local yangban association

Kullyang kamgwan 軍糧監官 military provisions supervisor

kŭmsu 禽獸 birds and beasts

Kŭmwiyŏng 禁衛營 Forbidden Guard Division

kŭn 斤 a measuring unit of weight

kun'gwan 軍官 military officers

kunhyŏn 郡縣 prefecture and county (Ch.: *jun-xian*)

Kunjagam Chŏng 軍資監 正 secretary of the Military Procurement Administration, Sr. 3

kwaesŏ sagŏn 掛書事件 incidents of posting seditious letters in public places

Kwanbansa 館伴使 escort of a Chinese envoy, Sr. 3

kwanch'ŏng singni 官廳殖利 public loan

Kwansŏ 關西 P'yŏngan Province

Kwŏn'gwan 權官 outpost officer, Jr. 9

kwŏnjŏm 圈點 placing a circle by the chosen candidate in the official selection process

kye 契 cooperative financial arrangement or mutual assistance association

kyo 校 military officers

kyoji 教旨 official appointment certificate

kyŏl 結 a constant measure of crop yield produced by an area that varied from 2.2 to 9.0 acres depending on the fertility of the land *kyŏllyŏm* 結斂 surcharges on land

Kyŏmsa 兼史 historian

kyŏnghwa sajok 京華士族 capital-based aristocracy

kyŏngyŏnghyŏng punong 경영형부농 entrepreneurial peasants

Kyosŏgwan 校書館 Office of Editorial Review

Kyosu 敎授 preceptor

Kyunyŏkch'ŏng 均役廳 Equal Service Bureau

maehyang 賣鄕 sale of local yangban association membership

mal 斗 1 *mal*=10 *toe*=5.96 liters

Manho 萬戶 subarea commander

mansang 灣商 Ŭiju merchants

millan 民亂 popular rebellions

min'go 民庫 people's fund

minjung 민중 mass

minjung hyŏngmyŏng ŭi sŏn'gu 민중혁명의 선구 the herald of people's revolution

minyo 民謠 folk song

moban taeyŏk yul 謀叛大逆律 punishment for high treason

mok cha mang chŏng ŭp hŭng 木子亡 鄭邑興 literally means that the tree character perishes and the chŏng town arises but symbolically meant the fall of the Chosŏn dynasty followed by a new dynasty founded by the Chŏng royal family

mollak yangban 沒落兩班 fallen yangban

mosa 謀士 strategist

Much'ŏng 武廳 Military Administration Bureau

munjae 文宰 a civil official

munkwa 文科 higher civil service examination

Munwŏn 文苑 Hongmun'gwan or Yemun'gwan

naesŏng 來姓 moved-in surname groups also known as *ipchin-sŏng* and *ipsŏng*

naeŭng 內應 fifth columnists

Namin 南人 Southerner Faction

namjŏngan 男丁案 military roster

nongmin hangjaeng 농민항쟁 peasant resistance movement

nongmin pallan 농민반란 peasant rebellion

Noron 老論 Patriarch's Faction

oebang yusaeng 外方儒生 students from a provincial area

o-haeng 五行 five phases

ŏnmun 諺文 the Korean vernacular

Owi Puhogun 五衛 副護軍 fourth deputy commander of the Five Military Commands, Jr. 4

Owijang 五衛將 commander at the Five Military Commands, Sr. 3

P'ach'ong 把摠 battalion commander

Paebijang 陪裨將 staff commander

Paeji 陪持 post-station runner

paengma changgun 白馬將軍 a general riding a white horse

Palchang 撥長 post-station chief

P'anggwan 判官 a junior fifth-rank military office

pangŏn 方言 dialect

Pangyŏng 防營 Defense Command

P'anyun 判尹 chief magistrate of the Capital District Office, Sr. 2

Pibyŏnsa 備邊司 Border Defense Command

pi-changgun 飛將軍 a flying general

p'il 疋 unit of cloth measurement

po 堡 defense station

po 步 paces

P'odoch'ŏng 捕盜廳 Police Bureau

pondo chŏllang 本道殿廊 positions such as the superintendent (Ch'ambong, Jr. 9) at the Kija shrine (Sunginjŏn) and Tan'gun shrine (Sungnyŏngjŏn) located in P'yŏngyang

Ponggyo 奉敎 a senior seventh-rank office at the Yemun'gwan

Pongsangsi Ch'ŏmjŏng 奉常寺 僉正 fourth secretary at the Bureau of Royal Rituals Jr. 4

pon'gwan 本貫 clan seat

pŏryŏl 閥閱 capital-based prominent yangban families in the late Chosŏn

puho 富戶 rich household

puho taego 富戶大賈 wealthy merchants

Pujangch'ŏng 部將廳 Office of Patrol

Pukchang-dae 北將臺 Northern Commander's Pavilion

Pumin-dogam 富民都監 superintendent of *min'go*

p'ungsok 風俗 customs

p'ungsu 風水 geomancy (Ch.: *feng-shui*)

pun'gwan 分館 initial assignment of traineeship for *munkwa* passers

Puwŏnsu 副元帥 assistant supreme commander

p'ye sa-gun 廢四郡 the area where four districts were located in the early Chosŏn period

Pyŏlchang 別將 garrison commander, Jr. 9

Pyŏlgam 別監 assistant director of the Bureau of Local Yangban

pyŏllan 변란 politically charged rebellions

pyŏl-yuho 別儒戶 quasi-yangban households

p'yŏnghan 平漢 the common rabble from P'yŏngan Province

Pyŏngjo 兵曹 Ministry of War

Pyŏngsa 兵使 provincial military commander

pyŏnjang 邊將 military office in border region

p'yŏnojiryu 編伍之類 commoners obliged to military service

pyŏnsinsul 變身術 occult arts

ri 里 a measuring unit approximately 3.3 miles or a subdistrict

sa 司 battalion

saaek sŏwŏn 賜額書院 royal-chartered private academy

saengwŏn 生員 a lower civil service examination degree or degree-holder

Saganwŏn 司諫院 Office of the Censor General

Sahŏnbu 司憲府 Office of the Inspector General

sahwan 使喚 a domestic servant

sain 士人 a scholar or yangban

sajok 士族 hereditary yangban

samasi 司馬試 triennial lower civil service examination

Samdo t'ongjesa 三道統制使 regional naval commander, Jr. 2

samsumi 三手米 rice surtax to support the three types of soldiers

sanghan 常漢 commoner

Sangjinch'ŏng 常賑廳 Ever-Normal Relief Bureau

Sangp'yŏngch'ŏng 常平廳 Ever-Normal Bureau

San guo zhi yan yi 三國志 演義 Romance of the Three Kingdoms

Sasongya 四松野 Four Pine Field

segŏji 世居地 semipermanent residence

Sejong sillok chiriji 世宗實錄地理誌 The Veritable Records of King Sejong Geographic Survey

silchik 實職 regular office

Sinan chido 新安地圖 Illustrated Map of Chŏngju

Sinan'gwan 新安館 the guesthouse of Chŏngju

singni 殖利 interest income from loaning out the people's fund

sinhae t'onggong 辛亥通共 joint-sale decree in 1791 which allowed unlicensed merchants to operate in the capital alongside the six shops

sinhyang 新鄉 local yangban or people with lesser social status who aspired to earn membership in a local yangban association

Sinjŭng tongguk yŏji sŭngnam 新增東國輿地勝覽 Augmented Survey of the Geography of Korea

Sinmirok 신미록 A Story of Sinmi Year

sinsa 神師 holy master

sŏch'i 서치 the common rabble from P'yŏngan Province

so-chunghwa 小中華 small civilization

sŏdang 書堂 village school

Sŏgigwan 書記官 document clerk

sogo-gun 束伍軍 *sogo* army which was modeled on the Zhejiang system of military organization of the late Ming period

Sohak 小學 The Elementary Learning

sohwa 小華 small civilization

sŏin 西人 P'yŏngan people

Sŏin 西人 Westerner Faction

sŏ-chi-han 西之漢 the common rabble from P'yŏngan Province

sŏm 石 1 *sŏm*=15 or 20 *mal*=1 picul of grain by volume= 89.464 or 119.285 liters

Sŏnbongjang 先鋒將 chief field commander

sŏnggwan chedo 姓貫制度 ancestral seat system

Sŏnggyun'gwan 成均館 Royal Academy

sŏn'gi 善騎 cavalrymen

sŏngin 聖人 a savior

Songnim 松林 Pine Grove

songsang 松商 Kaesŏng merchants

Sŏnjŏn'gwan 宣傳官 royal messenger

Sŏnjŏn'gwan ch'ŏng 宣傳官廳 Office of Transmission

sŏŏl 庶孽 nothoi or sons of yangban by slave or commoner concubines (sing.: nothous)

sorin 率人 houseguest

sŏtchok-nom 서쪽놈 the common rabble from P'yŏngan Province

sŏt'o 西土 P'yŏngan Province

sŏwŏn 書院 private academy

Such'an 修撰 sixth counselor of the Office of the Special Counselors, Sr. 6

Sumunjang 守門將 chief of gatekeepers

Sumunjang ch'ŏng 守門將廳 Gatekeeper's Office

Sunginjŏn 崇仁殿 Kija shrine in P'yŏngyang

Sŭngji 承旨 royal secretary of the Royal Secretariat, Sr. 3

Sŭngjŏngwŏn 承政院 Royal Secretariat

Sŭngmunwŏn 承文院 Office of Diplomatic Correspondence

Sungnyŏngjŏn 崇靈殿 Tan'gun shrine in P'yŏngyang

Sunmu Chunggun 巡撫中軍 deputy commander of the Circuit Pacification Army Headquarters

Sunmuyŏng 巡撫營 Circuit Pacification Army Headquarters

Sunmuyŏng chindo 巡撫營陣圖 Illustration of the Circuit Pacification Army Camp

Sunyŏng 巡營 Circuit Army Headquarters

Sunyŏng Chunggun 巡營中軍 dep-

uty commander of the Circuit
Army Headquarters
Tabok-tong 多福洞 Bountiful
Blessings Village
taedongmi 大同米 tribute rice
surtax
taedongpŏp 大同法 Uniform Land
Tax Law
Taegyo 待敎 a senior eighth-rank
office at the Yemun'gwan
taeŭi 대의 great principle
Taewŏnsu 大元帥 supreme
commander
tanggun 唐軍 Chinese soldiers
tangsanggwan 堂上官 officials
of the upper end of the hall;
high-ranking officials whose
rank reached higher than senior
third rank
to 道 the true way of Daoism or
Buddhism (Ch.: *dao*)
Todangnok 都堂錄 a final
candidate roster for the
Hongmun'gwan
toe 升 1 *toe*=10 *hop*=0.596 liter
t'ogwan chedo 土官制度 indigenous office and rank system
t'ogwanjik 土官職 indigenous
offices
t'oho 土豪 indigenous
power-holders
Tojihwisa 都指揮使 commander
in chief
Tonga ilbo 동아일보 *Tonga Daily*

tongjok purak 同族部落 same
surname village (J.: *dōzoku
buraku*)
T'ongjŏng taebu 通政大夫 a
senior third-rank title
t'ongmun 通文 a circular
T'ongnyewŏn 通禮院 Office of
Ceremonies
Tosa 都事 inspector, Jr. 5
t'osŏng 土姓 surname with geographical identification
ŭban 邑案 district yangban roster
ŭibyŏng 義兵 progovernment
militia
Ŭigŭmbu 義禁府 State Tribunal
unjech'ungch'a 雲梯衝車 Flying
War Cart
Wae 倭 Japanese
wŏnak hyangni 元惡鄕吏 corrupt
clerks
wŏn'an 原案 original roster
wŏnhyang 原鄕 original members
of the local yangban association
Wŏnsu-dae 元帥臺 Pavilion of the
Great General
wŏn-yuho 元儒戶 authentic yangban households
yang 兩 a monetary unit in the
late Chosŏn
yangban 兩班 a term referring to
social, political, and economic
elite of the Chosŏn dynasty
*yangbanja munmu kogwan chi
ch'ing ya* 兩班者文武高官之稱

也 yangban refers to high civil
and military officials

Yangmu-gong 襄武公 Duke of
Cultivating the Military

Yangŭi-gong 襄毅公 Duke of Cultivating Valor

Yejo 禮曹 Ministry of Rites

yejŏn 禮錢 monetary contribution

Yemun'gwan 藝文館 the Office of
Royal Decrees

yojik 要職 reputable positions

yŏksajŏk hwalgi 역사적 활기 historical energy

yong sinang 龍神仰 folk belief
in the dragon spirit

yŏngan 營案 provincial yangban
roster

Yŏngjang 營將 chief commander

yongnyŏ puin 龍女婦人 Madame
Dragon

Yŏngŭijŏng 領議政 chief state
councilor

Yugŭijŏn 六矣廛 six licensed
shops in the capital

yuhak 幼學 scholars in training
or Confucian scholar

yuho 儒戶 yangban households

Yujinjang 留陣將 chief
commander

Zhao Zilong 趙子龍 one of the
main characters from the *San
guo zhi yan yi*

Zhu-ge Liang 諸葛亮 one of the
main characters from the *San
guo zhi yan yi*

Bibliography

ABBREVIATIONS

CJI   *Chinjung ilgi* [A Diary at the Military Camp]. In *Han'guk minjung undongsa charyo taegye; 1811–1812 nyŏn ŭi nongmin chŏnjaeng p'yŏn, 3* [A Collection of Primary Sources in the History of the People's Movement in Korea; the Peasant War of 1811–1812, vo. 3]. Seoul: Yŏgang ch'ulp'ansa, 1985.

KP   *Kwansŏ p'yŏngnallok* [The Record of the Pacification Campaign of the Hong Kyŏngnae Rebellion]. 5 vols. Edited by Han'gukhak munhŏn yŏn'guso. Seoul: Asea munhwasa, 1979.

Sillok   All references to Kuksa p'yŏnch'an wiwŏnhoe [National Institute of Korean History], ed., *Chosŏn wangjo sillok* [The Veritable Records of the Kings of the Chosŏn Dynasty], 48 vols. (Seoul: Tongguk munhwasa, 1955), are noted according to the *sillok* (veritable record) of each king. The page reference is to the volume of the original folio edition, not to this 1955 edition, followed by the date in this form: year of king's reign.month.day and day in the sixty-day cycle in parentheses, e.g., *Chŏngjo sillok*, 44:20a, Chŏngjo 20.2.25 (*sinch'uk*).

SJ   Pang Ujŏng, *Sŏjŏng ilgi* [Records of the Pacification Campaign in P'yŏngan Province]. Seoul: Kuksa p'yŏnch'an wiwŏnhoe, 1964.

SSP   *Sunjo sinmi pyŏltŭngnok* [A Special Collection of Records of 1811]. In *Han'guk minjung undongsa charyo taegye; 1811–1812 nyŏn ŭi nongmin chŏnjaeng p'yŏn, 4* [A Collection of Primary Sources in the

History of the People's Movement in Korea; the Peasant War
of 1811–1812, vol. 4]. Seoul: Yŏgang ch'ulp'ansa, 1985.

SWI   Paek Kyŏnghae, *Suwa ilgi* [A Diary by Paek Kyŏnghae]. 2 *ch'aek*.
Kuksa py'ŏnch'an wiwŏnhoe Collection, B9I 89.

SWJ   Paek Kyŏnghae, *Suwajip* [Collected Works of Paek Kyŏnghae]. 8
kwŏn, 4 *ch'aek*. Kuksa p'yŏnch'an wiwŏnhoe Collection, D3B 263.

PRIMARY SOURCES

Allŭng ilgi [A Daily Reflection at the Anju Military Headquarters]. In *Han'guk
minjung undongsa charyo taegye; 1811–1812 nyŏn ŭi nongmin chŏnjaeng
p'yŏn, 4* [A Collection of Primary Sources in the History of People's Movement in Korea; the Peasant War of 1811–1812, vol. 4]. Seoul: Yŏgang
ch'ulp'ansa, 1985.

An Chŏngbok. *Sunam sŏnsaeng munjip* [Collected Works of An Chŏngbok].
Kwangju: An Chongyŏp, 1910? Harvard-Yenching Library Collection, K
5568.2 3423.

Anŭi Im ssi sebo [Genealogy of Anŭi Im]. Seoul: n.p., 1984.

Chinjung ilgi [A Diary at the Military Camp]. In *Han'guk minjung undongsa
charyo taegye; 1811–1812 nyŏn ŭi nongmin chŏnjaeng p'yŏn, 3* [A Collection of Primary Sources in the History of the People's Movement in Korea;
the Peasant War of 1811–1812, vol. 3]. Seoul: Yŏgang ch'ulp'ansa, 1985.

Cho Susam. *Ch'ujaejip* [Collected Works of Cho Susam]. Originally published
in 1939. Reprint, Seoul: Minjok munhwasa, 1980.

Chŏng Yagyong. *Kyŏngse yup'yo* [A Design for Good Government]. 3 vols.
Translated by Yi Iksŏng. Seoul: Han'gilsa, 1997.

———. *Yŏkchu mongmin simsŏ* [Essays from the Heart on Governing the
People, Translated and Annotated]. Translated and annotated by Tasan
yŏn'guhoe. Seoul: Ch'angjak kwa pip'yŏngsa, 1978.

Ch'ŏnggu yadam [Folk Tales of Korea]. Kyujanggak Collection, 2405 19 7.
Reprinted by Kyujanggak in 1999.

Chŏngju ŭpchi [Gazetteer of Chŏngju]. In *Chosŏn sidae sach'an ŭpchi*, vol. 48.
Seoul: Han'guk inmun kwahagwŏn, 1990.

Chŏngsin munhwa yŏn'guwŏn, comp. *Sama pangmok*. Dongbang Media, http://
www.koreaa2z.com/sama1/.

Chosŏn wangjo sillok [The Veritable Records of the Kings of the Chosŏn
Dynasty]. Edited by Kuksa p'yŏnch'an wiwŏnhoe [National Institute of
Korean History]. 48 vols. Seoul: Tongguk munhwasa, 1955.

Ch'uan kŭp kugan [Trials and Indictments]. Vol. 27, *Choein Chinch'ae*

tŭng ch'uan [Trial Records of Chinch'ae and Others], 1–182. Edited by
    Han'gukhak munhŏn yŏn'guso. Seoul: Asea munhwasa, 1978.

Chŭngbo Munhŏn pigo [Documents Compiled for Reference, Supplemented
    and Revised]. Compiled by Pak Yongdae et al. in 1908. Reprinted by Kojŏn
    kanhaenghoe. Seoul: Tongguk munhwasa, 1957.

Hadong Chŏng ssi sebo. Edited by Ch'ŏlsan Hadong Chŏng ssi chongch'inhoe.
    Seoul: Hoesangsa, 1971.

Hogu ch'ongsu [Population Data]. Reprint, Seoul: Seoul taehakkyo ch'ulp'anbu,
    1971.

Hong Kyŏngnae. In Yi Usŏng and Im Hyŏngt'aek, eds., *Yijo hanmun tanp'yŏn
    chip, ha* [Collection of Short Novels in Chinese During the Chosŏn Dynasty,
    vol. 3], 118–61 (Korean translation) and 366–84. Seoul: Ilchogak, 1978.

Hong Kyŏngnae imsin saryak [A Short History of Hong Kyŏngnae in 1812].
    An addendum to *Sok choya chipyo* [The Recapitulated History In and Out
    of the Court, Supplementary Edition], *kwŏn* 12, compiled by Chang Suyŏng,
    with preface by Yi Chŏnggu. Handwritten copy in 1932. Kyujanggak Collec-
    tion, ko.4250.104.12.

Hong Kyŏngnae kwan'gye t'ongmun [A Circular in Relation to Hong Kyŏng-
    nae]. Kuksa p'yŏnch'an wiwŏnhoe Collection, B14 84.

Hong Kyŏngnae pallangi [The Record of the Hong Kyŏngnae Rebellion].
    National Library of Korea (Kungnip chungang tosŏgwan) Collection, ko
    2518-93-2.

Hong ssi ilgi [A Diary about Mr. Hong]. In *Han'guk minjung undongsa charyo
    taegye; 1811–1812 nyŏn ŭi nongmin chŏnjaeng p'yŏn, 5* [A Collection of
    Primary Sources in the History of the People's Movement in Korea; the Peas-
    ant War of 1811–1812, vol. 5]. Seoul: Yŏgang ch'ulp'ansa, 1985.

Ilsŏngnok [Record of Daily Reflection]. 86 vols. Edited by Seoul taehakkyo
    Kyujanggak. Seoul: Seoul taehakkyo Kyujanggak, 1992.

Iryŏn. *Samguk yusa* [Memorabilia of the Three Kingdoms]. Edited by Ch'oe
    Namsŏn. Seoul: Sŏmun munhwasa, 1983.

Kang Hŭiyŏng. *Ilsŭng* [A Daily Record]. 1 *ch'aek*. Kyujanggak Collection,
    ko.4254.18.

Koryŏsa [History of the Koryŏ Dynasty]. 3 vols. Seoul: Asea munhwasa, 1972.

Kwangju No ssi chokpo [Genealogy of Kwangju No]. Compiled and published
    in 1898. Private Collection of No Unhŭi, Seoul, Korea.

Kwansŏ p'yŏngnallok [The Record of the Pacification Campaign of the Hong
    Kyŏngnae Rebellion]. 5 vols. Edited by Han'gukhak munhŏn yŏn'guso.
    Seoul: Asea munhwasa, 1979.

Kwansŏ sinmirok [The Trial Record of the Hong Kyŏngnae Rebellion]. In

Han'guk minjung undongsa charyo taegye; 1811–1812 nyŏn ŭi nongmin chŏnjaeng p'yŏn, 3 [A Collection of Primary Sources in the History of the People's Movement in Korea; the Peasant War of 1811–1812, vol. 3]. Seoul: Yŏgang ch'ulp'ansa, 1985.

Kwansŏ t'ongmun [A Circular to P'yŏngan People]. Kuksa p'yŏnch'an wiwŏnhoe Collection, GF 3757 (28-279-03).

Kwansŏ ŭpchi [Gazeteers of P'yŏngan Province]. In *Han'guk chiriji ch'ongsŏ ŭpchi*, vols. 14–17, *P'yŏngan-do 1–4*. Seoul: Asea munhwasa, 1986.

Man'gi yoram chaeyongp'yŏn [Handbook of Government Affairs, Finance]. Compiled by Sim Sanggyu and Sŏ Yŏngbo in 1808. Reprint, Keijō: Chōsen sōtokufu chūsūin, 1937.

Paech'ŏn Cho ssi sebo [Genealogy of Paech'ŏn Cho]. Seoul: Paech'ŏn Cho ssi chokpo p'yŏnch'an wiwŏnhoe, 1957.

Paek Kyŏnghae. *Suwa ilgi* [A Diary by Paek Kyŏnghae]. 2 *ch'aek*. Kuksa p'yŏnch'an wiwŏnhoe Collection, B9I 89.

———. *Suwajip* [Collected Works of Paek Kyŏnghae]. 8 *kwŏn*, 4 *ch'aek*. Kuksa p'yŏnch'an wiwŏnhoe Collection, D3B 263.

Paek Kyŏnghan. *Puhojip* [Collected Works of Paek Kyŏnghan]. Handwritten copy in 1933. Kuksa p'yŏnch'an wiwŏnhoe Collection, D3B 179.

Paek Siwŏn. *Nop'o sŏnsaeng munjip* [Collected Works of Paek Siwŏn]. Reprinted in *Han'guk yŏktae munjip ch'ongsŏ*, vol. 2948. Seoul: Kyŏngin munhwasa, 1999.

Pang Ujŏng. *Sŏjŏng ilgi* [Records of the Pacification Campaign in P'yŏngan Province]. Seoul: Kuksa p'yŏnch'an wiwŏnhoe, 1964.

P'yŏngsŏ ponmal [The Essence and Branch of Pacifying P'yŏngan Province]. 1 vol. in manuscript. East Asian Library, Asami Collection, University of California, Berkeley, Asami 15.23.

P'yŏngyang sokchi [The Gazetteer of P'yŏngyang, Revised]. In *Chosŏn sidae sach'an ŭpchi*, vol. 46. Seoul: Han'guk inmun kwahak yŏn'guwŏn, 1990.

Samguk sagi [History of Three Kingdoms]. Compiled by Kim Pusik in 1145. Reprint, Seoul: Minjok munhwa ch'ujinhoe, 1982.

Sejong sillok chiriji [The Veritable Records of King Sejong, Geographic Survey]. Keijō: Chōsen sōtokufu chūsūin, 1937.

Sinanji sokp'yŏn [The Gazetteer of Chŏngju, Continued]. Compiled in 1931. In *Han'guk kŭndae ŭpchi*, vols. 63 and 64. Seoul: Han'guk inmun kwahagwŏn, 1991.

Sinjŭng tongguk yŏji sŭngnam [Augmented Survey of the Geography of Korea]. Compiled and revised by Yi Haeng et al. in 1530. Reprinted by Kojŏn kan-haenghoe. Seoul: Sŏgyŏng munhwasa, 1994.

Sinmi kisa chŏnmal [A Detailed Account of the Incident in 1811]. 1 *ch'aek.*
   Yonsei University Collection.

Sinmirok [A Story of *Sinmi* Year]. Originally published in 1861. Reprinted in
   Chang Tŏksun and Ch'oe Chinwŏn, eds., *Han'guk kojŏn munhak taegye*
   [Collection of Classical Literature in Korea], vol. 1, 430–506. Seoul: Kyom-
   unsa, 1984.

Sinyŏk Chŏnggamnok [The Book of Chŏng Kam, New Translation]. Translated
   by Yi Minsu. Seoul: Hongsin munhwasa, 1985.

Sŏnu Hyŏp. *Tunam chŏnsŏ* [Collected Works of Sŏnu Hyŏp]. In *Han'guk munjip ch'onggan*, vol. 93. Seoul: Minjok munhwa ch'ujinhoe, 1992.

Suan Kye ssi inmaek po [Genealogy of the Suan Kye]. Seoul: Kye ssi inmaek
   yŏn'guso, 1974.

Sunch'ŏn Kim ssi Ch'ŏrwŏngong-p'a sebo [The Genealogy of the Sunch'ŏn Kim,
   Ch'ŏrwŏngong Branch]. Seoul: Sunch'ŏn Kim ssi Ch'ŏrwŏngong-p'a poso, 1980.

Sŭngjŏngwŏn ilgi [Records of the Royal Secretariat]. 126 vols. Edited by Kuksa
   p'yŏnch'an wiwŏnhoe. Seoul: T'amgudang, 1973.

Sunjo kisa [Annals of King Sunjo]. In Sim Nosŭng, ed., *Taedong p'aerim* [Unof-
   ficial History of Korea]. Seoul: Kukhak charyowŏn, 1983.

Sunjo sinmi pyŏltŭngnok [A Special Collection of Records of 1811]. In *Han'guk
   minjung undongsa charyo taegye; 1811–1812 nyŏn ŭi nongmin chŏnjaeng
   p'yŏn, 4* [A Collection of Primary Sources in the History of the People's
   Movement in Korea; the Peasant War of 1811–1812, vol. 4]. Seoul: Yŏgang
   ch'ulp'ansa, 1985.

Sunjŏllok [The Record of the Loyal Deaths]. In *Han'guk minjung undongsa
   charyo taegye; 1811–1812 nyŏn ŭi nongmin chŏnjaeng p'yŏn, 4* [A Collection of Primary Sources in the History of the People's Movement in Korea;
   the Peasant War of 1811–1812, vol. 4]. Seoul: Yŏgang ch'ulp'ansa, 1985.

Sunmuyŏng tŭngnok [The Records of the Circuit Pacification Army Head-
   quarters]. In *Han'guk minjung undongsa charyo taegye; 1811–1812 nyŏn
   ŭi nongmin chŏnjaeng p'yŏn, 1–2* [A Collection of Primary Sources in the
   History of the People's Movement in Korea; the Peasant War of 1811–1812,
   vols. 1 and 2]. Seoul: Yŏgang ch'ulp'ansa, 1985.

Suwŏn Paek ssi Chŏngju chokpo [Genealogy of the Suwŏn Paek of Chŏngju].
   3 vols. Suwŏn Paek ssi Chŏngju chokpo p'yŏnch'an wiwŏnhoe, 1940.
   National Library of Korea Collection, Han ko-cho 58 ka 26–22.

Taejŏn hoet'ong [Comprehensive Collection of Dynastic Code]. Reprint, Seoul:
   Pogyŏng munhwasa, 1990.

T'oegye sŏ chipsŏng [Collection of Yi Hwang's Letters]. 6 vols. Compiled with
   commentaries by Kwŏn Obong. P'ohang: P'ohang konggwa taehakkyo, 1996.

Tongguk wŏnsarok [The Record of Private Academies and Shrines in Chosŏn]. Harvard-Yenching Library Collection K 4976 7287.

U Hayŏng. *Ch'ŏnillok*. A selected translation with original text. Translation by Sariwŏn Nongŏp taehak. P'yŏngyang: Nongŏp ch'ulp'ansa, 1964.

Wagner, Edward W., and Song Chunho, comps. *The Wagner and Song Munkwa Roster of the Chosŏn Dynasty*. Dongbang Media, http://www.koreaa2z .com/munkwa/.

Yi Chunghwan. *T'aengniji* [A Guide to Select Villages]. Translated by Yi Iksŏng. Seoul: Ŭlyu munhwasa, 1993.

Yi Kŭngik. *Yŏllyŏsil kisul* [Record of Yi Kŭngik]. 6 vols. Kyŏngsŏng: Chosŏn kosŏ kanhaenghoe, 1912–13.

Yi Mungŏn. *Yangarok* [The Journal of Child Rearing]. Translated and annotated by Yi Sangju. Seoul: T'aehaksa, 1997.

Yi Sihang. *Hwaŭn sŏnsaeng munjip* [Collected Works of Yi Sihang]. Originally published in 1738. Reprinted in *Han'guk yŏktae munjip ch'ongsŏ*, vol. 636. Seoul: Kyŏngin munhwasa, 1998.

———. *Kim changgun yusa* [Records Regarding Commander Kim]. Compiled and published in 1738. Harvard-Yenching Library Collection, TK 2294.5 8161.

Yi Sŭnghyu. *Chewang un'gi* [An Epic of Emperors and Kings]. Originally published in 1287. Reprint in Kyŏngsŏng: Chosŏn kojŏn kanhaenghoe, 1939.

Yŏnan Kim ssi Kaesŏng Puyun-gong p'abo [Genealogy of the Yŏnan Kim, Kaesŏng Puyun Branch]. 2 vols. Taejŏn: Yŏnan Kim ssi chongch'inhoe, 1986.

Yŏngbyŏnji [Gazeteer of Yŏngbyŏn]. Originally published in 1944. Reprinted in *Han'guk kŭndae ŭpchi*, vol. 62. Seoul: Han'guk inmun kwahagwŏn, 1991.

Yongsŏng Ssangŭirok [Record of Two Loyal Subjects from Yongsŏng]. Compiled by Chŏng Sŏnghak and published in 1794. Kyoto University Kawai Collection, ri-10.

Yŏnil Sŭng ssi chokpo [Genealogy of the Yŏnil Sŭng]. Seoul: Yŏnil Sŭng ssi chokpo kanhaengso, 1962.

Yu Tŭkkong. *Kyŏngdo chapchi* [Miscellaneous Things in the Capital]. Kyŏngsŏng: Chosŏn kwangmunhoe, 1912.

SECONDARY SOURCES

Abelmann, Nancy. *Echoes of the Past, Epics of Dissent: A South Korean Social Movement*. Berkeley: University of California Press, 1996.

An Hwak. *Chosŏn munmyŏngsa* [The History of Korean Civilization]. Kyŏngsŏng: Hoedong sŏgwan, 1923.

An Pyŏngjik and Yi Yŏnghun, eds. *Matchil ŭi nongmindŭl* [Peasants of Matchil]. Seoul: Ilchogak, 2001.

Bernhardt, Kathryn. *Rents, Taxes, and Peasant Resistance: The Lower Yangzi Region, 1840–1950*. Stanford, Calif.: Stanford University Press, 1992.

Bix, Herbert P. *Peasant Protest in Japan, 1590–1884*. New Haven, Conn.: Yale University Press, 1986.

Byington, Mark Edward. "A History of the Puyŏ State, Its People, and Its Legacy." Ph.D. diss., Harvard University, 2003.

Ch'a Changsŏp. *Chosŏn hugi pŏryŏl yŏn'gu* [A Study of *Pŏryŏl* in the Late Chosŏn]. Seoul: Ilchogak, 1997.

Chang Tongp'yo. *Chosŏn hugi chibang chaejŏng yŏn'gu* [A Study of Local Finance in Late Chosŏn]. Seoul: Kukhak charyowŏn, 1999.

Cho Kwang. "19 segi millan ŭi sahoejŏk paegyŏng" [The Social Background of Popular Rebellions during the Nineteenth Century]. In *19 segi Han'guk chŏnt'ong sahoe ŭi pyŏnmo wa minjung ŭisik* [Changes of Traditional Society and Mass Consciousness in Korea during the Nineteenth Century], 181–236. Seoul: Kodae minjok munhwa yŏn'guso, 1982.

Cho Tongil. *Minjung yŏngung iyagi* [Stories of Popular Heroes]. Seoul: Munye ch'ulp'ansa, 1992.

Ch'oe Chinok. *Chosŏn sidae saengwŏn chinsa yŏn'gu* [A Study of *Saengwŏn* and *Chinsa* during the Chosŏn Period]. Seoul: Chimmundang, 1998.

Ch'oe Chongt'aek. "Chosŏn ch'o P'yŏngan Hamgil-do ŭi chibang seryŏk" [Local Power Groups in P'yŏngan and Hamgil Provinces in the Early Chosŏn]. *Tongbang hakchi* 99 (1998): 131–90.

Ch'oe Kilsŏng. "Koryŏ Chosŏn ŭi p'ungsu sasang" [The Geomantic Theory during the Koryŏ and Chosŏn Dynasties]. In *Han'guk min'gan sinang ŭi yŏn'gu* [The Study of Folk Beliefs in Korea], 223–42. Seoul: Kyemyŏng University Press, 1989.

Chŏn Haejong. "Ch'ŏngdae han-jung kwan'gye ŭi ilgoch'al" [A Study of Qing-Chosŏn Relations]. *Tongyanghak* 1 (1971): 229–45.

Chŏng Manjo. *Chosŏn sidae sŏwŏn yŏn'gu* [A Study of Private Academies in Chosŏn]. Seoul: Chimmundang, 1997.

Chŏng Okcha. *Chosŏn hugi Chosŏn chunghwa sasang yŏn'gu* [A Study of the Chosŏn *Chunghwa* Thought in the late Chosŏn Period]. Seoul: Ilchisa, 1998.

Chŏng Sŏkchong. "Chosŏn hugi Sukchong nyŏn'gan ŭi mirŭk sinang kwa sahoe undong" [The Belief in Maitreya Buddha and Social Movements during the Reign of King Sukchong]. In *Han Ugŭn paksa chŏngnyŏn kinyŏm sahak nonch'ong* [Historical Studies in Commemoration of Dr. Han Ugŭn's Retirement], 409–46. Seoul: Chisik sanŏpsa, 1981.

———. "Hong Kyŏngnae nan" [The Hong Kyŏngnae Rebellion]. In *Chŏnt'ong sidae ŭi minjung undong* [People's Movements in Traditional Society], 289–355. Seoul: P'ulbit, 1981.

———. "Hong Kyŏngnae nan kwa kŭ naeŭng seryŏk" [The Hong Kyŏngnae Rebellion and The Fifth Columnists]. *Kyonam sahak* 1 (Dec. 1985): 373–402.

———. "Hong Kyŏngnae nan ŭi sŏnggyŏk" [The Nature of the Hong Kyŏngnae Rebellion]. *Han'guksa yŏn'gu* 7 (1972): 151–206.

———. "Sukchong nyŏn'gan sŭngnyŏ seryŏk ŭi kŏbyŏn kyehoek kwa Chang Kilsan" [Chang Kilsan and a Conspiracy of Buddhist Monks During the Reign of King Sukchong]. *Tongbang hakchi* 31 (1982): 105–45.

Chŏng Yŏnghun. "*Sinmirok* yŏn'gu" [A Study of the *Sinmirok*]. Master's thesis, Ewha Women's University, 1993.

Chŏngju kunji [The Gazetteer of Chŏngju]. Edited by Chŏngju kunji p'yŏnch'an wiwŏnhoe. Seoul: Chŏngju kunji p'yŏnch'an wiwŏnhoe, 1975.

Chung, Chai-sik [Chŏng Chaesik]. "Chŏng Tojŏn: 'Architect' of Yi Dynasty Government and Ideology." In William T. de Bary and JaHyun Kim Haboush, eds., *The Rise of Neo-Confucianism in Korea*, 59–83. New York: Columbia University Press, 1985.

Duara, Prasenjit. *Rescuing History from the Nation: Questioning Narratives of Modern China*. Chicago: University of Chicago Press, 1995.

Deuchler, Martina. *The Confucian Transformation of Korea: A Study of Society and Ideology*. Cambridge, Mass.: Harvard University Press, 1992.

———. "'Heaven Does Not Discriminate': A Study of Secondary Sons in Chosŏn Korea." *Journal of Korean Studies* 6 (1988–89): 121–64.

Duncan, John B. "Hyanghwain: Migration and Assimilation in Chosŏn Dynasty Korea." *Acta Koreana* 3 (2000): 99–113.

———. *The Origins of the Chosŏn Dynasty*. Seattle: University of Washington Press, 2000.

Eggert, Marion. "A Borderline Case: Korean Travelers' Views of the Chinese Border (Eighteenth to Nineteenth Century)." In Sabine Dabringhaus and Roderich Ptak, eds., *China and Her Neighbours: Borders, Visions of the Other, Foreign Policy, 10th to 19th Century*, 49–78. Wiesbaden, Germany: Harrassowitz Verlag, 1997.

Elliott, Mark C. "The Limits of Tartary: Manchuria in Imperial and National Geographies." *Journal of Asian Studies* 59, no. 3 (Aug. 2000): 603–46.

Elman, Benjamin A. *Classicism, Politics, and Kinship: The Ch'ang-chou School of New Text Confucianism in Late Imperial China*. Berkeley: University of California Press, 1990.

Em, Henry H. "Nationalism, Post-Nationalism, and Shin Ch'ae-ho." *Korea Journal* 39, no. 2 (Summer 1999): 283–317.

Emmerson, Richard K. "The Secret." *American Historical Review* 104, no. 5 (Dec. 1999): 1603–14.

Esherick, Joseph W. "Symposium on Peasant Rebellions: Some Introductory Comments." *Modern China* 9, no. 3 (July 1983): 275–284.

Freedman, Maurice. *Chinese Lineage and Society: Fukien and Kwangtung.* London: University of London, the Athlone Press, 1966.

Goldstone, Jack. *Revolution and Rebellion in the Early Modern World.* Berkeley: University of California Press, 1991.

Haboush, JaHyun Kim. "Constructing the Center: The Ritual Controversy and the Search for a New Identity in Seventeenth-Century Korea." In JaHyun Kim Haboush and Martina Deuchler, eds., *Culture and the State in Late Chosŏn Korea*, 46–90. Cambridge, Mass.: Harvard University Asia Center, 1999.

Han Sanggwŏn. "1811 nyŏn Hwanghae-do Koksan chibang ŭi nongmin hangjaeng" [The 1811 Peasant Resistance Movement in Koksan, Hwanghae Province]. *Yŏksa wa hyŏnsil* 5 (1991): 189–241.

Han Young-woo [Han Yŏng'u]. "Kija Worship in the Koryŏ and Early Yi Dynasties: A Cultural Symbol in the Relationship Between Korea and China." In William T. de Bary and JaHyun Kim Haboush, eds., *The Rise of Neo-Confucianism in Korea*, 349–71. New York: Columbia University Press, 1985.

Han'guk yŏksa yŏn'guhoe, ed. *Chosŏn chŏngch'isa, 1800–1863, sang* [Political History of the Chosŏn Dynasty, 1800–1863, vol. 1]. Seoul: Ch'ŏngnyŏnsa, 1990.

Harrison, James P. *The Communists and Chinese Peasant Rebellions: A Study in the Rewriting of Chinese History.* New York: Atheneum, 1969.

Henthorn, William E. *A History of Korea.* New York: The Free Press, 1971.

Hill, Christopher. *The World Turned Upside Down.* New York: Penguin, 1972.

Hobsbawm, Eric J. *Primitive Rebels: Studies in Archaic Forms of Social Movement in the Nineteenth and Twentieth Centuries.* New York: W. W. Norton, 1959.

Hong Hŭiyu. "1811–1812 nyŏn P'yŏngan-do nongmin chŏnjaeng kwa kŭ sŏnggyŏk" [The Peasant War in P'yŏngan Province in 1811–1812 and its Nature]. In *Ponggŏn chibae kyegŭp ŭl pandaehan nongmindŭl ŭi t'ujaeng* [The Struggle of the Peasants against the Feudal Ruling Class], 47–120. P'yŏngyang: Kwahakgwŏn ch'ulp'ansa, 1963.

Hurst, G. Cameron III. "The Good, the Bad and the Ugly: Personalities in the

Founding of the Koryŏ Dynasty." *Korean Studies Forum* 7 (Summer–Fall 1981): 1–26.

Hwang, Kyung Moon. *Beyond Birth: Social Status in the Emergence of Modern Korea*. Cambridge, Mass.: Harvard University Press, 2004.

———. "From the Dirt to Heaven: Northern Koreans in the Chosŏn and Early Modern Eras." *Harvard Journal of Asiatic Studies* 62, no. 1 (June 2002): 135–78.

Hwang P'aegang. "Hanmun sosŏl *Hong Kyŏngnae chŏn* yŏn'gu" [A Study of a Classical Chinese Novel *Hong Kyŏngnae chŏn*]. *Tongyanghak* 18 (1988): 111–36.

Hyŏn Sangyun. "Hong Kyŏngnae." In *Chosŏn myŏngin chŏn* [Biographies of Famous People of Chosŏn], 374–400. Seoul: Chogwangsa, 1946.

———. *Hong Kyŏngnae chŏn* [Story of Hong Kyŏngnae]. *Tonga ilbo* 7/12/1931–8/20/1931.

Inaba Iwakichi, ed. *Heian hokudō shi, ge* [The History of Northern P'yŏngan Province, vol. 2]. Keijō: Chosŏn inswae chusik hoesa, 1938. Reprint, Seoul: Kyŏngin munhwasa, 1989.

———. *Heian hokudō shi, jō* [The History of Northern P'yŏngan Province, vol. 1]. Keijō: Chosŏn inswae chusik hoesa, 1938. Reprint, Seoul: Kyŏngin munhwasa, 1989.

Joe, Wanne J. *Traditional Korea: A Cultural History*. Seoul: Chungang University Press, 1972.

Karlsson, Anders. "Challenging the Dynasty: Popular Protest, *Chŏnggamnok* and the Ideology of the Hong Kyŏngnae Rebellion." *International Journal of Korean History* 2 (Dec. 2001): 253–77.

———. "The Hong Kyŏngnae Rebellion 1811–1812: Conflict between Central Power and Local Society in Nineteenth-Century Korea." Ph.D. diss., Stockholm University, Institute of Oriental Languages, 2000.

Kawarabayashi Shizumi. "1811 nyŏn ŭi P'yŏngan-do e issŏsŏ ŭi nongmin chŏnjaeng" [The Peasant War of 1811 in P'yŏngan Province]. In *Ponggŏn sahoe haech'egi ŭi sahoe kyŏngje kujo* [The Social and Economic Structure during the Period of Dissolution of the Feudal Society], 285–314. Seoul: Ch'ŏnga ch'ulp'ansa, 1982.

Kawashima, Fujiya. "A Study of *Hyangan*: Kin Groups and Aristocratic Localism in the Seventeenth and Eighteenth Century Korean Countryside." *Journal of Korean Studies* 5 (1984): 3–38.

———. "The Local Gentry Association in Mid-Yi Dynasty Korea: A Preliminary Study of Ch'angnyŏng *Hyangan* 1600–1838." *Journal of Korean Studies* 2 (1980): 113–37.

Kim Chaeho. "Nongch'on sahoe ŭi sinyong kwa kye: 1853–1934" [Credit and *Kye* in Rural Society: 1853–1934]. In An Pyŏngjik and Yi Yŏnghun, eds., *Matchil ŭi nongmin* [Peasants of Matchil], 300–31. Seoul: Ilchogak, 2001.

Kim Chongwŏn. "Chosŏn hugi taech'ŏng muyŏk e taehan ilgoch'al—chamsang ŭi muyŏk hwaltong ŭl chungsimŭiro" [A Study of Foreign Trade with Qing China in late Chosŏn—Trading Activities of Smugglers]. *Chindan hakpo* 43 (1977): 33–81.

Kim Chunhyŏng. *Chosŏn hugi Tansŏng sajokch'ŭng yŏn'gu* [A Study of *Sajok* in Tansŏng during the Late Chosŏn Period]. Seoul: Asea munhwasa, 2002.

Kim Hyŏllyong. *Han'guk munhŏn sŏrhwa 3* [The Documented Folk Tales of Korea, vol. 3]. Seoul: Kŏn'guk taehakkyo ch'ulp'anbu, 1999.

Kim Hyŏnyŏng. *Chosŏn sidae ŭi yangban kwa hyangch'on sahoe* [Yangban and Local Society in Chosŏn]. Seoul: Chimmundang, 1999.

———. "Ŭi, chŏm, mu: 16 segi ŭi chilbyŏng ch'iyu ŭi yŏrŏ yangsang" [Medicine, Divination, and Shamanism: Various Aspects of Curing Diseases in the Sixteenth Century]. *41 hoe chŏn'guk yŏksahak taehoe palp'yo yoji* (1998): 108–17.

Kim Ingŏl. "Chosŏn hugi hyangan ŭi sŏnggyŏk pyŏnhwa wa chaeji sajok" [Changes in the Nature of the Local Yangban Roster and Local Yangban in the Late Chosŏn]. In *Kim Ch'ŏlchun paksa hwagap kinyŏm sahak nonch'ong* [A Collection of Papers in Commemoration of Dr. Kim Ch'ŏlchun's Sixtieth Birthday], 525–60. Seoul: Chisik sanŏpsa, 1983.

———. "Chosŏn hugi hyangch'on sahoe pyŏndong e kwanhan yŏn'gu" [A Study of Changes in Local Society during the Late Chosŏn Dynasty]. Ph.D. diss., Seoul National University, 1991.

Kim Sŏkhŭi. "Sejojo ŭi samin e kwanhan koch'al" [A Study of the Population Relocation during the Reign of King Sejo]. *Pudae sahak* 2 (1971): 33–61.

Kim Sŏngyŏng. "Chosŏn hugi sansong kwa sallim soyugwŏn ŭi silt'ae" [Legal Dispute over Forest Lands and the Realities of Forest Land Ownership in Late Chosŏn]. *Tongbang hakchi* 77/78/79 (June 1993): 497–535.

Kim, Sun Joo [Kim Sŏnju]. "Chosŏn hugi P'yŏngan-do Chŏngju ŭi hyangan unyŏng kwa yangban munhwa" [The Management of the Local Yangban Roster and Elite Culture in Chŏngju, P'yŏngan Province, in the Late Chosŏn Period]. *Yŏksa hakpo* 185 (Mar. 2005): 65–105.

———. "In Defense of Regional Elite Identity and Culture." Paper presented at the conference "Korea as Cultural Imaginary: Discourse of Identity in Late Chosŏn Korea," Columbia University, New York, April 2005.

———. "Marginalized Elite, Regional Discrimination, and the Tradition of

266 *Bibliography*

Prophetic Belief in the Hong Kyŏngnae Rebellion." Ph.D. diss., University of Washington, 2000.

———. "Negotiating Cultural Identities in Conflict: A Reading of the Writings of Paek Kyŏnghae (1765–1842)." *Journal of Korean Studies* 10 (2005): 85–120.

Kim Taegil. *Chosŏn hugi changsi yŏn'gu* [A Study of Markets in Late Chosŏn]. Seoul: Kukhak charyowŏn, 1997.

Kim Tŏkchin. *Chosŏn hugi chibang chaejŏng kwa chabyŏkse* [Local Finance and Miscellaneous Surcharges in Late Chosŏn]. Seoul: Kukhak charyowŏn, 1999.

———. "Chosŏn hugi chibang kwanch'ŏng ŭi min'go sŏllip kwa unyŏng" [The Establishment of a People's Fund and its Operation by the Local Governments during the Late Chosŏn Period]. *Yŏksa hakpo* 133 (Mar. 1992): 63–93.

Kim Uch'ŏl. *Chosŏn hugi chibang kunje sa* [The History of Local Military System in Late Chosŏn]. Seoul: Kyŏngin munhwasa, 2000.

Kim Ungho. "Uri puja rŭl yŏkchŏk ŭiro moltani, Yi Kwal" [How Could My Son and I Be Accused of Treason? Yi Kwal]. In Han'guk yŏksa yŏn'guhoe, ed., *Moban ŭi yŏksa* [The History of Treason], 254–70. Seoul: Sejong sŏjŏk, 2001.

Kim Yongdŏk. "Chŏng Yŏrip yŏn'gu" [A Study of Chŏng Yŏrip]. *Han'guk hakpo* 4 (1976): 40–83.

Kim Yongsŏp. "Chosŏn hugi ŭi kyŏngyŏnghyŏng punong kwa sangŏpchŏk nongŏp." In *Chosŏn hugi nongŏpsa yŏn'gu: nongŏp pyŏndong, nonghak sajo* [Studies in the Agricultural History of Late Chosŏn: Changes in Agriculture and Trends in Agricultural Studies], 134–229. Seoul: Ilchogak, 1971.

Ko Sŏkkyu. "18 segimal 19 segich'o P'yŏngan-do chiyŏk hyanggwŏn ŭi ch'ui" [The Development of Local Power Relations in P'yŏngan Province during the Late Eighteenth and Early Nineteenth Centuries]. *Han'guk munhwa* 11 (1990): 341–406.

———. "19 segi chŏnban hyangch'on sahoe chibae kujo ŭi sŏnggyŏk" [The Nature of the Structure of Local Control in the Earlier Part of the Nineteenth Century]. *Oedae sahak* 2 (1989).

———. "19 segi chŏnban hyangch'on sahoe seryŏkkan ŭi taerip ŭi ch'ui— Kyŏngsang-do Yŏngyang hyŏn ŭl chungsim ŭro" [The Power Struggle in Local Society in the Earlier Part of the Nineteenth Century—Yŏngyang District in Kyŏngsang Province]. *Kuksagwan nonch'ong* 8 (1989): 147–81.

———. *19-segi Chosŏn ŭi hyangch'on sahoe yŏn'gu, chibae wa chŏhang ŭi kujo* [A Study of Local Society in Nineteenth-Century Chosŏn: The

Structure of Control and Resistance]. Seoul: Seoul Taehakkyo Chu'lp'anbu, 1998.

Ko Sŏnghun et al., eds. *Millan ŭi sidae* [The Era of Popular Rebellions]. Seoul: Karam kihoek, 2000.

Ko Tonghwan. *Chosŏn hugi Sŏul sangŏp paltalsa yŏn'gu* [A Study of the Development of Commerce in Seoul in Late Chosŏn]. Seoul: Chisik sanŏpsa, 1998.

Kuhn, Philip A. *Rebellion and Its Enemies in Late Imperial China: Militarization and Social Structure, 1796–1864.* Cambridge, Mass., and London: Harvard University Press, 1970.

Kwŏn Naehyŏn. "Chosŏn hugi P'yŏngan-do chaejŏng unyŏng yŏn'gu" [A Study of Financial Management of P'yŏngan Province in the Late Chosŏn Period]. Ph.D. diss., Korea University, 2003.

Kwŏn T'aehwan and Sin Yongha. "Chosŏn wangjo sidae in'gu ch'ujŏng e kwanhan ilsiron" [On Population Estimates of the Yi Dynasty, 1392–1910]. *Tonga munhwa* 14 (Dec. 1977): 287–330.

Ledyard, Gari. "Yin and Yang in the China-Manchuria-Korea Triangle." In Morris Rossabi, ed., *China among Equals*, 313–53. Berkeley: University of California Press, 1983.

Lee Ki-baik [Yi Kibaek]. *A New History of Korea.* Translated by Edward W. Wagner with Edward J. Shultz. Cambridge, Mass., and London: Harvard University Press, 1984.

Little, Daniel. *Understanding Peasant China: Case Studies in the Philosophy of Social Science.* New Haven, Conn., and London: Yale University Press, 1989.

Little, Daniel, and Joseph W. Esherick. "Testing the Testers: A Reply to Barbara Sands and Ramon Myers's Critique of G. William Skinner's Regional Systems Approach to China." *Journal of Asian Studies* 48, no. 1 (Feb. 1989): 90–99.

Mangwŏn Han'guksa yŏn'gusil 19 segi nongmin hangjaeng punkwa, ed. *1862 nyŏn nongmin hangjaeng—chungse malgi chŏn'guk nongmindŭl ŭi panbonggŏn t'ujaeng* [Peasant Resistance Movements in 1862—Antifeudal Peasant Struggle throughout the Country at the End of the Medieval Period]. Seoul: Tongnyŏk, 1988.

Michell, Tony. "Fact and Hypothesis in Yi Dynasty Economic History: The Demographic Dimension." *Korean Studies Forum* 6 (Winter–Spring 1979/1980): 65–92.

Moon, Seungsook. "Begetting the Nation: The Androcentric Discourse of National History and Tradition in South Korea." In Elaine H. Kim and

Chungmoo Choi, eds., *Dangerous Women, Gender and Korean Nationalism*, 33–66. New York and London: Routedge, 1998.

Morohashi Tetsuji. *Dai Kan-Wa jiten* [Great Chinese-Japanese Dictionary]. 13 vols. Tokyo: Taishukan Shoten, 1955–60.

Mun Ilp'yŏng. "Sasang ŭi kiin" [Famous Figures in History]. In *Hoam chŏnjip* [Collected Works of Mun Ilp'yŏng], vol. 1, 405–13. Seoul: Chosŏn ilbosa, 1939.

Mun Yongsik. *Chosŏn hugi chinjŏng kwa hwan'gok unyŏng* [The Relief Policies and Grain Loan Management in the Late Chosŏn]. Seoul: Kyŏngin munhwasa, 2000.

Murayama Chijun. *Chōsen no senboku to yogen* [The Prognostication and Prophetic Beliefs in Korea]. Keijō: Chōsen sōtokufu, 1933.

Nam Chidae. "Chungang chŏngch'i seryŏk ŭi hyŏngsŏng kujo" [The Structure in the Formation of Central Power Groups]. In Han'guk yŏksa yŏn'guhoe, ed., *Chosŏn chŏngch'isa, sang* [The Political History of the Chosŏn Dynasty, vol. 1], 129–65. Seoul: Ch'ŏngnyŏnsa, 1990.

Nam Yŏnsuk. "Chosŏn hugi hyangban ŭi kŏjuji idong kwa sahoe chiwi ŭi chisoksŏng, II" [Changes of Residence of Local Yangban and the Continuity of Their Social Status, II]. *Han'guksa yŏn'gu* 84 (Mar. 1994): 47–81.

Naquin, Susan. *Millenarian Rebellion in China: The Eight Trigrams Uprising of 1813.* New Haven, Conn.: Yale University Press, 1976.

———. *Shantung Rebellion: The Wang Lun Uprising of 1774.* New Haven, Conn.: Yale University Press, 1981.

No T'aedon, ed. *Tan'gun kwa Ko-Chosŏn sa* [Tan'gun and the History of Old Chosŏn]. Seoul: Sagyejŏl, 2000.

O Sŏng. "Insam sangin kwa kŭmsam chŏngch'aek" [Ginseng Merchants and Restrictive Policies on the Ginseng Trade]. In *Chosŏn hugi sangin yŏn'gu* [A Study of Merchants in the Late Chosŏn Period], 8–58. Seoul: Ilchogak, 1989.

O Such'ang. *Chosŏn hugi P'yŏngan-do sahoe palchŏn yŏn'gu* [A Study of Social Development in P'yŏngan Province during the Late Chosŏn Period]. Seoul: Ilchogak, 2002.

———. "Chosŏn hugi P'yŏngan-tomin e taehan insa chŏngch'aek kwa tomin ŭi chŏngch'ijŏk tonghyang" [The Personnel Administration Policy on the People from P'yŏngan Province and the Political Attitude of P'yŏngan Residents]. Ph.D. diss., Seoul National University, 1996.

———. "Chosŏn hugi P'yŏngyang kwa kŭ insik ŭi pyŏnhwa" [P'yŏngyang and Changing Perceptions of It in the Late Chosŏn]. In Ch'oe Sŭnghŭi kyosu chŏngnyŏn kinyŏm nonmunjip kanhaenghoe, ed., *Chosŏn ŭi chŏngch'i wa sahoe* [Politics and Society in the Chosŏn], 823–50. Seoul: Chimmundang, 2002.

———. "Hong Kyŏngnae nan ponggigun ŭi ch'oego chihwibu" [The Top Leadership in the Hong Kyŏngnae Rebellion]. *Kuksagwan nonch'ong* 46 (1993): 231–60.

———. "Hong Kyŏngnae nan ŭi chudo seryŏk kwa nongmin" [The Leaders and the Peasants in the Hong Kyŏngnae Rebellion]. In *1894 nyŏn nongmin chŏnjaeng yŏn'gu* 2 [Studies of the Peasant War of 1894, vol. 2], 141–84. Seoul: Yŏksa pip'yŏngsa, 1992.

———. "17, 18 segi P'yŏngan-do yusaengch'ŭng ŭi chŏngch'ijŏk sŏnggyŏk" [The Political Characteristics of Confucian Scholars of P'yŏngan Province during the Seventeenth and Eighteenth Centuries]. *Han'guk munhwa* 16 (Dec. 1995): 93–126.

O Yŏnggyo. "Chosŏn hugi chibang kwanch'ŏng kwa singni hwaltong" [Local Governments and Their Interest-Bearing Loans during the Late Chosŏn Period]. *Hangnim* 8 (1986): 1–68.

Oda Shōgo. "Kō Keirai ran no gairyaku to sono dōki ni tsuite" [An Outline and the Causes of the Hong Kyŏngnae Rebellion]. *Seikyu gakuso* 8 (1932): 1–18 and 11 (1933): 88–107.

———. *Shinbi Kō Keirai ran no kenkyū* [A Comprehensive Study of the Hong Kyŏngnae Rebellion of 1811]. Keijō: Oda sensei kōju kinenkai, 1934.

Ownby, David. "Chinese Millenarian Traditions: The Formative Age." *American Historical Review* 104, no. 5 (Dec. 1999): 1513–30.

Pae Hyesuk. "Yŏngjo nyŏn'gan ŭi sahoe tonghyang kwa min'gan sasang" [Social Trends and Folk Beliefs during the Reign of King Yŏngjo]. *Sangmyŏng sahak* 1 (May 1993): 81–102.

Paek Sŭngch'ŏl. *Chosŏn hugi sangŏpsa yŏn'gu* [A Study of the History of Commerce in Late Chosŏn]. Seoul: Hyean, 2000.

Paek Sŭngjong. "18–19 segi *Chŏnggamnok* ŭl pirothan kakchong yeŏnsŏ ŭi naeyong kwa kŭe taehan tangsidaeindŭl ŭi haesŏk" [Various Prophetic Records, including the *Record of Chŏng Kam*, in the Eighteenth and Nineteenth Centuries and the Understanding of Those Records by Contemporary Figures]. *Chindan hakpo* 88 (1999): 265–90.

———. "18 segi chŏnban sŏbuk chibang esŏ ch'ulhyŏnhan *Chŏnggamnok*" [The *Record of Chŏng Kam* that Emerged in the Northwestern Region in the Early Eighteenth Century]. *Yŏksa hakpo* 164 (1999): 99–124.

———. *Han'guk sahoesa yŏn'gu* [A Study of the Social History of Korea]. Seoul: Ilchogak, 1996.

Paek Tuhyŏn. "On the Correlation between Non-realization of T-palatalization

270 *Bibliography*

and Regional Identity in P'yŏngan Province." Paper presented at the workshop "The Northern Region, Identity, and Culture in Korea," Harvard University, Cambridge, Mass., June 12, 2004.

Pai, Hyung Il [Pae Hyŏngil]. *Constructing "Korean" Origins: A Critical Review of Archaeology, Historiography, and Racial Myth in Korean State-Formation Theories.* Cambridge, Mass.: Harvard University Press, 2000.

Pak Honggap. "Chosŏn chŏn'gi yanggye chŏngch'angmin ŭi sŏnggyŏk kwa ch'abyŏl ŭisik" [The Nature of Migrants to Two Border Regions in the Early Chosŏn Period and the Prejudice against Them]. In *Yi Sugŏn kyosu chŏngnyŏn kinyŏm han'guk chungsesa nonch'ong* [A Collection of Works on the Medieval History of Korea to Commemorate the Retirement of Professor Yi Sugŏn], 225–56. Seoul: Nonch'ong kanhaeng wiwŏnhoe, 2000.

Pak Hŭijin and Ch'a Myŏngsu. "Chosŏn hugi wa ilche sidae ŭi in'gu pyŏndong" [Demographic Trends in Late Chosŏn and Colonial Korea]. In Yi Yŏnghun, ed., *Suryang kyŏngjesa ro tasi pon Chosŏn hugi* [An Examination of Late Chosŏn from the Perspective of Economic History], 1–40. Seoul: Seoul taehakkyo ch'ulp'anbu, 2004.

Pak Hŭngsu. "Toryanghyŏng chedo" [Weights and Measures]. In *Han'guksa* [History of Korea], vol. 24, 599–625. Seoul: Kuksa p'yŏnch'an wiwŏnhoe, 1994.

Pak It'aek. "Sŏul ŭi sungnyŏn mit misungnyŏn nodongja ŭi imgŭm, 1600–1909" [Wages of Skilled and Unskilled Laborers in Seoul, 1600–1909]. In Yi Yŏnghun, ed., *Suryang kyŏngjesa ro tasi pon Chosŏn hugi* [An Examination of Late Chosŏn from the Perspective of Economic History], 41–107. Seoul: Seoul taehakkyo ch'ulp'anbu, 2004.

Pak Kiju. "Chaehwa kagyŏk ŭi ch'ui, 1701–1909" [The Analysis of Commodity Prices, 1701–1909]. In Yi Yŏnghun, ed., *Suryang kyŏngjesa ro tasi pon Chosŏn hugi* [An Examination of Late Chosŏn from the Perspective of Economic History], 174–223. Seoul: Seoul taehakkyo ch'ulp'anbu, 2004.

Pak Kyŏngja. *Koryŏ sidae hyangni yŏn'gu* [A Study of *Hyangni* in the Koryŏ Dynasty]. Seoul: Kukhak charyowŏn, 2001.

Palais, James B. *Confucian Statecraft and Korean Institutions: Yu Hyŏngwŏn and the Late Chosŏn Dynasty.* Seattle and London: University of Washington Press, 1996.

———. *Politics and Policy in Traditional Korea.* Cambridge, Mass.: Harvard University Press, 1975.

Pepper, Suzanne. "The Political Odyssey of an Intellectual Construct: Peasant Nationalism and the Study of China's Revolutionary History—A Review Essay." *Journal of Asian Studies* 63, no. 1 (Feb. 2004): 105–25.

Perry, Elizabeth J. *Challenging the Mandate of Heaven: Social Protest and State Power in China.* Armonk, N.Y.: M. E. Sharpe, 2002.

———. *Rebels and Revolutionaries in North China 1845–1945.* Stanford, Calif.: Stanford University Press, 1980.

Peterson, Mark A. *Korean Adoption and Inheritance: Case Studies in the Creation of a Classic Confucian Society.* Ithaca, N.Y.: Cornell University Press, 1996.

Pyŏn Kwangsŏk. *Chosŏn hugi sijŏn sangin yŏn'gu* [A Study of Licensed Merchants in Late Chosŏn]. Seoul: Hyean, 2001.

P'yŏngan-namdo chi [Gazetteer of Southern P'yŏngan Province]. Seoul: P'yŏngan-namdo chi p'yŏnch'an wiwŏnhoe, 1977.

P'yŏngan-pukto chi [Gazetteer of Northern P'yŏngan Province]. Seoul: P'yŏngan-pukto chi p'yŏnch'an wiwŏnhoe, 1973.

Robinson, Kenneth R. "From Raiders to Traders: Border Security and Border Control in Early Chosŏn, 1392–1450." *Korean Studies* 16 (1992): 94–115.

Robinson, Michael Edson. *Cultural Nationalism in Colonial Korea, 1920–1925.* Seattle: University of Washington Press, 1988.

Rogers, Michael C. "*P'yŏnnyŏn T'ongnok*: The Foundation Legend of the Koryŏ State." *Journal of Korean Studies* 4 (1982–83): 3–72.

Sahoe kwahagwŏn yŏksa yŏn'guwŏn [Institute of Social Science, Historical Research Department]. "1811–1812 nyŏn P'yŏngan-do nongmin chŏnjaeng" [Peasant War of 1811–1812 in P'yŏngan Province]. In *Chosŏn chŏnsa, 12, chungse-p'yŏn, Yijosa 5* [A Comprehensive History of Korea, vol. 12, Middle Age, History of Chosŏn Dynasty, vol. 5]. P'yŏngyang: Kwahak paekkwa sajŏn ch'ulp'ansa, 1980.

Schmid, Andre. *Korea Between Empires: Nationalism and Colonialism in East Asia, 1895–1919.* New York: Columbia University Press, 2002.

———. "Rediscovering Manchuria: Sin Ch'aeho and the Politics of Territorial History in Korea." *Journal of Asian Studies* 56, no. 1 (Feb. 1997): 38–43.

Scott, James. *Moral Economy of the Peasant.* New Haven, Conn.: Yale University Press, 1976.

Shultz, Edward J. *Generals and Scholars: Military Rule in Medieval Korea.* Honolulu: University of Hawaii Press, 2000.

Silberman, Bernard S. *Ministers of Modernization: Elite Mobility in the Meiji Restoration 1868–1873.* Tucson: University of Arizona Press, 1964.

Shin, Gi-Wook [Sin Kiuk]. *Peasant Protest and Social Change in Colonial Korea.* Seattle and London: University of Washington Press, 1996.

Skocpol, Theda. *States and Social Revolution: A Comparative Analysis of France, Russia, and China.* Cambridge: Cambridge University Press, 1979.

Sŏ T'aewŏn. *Chosŏn hugi chibang kunje yŏn'gu—Yŏngjangje rŭl chungsim ŭro* [A Study of Local Military System in Late Chosŏn—the System of the Yŏngjang]. Seoul: Hyean, 1999.

Sŏ Yŏngdae. "Chŏnt'ong sidae ŭi Tan'gun ŭisik" [The Understanding of Tan'gun in Traditional Korea]. In No T'aedon, ed., *Tan'gun kwa Ko-Chosŏn sa* [Tan'gun and the History of Old Chosŏn], 157–82. Seoul: Sagyejŏl, 2000.

Somerville, John N. "Stability in Eighteenth Century Ulsan." *Korean Studies Forum* 1 (1976–77): 1–18.

Son Pyŏnggyu et al. *Tansŏng hojŏk taejang yŏn'gu* [The Study of Household Registers of Tansŏng]. Seoul: Sŏnggyun'gwan taehakkyo taedong munhwa yŏn'guwŏn, 2003.

Song Ch'ansŏp. *Chosŏn hugi hwan'gok chedo kaehyŏk yŏn'gu* [A Study of Reform Policies of the Grain Loan System in Late Chosŏn]. Seoul: Seoul taehakkyo ch'ulp'anbu, 2002.

Song Chunho. *Chosŏn sahoesa yŏn'gu* [A Social History of the Chosŏn Dynasty]. Seoul: Ilchogak, 1987.

Song Kiho. "Current Trends in the Research of Palhae History." *Seoul Journal of Korean Studies* 3 (Dec. 1990): 157–74.

———. "Several Questions in Studies of the History of Palhae." *Korea Journal* 30, no. 6 (June 1990): 4–20.

Sorensen, Clark. "National Identity and the Creation of the Category 'Peasant' in Colonial Korea." In Gi-Wook Shin and Michael Robinson, eds., *Colonial Modernity in Korea*, 288–310. Cambridge, Mass.: Harvard University Asia Center, 1999.

Tai, Hue-Tam Ho. *Millenarianism and Peasant Politics in Vietnam*. Cambridge, Mass.: Harvard University Press, 1983.

Tilly, Charles. *From Mobilization to Revolution*. New York: McGraw-Hill Publishing Company, 1978.

———. *The Vendée*. Cambridge, Mass.: Harvard University Press, 1964.

"Toryanghyŏng" [Weights and Measures]. EncyKorea, http://www.encykorea .com.

Tsurusono Hiroshi. "Heian-dō nōmin sensō ni okeru sankasō" [The Participants in the Peasant War of P'yŏngan Province]. *Chōsen shisō* 2 (1979): 57–105.

Wagner, Edward W. "The Civil Examination Process as Social Leaven: The Case of the Northern Provinces in the Yi Dynasty." *Korea Journal* 17, no. 1 (Jan. 1977): 22–27.

———. "The Ladder of Success in Yi Dynasty Korea." *Occasional Papers on Korea* 1 (1972): 1–8.

————. "Yi Dynasty Munkwa Examination Passers." Computer printout, Cambridge Computer Association, n.d.

Walraven, Boudewijn. "Popular Religion in a Confucianized Society." In JaHyun Kim Haboush and Martina Deuchler, eds., *Culture and the State in Late Chosŏn Korea*, pp.160–98. Cambridge, Mass.: Harvard University Press, 1999.

Wells, Kenneth M., ed. *South Korea's Minjung Movement: The Culture and Politics of Dissidence*. Honolulu: University of Hawaii Press, 1995.

White, James. *Ikki, Social Conflict and Political Protest in Early Modern Japan*. Ithaca, N.Y.: Cornell University Press, 1995.

Wigen, Karen. "Culture, Power, and Place: The New Landscape of East Asian Regionalism." *American Historical Review* 104, no. 4 (Oct. 1999): 1183–201.

————. *The Making of a Japanese Periphery, 1750–1920*. Berkeley: University of California Press, 1995.

Yamauchi Kōichi. "Chōsen o motte tenka ni ō tarashimu—Gakushūin daigauzō *Kija p'alchoji* ni miru zaiya Rorōn chishiki-jin no yume" [The Desire to Enthrone Chosŏn as the Son of Heaven—A Dream of Out-of-Power Intellectuals of Patriarch's Faction as Seen in the *Kija P'alchoji*, a Gakushūin University Collection]. *Tōyō gakuhō* 84, no. 3 (Dec. 2002): 1–31.

Yi Chaeryong. "Chosŏn ch'ogi ŭi t'ogwan e taehayŏ" [An Examination of the *T'ogwan* in the Early Chosŏn Dynasty]. *Chindan hakpo* 29/30 (1966): 118–28.

Yi Ch'ŏlsŏng. *Chosŏn hugi taech'ŏng muyŏksa yŏn'gu* [A Study of Foreign Trade with Qing in the Late Chosŏn Period]. Seoul: Kukhak charyowŏn, 2000.

————. "17 segi P'yŏngan-do kangbyŏn 7 ŭp ŭi pangŏ ch'eje" [The Defense Structure of Seven Districts along the Border in P'yŏngan Province in the Seventeenth Century]. *Han'guksa hakpo* 13 (Sept. 2002): 299–353.

Yi Chongil. *Taejŏn hoet'ong yŏn'gu, kwŏnsu ijŏn p'yŏn* [A Study of *Comprehensive Collection of Dynastic Codes*, Introductions and the Code of Personnel]. Seoul: Han'guk pŏpche yŏn'guwŏn, 1993.

Yi Chonhwi. *Chosŏn sidae chibang haengjŏng chedo yŏn'gu* [Studies of Local Administration System in Chosŏn]. Seoul: Ilchisa, 1990.

Yi Chun'gu. "Chosŏn hugi hallyang kwa kŭ chiwi" [Social Status of *Hallyang* during the Late Chosŏn Dynasty]. *Kuksagwan nonch'ong* 5 (1989): 147–73.

Yi Haejun. "Chosŏn hugi Chinju chibang ŭi yuho ŭi silt'ae—1832 nyŏn Chinju hyanggyo suri kirok ŭi punsŏk" [The Conditions of Yangban Households in Chinju in the Late Chosŏn Period—An Analysis of the Renovation Record of Chinju Local School]. *Chindan hakpo* 60 (1985): 79–100.

———. *Chosŏn sigi ch'ollak sahoesa* [The Social History of Villages in the Chosŏn Period]. Seoul: Minjok munhwasa, 1996.

Yi Hoch'ŏl. "19 segi nongŏp munje ŭi sŏnggyŏk" [The Nature of Problems in Agriculture in the Nineteenth Century]. In *19 segi han'guk chŏnt'ong sahoe ŭi pyŏnmo wa minjung ŭisik* [Changes of Traditional Society and People's Consciousness in Nineteenth-Century Korea], 33–90. Seoul: Koryŏ taehak-kyo minjok munhwa yŏn'guso, 1982.

Yi Hoch'ŏl and Pak Kŭnp'il. "19 segi ch'o Chosŏn ŭi kihu pyŏndong kwa non-gŏp wigi" [Climatic Change and Agricultural Crisis in Early Nineteenth Century Chosŏn]. *Chosŏn sidaesa hakpo* 2 (June 1997): 123–91.

Yi Hŏnch'ang. "Kim Yuk ŭi kyŏngje sasang kwa kyŏngje chŏngch'aek" [Economic Philosophy and Policies of Kim Yuk]. Unpublished paper provided by the author in August 2005.

Yi Hongjik. *Han'guksa taesajŏn, ha* [Encyclopedia of Korean History, vol. 2]. Seoul: Kyoyuk tosŏ, 1991.

———. *Han'guksa taesajŏn, sang* [Encyclopedia of Korean History, vol. 1]. Seoul: Kyoyuk tosŏ, 1991.

Yi Hŭigwŏn. "Chŏng Yŏrip moban sagŏn e kwanhan koch'al" [A Study of the Conspiracy of Chŏng Yŏrip]. *Ch'angjak kwa pip'yŏng* 10, no. 3 (1975): 204–18.

Yi Hunsang. *Chosŏn hugi ŭi hyangni* [The *Hyangni* during the Late Chosŏn Period]. Seoul: Ilchogak, 1990.

Yi Inyŏng. "Yi ssi Chosŏn Sejo ttae ŭi pukpang imin chŏngch'aek" [The Migration Policy to the North during the Reign of King Sejo in the Chosŏn Dynasty]. *Chindan hakpo* 15 (1947): 90–113.

Yi Kisun. "Chosŏn hugi Koryŏng Sin ssi ŭi kajok kyumo" [Family Structure as Represented in the Genealogy of the Koryŏng Sin Descent Group in the Late Chosŏn Period]. *Paeksan hakpo* 58 (2001): 225–74.

———. "Pongsan Yi ssi chokpo rŭl t'onghaesŏ pon Chosŏn sidae kajok kyumo" [Family Structure as Represented in the Genealogy of the Pongsan Yi Descent Group]. *Hongik sahak* 6 (1996): 1–16.

Yi Kyŏngsik. "Chosŏn ch'ogi ŭi pukpang kaech'ŏk kwa nongŏp kaebal" [The Reclamation of the Northern Area and Agricultural Development during the Early Chosŏn Period]. *Yŏksa kyoyuk* 52 (Dec. 1992): 13–29.

Yi Pokkyu. "Chosŏn chŏn'gi sadaebuga ŭi chŏmbok kwa tokkyŏng—Yi

Mungŏn ŭi *Mukchae ilgi* rŭl chungsim ŭiro" [Divinations and Shamanistic Chantings in a Yangban Household in the Early Chosŏn—An Examination of *Yi Mungŏn's Diary*]. *Han'guk minsok hakpo* 10 (1999): 1–17.

———. "Chosŏn chŏn'gi sadaebuga ŭi musok—Yi Mungŏn ŭi *Mukchae ilgi* rŭl chungsim ŭiro" [Shamanistic Beliefs in a Yangban Household in the Early Chosŏn—An Examination *of Yi Mungŏn's Diary*]. *Han'guk minsok hakpo* 9 (1998): 5–29.

Yi Pyŏngdo. "Hong Kyŏngnae nan kwa Chŏngju sŏngdo" [The Hong Kyŏngnae Rebellion and the Map of Chŏngju]. *Paeksan Hakpo* 3 (1967): 379–400.

———. *Koryŏ sidae ŭi yŏn'gu* [A Study of the Koryŏ Dynasty]. Seoul: Asea munhwasa, 1980.

Yi Sangbae, *Chosŏn hugi chŏngch'i wa kwaesŏ* [The Politics in Late Chosŏn and Seditious Letters]. Seoul: Kukhak charyowŏn, 1999.

———. "Chosŏn hugi Hansŏng-bu kwaesŏ e kwanhan yŏn'gu" [A Study of the Incidents of Posting Seditious Letters in Seoul during the Late Chosŏn Period]. *Hyangt'o Seoul* 53 (1993): 153–86.

———. "Sukchongjo kwaesŏ e kwanhan yŏn'gu" [A Study of Incidents of Posting Seditious Letters during the Reign of King Sukchong]. *Kangwŏn sahak* 5 (1989): 33–68.

———. "Yŏngjojo Yun Chi kwaesŏ sagŏn kwa chŏngguk ŭi tonghyang" [The Conspiracy of Yun Chi and Political Trends during the Reign of King Yŏngjo]. *Han'guksa yŏn'gu* 76 (1992): 77–98.

Yi Sanghyŏp. *Chosŏn chŏn'gi pukpang samin yŏn'gu* [A Study of the Relocation of Population to the North in Early Chosŏn]. Seoul: Kyŏngin munhwasa, 2001.

Yi Sŏngmu. *Chosŏn ch'ogi yangban yŏn'gu* [A Study of Yangban in the Early Chosŏn Period]. Seoul: Ilchogak, 1980.

Yi Sugŏn. "Chokpo wa yangban ŭisik" [Genealogy and Yangban Consciousness]. *Han'guksa simin kangjwa* 24 (1999): 20–49.

———. "Chosŏn hugi sŏnggwan ŭisik kwa p'yŏnbo ch'eje ŭi pyŏnhwa" [Perceptions on Surname and Clan Seat in Late Chosŏn and Changes in the Compilation of Genealogies]. In *Kugok Hwang Chongdong kyosu chŏngnyŏn kinyŏm sahak nonch'ong* [A Collection of Historical Studies in Honor of Professor Hwang Chongdong's Retirement], 395–420. Taegu: Kugok Hwang Chongdong kyosu chŏngnyŏn kinyŏm sahak nonch'ong kanhaeng wiwŏnhoe, 1994.

———. *Chosŏn sidae chibang haengjŏngsa* [The History of Local Administration System in Chosŏn]. Seoul: Minŭmsa, 1989.

———. "Chosŏn Sŏngjongjo ŭi pukpang imin chŏngch'aek" [The Migration Policy to the North during King Sŏngjong's Reign in the Chosŏn Dynasty]. *Asea hakpo* 7 (1970): 184–208 (part 1) and 8 (1970): 76–112 (part 2).

———. *Han'guk chungse sahoesa yŏn'gu* [Studies in the Social History of Medieval Korea]. Seoul: Ilchogak, 1984.

———. *Yŏngnam hakp'a ŭi hyŏngsŏng kwa chŏn'gae* [The Formation and Development of the Yŏngnam School]. Seoul: Ilchogak, 1995.

Yi Sŭnghun. "Sŏbugin ŭi sugwŏn sint'ong" [Old Resentment and New Grief of People from P'yŏngan Province]. Originally in *Sinmin* [New People] 14 (June 1926). Reprinted in Chŏngju kunji p'yŏnch'an wiwŏnhoe, ed., *Chŏngju kunji* [The Gazetteer of Chŏngju], 363–4. Seoul: Chŏngju kunji p'yŏnch'an wiwŏnhoe, 1975.

Yi Sun'gu. "Chosŏn ch'ogi chongpŏp ŭi suyong kwa yŏsŏng chiwi ŭi pyŏnhwa" [The Propagation of the Agnatic Principle and the Changes in the Status of Women during the Early Chosŏn Dynasty]. Ph.D. diss., Han'guk chŏngsin munhwa yŏn'guwŏn, 1994.

Yi T'aejin. "Chosŏn hugi yangban sahoe ŭi pyŏnhwa" [Changes in Yangban Society in the Late Chosŏn Period]. In Chu Podon et al., *Han'guk sahoe palchŏnsa non* [Studies on the Development of Korean Society], 129–226. Seoul: Ilchogak, 1992.

———. "Sŏŏl ch'adae ko" [A Study of Discrimination against *Sŏŏl*]. *Yŏksa hakpo* 27 (1965): 65–104.

Yi Tonhwa [Paektu-sanin]. "Hong Kyŏngnae wa Chŏn Pongjun." *Kaebyŏk* (Nov. 1920): 39–47.

Yi Usŏng. "A Study of the Period of the Northern and Southern States." *Korea Journal* 17, no. 1 (Jan. 1977): 28–33.

Yi Yŏnghak, "Tambae ŭi sahoesa" [Social History of Tobacco]. *Yŏksa pip'yŏng* 12 (Spring 1991): 121–35.

Yi Yŏnghun. "18.19 segi Taejŏ-ri ŭi sinbun kusŏng kwa chach'i chilsŏ" [The Status Composition and Self-Governing Orders in Taejŏ-ri in the Eighteenth and Nineteenth Centuries]. In An Pyŏngjik and Yi Yŏnghun, eds., *Matchil ŭi nongmin* [Peasants of Matchil], 245–99. Seoul: Ilchogak, 2001.

———, ed. *Suryang kyŏngjesa ro tasi pon Chosŏn hugi* [An Examination of the Late Chosŏn from the Perspective of Economic History]. Seoul: Seoul taehakkyo ch'ulp'anbu, 2004.

Yŏm Chŏngsŏp. *Chosŏn sidae nongpŏp paltal yŏn'gu* [A Study of the Development in the Agricultural Technologies in the Chosŏn Dynasty]. Seoul: T'aehaksa, 2002.

Yŏnse taehakkyo kukhak yŏn'guwŏn, ed. *Han'guk kŭndae ihaenggi chungin yŏn'gu* [Studies of *Chungin* in the Modern Transitional Period in Korea]. Seoul: Sinsŏwŏn, 1999.

Yoon, Hong-key [Yun Honggi]. "The Image of Nature in Geomancy." *GeoJournal* 4, no. 4 (1980): 341–48.

———. "P'ungsu chirisŏl ŭi ponjil kwa kiwŏn mit kŭ chayŏn'gwan" [The Essence and Origin of Geomancy and its Image of Nature]. *Han'guksa simin kangjwa* 14 (1994): 187–204.

Yoshikawa Tomotake. "Kō Keirai no ran ni okeru hanran shudobu no senryaku to ishiki" [The Strategy and Consciousness of Leaders in the Hong Kyŏngnae Rebellion]. *Chōsen Gakkai* 166 (1998): 81–118.

Yu Sŭngju. "Chosŏn hugi kwangŏpsa ŭi sidae kubun e kwanhan ilsiron" [A Study of Periodization in the History of Mining During the Late Chosŏn Period]. In *Chosŏn hugi sahoe kyŏngjesa yŏn'gu immun* [An Introduction of Social and Economic History of Late Chosŏn], 124–69. Seoul: Minjok munhwasa, 1991.

Yu Sŭngju and Yi Ch'ŏlsŏng. *Chosŏn hugi chungguk kwa ŭi muyoksa* [History of Trade with China in the Late Chosŏn Period]. Seoul: Kyŏngin munhwasa, 2002.

Yu T'agil. *Sŏngho hangmaek ŭi munjip kanhaeng yŏn'gu* [A Study of Publications of Collected Works by Yi Ik and His Disciples]. Pusan: Pusan taehakkyo ch'ulp'anbu, 2000.

Zenshō Eisuke. *Chōsen no seishi to dōzoku buraku* [The Surnames and Single Surname Villages in Chosŏn]. Tōkyō: Tōkō shoin, 1943.

———. *Chōsen no shūraku* [Villages of Chosŏn Korea]. 3 vols. Keijō: Chōsen sōtokufu, 1933–35.